Behind the Silence

ASIAN VOICES

A sub-series of Asia/Pacific/Perspectives

Series Editor: Mark Selden

Behind the Silence

Chinese Voices on Abortion

Nie Jing-Bao

ROWMAN & LITTLEFIELD PUBLISHERS, INC.
Lanham • Boulder • New York • Toronto • Oxford

Author's note:

For reasons of confidentiality, the names of all informants are pseudonymous. All identifying individual and geographic information has been altered or omitted.

All Chinese names, including the cited Chinese authors of Chinese publications, are treated in the Chinese way, that is, the family name first and the given name last. The cited Chinese authors of English publications are put as they appear in the original publications, often in the Western way, that is, the given name first and the family name last.

Except as specifically acknowledged, all English translations of Chinese materials in this book are the author's.

ROWMAN & LITTLEFIELD PUBLISHERS, INC.

Published in the United States of America
by Rowman & Littlefield Publishers, Inc.
A wholly owned subsidiary of The Rowman & Littlefield Publishing Group, Inc.
4501 Forbes Boulevard, Suite 200, Lanham, Maryland 20706
www.rowmanlittlefield.com

P.O. Box 317, Oxford OX2 9RU, UK

British Library Cataloguing in Publication Information Available

Library of Congress Cataloging-in-Publication Data

Nie, Jing-Bao, 1962–
  Behind the silence : Chinese voices on abortion / Nie Jing-Bao.
    p. cm. — (Asian voices)
  Includes bibliographical references and index.
  ISBN 0-7425-2370-5 (cloth : alk. paper) — ISBN 0-7425-2371-3 (pbk. : alk. paper)
  1. Abortion—China. 2. Abortion—Moral and ethical aspects—China. 3. Birth control—China. 4. China—Population policy. I. Title. II. Series.
HQ767.5.C6N54 2005
363.46'0951—dc22   2005009543

Printed in the United States of America

♾™ The paper used in this publication meets the minimum requirements of American National Standard for Information Sciences—Permanence of Paper for Printed Library Materials, ANSI/NISO Z39.48-1992.

Contents

v

The fact that people don't speak out [publicly and privately] doesn't mean they have nothing to say [*bushuohua budengyu meihuashuo*, literally, "no speaking is not tantamount to nothing to speak"].

—Chinese physician-scientist and Party member

So long as it doesn't come forth, nothing happens. But when it does, then ten thousand hollows begin crying wildly. Can't you hear them, long drawn out? In the mountain forests that lash and sway, there are huge trees a hundred spans around with hollows and openings like noses, like mouths, like ears, like jugs, like cups, like mortars, like rifts, like ruts. They roar like waves, whistle like arrows, screech, gasp, cry, wail, moan, and howl, those in the lead calling out yeee!, those behind calling out yuuu! In a gentle breeze they answer faintly, but in a full gale the chorus is gigantic. And when the fierce wind has passed on, then all the hollows are empty again. Have you never seen the tossing and trembling that goes on?

—Zhuang Zi (Chuang Tzu), a founder of Daoism (Taoism)

To my parents

For my motherland China

Foreword

In the early 1980s, I was conducting research in China at the Hunan Medical University (formerly Yale-in-China Medical School, and more recently part of Central South University). One memorable day, while interviewing patients in a psychiatric outpatient clinic at the Medical School's Second Affiliated Hospital, the vice director of the hospital as well as the leading members of the Department of Psychiatry asked me to help them interpret for a visiting group of mental health professionals from the United States who were in the midst of a professional visit to psychiatric institutions in China. "You speak Chinese; you know our hospital. You can help us," they implored.

Hence I found myself in the strange situation of being introduced to my fellow Americans as a visiting member of the work unit who would interpret between the visitors and my Chinese colleagues. The emphasis was that I was a member of the hospital who could help explain to my fellow countrymen local problems and practices. The American group had its own translator, of course, but he clearly had trouble with the mental health terminology and concepts, and he took a backseat as I mediated the meeting. Everything went well for the first half hour or so, but then a child psychologist from New York asked me, in a low-key voice, what my Chinese colleagues would do if an adolescent with serious mental retardation in their care became pregnant. Would they recommend abortion? Would the patient undergo sterilization?

I remember the question was asked innocently enough, and it was so outside my own area of expertise that without modification or any qualifying information I simply translated the question into standard Chinese for my colleagues, at least half of whom understood English well enough that they—although not the hospital's senior administrative cadres, who were also present—almost certainly understood the drift of the question in English. My colleagues replied in equally straightforward words that they would advise the young woman and her family it would be best if she underwent an abortion because she would not be able to care for the infant and her parents were so limited in the time and resources they had, nor could they take on the heavy responsibility to raise another child. For more or less the same reasons, with the consent of the young, cognitively impaired woman and her parents, and because of her vulnerability to further sexual misadventures, they would recommend sterilization via tubal ligation. I translated the words almost verbatim and had prepared myself for the next question, when with great passion and in rising tones of someone who is morally outraged, the questioner said something such as, you are telling us they would force this mentally disabled woman to undergo abortion and sterilization? I didn't say that, I protested. I didn't say force. But it amounts to that, doesn't it, in this repressive atmosphere, he riposted. And then the entire meeting got side-tracked on this issue, with those on the Chinese side about as upset as the American visitors. I remember shaking my head in utter amazement. With good intentions, I had either created havoc in intercultural communication or, put in other terms, had watched play out a seminal cultural misunderstanding between Chinese and Westerners.

Nie Jing-Bao's important book would have greatly helped both groups of interlocutors. It would have informed them about what is so deeply at stake in the moral experience and ethics of abortion for different groups of Chinese and Westerners, particularly Americans, that they cannot understand each other. And this book succeeds not by simplifying a complex social reality but by showing how pluralistic, multisided, and contested the issue of abortion is within China and among Chinese. I am not aware of another book that gives voice to all the players engaged with abortion in China: women who have undergone the procedure in urban and rural China, their family members, their doctors (both generalists and specialists), the family planning professionals, the ethicists, the silent majority, the state, and so on.

By providing survey and ethnographic information about the lived moral experience of abortion, Nie Jing-Bao frames the ethical issues with the key social, cultural, psychological, political, and religious forces that are at work, as well as the historical experiences that form the background to contemporary debates. We come to understand the different perspectives, what they are based on, and their implications. And in so doing, we see why local moral experience is so troubled and troubling. This is because it forces theorists to come to terms with suffering as the outcome of large-scale political and economic transformations on the always dynamic relationship between cultural representations, collective experiences, and subjectivity. The silences and voices are themselves expressions of this set of relationships. This book clarifies the plurality and divided nature of the cultural representations, the grounding of experience in local worlds, and the multisided subjectivities of ordinary Chinese confronting abortion. I believe it is one of the most important books written on morality and ethics in China and that it will also be widely read and commented on by China scholars generally.

Moral experience, as this book shows, is always about things that are most at stake for us when encountering the very real dangers of the social world. Those dangers, in turn, force us to confront the possibility that our commitments will be challenged, undermined, even lost. In turn, we ourselves become dangerous as we strike back to defend what is at stake. The abortion controversy in America has created this cascade of dangers, whereas in Chinese society the popular silence about abortion has led observers to believe that this intensification of social and subjective danger has been averted. The research presented in the pages that follow challenges this perspective. Voices and stories show just how morally and emotionally and politically charged the topic of abortion is in China today. In this respect, Nie Jing-Bao's achievement is not just to tell us about what people have practiced and how they have reacted to abortion. Even more, this book opens a window on contemporary Chinese society that provides a better sense of how ordinary Chinese negotiate social dangers and endure and transform moral experience.

Arthur Kleinman
Harvard University

Introduction

ONE DOCTOR AND TWO WOMEN THUS SPOKE

Dr. Ying Zhonghua: "Everything I've Said Is the Truth I Believe In (*dushi da shihua*)"

Now in her fifties, Dr. Ying had been an obstetrician and gynecologist for more than thirty years and had performed numerous abortions. At first, she was reluctant to be interviewed, claiming that she was not a good speaker. Eventually, encouraged by her coworkers, she agreed to answer a few questions. She proved to be a compelling interlocutor whose laughter was contagious. Without prompting, she began by giving a vivid description of her joy in delivering babies, especially her excitement and the feeling of achievement after a difficult but successful birth. "You can never imagine how proud and happy an obstetrician feels in her heart when she sees the baby she delivered grow up to become a pillar of the nation (*guojia de dongliang zhicai*)," she said with enthusiasm.

Dr. Ying had hoped to specialize in surgery, but was assigned to her hospital's department of obstetrics and gynecology. At first, she had a difficult time because of her initial dislike of her specialty. But she gradually began to love her work, which routinely included abortions. For Dr. Ying, her job carried a strong sense of social responsibility. Asked whether she felt differently about performing abortions and delivering babies, she laughed as if she considered the question ignorant, if not silly. She saw delivering babies and performing terminations as two totally different matters. Performing abortions was a task she undertook to help implement the national birth control policy. Although she believed that abortion, medically speaking, was

1

quite safe, she considered it "a remedial measure when contraception fails—abortion is a solution when there is no other alternative. A major aim of family planning work is to reduce the abortion rate."

Dr. Ying was a strong supporter of the national population policy. When asked what she would do if a woman wanted to continue her pregnancy but the policy would not permit it, she commented that I was "a very perverse person" (*ben pianmian*, one-sided or lopsided). She told me with charming candor that, despite the fact that I had been born in China and lived there for nearly thirty years, I knew nothing about the family planning program and suggested that I pay a visit to the city's Family Planning Commission. (I later did, though in a different city.) In her eyes, many Westerners lacked basic knowledge of the realities of contemporary China:

> Westerners just don't understand the Chinese family planning program. It isn't that women are forced to have abortions as they [foreigners] say. I never encountered a case in which the woman wasn't willing to have an abortion—very rarely. As far as my experience is concerned, no one was ever forced. No one grumbled. Americans simply are completely ignorant (*wuquan budong*). The actual situations of the two countries [China and the United States] are different. If everyone just carries on having children, how will China develop industry, agriculture, and advanced technology?

She offered an example to illustrate China's overpopulation problem. In the year when the interview took place (1997), junior high school children were having great difficulty getting into high school—there simply weren't enough places for the children of the early 1950s baby boomers. For Dr. Ying, the shortage of schools for these junior high graduates was a direct consequence of the earlier failure to implement effective birth control.

Dr. Ying said that as a Chinese student in the United States, it was my duty to help the world, especially the West, understand the "national reality" (*guoqing*) of China and the truth about China's population program. She emphasized that the state only advocates (*tichang*)—rather than demands—"one child per family" and family planning. It is neither a universal policy nor a law. She mentioned some exceptions to the rule—a couple could have a second child if the father was the only son in his extended family, and ethnic minorities could have more than one child. She further noted that prevention in the form of contraception was the major method for carrying out family planning. If that failed, the emphasis shifted to the early stages of the pregnancy. "In our area, late abortion hardly exists. But I couldn't say what the situation is in remote areas." Dr. Ying favored compulsory premarital examination as a eugenic (*yousheng*, literally, good or excellent birth) measure, and this was a routine part of her work. In a tone that left no room for doubt, she declared: "The mentally retarded and people with genetic diseases shouldn't bear children—the state doesn't allow it, either. For them to have children is harmful to society, the country, the family, and the individual." (The new marriage law, effective from October 1, 2003, no longer stipulates compulsory medical examination for marriage registration.)

When I thanked her at the end of the interview, Dr. Ying's final comment, accompanied by hearty laughter, was: "Everything I've said is the truth I believe in (*dushi da shihua*)." Her emphasis was obvious not only by her use of *da* (literally, thorough, only, very, or all-out) before *shihua* (truth), but by her tone as well. Never doubting her integrity, I took this to mean that she was not merely paying lip service to the official position on these issues, nor was she mincing her words.

Ms. Li Xiaohua:"Shouldn't This Be Regarded as Murder (*mousha*)?"

A woman such as Li Xiaohua, who has an abortion in middle or late pregnancy, sometimes sees herself—and is treated by family members—as having given birth to a child. In China there is a deeply rooted and still widely practiced custom called *zhu yuezi* (sitting out the month after childbirth). According to this custom, a woman should remain at home for a month of convalescence after childbirth. The period of recuperation varies from *xiaoyue* ("small month," literally a full month) to *dayue* ("big month," literally forty-five days). During this time, women must obey rules such as following a special nutritious diet by consuming foods such as chicken soup, abstaining from sex, staying inside, avoiding contact with cold water and wind, and abstaining from baths (especially cold ones) and from washing the head, even in warm water. These things are done mainly in the interest of postpartum care—to ensure the mother's recovery from labor and especially to ensure her future health. It is also believed that after giving birth a woman may bring bad luck to others or offend the gods as a result of continued bleeding. The woman needs a *dayue* to recover fully and become "normal" again (see Pillsbury 1978 for an anthropological study of the Chinese rationale and a Western biomedical evaluation of this custom).

The doctor and nurses caring for Ms. Li viewed her as a patient for an abortion (*renliu*) service. After the induced birth (*yinchan*), this "patient" lay on a bed in a ward shared with another patient at the Clinic for Maternal and Infant Care in a county town of an inland province. Her head was wrapped in a bandage made from a blue handkerchief, a common social marker for a woman who is "sitting out the month." The towel also has a practical purpose as, after giving birth, women are believed to be especially vulnerable to headaches induced by exposure to cold air.

Ms. Li was reluctant to be interviewed. When her doctor introduced me, she nodded slightly and motioned us to sit down. Her voice was barely audible. The procedure for inducing birth at five months' pregnancy had left her already very fair face even paler, and left her lips bloodless.

Ms. Li had been married for about a year. Local government policy in her area required that the wife be twenty-three and a half years of age to obtain a permit for bearing a child. One year younger than the required age, Ms. Li was denied the necessary permission. Although her husband was over thirty, the family planning official she dealt with recognized only the age of the mother.

> We really wanted this child. My husband and I tried our utmost to obtain a birth permit. But we failed. The family planning policy was implemented very strictly. Finally, we had no choice but to come to this clinic to have an abortion. I came here with my husband. I'm still young—I believe that I'll be able to have another child later.

When asked how she felt about the abortion, tears welled up in her eyes. Like a good number of the women interviewed, she viewed the aborted fetus as a part of her own body. Between sobs, Ms. Li said,

> How could I feel? How do you think I felt? It'd be better if I had no feelings at all. No words can describe what I've gone through. First, drugs were injected into my womb to kill the child, to make it dead. Then I had to wait for the fetus to descend. When it came down, I asked the doctor to show me the aborted baby. How brutal this is! I felt extremely sad. The baby is a part of my bone and flesh (*gurou*). But I couldn't do anything to protect my baby, my child. Only a few months later and the baby would have been born and become a child. Shouldn't this be regarded as murder (*mousha*)?

With the exception of three Catholic priests, a Protestant pastor, and a couple of lay Christians, Ms. Li was the only Chinese I met in the course of my field research who wondered whether abortion could be considered murder. The particular context of her coerced abortion makes her question all the more poignant.

Yet in spite of all the suffering she had just been through, Ms. Li still supported the national family planning program:

> Our country must carry out family planning. Our nation has so many people. It's crowded everywhere. My husband and I had no intention of having more than one child. The "one-child" policy is necessary for our country. It's also good for women. But should the policy be carried out so rigorously? In my case, I'm just one year younger than the required age. Why didn't they grant me a birth permit?

Her voice, though very weak and soft, betrayed her anger and frustration. Her eyes and face exposed her helplessness. After remaining silent for a while, she said apologetically: "I've been in pain for over twelve hours. I'm really very tired now." She gave a bitter smile and turned her face away from me.

Her husband came in with a pot of soup cradled in his hands as I, with Ms. Li's physician, left the ward. Her doctor, a dour woman in her early forties, seemed lacking in sympathy for her patient. Perhaps she had seen too many cases like this one, or even worse ones. As soon as we were out of the room, she said: "Did you notice that she's married a man much older than she is? He looks very wealthy." Her tone and gesture suggested that to her Ms. Li was actually one of life's winners.

Ms. Liu Liping: Feeling Guilty (*neijiu*) about the Aborted Child

As we talked, Ms. Liu Liping was waiting for insertion of an intrauterine device (IUD)—the most common method of contraception for married women in China, especially those who have already given birth to one or two children. Although she and her partner had obtained a marriage license, they were not yet married in society's eyes, as the wedding was still to come. Nevertheless, she addressed her partner as *laogong* (literally, old man)—a common term in the North for one's husband. Earlier, her *laogong* had asked her to have an IUD inserted, but she had ignored his advice. However, after one termination, Ms. Liu was motivated to protect herself from future unwanted pregnancies.

Ms. Liu had agreed to an abortion because she and her partner believed they were not yet ready for a child. She said:

> I'm just twenty-six and still young. I really want to *wan* (play, or enjoy life) for a few more years. And our economic situation isn't stable yet. We want to travel and see all those famous mountains and rivers. I run my own business, but things are rather slow at the moment. So we had no hesitation in deciding to terminate the pregnancy. I'd prefer to have a child in my early thirties. Giving birth too late [after this period] is no good for the child.

Ms. Liu remarked that no one among her college classmates had yet started a family. She compared having a baby to "being fastened on a rope." For her and her partner, a child meant heavy responsibilities—but it never occurred to them to remain permanently childless in order to escape these burdens. Indeed, Ms. Liu commented, "Every family needs to have a child. Otherwise, life would be too boring." Moreover, she considered it better for the child to have a brother or sister. "One boy and one girl would be the ideal." She used her parents' experience to support the idea: "I can't imagine how dull my parents' life would be if they had no sisters or brothers."

Asked how she felt after her abortion, Ms. Liu replied without hesitation, "I feel conscience-stricken (*neijiu*, or guilty)." Asked for whom the guilt was felt, she exclaimed, "The aborted child, of course." She continued: "It was really too cruel. It should have been born, but was destroyed by its own parents." She added that she occasionally thought of the aborted fetus. She sometimes joked with her partner that, when they did have a child, she would let it know that it would never have been born were it not for the earlier abortion. "How absurd life is!" Ms. Liu sighed heavily.

APPROACHING THE VOICES BEHIND THE SILENCE

This book is about abortion in mainland China—specifically, the attitudes of contemporary Chinese to the artificial termination of pregnancy and such related issues as fetal life and the birth control program.

Induced abortion—deliberately terminating a pregnancy or, in the eyes of critics, intentionally destroying a growing human life—has been practiced in every society throughout history, regardless of whether it has been sanctioned by mainstream morality, religion, and law. In China today, abortion is undertaken for a wide range of reasons, from unwanted pregnancy and personal convenience to preference for a male child (which is illegal) and the requirements of the national population policy. The Chinese language, from classical to modern times, has included numerous terms for terminating pregnancy. The current and most widely used are *rengong liuchan* ("induced slippery delivery" or artificial termination), abbreviated as *renliu* ("slippery delivery" or abortion), and *duotai* (dropping the fetus). Variations include *duoshengtai* (dropping the living fetus), *datai* (beating the fetus), *qutai* (expulsion of the fetus), and *xiatai* (bringing the fetus down). Spontaneous abortion or miscarriage is called *xiaochan* ("small delivery" or "small labor"). While *rengong liuchan* (induced abortion) or *renliu* (abortion) usually denotes termination at any stage, it can also refer more specifically to termination in early pregnancy, that is, before fourteen weeks. Another term—*yinchan* (induced birth or induced labor)—is used to refer to termination in the middle and late stages of pregnancy, that is, fourteen to twenty-seven weeks and especially after twenty-eight weeks.

Despite this terminological richness, Chinese moral perspectives on abortion remain an unknown landscape awaiting discovery and understanding. Western public concerns over abortion in contemporary China, as indicated in academic discussions and the mass media, notably in the United States, have virtually fixated on coerced abortion in the birth control program (see chapter 1). And numerous publications criticize the Chinese practice from the perspective of human rights. While these criticisms are often cogent, a significant factor is usually missing—sensitivity to and awareness of Chinese people's perspectives on abortion, fetal life, and the state's birth control policies. The international debate over Chinese population control and abortion practices has, in short, proceeded without paying sufficient attention to Chinese views and experiences. In fact, due to the absence of serious studies and the influence of stereotypes of Chinese people and culture—both in the West as well as in China—the moral and sociocultural dimensions of abortion in Chinese society are surrounded by unexamined assumptions, superficial observations, misunderstandings, and myths. To list only a few here: "Chinese have a distinctive and monolithic perspective, very different from the Western one, on the ethical grounds for abortion, as on many other issues." "The typical Chinese response to the moral aspects of abortion is indifference." "Abortion is acceptable in China because human life in Chinese culture is not respected as highly as in Western culture and because most if not all Chinese consider that human life starts at birth." "Most people in China want more than one child and thus oppose the national birth control program." This book will closely examine all these and more.

Around the world, moral assessments on aborting the fetus by artificial means have always been diverse, just as abortion laws vary from strict prohibition to complete license. Ethical and legal standpoints on abortion have also varied from one historical period to another. At some times and in some places, notably in the contemporary United States, abortion issues give rise to intense and intractable moral, social, legal, and political controversies. In striking contrast, as Westerners as well as Chinese have often observed, many Chinese appear to be extraordinarily complacent about the issue, especially in the public sphere (see chapter 1).

Appearances, however, can be deceiving. When asked why Chinese people are silent on the issue, a physician–researcher and member of the Chinese Communist Party replied unhesitatingly: "The fact that people don't speak out doesn't mean they have nothing to say (*bushuohua budengyu meihuashuo*)." Indeed. This book is a result of my attempt to listen to the apparent Chinese silence and the voices behind it.

Although as a child in the late 1960s and early 1970s I had heard village women in the South talking about abortion and as a medical student in the early 1980s had studied abortion, it was not until the late 1980s that I became aware that it might be morally and socially proscribed in some quarters. In preparing to study in North America, I read several American, British, and Chinese authors on how to "survive" in the West, including suggestions about topics best avoided in conversations with Westerners. One book advised against asking a Westerner's position on abortion. Other topics to be avoided included the person's age (especially in the case of a woman), income, religious beliefs, and political views. Avoiding the topic of abortion was recommended because many Westerners opposed it on religious grounds. At the time, I thought to myself: "OK. Westerners are different. I will have no problem avoiding the issue." I wondered who would be curious about it, anyway.

Even though in the late 1980s I had taught the medical humanities at a traditional-style medical school in China and undertaken research in the philosophy of medicine, it was not until the autumn of 1993 when I had studied for two years in North America that I realized that abortion could be an important moral problem deserving of serious academic attention. Even then, abortion, whether in China or in the West, never occurred to me as a possible research topic. Not until the fall of 1995, after much ambivalence, hesitation, anxiety, and even fear, did I decide to conduct a systematic study of Chinese perspectives on abortion. The main source of my anxiety and fear lies in its political sensitivity, especially in its direct relevance to China's birth control program. Even after committing to the project, for a long time I restricted myself to abortion per se and avoided the issue of population control as much as possible, skirting around the topic when interviewing people for the pilot study and in my fieldwork. Only much later did I realize that this is an unavoidable part of the subject.

A project that came to me as a surprise has since brought even more surprises. This journey, as both a blessing and a burden, has been intellectually, emotionally, and even spiritually challenging and rewarding for me. One of the most gratifying aspects has been discovering the existence of so many different voices. During my field research, I was constantly impressed by the willingness of people to be interviewed and by the sheer variety of their perspectives. For instance, on one occasion about ten rural people—men and women, young and old—gathered in a village house to fill out the questionnaires I had given them. After completing the forms, several of them started to debate the items listed in the questionnaire passionately. This fascinating discussion revealed that the two most divisive issues were whether aborting a fetus was equivalent to taking a life and the question of when human life began. They could not agree on whether human life started at conception, at birth, or at some time in between.

As the first systematic and in-depth study in any language on the subject, this book provides compelling evidence that Chinese have diverse and often opposing views, strong feelings, myriad experiences, and nuanced attitudes on abortion, the moral status of fetal life, and the birth control program. It also explores the complex political, sociocultural, and historical terrain that shapes their perplexing silences and diverse perspectives. As a perennial human activity like sex and childbirth, abortion is associated with fundamental aspects of life, including reproduction, medicine, health care, gender, sexuality, family, religion, culture, and the role of the state. Just as the abortion controversies in the United States reflect essential features of American society and culture—its moral discourses, religious traditions, legal systems, political ideals, methods of academic and intellectual inquiry, and the nature of the public and private domains—so contemporary Chinese attitudes to abortion serve as a unique window onto the moral and sociocultural life of China today. As a preliminary guide to Chinese perspectives on abortion, this work, I hope, will convey firsthand information essential for understanding contemporary Chinese society, including attitudes and values, and issues as diverse as morality, politics, reproduction, population control, eugenics, state power, cultural traditions, gender and the status of women, the place of the individual in society, the medical profession, and the physician–patient relationship.

This study uses methods widely employed in the social sciences for gathering reliable information about people's beliefs. Empirical information presented in this book is primarily based on fieldwork that took place in five Chinese cities—Qingdao, Dalian, Beijing, Changsha, and Guangzhou (three in the North and two in the South)—and three villages in an inland southern province, Hunan, from August through September 1997. Using semistructured interviews, I formally spoke with thirty women who had experienced abortion and thirty doctors who had performed terminations. In addition, 601 questionnaires were collected from a range of individuals, including urban residents, rural people, Catholics, Protestants, Buddhists, doctors, biomedical and traditional Chinese medical students, university students, and scholars of the medical humanities and ethics. A pilot study had been conducted among twenty Chinese students and scholars living in the United States, most of them in Galveston, Texas, in the late spring and early summer of 1997. Since all the interviewees in the pilot study were educated and worked in China, the views of these well-educated overseas Chinese offer a fascinating slant on the issue. In addition, the book draws on my personal experience of growing up in a remote village in south-central China and living for thirteen years in Changsha, the capital of Hunan Province. (Additional information about the interviews, the survey, and the pilot study can be found in the appendix.)

This book is not so much something of mine as something of those Chinese—nearly seven hundred in total—who participated directly in the research. My primary burden is not prescriptive, but to present the varied "native" Chinese viewpoints on abortion. The basic approach is interpretative or humanistic rather than scientific, phenomenological rather than positivistic, descriptive and informative rather than normative, sympathetic rather than critical and judgmental. The book does not aim to be an "objective description" of or "scientific report" on contemporary Chinese understandings of abortion, both because I do not think pure objectivity can ever be achieved in studying humans and their societies and because data collection was necessarily circumscribed by the nature of the opportunities afforded in Chinese society. Moreover, it is neither possible nor desirable for anyone who studies a subject such as abortion to remain ethically neutral or emotionally indifferent. In general, any description or vision of "the reality of China," though not necessarily equally valid as its alternatives, is always limited by human capacities of knowing and contaminated with political interests and group or individual biases—apparent, implicit, unconscious, as well as deliberately concealed.

What really matters for me is thus *faithfulness, truthfulness,* and *authenticity,* rather than objectivity. I have tried my utmost throughout this study to be a faithful witness to the hundreds of participants' voices I was privileged to hear. I would like this book to be read as *my faithful testimony* to Chinese views and experiences of abortion. The major task for me as author is to be a good interpreter, a task not necessarily easier than being an objective reporter. This does not at all mean that I wish to serve as a spokesperson for Chinese people, although I am a Chinese citizen by birth and choice. For far too long, Chinese people and their perspectives have been misrepresented and even hijacked by too many different individuals, organizations, and institutions. The diverse voices presented in this book illustrate not only the basic fact that Chinese people can speak for themselves, but also the urgent need for China to develop effective political and institutional channels so that these voices can be adequately expressed.

Chinese opinions and narratives on abortion are so complex and diverse that generalizations will inevitably distort their profound humanity, distinctiveness, and sophistication. Generalizations and interpretation of any kind run the risk of failing to grasp the full and often conflicting personal, interpersonal, political, social, cultural, moral, and even existential meanings raised by this issue, including the individual uniqueness and universal appealing, the unimaginable and admirable struggles, the courage and weakness, the complexity of local texture and general social-cultural context, as well as the hopes these Chinese voices embody. At the same time, generalizing, interpreting, and contextualizing are essential to making sense of the meanings of Chinese voices, spoken and unspoken. Because people in the West as well as China are so accustomed to interpreting Chinese beliefs and experience in the light of various myths and stereotypes, in this book I have made an effort to resist ethnic generalizations. Rather, while highlighting many genuinely shared features, I will focus on the enormous diversity contained in the Chinese experience of abortion.

However difficult the task, we should strive to understand Chinese opinions and experiences at both collective and personal levels on abortion and related issues. The more widely and attentively these voices are heeded, the more likely the prospects are not only for reforming related social practices and public policies related to abortion and birth control, but also in general for resisting all kinds of dehumanized human relationships, for helping the societies we individually are a part of to become a bit more sound morally, and for improving cross-cultural communication in this age of globalization. However ineffective and flawed this book is, I know how authentic my testimony is and how hard I have tried at least not to be "perverse" in approaching the subject, as Dr. Ying had provokingly urged. Although it is impossible for me, indeed any human being, to avoid one-sidedness in approaching any matter, especially any social issue such as abortion, I have tried hard not to fall too much into this inevitable sin by keeping in my mind and heart the ideal all-sided perspective. Assessment of my performance as a not-that-one-sided interpreter or messenger will have to be left to the readers of this book, including Chinese people, for whom a Chinese version is planned. As for how much I have perceived and testified to the *ultimate truth* about Chinese views and experiences of abortion as well as the reality of China, Heaven (*tian*) or God (*shen*) only knows.

In the following pages, I weave together survey results, individual narratives, personal experience, historical investigation, sociological inquiry, cultural understanding, political analysis, cross-cultural comparison, and ethical discussion. Together providing a general background, the first three chapters respectively explore the complex meanings of the Chinese silence on abortion, present the contemporary official and dominant discourse, and revisit forgotten controversies over abortion and fetal life in imperial times. Being the core of this book, chapters 4, 5, and 6 demonstrate popular beliefs of a number of groups and present detailed personal narratives of both women and doctors involved in abortion, gathered from the survey and interviews. As a part of my own initial effort in drawing out some normative conclusions, the last two chapters first offer a sociological and ethical inquiry into coerced abortion associated with the birth control program and then illustrate, by the use of abortion as an example, the importance of taking seriously the internal plurality of China in a more effective cross-cultural dialogue.

Let us first of all listen attentively to the silence itself.

1

Listening to the Silence: The Absence of Public Debate and Its Meaning

> The soil, the sentences, all life
> and suffering
> chase us
> toward the clouds and the silence of the South
>
> —Haizi, "The Pondering Chinese Gate"

"Abortions: No Questions Asked," proclaims the heading of a *Time* magazine article (Drake 2001) on abortion clinics at public hospitals in Guangzhou, a southern coastal city near Hong Kong. According to journalist Kate Drake, "No one cares who you are or why you're there" because in China "abortion is treated as a human right, rather than a metaphysical question." A gynecologist at Guangzhou People's Hospital is quoted as saying, "Girls and women of all ages come in here every day for treatment. . . . I don't ask for reasons or home towns." Many Hong Kong women go to Guangzhou for treatment "all the time," and not just because the service is cheap (the fee is $60 per patient, all inclusive).[1] According to the short report, hospitals in the region attracted women from Hong Kong and even Beijing and Singapore because the procedure offered there was painless. In other parts of China, by contrast, general anesthesia was rarely used for early abortions, being reserved almost solely for late-term abortions or patients under extreme stress.

Drake's characterizing of abortion in China as a human right might have been meant ironically or even sarcastically since, in Western practice, the silence implied in the failure to question patients indicates precisely the opposite. In his best-selling book *Abortion: The Clash of Absolutes*, U.S. constitutional authority Laurence Tribe sets this feature of abortion in

13

China—the apparent lack of concern for individual rights—in international perspective:

> As in Stalin's Russia and Nazi Germany, in the Chinese context neither those advocating abortion nor those opposing it use the language of "rights" that characterizes the abortion debate in the United States. Scant attention is paid either to the rights of the women to have her child or to her right to terminate her pregnancy—or to any right of the fetus to be born. Rather, the conflict is structured almost wholly in terms of corporate groups, like the state and the family, and centers on the needs of and the duties owed to such groups. (Tribe 1990: 63)

Tribe's view seems to be widely shared in the West.

Whether or not abortion in China is treated as a human right, both Drake and Tribe, together with many other Western observers and indeed many Chinese, agree that Chinese, unlike Westerners, have little if any concern with the morality of terminating pregnancy. In the most recent comprehensive review of population policy and demographic developments in China in 1949–2000, German scholar Thomas Scharping summarizes this common perception:

> [B]ecause popular medical knowledge continuously pre-dating the beginning of life is unknown, because modern psychology bestowing a soul to infants has not entered the peasant mind and because basic religious ideas are different, the question of abortion in China does not lead to the passionate pro and con arguments we witness in the West. (Scharping 2003: 12)

Chinese medical ethicist Ya-li Cong (Cong Yali) in her recent review of bioethics in China for Western audiences, asserts:

> The reality of abortion in China is that most people do not regard it as an ethical issue. This is related to the policy of family planning but also to the traditional idea that a human being begins at birth. (Cong 2003: 252)

But, as I show later in this chapter, a variety of voices can be heard, even in the public discourse in China. The paucity of public discussion should not, therefore, automatically be presumed to indicate a lack of interest in or concern with the issue on the part of Chinese people. In other words, the common view that Chinese do not view abortion as a serious ethical issue is misleading, appearances to the contrary notwithstanding. Anyone interested in a better understanding of Chinese attitudes to abortion needs to do what the contemporary Chinese poet–philosopher Zhou Guoping enjoins us to do: "Let us learn to listen to the silence. . . . One who listens to words only is a deaf person whose ears are blocked by too much noise" (Zhou 1997: 229).

THROUGH WESTERN EYES

Many Americans and other Westerners have expressed shock at the use of coercion in implementing an aggressive national population policy whereby the state forces women to terminate pregnancies, even very late-term ones. In addition, Western observers have been surprised by the apparent silence of Chinese on related ethical issues. This seems to confirm the assumption that China belongs to a different ethical universe.

Although the Chinese birth control policy does not lack Western supporters, forced abortion and sterilization have been almost universally condemned. In American media and intellectual circles, forced abortion and sterilization have aroused deep and indignant criticism. The intense outrage expressed at forced abortion and other coercive measures associated with China's birth control program is probably second only to the political and moral outpourings over the Tiananmen Square massacre of 1989. For many international observers, particularly Americans, coerced abortion is nothing less than forcing a woman to kill her unborn child. It is simply unacceptable in the Western liberal tradition for the state to forcibly intervene in matters of individual reproduction. Abortion itself, even voluntary abortion, is viewed at a minimum as a *moral problem* by many and as a *moral crime* in certain Western religious traditions. What possible justification could there be for coerced abortion? Just as the Tiananmen Square massacre shattered American liberal illusions concerning China (see Madsen 1995), so forced abortion directly challenges moral, religious, social, and political values—including the sanctity of human life and the liberty of the individual—that are widely and dearly held by the great majority of Americans.

In 1995 and 1998, two hearings on forced abortion and coercive population control in China were held before the Subcommittee on International Operations and Human Rights of the Committee on International Relations in the U.S. House of Representatives. A resolution by the subcommittee condemned forced abortion as a crime against humanity. Chairman of the Judiciary Committee Henry J. Hyde called forced abortion a "double insult to humanity" (U.S. House of Representatives 1998). For Hyde, abortion for whatever reason is "dehumanizing" because it means "a life member of the human family extinguished." He added, "But it's doubly dehumanizing when the mother who wants to have her child is forced by the government to exterminate her child" (U.S. House of Representatives 1998). In his opening statement at the 1998 hearing, subcommittee chairman Christopher H. Smith gave his view of the situation in China:

> We knew that when a woman has an unauthorized pregnancy, she is typically brought to the family planning center and subjected to intense psychological pressure, often with the personal involvement of her boss and other people

who hold power over her, until she agrees to the abortion. We knew that when the psychological pressure does not work, women are sometimes dragged physically to abortion mills and that physical force is often also employed against both men and women when they refuse to be sterilized. . . .

The world has not known . . . that family planning centers engage in Gestapo-like record keeping about the sexual history of every woman within their jurisdiction. Perhaps most stunning, the world has not known that these so-called family planning centers actually contain cells, detention centers with prison bars, to hold those who have resisted abortion or sterilization. (U.S. House of Representatives 1998: 2–3)

Since forced abortion "was rightly denounced as a crime against humanity by the Nuremberg war crimes tribunal," Smith proposed that "the United Nations should be organizing an international tribunal to investigate and prosecute the perpetrators of the Chinese population control program" (U.S. House of Representatives 1998: 3). After hearing testimonies from witnesses, including a victim and a former administrator of Chinese family planning programs, Smith concluded by pointing out that he himself and three of his children would never have been born had his family lived in China. He pleaded with Americans and other people in the Western world to "wake up . . . to this shame and the dishonor of a policy and the cruelty of a policy that makes brothers and sisters illegal" (U.S. House of Representatives 1998: 26). Such emotionally charged remarks by politicians doubtless represent the views of a fair number of Americans, though how representative they really are is unknown.

John S. Aird and Steven W. Mosher are prominent among American scholars and activists who condemn forced abortion and the coercive nature of the Chinese birth control program. In a highly controversial journalistic report on conditions in rural China, Mosher (1983: 22–261) describes what he saw as the horrors of birth control. Later, based on the life story of a Chinese woman who emigrated to the United States, Mosher (1993) reported in detail on what he perceived as the heroic fight of a mother against the "one-child" policy. The title of Aird's influential monograph on birth control in China, *Slaughter of the Innocents*, leaves no room for misinterpretation. The first sentence reads: "China's birth control program has earned a worldwide reputation as the most draconian since King Herod's slaughter of the innocents" (Aird 1990: 1). While Aird's biblical comparison may be an exaggeration even for most Westerners, his contention is accurate that, for most Westerners, forced abortion and sterilization demand extremely strong moral justification and are generally neither ethically nor politically acceptable.

The fact that abortion is legal in China does not necessarily mean that it is regarded as a human right. Despite the fact that, unlike in the West, in China moral norms are expressed in administrative regulations, customs, and unspoken rules rather than in statute law, law can still be a useful indicator of morality in China. In his review of abortion laws as measures of women's rights in the former Soviet Union and the People's Republic of China, Mark Savage (1988: 1107) concludes that, although a woman "enjoys" the right to abortion in these two countries, she "has no human or natural right to decide whether she will have an abortion. . . . Her substantive and procedural legal rights and remedies under the laws on abortion are subordinated to the needs of the state and vary as those needs vary." Therefore, her rights to abortion are "not rights per se," but more properly reflect "women's duties as child-bearers." Savage suggests that understanding abortion law in these two socialist countries "requires every effort to take the point of view internal to the foreign culture and its legal system" (1028–29). It is from Savage's work that Tribe drew his hostile generalizations.

Chinese attitudes toward abortion and fetal life often appear so alien to outsiders that Westerners exposed to the "silence" around the issue feel like "anthropologists on Mars" (to borrow an expression made famous by American psychiatrist Oliver Sacks). Susan Rigdon and William Jennings are among many American scholars who have visited, researched, and lectured in China since the normalization of relations in the early 1970s, and especially since the openness policy was initiated in the late 1970s. Rigdon, an anthropologist, taught a graduate seminar in China on American political life in 1989–1990, while Jennings, an expert in religious studies, taught a course on U.S. medical ethics at a university in Shanghai in the autumn of 1996. In introducing their Chinese students to the American abortion controversy, both Rigdon and Jennings were surprised by the reaction of their audience (Rigdon 1996; Jennings 1999). First, there was a striking lack of interest in the subject. Jennings called his following experience "revealing":

> Many of the fifty-some students said they had never heard abortion discussed in a class and never thought of it as controversial. When asked if the American debate related to the Chinese situation, they said "no" because America has a smaller population and can afford the luxury of the debate. They felt China has too many people and must have abortions to control population. (Jennings 1999: 476)

In contrast with their great interest in, and relaxed discussion of, such issues as AIDS, homelessness, or the U.S. savings and loan scandal, Rigdon's students responded with "blank stares" to the U.S. abortion debate. Abortion was not interesting or controversial unless it was placed in specific contexts such as the Sino-American relationship or the Chinese family planning program.

One of Rigdon's students, who chose the American abortion rights movement as the topic of his seminar paper, complained of his difficulty in making a comparison with China because "he could not find materials in the library and because abortion is rarely discussed." He wrote that the abortion debate was a "purely American story" and found it "amusing to watch Americans fighting an internal war among themselves." The student asserted confidently: "I dare say that for the vast majority of Chinese, intellectuals included, the debate on abortion is meaningless. . . . The lack of religious tradition [in China] determines that abortion is only a medical procedure. No Operation Rescue here." Strongly supporting China's national population control policy, he wrote that, unlike the situation in "rich" America, it is "inhumane to [have] kids you cannot feed and clothe." If a couple or an individual mother-to-be were to be free to decide the timing and size of their family, he believed that "our economy [would] collapse and our living standards [would] slide."

Second, according to Rigdon and Jennings, their Chinese audience had no concern for the moral status of the fetus. Rigdon's students mistook the phrase "life begins at conception" for "life begins with the idea [of having a baby]"—and not because of their insufficient grasp of English. Even when they were told the meaning of the word "conception," the phrase still "made little more sense to them than it did with their own translation." For Rigdon, this "little incident" (Rigdon 1996: 543) indicated how difficult it was for most of her Chinese students "to consider the abortion issue in the larger context of human rights and civil liberties in which it is generally placed by all sides in the abortion debates in the U.S." When Jennings outlined fetal development in class, "students listened" but saw no relationship between abortion and what was "taking place in the womb." His students told him: "In China we have always thought life begins at birth" and "China has decided that life in the womb is not yet human." Jennings further points out, correctly, the lack of attention given to the moral status of the fetus in an earlier discussion of forced abortion by the present author (Nie 1999c) and in the treatment of late abortions by other Chinese scholars (Qiu, Wang, and Gu 1989).

Third, both Rigdon and Jennings exclude "fear" as the main reason for the lack of interest in the subject among Chinese students. Jennings observes:

> There is more openness in China than is often reported and students would find ways to express concerns about abortion if they wished. They openly discuss topics as varied as euthanasia and official corruption. On abortion they acquiesce, it seems, because they strongly support China's current economic policies and see enforced abortion as essential to those policies. (Jennings 1999: 475)

Rigdon dismisses fear of reprisal as the probable reason for her students' failure to speak out as the subject under discussion was abortion politics in the United States, not in China, and because the discussion of other policy-sensitive topics such as AIDS engendered active interest. She attributed the "silence" over abortion to "the students' inability to grasp the political context in which abortion became an issue in U.S. politics" and, modestly, to her own "inability to move the discussion on to a plane where the vocabulary and concepts were mutually intelligible" (Rigdon 1996: 543).

The great majority of Chinese—nearly one billion in 2005—live in the countryside. Anthropological studies have reported that, like university students, rural Chinese do not consider abortion as the taking of a human life and thus morally problematic. As early as the 1970s, Elizabeth Johnson, who studied childbearing practices in a village in the New Territories of Hong Kong, noticed that most village women thought of abortion in relation to the physical health of women rather than as involving the killing of a human being.

> No one raised moral objections; the taking of life at this stage appears not to be considered immoral. Abortion is inadvisable, almost all the women said, because it is dangerous to the mother's health. The threat to the mother's health was the overwhelming concern. (Johnson 1975: 236)

In the words of one female informant, abortion might mean that a woman "could have no babies afterward, and it might kill her, because of infection. Some dirty things might be left in her womb, which would make her weaker and weaker." In another village woman's words, "An abortion is not good. It hurts the woman. It is like picking an unripe papaya, which hurts the tree. It is better to pick it when ripe" (Johnson 1975: 236–37).

The most detailed study of cultural assumptions about abortion in contemporary rural China comes from two other anthropologists, Sulamith and Jack Potter, who from the late 1970s through the mid-1980s studied family planning practices in a Cantonese village. The Potters (1990) discovered that while villagers resisted pressure to have abortions, this was not for the reasons registered by antiabortionists in the United States; and while they accepted the morality of abortion, it was for different reasons than those espoused by Western pro-choicers. As the Potters saw it, "Valuing a child as a 'human life,' in isolation from its significance to the family and to society, is a senseless abstraction when considered in terms of Chinese ideas about what it means to be a person" (230). "The Chinese do *not* have a concept of birth as legitimately the personal decision of a woman about her body" (231, original emphasis). They warned that attempts to impose categories that reflect "specifically American cultural concerns" (such as "prochoice" versus "prolife") onto traditional Chinese birth planning "leads only to misunderstanding" (231). To make sense of Chinese methods of family planning, it is crucial "to stand aside from the emotionally powerful connotations that abortion has in American society" (239) and to grasp the "culturally specific assumptions" relating to birth and abortion in China.

In summary, normatively speaking, Western commentators cited above adopted diverse and even opposite positions: a clear condemnation or moral superiority to China's practice on the one end and sympathy or antiethno-centrism on the other. But they all agree on one "matter of fact": the Chinese silence on the subject indicates that Chinese have little or no concern for the morality of abortion.

The strong reactions—from shock to surprise—to Chinese abortion prac-tices, from the general public and intellectuals alike in the United States, says more about the U.S. abortion debate and its sociocultural and intellectual underpinnings than about the realities of the Chinese situation. In the West, abortion has been one of the most contentious ethical, religious, social, and political issues of the twentieth century. In the United States, abortion and re-lated issues have been fervently addressed on television, in newspapers and magazines, in classrooms, lecture halls, and conferences, in courtrooms, in churches, in the halls of Congress, on the street, in bars, and in homes. Nu-merous scholars, theologians, moral philosophers, lawyers, social activists, religious leaders, policy makers, and citizens of diverse religious and philo-sophical beliefs and different national origins have all taken up the issue. Mountains of articles, pamphlets, books, monographs, and theses have ap-peared, and their numbers continue to grow. Still, abortion remains morally controversial and politically divisive. Americans are vocal in their protests on both sides of the issue. Bumper stickers illustrate the polarization involved: "Abortion: An American Holocaust!" versus "A Woman's Right to Choose!" Even devoted couples, such as former President George H. W. Bush and his wife, may hold entirely opposite views. Despite the occasional changing of sides, no sign of a respite, much less a permanent resolution, is discernible in this ongoing conflict. This battle between two fundamental American values—life and liberty—is unlikely to end anytime soon.

Violence, including bombings and shootings, has been directed at abortion clinics and physicians who provided abortions. On the day I first drafted this sentence for my Ph.D. dissertation (January 29, 1998), the media reported an abortion clinic bombing in Birmingham, Alabama—a policeman died and an-other person was injured. After the injured clinic worker was released from the hospital, she claimed that violence would never stop her from doing her job—helping women who needed abortions. And on the day I finished preparing for the oral defense of my dissertation (October 23, 1998), the mur-der of a New York abortion physician—Dr. Barnett Slepian—was reported. He was shot by a sniper through the window of his home at night.

The only consensus on abortion in the United Sates is that it is one of the thorniest ethical issues of the day, if not *the* most difficult. In their historic de-cision in the *Roe v. Wade* case in 1973, the judges of the U.S. Supreme Court ruled that the right of privacy protected in the American Constitution "is broad enough to encompass a woman's decision whether or not to terminate her pregnancy" (collected in Shapiro 1995: 60). Before presenting the major-ity view, the court first stated:

We forthwith acknowledge our awareness of the sensitive and emotional nature of the abortion controversy, of the vigorous opposing views, even among physicians, and of the deep and seemingly absolute convictions that the subject inspires. One's philosophy, one's experiences, one's exposure to the raw edge of human existence, one's religious training, one's attitudes toward life and family and their values, and the moral standards one establishes and seeks to observe, are all likely to influence and to color one's thinking and conclusions about abortion. . . . In addition, population growth, pollution, poverty, and racial overtones tend to complicate and not to simplify the problem. (In Shapiro 1995: 46)

Sixteen years later, when in the eyes of its defenders a woman's "fundamental constitutional right" to abortion was challenged in the 1989 *Webster v. Reproductive Health Services* case, abortion was described by Justice Blackman as "the most politically divisive domestic legal issue of our time" (in Shapiro 1995: 183). Theologian Richard A. McCormick summarizes the troubling abortion issue in the United States in eloquent terms:

Abortion is a matter that is morally problematic, pastorally delicate, legislatively thorny, constitutionally insecure, ecumenically divisive, medically normless, humanly anguishing, racially provocative, journalistically abused, personally biased, and widely performed. (Quoted in Rodman, Sarvis, and Bonar 1987: xiii)

Philosopher Daniel Callahan, one of the founders of bioethics, begins his book on the law and morality of abortion by describing it as "a nasty problem. . . . If many individuals have worked through a position they find satisfactory, the world as a whole, and most societies, have not" (Callahan 1970: 1). For some Westerners, abortion is simply an insoluble moral and legal challenge.

Given this intense polemical background, it is not surprising that Western observers are surprised by the Chinese silence on abortion and puzzled that the issue has not sparked serious public debate in China. Chinese people appear to be far from sharing the American experience that abortion is a serious moral problem and has brought about a fundamental clash of values.

Why then does abortion, a topic heatedly debated on one side of the Pacific, seem to be morally and politically insignificant on the other? The more profound question is: What does the Chinese silence really mean and how should it be interpreted?

ATTITUDES OF OVERSEAS CHINESE

Often self-labeled as people at the "cultural margins," thousands of mainland Chinese students, scholars, doctors, scientists, and their families have arrived in the West, especially the so-called melting pot of the United States, to live, study, and work since the 1980s. In coming to the West, they were willing to face the challenges of a different society and culture. At the same time, like other new immigrants, they hoped to maintain some of their native social and cultural values. As a result, the views of overseas Chinese students and scholars expressed in the pilot study conducted in Galveston, Texas, reflect not only Western influence but also original Chinese perspectives. Their opinions reflect both the apparent lack of concern about abortion among Chinese and the diverse views sheltered behind the silence— mirroring the complexity of mainland Chinese views on abortion and related issues.

Certainly, I encountered silence and lack of interest in the course of the pilot study, as the following case illustrates. I sat with Dr. Lu in a corner of the University of Texas Medical Branch library in Galveston, where Chinese newspapers and magazines published both on the mainland and abroad were displayed. Dr. Lu was a former biomedical researcher and had lived in the United States for several years. When I asked about interviewing her for a study of Chinese attitudes on abortion, she looked at me as though I were an alien. "What are you studying? Are you a student *here* [at a medical school]?" she asked, incredulous. I informed her that I was trained in Chinese medicine in China and was currently a graduate student in medical humanities at the school. "Why are you interested in this topic? I performed abortions once. I once had an abortion myself. But, except for the medical aspects, there's nothing worth talking about." Referring to the U.S. controversies, she continued: "Some Americans are ridiculous. Abortion and killing are two totally different things. The fetus is not a human being." She then turned to her newspaper. The "interview" ended there.

Dr. Lu was not alone in perceiving the American debate as "ridiculous." The interviewees in the pilot study were asked to comment on abortion in the United States. Just as American responses to abortion in China say more about American understandings of the issue, Chinese informants' comments on the U.S. abortion debate say more about Chinese or, to be exact, their own perspectives. Nearly one-third (five out of eighteen) of informants dismissed the Western abortion controversy as "meaningless," "ridiculous," or "totally unnecessary." Some of their responses are given below, in their own words. "The debate is meaningless. The circumstances [under which a woman has an abortion] should be analyzed differently." "The controversy is ridiculous. Take, for example, the case in Ireland where a girl who had been raped had to go abroad to have an abortion." "I have little knowledge about the debate. I've got very little interest in it. I'm for abortion. Women should have the right to make their own decisions." "There are two opposite views. But debate about it is totally unnecessary. The woman can make her own decision." "It's too much to equate abortion to killing and even murder. People place too much importance on abortion. Some even decide on their presidential candidate on this issue alone."

Some criticized the way Americans dealt with related issues such as teen pregnancy. One man stated: "In the United States, there are no restrictions. Many teenagers go to school with their own children. This is no good, even for the teenagers. This is not a mark of progress. Moreover, babies born to immature [adolescent] parents are usually vulnerable to disease—this is supported by medical research." For this informant, abortion was preferable to a teen pregnancy resulting in birth.

Most respondents stressed that religion was the major ground for American opposition to abortion. Two men supported this view: "I know that many people oppose abortion. I guess that people's religious beliefs are the main reason." "I'm not clear about the debate. Usually, they oppose abortion because of their religious beliefs. They believe that life is created by God." Two women specifically pointed out the role of Roman Catholicism in the debate: "The Catholic Church opposes any abortion and even contraception. Aborting the fetus after two months is seen as murder." "It's mainly a religious issue. Catholics consider abortion to be killing, even murder."

Most interviewees also attributed the different attitudes to abortion to discrepancies between the United States and China in demographics, economic development, and human rights. One woman observed: "Every country has different customs, culture, values, and beliefs, as well as unique circumstances. The United States is richer than China. Americans can afford [many children]. Besides, the population of the United States is much smaller than that of China." One man said: "China and the United States are not at the same social and economic level. The key is not the political system, but economic and social development. Society is always changing. In the old days, a woman wearing a bikini could be sent to jail in China. It [American opposition to abortion] must have something to do with human rights. I can't say clearly."

Several informants considered the U.S. abortion debate to be positive, indicative of the fact that greater respect was placed on human life in the United States than in China. One man (a medical scientist and Party member who believed that the Chinese silence on the subject stemmed from the "cheapness" of human life in China) argued that the American abortion debate reflected the sociocultural premium placed on human life there, rather than economic conditions or population factors.

Some expressed misconceptions about abortion in the United States. A young woman who had arrived in the United States less than a year earlier commented: "I don't know much about the debate. I think it's illegal here. You have to go to a 'back street' or 'black market' doctor to have one." She understood, however, that many "Americans believe that the fetus is a human life" that should be respected as such.

One of the questions I asked in the pilot study was: "Why, in your view, do Chinese people remain silent on the abortion issue and not debate it as Americans do?" Interestingly, the responses of overseas Chinese to the question indicated that Chinese were not as silent as the question implied. The following answers were given to account for the "silence": political repression; the lack of a religious tradition such as Christianity that values human life highly; the scant attention paid to human life due to social-economic conditions; the cultural taboo associated with sex; the low rate of illicit—premarital and extramarital—sex; and the fact that the issue itself is not necessarily controversial. Many informants listed more than one factor.

Political factors, especially the national population control policy, were mentioned by several respondents as the most important reason for the silence: "The state has a national policy. It's useless to talk about it. You can't write an article against abortion, can you? I guess religious believers in China oppose abortion." "The government doesn't permit [public discussion]. It wants to control. There will be debate and discussion only if the government allows it—I know that because I was once a member of a medical team in the family planning program. But, even though you and I are friends, I'd prefer not to tell you about that experience of mine." "The one-child policy doesn't allow for any debate. Abortion is essential to the birth control policy. Chinese women have no choice. They have no real desire to choose, either. And it's not really necessary to discuss abortion." "People can't voice their opinions even though they all have different views. We all see things from different angles, although we all live under the sun. But, because of the political system, people like officials and workers daren't speak out."

A biomedical scientist and Party member spoke out about political repression:

> The fact that people don't speak out doesn't at all mean that they have nothing to say. People have opinions about abortion. The family planning program is a national policy. You know the situation in mainland China—it's a centralized state power. All policies are made by the government. If the government claims something is black, it's black. The "small reason" [i.e., individual interests] must always be subordinated to the "big reason" [the national and collective interest]. Even though you have opinions, the political system doesn't allow you to speak. In the West, the air is comparatively free.

Some thought that the absence of religious traditions such as Christianity, which emphasizes the value of human life, had resulted in the social acceptance of abortion in China and the general silence on the issue. A woman who had become a Baptist several years earlier, after coming to the United States, said:

There are deeper cultural reasons. There isn't a religion like Christianity in China. The Chinese don't believe in God and don't know that the fetus comes from Jehovah. As a result, they want to control and take responsibility [for the fate of the fetus] into their own hands. Chinese think abortion is acceptable and reasonable. They take it for granted and view it as a natural thing. They don't have a sense of respect for life. For example, Chinese contains phrases like "deserving death"; it's considered OK to save good people but kill the bad guys.

The medical scientist in the group, who supported coercive measures in implementing the national birth control policy, also harshly criticized the lack of respect for human life in Chinese society and culture, and attributed the silence to this ethical void. But unlike the Baptist woman, he saw this lack of respect deriving not from the absence of religious beliefs, but from the low level of social, mainly economic, development:

> Chinese society has not developed to the level where the value of life is given prominence. The whole country is basically ignorant about the importance of life. People's deaths are not seen as that serious. The situation in China is different from that in the West. In *The Romance of Three Kingdoms* [a classical novel], killing a person is a small matter. In the U.S., executing a person, a criminal, is a big issue. But in China, executing a bunch of bad guys is often spoken of as [being done to] "the immense satisfaction of the people" (*dakuai renxin*).

Some informants considered China's cultural taboo on sexuality as the primary factor contributing to the silence. One woman observed: "Sex is viewed as a taboo, as a bad and dirty thing; this custom dates back thousands of years. It's embarrassing to talk about these things—it's shameful." One man asserted: "Sex is a shameful issue. Chinese tradition considers sexuality a forbidden area. Women may discuss it with each other. Men sometimes joke with one another about abortion." Another man said: "Abortion is a private thing and so, like sex, it's rarely discussed publicly; people don't talk about issues related to sex in public. It's a taboo topic. People talk about birth control, but they don't discuss the specifics." One informant disagreed with the view that Chinese people are silent about abortion: "People do talk about it. For instance, the radio has a special program on sex called 'Whisper at Midnight.'" While his example confused abortion and wider sexual issues, he was right that sex has ceased to be a taboo subject in China over the past two or three decades. China has been experiencing its own sexual revolution, probably due not so much to the influence of Western values, as is often asserted, as to the revival of traditional Chinese sexual culture.

Two men attributed the cultural silence to the low rate of illicit sex and the lack of sexual permissiveness in China: "There are fewer premarital pregnancies in China than in the United States. There is not as much illicit sexual behavior in China as here in the United States." "Abortion is a big problem in the United States as a result of sexual liberation. But it is not a big problem in China, since China has not experienced sexual liberation." However, as I show in chapter 6, the level of premarital pregnancies among Chinese youth has increased in recent years.

Some informants claimed that abortion in China was so socially acceptable that there was simply no need to discuss it. One woman said: "No one is interested in it. There's nothing worth discussing about abortion." And one man observed: "Chinese people consider abortion acceptable. It's just too convenient to have abortions. [A woman] will come up against social pressure if she doesn't have an abortion."

In summary, like the Chinese informants cited by Western commentators discussed above, these overseas Chinese generally considered their fellow Chinese to be unconcerned with the morality of taking a fetal life. The fact that Chinese apparently have little to say about abortion, especially in public discourse, indicated to both my interview subjects and the Western observers quoted above that Chinese have minimal opinions on the issue. Although often critical of both Western and Chinese attitudes, respondents seemed willing to accept such Chinese stereotypes as a low level of respect for individual human life and conservative norms about sex. Nevertheless, their own diverse views indicate the existence of a variety of voices on these issues among overseas Chinese that reflects the situation on the mainland. Further results of the pilot study are discussed in the analysis of the wider survey data in chapter 4.

THE HIDDEN DEBATE IN THE PUBLIC SPHERE

No systematic treatment on the ethics of abortion and the moral status of the fetus is to be found in contemporary China. While extensive medical and demographic research on abortion has been conducted in China, few studies assess the moral or philosophical aspects. And the secondary literature on abortion in China in English, albeit limited in scope, far exceeds that in Chinese, as witnessed by the reference list for the present study. The only substantial ethical treatment of abortion by a Chinese author is found in the 1987 book *Shengming Lunlixue* (Bioethics), by Qiu Renzong (known as "Ren-Zong Qiu" in the West), a leading Chinese bioethicist and philosopher of science. In this first and most influential text published in Chinese in this new field, Qiu introduces Chinese audiences to American bioethics research on assisted reproduction, birth control, genetics and eugenics, impaired infants, issues surrounding death and euthanasia, organ transplantation, behavioral control, and public policy and ethics. Each topic discussed is related to Chinese cultural norms and social realities. Chapter 3 includes a discussion of the ethics of abortion (Qiu 1987: 76–99) as well as contraception, sterilization, and research involving fetuses. In the space of some twenty pages, Qiu outlines the Western abortion controversies, what he calls "the biggest bioethical debate" (Qiu 1987: 77). He takes the ethical position that the fetus is a human being in the biological sense but not a person in the moral and social sense. Citing two influential ancient Chinese philosophers, Xun Zi and Hanfei Zi, Qiu reasserts the traditional Chinese belief that the fetus becomes a human being only at birth (85, 90; see also his English work, Qiu 1992: 169). For Qiu, the fetus has mainly "external value," supporting the view that abortion is ethically acceptable as a measure of birth control, especially in the context of China's population problems.

Since the late 1970s and early 1980s, medical ethics as an academic discipline has developed rapidly in China. It is also increasingly prominent in public discourse; such topics as euthanasia and assisted reproduction have gained enormous coverage in the mass media and are widely discussed in popular forums (for the English-language literature on medical ethics in contemporary China, see, e.g., Fox and Swazey 1984; Qiu 1992; Nie 2000; Döring 2002a; Döring and Chen 2002; Cong 2003; Döring 2003; Qiu and Jonsen 2003; Schwarz and Stern 2004; Fan and Tao 2004; Qiu 2004; Nie forthcoming-a). The two premier journals in the fields of medical ethics and medical humanities in contemporary China, *Yixue Yu Zhexue* (Medicine and Philosophy) and *Zhongguo Yixue Lunli* (Chinese Medical Ethics), were launched respectively in 1979 and 1988. Their audience includes academics and medical students as well as medical professionals and health-care administrators. Yet, except for a few brief reports on the abortion debate in the West (e.g., Li and Leng 1993), neither journal has published any serious ethical or philosophical inquiry on the subject.

As a compulsory subject for medical students, medical ethics is taught in almost all medical schools in China, whether traditional Chinese or modern institutions (see Döring 2003; Nie 2003; and several articles in Reiser and Wang 2004 on medical ethics education in China). Dozens of medical ethics textbooks, with extremely similar structures and contents, have been published in China since the 1980s. Some, especially those published since the 1990s, have a section on the ethical issues surrounding abortion. Especially if the topic is only briefly touched on, the context is always birth control and the text always states unambiguously that abortion is morally acceptable and necessary for carrying out the national population policy. The reasons generally given for abortion include: (1) to save the life of the mother; (2) to prevent physical and mental harm to the mother; (3) to avoid the birth of a seriously impaired infant; (4) to terminate pregnancies resulting from rape, incest, or illicit sex; (5) to facilitate the personal choice of limiting family size; and (6) to meet the societal needs of controlling population growth (see Qiu 1987: 76; Zhang and Zhang 1995: 191–92; Cao, Qiu, and Fan 1998: 153–55; Shi, He, and Huang 1998: 277; Lu 1999: 196; Bu 2003: 83).

In the second edition of their medical ethics textbook, the three Chinese scholars Shi, He, and Huang state:

> In our country, both the medical profession and the public take an enlightened (*kaiming*) and permissive (*kengding*) attitude toward induced abortion. Usually, ethical disagreements over the issues involved have not undermined the practice of abortion. All this has not been not achieved (*nandede*) easily. Success in this area is attributable (*guigongyu*) to the long-term development of our country's family planning work, and the publicity and propaganda associated with it, which has brought about a change in people's beliefs. (Shi, He, and Huang 1998: 278)

They set out the grounds on which "the legitimacy of abortion can be proven," based on their perception of individual rights. First, the fetus lacks the rights of a human being because what they call the "conceived body" or "conceived existence" (*shouyunti*) does not represent the beginning of human life. Second, even if the "conceived existence" has a right to life, this right is not absolute. Third, the interests of the state and the needs of society require population control, for which abortion can legitimately be used as a remedial measure after contraceptive failure. Fourth, because every couple has a right extended by society to give birth to a healthy child, there are ethical, personal, and social reasons (not spelled out in the text) for aborting the fetus if a serious disability is present. Finally, the three authors give a rosy but medically erroneous picture of the technical side of abortion, asserting that the modern medical techniques have made abortion "more and more perfect, convenient, safe, and painless," so that carrying a pregnancy to term can be more dangerous than an "almost risk-free" abortion (278).[2]

Despite this, one must exercise caution in drawing conclusions from the lack of serious debate about abortion in the prevailing discourse in China. The Chinese emphasize that one should discern essences from small clues (*jianweizhizhu*). Many clues in the public discourse that appear trivial at first sight can alert us to a fuller conversation, especially if we are aware of the context in which they arise.

Such clues can even be discovered in medical ethics texts. One recent standard medical ethics textbook for continuing medical education, published by the national Higher Education Press in Beijing, distinguishes late abortion from the other stages while affirming that abortion in general is necessary for China's birth control policy. As pointed out in the introduction, the standard term for abortion in Chinese, *rengong liuchan* (induced abortion), usually refers to a termination at any time before birth, but more specifically to termination in early pregnancy. Generally, a different term—*yinchan* (induced birth or induced labor)—is used to refer to termination in the middle and especially the later stages. The textbook expresses clear reservations about permitting abortion at any stage merely for social and economic reasons:

[I]t damages the sentiment or feeling (*qinggang*) of humankind if, due to social and economic interests, no restriction is placed on abortion. This is especially the case with abortion at the late stage (*dayufeng liuchan*, literally, abortion beyond several months of pregnancy) when the fetus is viable. From the perspective of the sanctity of life (*shengming shenshang*), we should think over the matter carefully and should not simply perform any abortion indiscriminately (*yidaoqie*, literally, cutting with one blow). (Bu 2003: 84)

I do not want to suggest that, in justifying abortion, Chinese medical ethicists regularly exclude later terminations, as is done here. Most probably do not make distinctions according to the different stages of pregnancy and usually use the general term *rengong liuchan*.

Generalizations are difficult to make. One the one hand, one medical ethics textbook in a nonspecialist series edited by the Ministry of Education's Department of Higher Education and intended for university and college students discusses both abortion (*rengong liuchan*) and induced birth (*yinchan*) without making any ethical distinction between them (Lu 1999: 196–97). On the other hand, this same textbook stresses the voluntary consent of women and their families:

> Medical professionals who perform the operations of abortion and induced birth must resolutely oppose any form of coerced abortion (*jianjue fandui renhe xingshi de qiangzhi duotai*), and must make the consent of the patient and her family or husband a prerequisite. Besides dissuading women from coerced abortion or induced birth by all means necessary, medical professionals should refuse to participate in such operations so as to safeguard the dignity of women and the integrity of medical ethics. (167)

Certainly, the view that any form of coerced abortion is morally unjustifiable is not a popular one in China. Many medical ethics texts often more than hint that coerced abortions, such as those performed in the interests of the national population policy, are a necessary evil for the sake of the greater social good and, thus, ethically permissible. Still, different voices, however weak and hesitating, can be detected even in the public sphere. The biomedical context in which "small clues" are placed reminds us that people are quietly aware (*xinzhao buxuan*) that coerced abortion (including forced induced birth) is widely performed in China.

Some voices are heard more loudly than others. The government exercises much tighter control over the mass media, and especially over studies linked to the social sciences, than it is able to exercise over literary works. As a result, creative writers enjoy greater freedom of speech in China today than scholars in the humanities and social sciences, and literary works often constitute the best window into the concerns and opinions of ordinary people on many social issues. While a medical humanities scholar may fail to find an outlet for an article that argues that abortion is ethically wrong, a fiction writer may sometimes be able to express a similar opinion without falling afoul of the authorities.

Two contemporary Chinese literary works that express contrasting views can serve to introduce us to the hidden abortion debate in the public sphere.[3] The first is a popular movie based on the widely acclaimed novel *Once Deceived*. The hero of the story is a young teacher at a senior middle school in a city in North China. When one of his students becomes pregnant by a rich businessman from Hong Kong, the teacher signs an official document for the girl to have an abortion. As a result, he is falsely charged by her parents and by the school authorities with having had illicit sex with her. Both the novelist and the filmmakers applaud the teacher for procuring an abortion for his student—his actions reflect his virtues as a good teacher and caring individual. Both take it for granted that abortion is the best choice for a pregnant, unmarried teenager. Continuing her pregnancy is viewed as a threat to her health and especially to her future well-being. The government's population policy is seen as much less morally significant than the harm done to her future prospects. Given the bleak prospect for a single mother in China, the girl involved also favors an abortion.

The second story, "The Lonely Grave Mound," published in a prestigious Chinese literary magazine, conveys a different message (Du 1997: 174). This fictional but realistic account is set in late-1960s China at the start of the Cultural Revolution. The heroine is a lecturer at an urban university, still single at thirty. When her father is falsely accused of being a spy for Taiwan and is humiliated in "struggle" meetings, one of her students responds by revealing his feelings for her. But after having sex with her, he betrays her for the sake of his own political prospects by reporting information she has confided to him. Her father commits suicide, and she is banished to the remote countryside. Discovering that she is pregnant, her first thought is to go to a hospital and have an abortion, wiping out the painful memories of the lover who betrayed her. But on second thought, she realizes that the fetus in her womb is "guilty of nothing" and has "every right to survive." "Half of the blood in the fetus's veins was my own blood," she muses. As a mother she "had no right to kill it." With help from the villagers, especially from a woman and a mute man, she gives birth and raises a baby boy. Clearly, the author of this story presents abortion as the killing of an innocent human being and, as such, morally offensive. Furthermore, he affirms the right of a woman to bear and nurture a child resulting from extramarital sex as a single parent.

Although the apparent silence of Chinese is astounding if the U.S. controversies are taken as a reference point, absence of public debate does not necessarily signal an absence of concern among the public over the issue. As Shi, He, and Huang hinted in their textbook, the widespread acceptance of abortion is something "not easily achieved," and the lack of significant resistance to the party line is a result of painstaking propaganda. It is not that Chinese lack any moral concern about abortion. Rather the official standpoint dominates the voices of the silent majority so that they are scarcely audible.

In the past two decades, more and more attention in both the public and intellectual spheres has been given to the ethics of abortion and related issues. This development should not be interpreted merely as a result of Western influence, no matter how crucial this influence may be. As chapter 3 shows, this development should also be understood as a revival of long-neglected traditional Chinese ethical beliefs on abortion and fetal life. It is wrong to conclude that, because of the contemporary lack of serious public debate, abortion has always been acceptable in Chinese culture. Chinese soil *is* a fertile medium for Western views opposing abortion. But if the present Chinese state has adopted a firm pro-abortion position, many individual Chinese, past and present, have disagreed radically on abortion and especially on the moral status of the fetus.

WHAT THE SILENCE SPEAKS

Not only do diverse voices underlie the deceptive silence, but also the silence itself speaks. The public and private silence surrounding abortion has such intricate personal and sociocultural meanings that any single explanation will inevitably simplify and distort its complexity. People remain silent or reticent about abortion in different ways and for different reasons. For a particular individual, silence might signify self-protection, fear, helplessness, self-censorship, anger, shame, anxiety, bitterness, acceptance, embarrassment, indifference, resistance, disagreement, a desire for secrecy, privacy, or escape, or simply having nothing to say. Various political or personal reasons may compel one to be silent, to "choose" not to speak out. A person may lack the capacity to speak out, or lack the vocabulary to discuss the subject. The dynamics and multiple meanings of an individual's silence can never be fully understood or articulated. To comprehend even one individual's silence, one must enter a unique life world.

In my fieldwork as in the pilot study, I met many instances of silence that spoke volumes. Sometimes, the silence is difficult to interpret, though one is certain that it is meaningful. One such encounter took place in the living room of a plain wooden house in a southern inland village. Two women, one in her twenties and the other in her thirties, were filling out the questionnaires. Several children were playing and reading out parts of the questionnaire for fun. I was trying to talk to a third woman who was probably in her seventies or eighties. I spoke to in her local dialect. She kept smiling and nodding without saying a word. The children sometimes restated what I was asking her. Sometimes her mouth moved and she looked as though she wanted to say something, but nothing came out. After a while, the two young women finished their questionnaires and three research assistants came to take me to another site. When I was ready to leave, I thanked the older woman, wished her good health and longevity, and bid her farewell while I held her hands in mine. She said "*hao, hao*" (good, good) in a trembling voice in her southern accent. As we walked into the field and I looked back at the house, she still stood there—near the main entrance—following our departure.

This elderly woman, probably uneducated like most women of her age, might have wished to ask some questions of me, a stranger, but did not find an appropriate way to do so. She might once have had an abortion herself and wanted to tell me her own story, but did not know where to start. Or she might have been amazed that strangers from far away were interested in the opinions of villagers like herself. I will never know for sure. Yet I can still feel her trembling voice and lovely gaze, which somehow validated the whole project.

In China, silence often means that people do not consider it prudent to talk, out of fear or simply to avoid trouble, as the following two cases show. I met a man in his late thirties or early forties who had been trained in biomedicine and become a government official. I got to know him through a friend who informed me that he had been in charge of family planning for a couple of years while serving as a deputy township head in the countryside. The man straightforwardly rejected my request for an interview about his experiences in the township. "Yes, I have seen and experienced a lot. I have also been closely involved in persuading and forcing rural women to have abortions. It was a difficult job. But I really don't want to talk about my experience and feelings. As a matter of fact, I rarely talk to anyone about it, even my wife and close friends."

A young woman had come to a family planning clinic for an abortion. Her doctor introduced her to me because she had had an earlier abortion. After gaining her permission, I began to interview her and take notes. She said that she would continue her current pregnancy if she could. It was not clear whether she had come to the clinic because of the policy or through a personal decision. She often thought about her aborted fetus by imagining how old the child would be now. Her first abortion had been physically painful, and she was very much afraid of having another termination. Although she agreed to be interviewed, she was very reluctant to talk. Picking up on her fear and nervousness, I emphasized again the anonymity in my research project. She retorted that the doctor had all the information about her abortion and I could get it from her. When I asked whether she wanted me to return the notes I had taken, she hesitated. Although she seemed willing to help, she looked uncomfortable and even slightly fearful. Tearing the page from my notebook, I handed it over with some words of reassurance: "I really don't want you to worry about anything." She left with the piece of paper in her hand. I could not pinpoint the source of her fears, whether it was her distrust of me, the medical profession, or others.

While experiencing people's willingness to speak out in the course of my field research, I also witnessed fear, caution, hesitation, reservation, and reluctance everywhere I went—from the north to the south, from the cities to the villages, among the well-educated as well as semieducated and illiterate people, among officials and common citizens. Many people preferred either to keep quiet or to say little so as to avoid political repercussions. Repression by the authorities—central and local—is one clear explanation for the Chinese silence concerning abortion, the absence of public debate on the issue. As we saw above, this is the reason most frequently given by overseas Chinese academics. In a society where censorship is an everyday practice; where freedom of speech is no more than words on paper; where public criticism of state policies may result in punishment, including loss of one's job, imprisonment, and even the death penalty; and where academic activities are tightly controlled, ordinary people and intellectuals alike find it prudent to remain silent on many social issues and policies, at least in the public domain. The issues are particularly sensitive with respect to birth control, not only because the population program is a national priority, but also because the Chinese state, responding to Western attacks on its social policies, vociferously denies that it practices coerced abortion.

This silence or reticence issues not only from official directives but also from a ubiquitous, nameless fear that permeates Chinese society, resulting in a pervasive self-censorship. As several interviewees told me, the government has issued guidelines warning Chinese citizens, especially Communist Party members and officials, from public criticism of the national family planning program. More disturbing, however, is a general atmosphere of fear and anxiety that prevents people from fully speaking their minds. The case of Dr. Wei and her husband brings this point to life.

Dr. Wei was a recently retired gynecologist/obstetrician. I obtained consent to interview her at home through a colleague of a friend. Like most Chinese urban people, Dr. Wei lived in an apartment assigned by her work unit. As I approached the gate to the building, a middle-aged man challenged me: "Where have you come from? Who are you looking for?" Told that I was a guest of Dr. Wei, he inquired on the nature of my relationship with Dr. Wei. Despite my rather evasive reply, he allowed me to enter the building. It is not unusual for a work unit in a Chinese city to arrange for a security guard to monitor its apartment complex. Although mainly aimed at crime prevention, this practice is sometimes used for political surveillance, although on a much lesser scale than it was prior to the 1980s.

I climbed the stairs to Dr. Wei's apartment on the top floor, since the six-story building had no elevator. Dr. Wei invited me into the living/dining room and offered me tea. I politely declined the cigarette offered by her husband, following local custom. The couple, especially the husband, looked very serious, even nervous. After some small talk, they asked me about my life in the United States and where I had grown up and worked in China. Then I introduced my research project. In an effort to ease their obvious anxiety, I emphasized that I was interested in what Chinese people actually think about abortion, not about the family planning policy per se, and that my research might contribute to better policy making. I was aware that people in China, especially local officials, are usually more comfortable responding to factual questions than offering personal opinions.

Both Dr. Wei and her husband warned me that my research project would be extremely difficult to carry out, since it was related to the birth control policy. Dr. Wei's husband told me in no uncertain tones: "People will not be willing to talk to you. Even if they do talk to you, what they say will definitely not be meaningful." In his view, people would find it impossible to communicate their true feelings and genuine thoughts on the subject. However, Dr. Wei did not refuse to be interviewed, nor did her husband ask that I not interview his wife, perhaps out of a sense of obligation to the people who had introduced me. Even before I had asked her anything, Dr. Wei told me in an apologetic tone: "I'll just say something very general. I can't talk about concrete details. I can't dig deep."

Yet Dr. Wei actually spoke at length. She strongly believed that abortion seriously affected women's health. She mentioned a well-known senior clinician who had written a book about the health problems experienced by women who had had abortions. Dr. Wei said that, in the past, the OB/GYN department where she worked had performed more than two hundred middle- and late-term abortions every month, about ten cases a day. Recently, this type of abortion had been reduced to about ten cases a month, with some months showing no statistics for late-term abortions.[4]

Asked about the fate of live babies resulting from late abortions, she replied without hesitation: "They shouldn't be living. They must die." She added that, although some hospitals let them live, their life span was limited by the heavy dosages of drugs injected into their skulls.

Neither Dr. Wei nor her husband indicated that they had any reservations about the family planning policy in general. They did not express any opposition to using abortion in the population control program. However, the husband strongly criticized the policy differentiation between the rural and urban areas, which permitted most rural people to have two children. He believed this was unfair and became very angry when discussing it. He had no comment on the enormous inequities in economic, cultural, educational, and health-care opportunities that favor the cities over the countryside.

Later, the pair who had arranged the interview asked me how it had gone. I told them that while Dr. Wei and her husband appeared reticent, they actually talked quite a lot. My friend attributed this to the personalities of the couple, especially the husband, who had been a long-serving official, and said that they were always overcautious (*jingxiao shenwei*). Seeing their disappointment, I stressed that the interview would nevertheless be very useful in helping me understand how people actually feel and think about the topic.

It would be simplistic to attribute the reluctance of this couple and many other interviewees to talk freely to an "overcautious nature," for in the course of the twentieth century millions of Chinese have been humiliated, punished, and even executed for speaking out. Guarding one's tongue is a basic survival strategy in an authoritarian regime. In general, I found that better-educated people seemed more inclined to speak out than the less educated, university students more than the general public, urban residents more than rural people, physicians more than patients, and professionals and ordinary citizens more than officials. While excessive reticence may well be an individual trait in some cases, we must still ask why so many Chinese have developed this characteristic. From ancient times to the present, the emperor and the state have controlled people not only through official decrees and institutions, such as the police system and state censorship, but also through widespread fear, self-censorship, and the silent compliance of the masses. Reticence is thus an ingrained habit among Chinese, even when the authorities have not imposed direct restrictions.

The Chinese silence on abortion can thus be interpreted as reflecting not only China's current political system but also the fundamental dimensions of Chinese society—its ancient and modern history, moral values, social structure, and cultural traditions, and its definition of the relationship between state and society and between society and the individual. For example, Chinese put a high value on consensus shaped by tradition and secular authority, rather than through public debate. This helps explain the perception that Chinese willingly respect and accept authority and the customs, norms, attitudes, and interests authorized by the state and the extant social order. Chinese philosophical and literary traditions have placed a high value on silence. In Daoist thought and Chinese Zen Buddhism, silence is treasured as one of the highest spiritual, psychological, aesthetic, and even ethical states to which a person can aspire. Whether shaped by these traditions or for other reasons, collectively and individually Chinese place a particular value on silence—in the face of good and bad, happiness and sadness, justice and tyranny, joy and suffering, moral difficulties and dilemmas. Chinese society values such silence even more than the freedom of expression so highly vaunted in the West.

In making these points, however, we should take care to avoid reinforcing current stereotypes of China and the Chinese. We must avoid confusing the limits on free speech imposed by particular political systems with something innate to the culture. In their tens of millions, Chinese have fiercely debated a whole variety of issues—for example, during the Cultural Revolution of 1966–1976 and the prodemocracy movement of 1989—and they continue to do so. The achievements of Chinese in Hong Kong and Taiwan during the last century constitute a powerful counter to the stereotypical view that Chinese are incapable of public debate on vital social issues.

Even if we assume that the stereotype contains some grains of truth, silence can itself speak volumes, often more powerfully than words. Silence can be another way of speaking, especially if the subject is politically sensitive, morally ambiguous, intellectually overwhelming, or emotionally intractable. For instance, every year since 1989, the online magazine *China's New Digest* (CND), popular among overseas mainland Chinese academics, has commemorated the Tiananmen Square massacre in its May and June issues. In 2003 and 2004, the front page of the CND website featured two phrases consisting of eight Chinese characters displayed under the image of the statue of the goddess of democracy that once graced the square: "Rarely mention it, but never dare to forget" (*bucheng diqi, weigang wanji*). If one assumes that this case means people have nothing to say, he would be "a deaf person whose ears are blocked by too much noise." Silence has often been associated with sadness, despair, bitterness, helplessness, and resistance in Chinese culture. Does the Chinese silence on abortion mean that, rather having nothing to say, those involved find the subject too difficult even to begin talking about? However novel this interpretation may seem, what follows, in particular in chapters 4, 5, and 6, will demonstrate the bitter pain of abortion for many Chinese people, a pain that goes beyond what words can describe.

CONCLUSION

The absence of public debate on abortion in contemporary China has been interpreted as meaning that Chinese people are unconcerned with the morality of terminating pregnancy. But, if we listen closely, we can discern a wide range of voices, however weak, hesitant, or suppressed, even in the public sphere. Although the overseas Chinese in the pilot study reported a lack of concern among their fellow Chinese, their own critical voices have broken this apparent silence. Even more importantly, the silence itself speaks. Among the many contributors to the Chinese silence on abortion is political repression, direct and indirect, especially the widespread and nameless fear of speaking freely. It is not uncommon for Chinese to remain silent when they have too much on their minds and hearts regarding a tragic event or difficult subject.

The following pages will demonstrate that, contrary to the common Western observation, Chinese are far from morally blind about abortion and fetal life. Comments suggesting that people in China are ethically oblivious to abortion are true only for some Chinese. It is simply incorrect to claim that abortion in China is merely a medical procedure and that ethical concern over terminations is a "purely American story." To the Chinese student of American anthropologist Susan Rigdon, the notion that a human life begins at "conception" made no more sense than the proposition that life begins with an "idea." But this is definitely not the case for most Chinese. The survey results show that the majority of Chinese believe that the fetus is a human life, and nearly half of respondents held that human life starts at conception. The narratives and experiences of women and doctors directly involved in abortion further show that, for some at least, the fetus is a special entity—if not a child then at least a potential human being.

In sum, under their dome of apparent silence, contemporary Chinese are able to articulate surprisingly diverse and complex viewpoints. But before the voices of the silent majority are examined in detail, we need to pay close attention to the official and dominant ideology of abortion in the context of birth control in contemporary China. For without a firm grasp of this ideology, the diverse perspectives exhibited by Chinese will never be properly understood.

NOTES

1. But this is not cheap according to mainland China's standard. At a hospital located in a less-developed northern coastal city in 1997, suction curettage and abortion at the sixth month cost about $12 (100 yuan or Chinese dollars), drug abortion nearly $10 (80 yuan or Chinese dollars). A doctor in the countryside informed me that it cost less than $4 (30 yuan or Chinese dollars) for an abortion in her area. The difference in abortion prices reflects differences in economic levels and living standards in diverse parts of China.

2. Responses of some my Chinese colleagues to my research topic confirm that the ethics of abortion has yet to be treated as a legitimate academic and intellectual issue in the public discourse. While conducting fieldwork in China in 1997, I met many physicians, medical scientists, and scholars in medical ethics and medical humanities. I sometimes experienced great difficulty in communicating with Chinese colleagues about the project. Some mistook it for a study of the Chinese family planning program from the human rights perspective—which for them made sense since I was pursuing a doctoral degree at an American university. Others had no problem in understanding the topic, but they hardly saw abortion per se as a legitimate moral problem. Although no one ever told me directly, it was apparent that quite a few considered my research "exotic," "weird," or even "pernicious." In contrast, for almost all the Americans and international friends and colleagues with

whom I have discussed the project, its theoretical and practical significance seems obvious.

3. It should be pointed out that I became aware of these two literary works not through any systematic and careful survey of related literary works, however significant this undertaking would be, but simply by chance. I happened to encounter them.

4. In general, the rate of late-term abortions in the 1980s (not necessarily coerced by the state birth control policy) was much higher than in the 1990s, although detailed statistics are very difficult to obtain. The figures given by Dr. Wei indicate that a single OB/GYN clinic could perform 2,400 middle- or late-term abortions per year.

2

"Instructions" from Above: Official Positions

> Debasement is the password of the base
> Nobility is the epitaph of the noble
> See how the gilded sky is covered
> With the drifting twisted shadows of the dead
>
> —Bei Dao (during the Cultural Revolution): "The Answer"

The previous chapter presents some evidence of political repression—direct and indirect—as a major cause for the Chinese silence on abortion in the public sphere. The Chinese government firmly rejects most criticism of its birth control policies emanating from overseas, especially from the United States. Official publications have variously described Western critics as "imposing their own values on China," "interfering in the internal affairs of China," "maliciously attacking China," "viciously slandering," and "irresponsibly exaggerating or wantonly distorting the facts." State authorities accuse foreign critics of being ignorant of Chinese realities such as the crisis of population–resource ratios, "being surprised or alarmed by normal things" (*dajing xiaoguai*), having a political axe to grind, "having ulterior motives" (*bicyou yongxin*), being hostile to China and the Chinese people, or even "entertaining most evil designs" (*yongxin jiqi edu*) (see, e.g., Peng 1997: 403).

As for the political explanation of the public silence on abortion, the Chinese authorities consider it "totally groundless" (*haowu genju*) and accuse Chinese who publicize political repression of "being one-sided and ignorant" (*pianmian wuzhi*), "viciously attacking the Party and government" (*edu gongji dang he zhengfu*), "confusing people's minds by demagogy" (*guhuo renxin*), or even the crime of "subverting the state" (*dianfu guojia*). The government claims that contemporary Chinese enjoy not only unprecedented

39

freedom when compared to the Qing and Republican periods, but also a higher form of democracy than is found in the West, America included. While acknowledging that democracy with Chinese characteristics is still developing, and thus still imperfect, it insists that any problems should be treated as issues to be resolved in the course of the nation's development, rather than something inherent in the socialist political system. In a word, systematic political repression does not exist in socialist China.

The official discourse on abortion provides the general political-social framework for the views expressed by individuals. Many Chinese support or accept the official viewpoint to some extent. In addition, although the official response has been to unequivocally reject Western criticisms, the Chinese authorities have not completely ignored international concerns about aspects of China's birth control program: the social role of abortion, abortion for sex selection, the unbalanced ratio of male to female infants, and the problem of female infanticide and abandonment have all come in for scrutiny. Indeed, many of these issues have been central to official adjustment of birth control policies over the past quarter century. After all, Chinese cultural norms value what is called "presenting the facts and reasoning things out" (*bai shishi, jiang daoli*), which is more than merely rhetoric.

This chapter, therefore, examines Party and government views on abortion and birth control. It begins with a brief historical review of abortion policies and laws, especially the dramatic shift—from prohibitive to permissive—that occurred in the early 1960s. Because compliance with the national population policy is the reason most frequently cited for abortion, I summarize official standpoints on birth control in general and coerced abortion and infanticide in particular. Special attention is paid to the moral arguments used both explicitly and implicitly in the official discourse for promoting birth control and accepting abortion—a collectivist and statist ideology in which the value of the individual, and fetal life in particular, is readily subordinated to the interests of society, specifically the nation-state.

There is a vast English-language literature on the Chinese population control program (see, e.g., Croll, Davin, and Kane 1985; Banister 1987; Kane 1987; Aird 1990; Tien 1991; Poston and Yaukey 1992; Milwertz 1997; Scharping 2003). This chapter, however, draws mainly on Chinese official and semiofficial materials. Prominent among them is an anthology entitled *Zhongguo Jifa Shengyu Quanshu* (The Complete Sourcebook of Family Planning in China), edited by Peng Peiyun and published in 1997—the most authoritative and comprehensive Chinese source on the subject. The volume has nearly 1,500 pages and over thirty-three million Chinese words. It includes almost all the relevant national laws and policies on abortion and population control from 1949 to the mid-1990s. It also collects relevant speeches by national leaders, editorials from official newspapers, and significant semiofficial articles and research papers. Moreover, the chief editor is herself a national leader and former chair of the National Commission for Family Planning—the body responsible for administering the population control program. Besides being prefaced by a national leader, Song Ping, the book is calligraphically inscribed by words from Jiang Zemin, then president of China and general secretary of the Central Committee and the Central Military Committee of the Chinese Communist Party (CCP); Li Peng, then prime minister and later head of the People's Congress; and a number of other national leaders. Jiang wrote: "Carrying out family planning is a long-term and fundamental national policy for our country."

POLICIES AND LAWS SINCE 1949

According to the official line—the orthodox view to which Chinese have been subject for more than half a century—the establishment of the People's Republic in 1949 was the greatest event in the history of China, representing the beginning of a new society in which all Chinese people, emancipated by the Party, "at last stood up." In contrast with the preliberation society, people in the new China were no longer oppressed and exploited by internal feudalism and foreign imperialism. Chinese people had finally become masters of their own affairs and destiny under the most democratic political system possible: "democratic dictatorship of the people"—a system in which the masses of the proletariat "dictate" to the remaining class enemies, excluded from the category of "the people." Now, the current official discourse admits that serious mistakes occurred in Mao Zedong's era, which was characterized by constant political upheavals, and that the ten-year Cultural Revolution (1966–1976) was especially disastrous. Still, Mao's reign (1949–1976) is portrayed as positive overall. Any mistakes were defined as bumps on the road to progress, a necessary "tuition fee" for success, and thus excusable. On this view, any excesses were not the result of flaws inherent in the political system, but of excusable personal errors stemming from Mao's old age ("the errors of a great revolutionary and leader"), the emergence of anti-Party cliques such as Lin Biao and the Gang of Four, and the remnants of feudalism and foreign-inspired bourgeois culture among the masses, as well as Western imperialist, China-hostile, reactionary forces. In the official discourse, the massive famine of 1959–1962 that was a direct result of the Great Leap Forward Movement and the fanatical utopianism associated with it, in which twenty to forty million rural Chinese died, was referred to as "the three-year period of difficulty" caused by natural disasters and the betrayal of the Soviet Union. Despite shifts in terminology, socialism and the leadership of the Communist Party were (and still are) the right choice for Chinese people, and any Chinese who dares to challenge their legitimacy should be punished. The remarkable achievements in economic development and social reform from the late 1970s and early 1980s "once again prove" that, as the only repository of leadership in China, the Party is "great, glorious, and correct," always serving the people and representing the fundamental interests of the great majority of Chinese.

However we might evaluate these claims, it is undeniable that political and economic life, social institutions, cultural norms, and even the language itself (the replacement of the traditional writing system by simplified characters) have all been subject to radical change during the past half century. Radical change has also marked the regulation and practice of abortion in China since 1949.

In the early 1950s, government policy greatly restricted abortion, along with sterilization and the provision of contraceptive drugs and instruments. The mouthpiece of the central Party, *Renmin Ribao* (*The People's Daily*), summarized the rationale neatly in 1951: while imperialist and capitalist states endorse birth control, socialist and democratic societies promote childbearing (cited in Sharping 2003: 30). Abortion in general was thus proscribed by the Ministry of Health and by the Culture and Education Committee in 1950 and again in 1953. Abortion was permitted in only three situations: (1) when the presence of conditions such as tuberculosis, heart disease, kidney disease, and pernicious anemia meant that continuing the pregnancy would threaten the mother's life and seriously damage her health; (2) when traditional Chinese medicine administered to "pacify" and restrict movement of the overactive fetus had no effect and spontaneous abortion was imminent; or (3) when the mother had already undergone two or more Cesarean births (Peng 1997: 59, 889–90). These regulations also stipulated penalties for performing or having an illegal abortion.

In 1954 and 1956, the Ministry of Health extended the scope for legal abortion to include other maternal disabilities (such as hypertension, epilepsy, nervous and mental diseases, pernicious vomiting while pregnant, amputation, and blindness); special occupational categories (such as women working or studying abroad); and domestic stress where the mother already had four or more children or became pregnant again within four months of giving birth (Peng 1997: 889–91). Nevertheless, all the regulations promulgated between 1950 and 1956 required that strict administrative procedures be followed. Except in cases of emergency, applications for an abortion had to be signed by both husband and wife, certified by the attending physician, authorized by the leader of the pregnant woman's work unit, and finally, approved by the hospital.

The severe restrictions placed on abortion by the Ministry of Health reflected a number of wider social purposes. Concern for the safety and health of the mother was paramount because termination was believed to be especially risky in first pregnancies. It also concealed a political motive—a large and growing population was seen as essential for national economic development and the strength and prestige of the nation. Interestingly, the 1950 regulations also stated that termination should be prohibited to "ensure the life of the next generation" (Peng 1997: 889). This should not be understood as affirming the intrinsic value of fetal life per se, but as another way of emphasizing the importance of continuing population growth in China. This said, the phrase does imply that abortion is a way of destroying the life of the next generation, morally justifiable or not.

Even as these prohibitive regulations were being promulgated, some officials and scholars were urging that population growth be controlled. The most articulate spokesperson for these views was the demographer Ma Yinchu. Ma's rationale was Malthusian (although for political reasons he never made this explicit): China's economic production was simply unable to keep pace with population growth. Yet although Ma advocated controlling fertility to check population growth, he strongly opposed abortion as a method of birth control. Believing instead that widespread dissemination of contraception was the most effective means of achieving this aim (Peng 1997: 551–56), Ma viewed abortion as "destroying life" and asserted that it should be considered only where the mother's health was compromised. He also believed that it damaged a woman's health and made her more susceptible to disease. Ma held that, from the time that the child is formed in the mother's body, it has the right to life (*shengming quan*).

Ma's proposals for population control were initially rejected by the Party dominated by Mao. Ma was officially condemned as part of the 1957 "Antirightist Movement," a political campaign to eliminate dissidence among intellectuals. Nevertheless, the idea of controlling population was gradually adopted by the government. Late in 1957, the government began tentatively encouraging people to practice birth control. Contraception information programs were initiated on a limited scale, and research was carried out on birth control. Restrictions on abortion and sterilization were relaxed correspondingly. A 1957 Ministry of Health regulation permitted abortion in (vaguely defined) circumstances that made continuation of pregnancy difficult. The grounds for termination were considerably liberalized: it was permitted as long as it was carried out within the first trimester, no second abortion occurred within one year, and medical contraindications were not present. Previous requirements, such as approval from the mother's work unit leader, were no longer stipulated.

In the early 1960s, abortion and sterilization policy in China were relaxed still further. In 1962, the Central Committee of the Party and the State Council released the first specific document on birth control, which instructed the departments of medicine and public health to "devise practical methods and work energetically to bring abortion and sterilization procedures to the masses" (Peng 1997: 5). A major reason was "to protect the masses from lifelong illness or injury or death through the use of illegal abortion rather than scientific abortion methods." The document also stressed the need to inform the people about the dangers of abortion and the advantages of contraception. As a response to this directive from the central government, the Ministry of Health issued a new regulation that required hospitals and clinics to undertake terminations on request and "as soon as possible," provided there were no medical contraindications (Peng 1997: 895). Hospitals and clinics were required to plan their operating schedules carefully to avoid backlogs. While termination within the first trimester was preferable, abortions could be performed up to the fifth month of pregnancy—although terminations beyond this period were not specifically prohibited. Like all previous regulations, the new edict emphasized that abortions must be performed by authorized and experienced personnel only—physicians in obstetrics and gynecology or urological departments, surgeons, and trained midwives (Peng 1997: 895).

This dramatic transformation in policy was inspired by many social, political, technological, and economic factors. For instance, surgical advances made both early and late terminations safer. Social attitudes were also changing, and the demand for abortion was increasing. But the most significant factor was the introduction of the national birth control program. In fact, the Health Ministry's 1963 regulation was specifically designed to implement the "Instruction on Advocating Family Planning" promulgated by the Party and central government the previous year.

Although induced abortion as a social practice among Chinese is not unique to contemporary China, the use of abortion as an indispensable instrument of the national population control agenda is historically unprecedented. As we have seen, the program began to gather momentum in the early 1960s in order to combat rapid population growth. Since the late 1970s, as I show below, the Chinese government has been carrying out the most rigorous, comprehensive, and ambitious birth control program in the world. Late marriage, contraception, sterilization, and abortion have all been employed under this strict regime. The restrictive abortion policies of the first decade of communist China have been replaced by their antitheses: even coerced and late-term abortion has become an inevitable part of this "great social project." Officially and euphemistically, abortion is called a "remedial measure" (*bujiu cuoshi*) in the context of the birth control program.

THE BIRTH CONTROL PROGRAM

As a "great project of social engineering," China's national birth control program is unprecedented and unrivaled in its massive scale and profound demographic and social impact. From its beginning, the program has had two aims: *to control the quantity of the population* and *to improve or enhance the quality of the population.* China has been carrying out this "long-term," "fundamental," and "strategic" national policy for two or three decades now. The Chinese term for the program is *jihua shengyu* (literally, "planned reproduction"), which has been translated into English as "family planning," "birth planning," "birth control" or "planned fertility." The English translation endorsed by the Chinese authorities is "family planning."

In her now classic social history of birth control in the United States, Linda Gordon stated that "birth control has always been primarily an issue of politics, not of technology" (Gordon 1977: xii). Gordon's assessment is even more true of birth control in contemporary China.

Between 1949 and the late 1970s, Mao Zedong's personal preferences and his utopian social ideals dominated Chinese society and dictated its direction. Mao's influence and control extended from the running of the nation to cultural life and the lifestyle of ordinary people, as well as to the population policy. Although Mao is still officially credited with initiating the family planning program, this claim resembles *la daqi zuo hupi* (using a tiger skin as a banner to intimidate people, or draping oneself in the flag to impress the audience). In actuality, it seems that Mao was never really convinced that a big population constituted a serious problem for China, even though he talked about the importance of population control. Until the late 1950s and early 1960s, Mao stressed that the greater the population, the greater the energy available for socialist revolution and reconstruction. Partly due to Mao's personal preferences, the importation of contraceptives was restricted and abortion all but prohibited in the first decade of Communist rule. Mao's attitudes contributed to arresting the development of a wholesale national population control program until after his death. His limited advocacy of population control did not mean, however, that he disapproved of state interference in population issues. On the contrary, from the very beginning, Mao strongly opposed what he called "the anarchy of human reproduction." He said: "I think human beings don't know how to manage themselves at all. . . . Mankind doesn't have any kind of plan for reproducing itself. This is anarchy—no government, no organization, no discipline" (Peng 1997: 131). In other words, Mao was certainly in favor of state controls on population size—whether to restrict or increase it—and human reproduction in general.

After the death of Mao in 1976, and especially since the early 1980s, China has carried out its family planning program in a thoroughgoing way. The neglect of birth control in former decades is described as a "historic mistake." The appearance of the "one-child-per-couple" policy, officially announced in 1980 in an open letter from the Central Committee of the Party to the country's youth, marked an important watershed. The "Public Letter to all Members of the Communist Party and Communist Youth League on Controlling Population Growth in Our Country" (abbreviated as "The Public Letter") set out the government's ambitious aim: the national population should not exceed 1.2 billion people by the year 2000 (Peng 1997: 16–17). The population policy pursued by the Chinese government from the early 1980s to the present has been summarized as: "to advocate late marriage, late childbearing, fewer births, and good birth; to advocate one child only for each couple" (Peng 1997: 19, 34, 121). This is often referred to even more simply as the "one-child-per-couple" policy (*dusheng zinü zhengce*) or "one-child" policy (*yitai hua*, literally, one-childization).

Though widely known and used, the expression "one-child policy" is misleading because the policy allows many exceptions, even several structural exclusions. The Chinese population program is often misunderstood in the West as being based on an absolute policy admitting no exceptions. An American I once met raised the case of twins. The official policy is flexible in its application and allows for numerous (though limited) exceptions. Strictly speaking, China has never carried out such a policy as a national and universal rule. The number of children allowed to an individual couple varies according to areas of residency, employment, and ethnicity. A 1991 government document sets out three general categories:

> [I]n the case of state-employed cadres and workers and urban residents, a couple can have one child only, except in some special situations and with official approval. In rural areas, although couples should still be encouraged to have only one child, those who would suffer hardship as a result of this restriction may have a second child after a certain interval and with approval. In areas populated by minority ethnic groups, family planning should be advocated in order to advance economic and cultural levels and improve the genetic stock. However, detailed arrangements should be made by the autonomous region or province concerned. (Peng 1997: 34)

The first exception listed here allows rural people more freedom of choice than urban folk. A rural couple can usually get permission for a second child, especially if their first child is a girl. The second largest exceptional category applies to more than fifty minority ethnic groups, including Tibetans. Although the one-child policy is not enforced among them, these groups are encouraged to practice family planning. And even state-employed workers and urban residents may have a second child under special circumstances, such as when the first child is physically or mentally disabled. Furthermore, it is possible to have additional children, whatever one's residency, on payment of fines or other penalties—including losing one's job.

Chinese nationals studying and living overseas are treated as a special group. According to a document issued in 1989 by the National Committee on Family Planning and the National Committee on Education, penalties should not be imposed on students and scholars who give birth to more than one child while abroad (Peng 1997: 719). These concessions reflect the government's recognition that a restrictive policy would be very difficult to enforce with this group. The concessions may also stem from the idea held by some Chinese that well-educated people should be allowed and even encouraged to have more children as a way of improving the quality of the general population.

Of the Chinese birth control program's two major aims—reducing rapid population growth and improving the "quality" of the population—more emphasis has been given since the 1990s to quality, to "superior birth and superior child-raising" practices (*yousheng youyu*). In 1994, for example, the Eighth National People's Congress passed a law governing the health care of mothers and infants popularly known as the "eugenics law" (Peng 1997: 54–56). Its first article states that the law "is formulated in accordance with the Constitution with a view to ensuring the health of mother and infant and improving the quality of the new-born population" (official translation with modifications). The law stipulates that all medical and health-care facilities must provide citizens with premarital health care (including sex education, premarital health consultations, and the medical examination required for an engaged couple to obtain their marriage certificate) and prenatal and lying-in services (including instruction in maternal and infant care, the health protection of the pregnant and the lying-in woman, prenatal care, the care of the newborn, and prenatal diagnosis and examination). The fourteenth article of the law refers to the care of the fetus as "monitoring, consultancy and medical advice on the development of the fetus." Article 18 stipulates that the physician "shall explain the situation to the married couple and give them medical advice on a termination of gestation" if the prenatal medical examination discloses any of the following conditions: "(1) The fetus is affected by a genetic disease of a serious nature; (2) the fetus has a defect of a serious nature; or (3) continued gestation may jeopardize the life of the pregnant women or seriously impair her health as a result of a serious pre-existing condition." The first supplemental provision, Article 38, defines "genetic disease of a serious nature" as "diseases that are caused by genetic factors congenitally, that may deprive the victim of the ability to live independently either totally or partially, that are highly likely to recur in future generations, and that would make reproduction inappropriate on medical grounds." "Pre-natal diagnosis" refers to "diagnosis of the fetus regarding congenital defects and hereditary diseases." Most notably, Article 19 states: "Termination of gestation . . . practiced in accordance with the provisions of this Law should be subject to the consent of the individual affected. If that individual lacks the capacity for civil conduct, it shall be performed subject to the consent of the former's guardian."

The government has made it clear on many occasions that the national family planning program will continue indefinitely. In both official documents and speeches, national leaders have repeatedly emphasized that the program is a long-term, fundamental strategic policy for China. Adopted at the twenty-fifth meeting of the Ninth Standing Committee of the National People's Congress on December 29, 2001, the Law on Population and Family Planning became effective on September 1, 2002. The first national law to be enacted on the subject, which supersedes all provincial regulations, this self-styled "human-oriented" law makes birth control a legal duty of Chinese citizens. Drawing on the experience of the past two and a half decades, the Law on Population and Family Planning is a milestone in China's birth control program, marking the transition from a period of ad hoc administrative decree to an era in which the legal system and legislative measures are paramount.

In fact, the duty of citizens to follow state birth control policies has long been mandated in Chinese law. In 1980, the Fifth National People's Congress passed a revised marriage law that obligated both partners to practice family planning (Peng 1997: 41). In 1982, the same body passed a new constitution that set out the government's aims very clearly: "The state's family planning program is designed to ensure that population increase keeps pace with its plans for economic and social development"; and on the family level, "Both the husband and the wife have an obligation to practice family planning" (Peng 1997: 43).

On the role of abortion in population control policy, the government insists that abortion is not preferred as a method of family planning and birth control. It has repeatedly emphasized that abortion is a "remedial measure" or "back-up method" (*bujiu cuoshi*). In the words of the Chinese government's White Paper on human rights in China, the family planning policy,

> has consistently given first place to contraception and the protection of women's and children's health. . . . The government strongly opposes any form of coerced abortion. Abortion is only a remedial measure when contraception fails, and is performed under voluntary and safe and secure conditions. (Peng 1997: 116)

The White Paper on family planning points out that as the birth rate in China has fallen sharply, the ratio of abortions to live births remains at approximately 0.3:1—making China's abortion rate about average compared with other countries (Peng 1997: 123).

Contrary to the impression of many Westerners, not all abortions are legal in China. Termination for the purpose of sex selection, which has been made easier through modern methods of prenatal sex diagnosis, is clearly prohibited by various regulations. For many reasons, including the traditional value placed on male offspring to continue the bloodline and the need for security for elderly people, especially in countryside, many Chinese still prefer to have at least one male child. Over the centuries, Chinese doctors have pursued many methods of predicting the sex of the fetus, including taking the pulse of the pregnant woman. According to traditional Chinese medicine, male and female fetuses produce different pulse patterns in mothers. While the accuracy of such traditional methods is doubtful, advances in modern biomedical technology, such as B ultrasonic, have made relatively accurate prenatal sex diagnosis both possible and financially feasible.

Prenatal diagnosis of sex and selective abortion for males has been outlawed in a series of regulations. As early as September 1986, the National Commission for Family Planning and the Ministry of Health circulated a regulation promulgated by the authorities in Beijing that prohibited prenatal diagnosis at the request of the mother, except when used by authorized hospitals to diagnose certain hereditary diseases. Individuals or clinics violating this ban were liable for penalties (Peng 1997: 939). In May 1989, September 1990, and April 1993, the 1986 decree was reaffirmed in the circulars issued by the two national authorities (Peng 1997: 959, 984). Sex identification of the fetus using medical techniques (except when necessary on medical grounds) and selective abortion for nonmedical reasons are strictly prohibited in the Law on Maternal and Infant Health Care (1994), the Law on Population and Family Planning (2001), and the comprehensive regulation on this subject issued jointly by the National Committee for Family Planning, the Ministry of Health, and the National Administrative and Supervisory Bureau of Drugs in 2002.

Taken together, these regulations offer three grounds for prohibition (Peng 1997: 939, 959, 984). First, prenatal diagnosis presents a threat to the family planning program, as some pregnant women, motivated by preference for a boy, would continue with an unauthorized pregnancy if they knew the fetus was male. Second, prenatal screening would lead many to abort female fetuses, creating an unbalanced sex ratio that would eventually produce serious social problems and endanger the long-term stability of the nation. Third, the use of such medical techniques is said to constitute a serious breach of medical ethics on the part of the physician involved—although the precise nature of the breach is not specified.

However, the current extraordinarily high ratio of male to female newborns in China shows that these regulations have proved much less effective than policy makers intended. According to censuses taken in 1983 and 1990, in the 1980s the ratio of male to female newborns varied between 108.5 (1981) and 113.8 (1989). The ratio has since spiraled to 117 in 2000, resulting in much concern and discussion. In a semiofficial article, demographer Tu Ping attributes the increasing incidence of male births to two factors: failure to report female births and selective abortion (Peng 1997: 662–64). For Tu, "The abnormality of sex ratios among newborns and infants in our country has profound social, economic, cultural, and historical causes. . . . We cannot attribute this problem simply to the implementation of the family planning program" (Peng 1997: 662–64). The author deplores the statistical distortion resulting from the underreporting of female newborns. He further argues that selective abortion and the high mortality of female infants constitute an even graver problem because it disrupts the gender balance. Despite drawing attention to the abnormally high mortality rate among female children under five, and especially under one, the author never mentions infanticide as a possible cause.

In addition to the use of contraception and abortion, many societies have resorted to infanticide and child abandonment as methods of limiting family size. The killing and abandonment of infants, especially females, has been practiced from very early times in China. For centuries, infanticide was not deemed a straightforward illegal act, partly because the social, moral, and legal control exercised by parents over their children extended to the power of life and death. Although clearly illegal in contemporary China, infanticide and abandonment still occur. Just as the demand for selective abortion is often attributed to the traditional valuing of males over females, infanticide is officially defined as a "feudalistic evil." The White Paper on human rights in China expressed the official position:

> Infanticide through drowning and abandoning female babies is an evil custom left over from feudal times. Although the practice has been greatly reduced, it still lingers on in a few remote places. Chinese laws explicitly forbid the drowning of infants and other actions that would harm them. China has adopted practical and effective measures to wipe out infanticide as well as to investigate and prosecute offenders. (Peng 1997: 116)

Chinese law does in fact proscribe killing, abandoning, or abusing infants. The Marriage Law of 1980 prohibits "the drowning of infants and other actions that would lead to injury or death" (Peng 1997: 41). The 1982 Constitution extends the protection of the state to the family, including the mother and child, and prohibits abuse of the elderly, women, and children (Peng 1997: 43). In the official discourse, therefore, just as the abnormally high ratio of male to female newborns bears no relation to the birth control program, it is the "pernicious influence of feudalism" that is responsible for the killing and abandonment of female infants. Given the existence of the practice for centuries in China, it is certainly wrong to say that all contemporary cases of infanticide are a direct result of the birth control program. Nevertheless, it is inconceivable to deny any connection between female infanticide and family planning policies. Of course, the continuation of female infanticide as well as the severely unbalanced birth ratio were never intended by policy makers. But any social policy has the potential to yield unintended negative consequences as well as intended benefits.

STATISM AND COLLECTIVISM

In spite of the radical change in abortion policies in the People's Republic China—the shift from a restrictive to a permissive and even coercive stance—the moral reasoning or ideology behind the different edicts remain the same: a collectivist and statist ethics. It is collectivist because in China the interests of the country and collective enterprises are always given priority over the personal interests of individuals. It is statist because the state or Party or government (the three terms are used interchangeably in the official discourse) represents the highest interests of China as a country and the Chinese people as a whole. According to the standard Chinese textbooks on ethics (Luo, Ma, and Yu 2004 [1986]: 159–61; see also Luo 2002 [1989], 150–60), the fundamental communist ethic has been summed up in the phrase: "a collectivism that is loyal to the communist cause." The essential points of collectivist morality can be summarized in three principles: (1) the total interests of society (*shehui zhengdi liyi*) are superior to the personal interests of individuals (*geren liyi*), or loyalty to the communist cause is the central purpose and yardstick of both social and individual morality; (2) the realization of individuals' personal interests should always be subordinated to the wider interests of society, or the best way to realize personal interests is to integrate them with the wider interests of society; and (3) when the interests of the society and the individual are in conflict, one should "consciously and unconditionally subject personal interests to the wider interests of society." (Luo, Ma, and Yu 2004 [1986]: 159) The authors note that this understanding of "collectivism" did not originate in the works of Marx and Engels—the founders of Marxism and communism—but was first put forward by Stalin and further developed by Mao Zedong.

The moral justification for China's birth control program is grounded in these collectivist and statist ethics. A number of reasons, explicitly stated and implicitly assumed, are given to justify the birth control program. From the beginning, the program has presupposed two fundamental "matters of fact." First, overpopulation and rapid population growth are seen as the most serious social problem in China today. National leaders continue to assert that population is the primary social problem China faces. As former Prime Minister Li Peng put it: "Foreign guests . . . often ask me what the biggest problem in China is. I tell them that the biggest problem . . . is the population problem" (Peng 1997: 246). Second, the problem is so severe that forceful and continuing intervention by the state is the best and only solution.

This conception of the collective and social good of present and future generations, and of China as well as the world, provides the ethical grounds on which Chinese officials and scholars defend fertility control in general and coerced abortion in particular. First, whether or not we agree that overpopulation is the primary social problem in contemporary China, it is indisputable that China's large population—one-fifth of the world's—and its rapid growth must be seriously addressed. It is widely regarded as necessary to control the geometric rate of increase in population in order to raise living standards, given China's limited natural resources and agricultural capacity. The rationale here is very simple: accelerating population growth threatens the whole society, and individuals must make sacrifices for the sake of the common good. The government thus insists that citizens have an obligation to follow family planning practices—using efficient birth control methods and having abortions in the case of unplanned pregnancy. In the interests of the common good, birth control campaigns have been vigorously pursued in controlling population growth, adjusting population structure, and improving the "quality" of human resources. Moreover, the argument for the social good is extended to include future generations: people living now have an obligation to ensure that their successors will inherit a livable world. Finally, fertility control is considered a social good not only for China but also for the world since overpopulation is a global rather than a national problem. The social good argument will be further developed and critically assessed in chapter 7.

The Party's Public Letter of 1980, the first official pronouncement on the issue, foreshadowed the one-child policy in purely economic and utilitarian terms:

> As far as the country as a whole is concerned, as long as the rate of labor productivity in industry and agriculture is still rather low, and as long as we have not reached a state of abundance in the production of material resources, the rate of population growth will directly affect the accumulation of the capital funds necessary for the construction of modernization. A much too rapid growth of population will mean a reduction in the accumulation of capital funds, while a slowdown in population growth could mean an increase in the accumulation of capital funds. With the growth of the population, in addition to the fact that the families and households would need to expend an increased amount of money to take care of the children, in order to resolve the problems of their education and employment and so on, the state would also need to increase its budget for education, and its investment in equipment and in the society's public facilities, and so on. (Peng 1997: 16; English translation in White 1992: 12–13)

The Public Letter further pointed out that rapid population growth made it "very difficult to improve people's standard of living" and to maintain food production on China's limited arable land.

The first paragraph of the 1995 government White Paper on family planning, "A Strategic Policy for National Conditions," makes the point that population control serves the wider interests of the entire country:

The population problem has important implications for the survival and development of the Chinese nation and the success or failure of China's modernization drive—as well as maintaining a balance between the demands of population growth on the one hand, and the viability of economic, social, material, and environmental resources on the other. The Chinese government has established policies to implement family planning, control population growth, and improve the quality of the population. It is a necessary choice in order to make the country strong and powerful, the nation prosperous, and the people happy. (Peng 1997: 118)

At the end of its first section, the White Paper looks to the needs of future generations:

It is precisely in order to bring about sustained economic growth and sustainable development, to satisfy the increasing material and cultural demands of the people, and to guarantee the long-term interests of both the current generation and their posterity, that the Chinese government has chosen the strategic policy of family planning. The facts have shown . . . that, alongside major efforts to develop the economy, the comprehensive promotion of family planning was the correct policy decision . . . bringing benefits to the present and performing a great service for the future. (Peng 1997: 119)

The paper argues with interesting logic that, because the birth control program embodies the long-term interests of society, it is supported by the great majority of Chinese people. It makes the further claim that the population control program accords not only with internationally acknowledged principles such as human rights, but also with Chinese moral concepts. The White Paper elaborates:

Family planning in China is pursued in complete accordance with the relevant principles and human rights requirements designated by the international community. China's family planning policies and programs combine the rights and duties of its citizens, joining the interests of the individual with those of society. These conform to the basic principles laid down by various international population conferences and reflect the understanding of interpersonal interests under socialism. Rights and duties have never been absolute in any country—rather, they are seen as relative. Duties cannot be separated from rights, nor rights from duties. When conflict arises between social needs and individual interests, mediation must be sought. This is the responsibility of the government of every sovereign country. As China has a large population, the government reserves the right to limit births in the interests of the continuing prosperity of the nation as a whole—rather than serving the private interests of a few individuals. This is wholly justifiable and entirely consistent with the ethical concepts embraced by Chinese society. To talk about the rights and duties of citizens in an abstract and absolute way, divorced from reality, is not a realistic option either for China or for any other country. In a heavily populated developing country

such as China, if the reproductive freedom of individuals is emphasized at the expense of their responsibilities to family, children, and society, unplanned and unlimited population growth will inevitably ensue. The interests of the majority, including those of new-born infants, will be seriously harmed. (Peng 1997: 124–25)

The White Paper hammers home the point that individual rights and freedom of reproduction can never be seen as absolute and separate from one's duty to society. Although the document claims that government population policy is "consistent with the ethical concepts embraced by Chinese society," it does not explain what exactly these concepts might be.

The collectivist and statist ethics expressed by the White Paper is reflected in the work of contemporary Chinese scholars in the field of medical ethics. An influential textbook, *Modern Biomedical Ethics*, written by a group of teachers of medical ethics from several medical schools in China, includes a discussion of the importance of eugenics:

If we fail to reduce the birth rate of infants with serious genetic and inherited diseases, simply reducing the size of the population will be of limited use. On the contrary, a mere reduction in population will influence the quality of the population negatively and harm the fundamental interests of the country, the people, and society. Reproduction is not only a right, but also an obligation. While the individual has the right to bear children, this right of the individual to reproduction must be limited, i.e., the individual must also accept an obligation to society and humankind. Society is able to make demands on the individual's capacity for reproduction in terms of both quantity and quality; only if both requirements have been met are the rights and obligations of the individual integrated. If the rights or freedom of the individual go beyond the bounds set by society, then society has the right to interfere. Hence, the individual's capacity for reproduction entails responsibilities not only to himself or herself, but also to others, to society, and to future generations. This is the unshakable genetic duty [of the individual]. (He and Shi 1989: 142–43)

In presenting their views on eugenics and reproduction, these academic writers echo the official and dominant Chinese logic on the relationship between the individual and society as expressed, for example, in the 1995 White Paper quoted at length above.

Many Chinese medical ethicists support this prioritizing of the common good and use the concept to justify the state family planning program. The author of *Essentials of Medical Ethics* is typical: "When prenatal care [of a continuing pregnancy] comes into conflict with birth control and eugenics, it must be subordinated to the needs of the latter, because these are in the interest of the whole nation and of humanity, as well as in accord with the highest morality" (cited in Qiu, Wang, and Gu 1989: 191–92). Given this theoretical perspective, it is not difficult to morally justify even coercive measures for the good of society. Neither is it hard to understand why, in the light of the overpopulation issue, many academics as well as government officials believe the central government should enforce a population control program.

"Common good" arguments are regularly used by family planning cadres to convince people to comply with the birth control policies and to justify the use of coercive measures when necessary. For instance, a rural cadre, a villager himself, addressed in these terms a family planning meeting that women pregnant with a third or later child were required to attend: "China must develop, and we will gradually mould China into a strong socialist state. . . . But whether or not we develop depends on controlling our population." He continued:

> We know that you want a son in order to be secure in your old age. But remember that you are still young. As the country develops, it will create welfare programs. By the time you are old, you won't have to worry about who is going to support you. The government will support you.
>
> We are not forcing you to abort. . . . The decision to undergo an abortion has to be made by you yourselves. But in making this decision, you have to consider not only yourselves but the country and the collective as well. Obviously the country needs to control its population for the sake of the Four Modernizations [modernizations of agriculture, industry, national security, and science and technology]. The collective, as well, needs to limit its population.

The cadre concluded: "There is already only one-sixth of an acre for each person in the village. . . . Having more children is only going to make it more difficult for all of us to make a living" (quoted in Mosher 1983: 227). Whether or not these words were effective in persuading the villagers, the local cadre couched his appeal in well-established collectivist and statist moral terms.

In considering these issues, it is important to note that the Chinese terms for "country" (*guojia*, literally, the country and family), "people" (*renming*), and "society" (*shehui*) are used interchangeably with the terms for "state" (*guojia*), "government" (*zhengfu*), and even "the Party" (*dang*, i.e., CCP, literally and originally meaning "a group of people"). Not only is this is a feature of everyday language, but also it is often found even in intellectual circles. Whether intentionally or not, the two different meanings of "*guojia*," one referring to the country and the other to the state, are regularly conflated in official propaganda. Official ideology always insists that the latter (state, government, and the Party) represents the fundamental interests of the former (the whole country, the whole or at least the great majority of the people). As a result, any Chinese who dares to criticize official policies openly, especially the legitimacy of the Party and the government, can be labeled a traitor; and any foreigner who does the same thing can be labeled an enemy of China.

COERCION AS A LESSER EVIL

The most common criticism leveled by the West against China's population control program is directed against its coercive nature, in particular the use of forced abortion and sterilization. These criticisms are countered in official and semiofficial sources both directly or indirectly, first by denying the use of coercion as the primary approach to birth control and then by arguing that coercion, where it is used, is the lesser of two evils.

Two arguments are used to downplay the use of forced abortion and other coercive measures: first, that coercion has no place in the population program, as the program is supported by the great majority of Chinese and founded on voluntary participation; second, that coercion is not an essential element of the policy but rather results from unsatisfactory performance on the part of local cadres. It is claimed that the family planning program is "the choice of all Chinese people." The government insists that the basic principle of the family planning program is to "combine the guidance of the state and the voluntarism of the masses." It argues that, since the program amounts to an enormous social enterprise involving every family and individual in the country, it would be impossible to implement it through coercion, compulsion, or directives alone. Official and semiofficial documents regularly proclaim that, "under the principle of voluntarism on the part of the masses, with state guidance," couples of childbearing age adopt fertility control methods, including abortion, entirely voluntarily or, sometimes, through persuasion—but not through coercion. It is true that official policies favor education and contraception over the use of force and induced abortion. At times, national leaders have even criticized the coercive methods used by some local officials (Peng 1997: 144, 152, 155, 169). Later chapters will demonstrate that there is much truth to the claim that persuasion is preferred to coercion; the Chinese birth control program is indeed widely accepted by Chinese people, for whatever reasons.

That there exist many cases of forced abortion does not necessarily mean that an explicit coercive abortion *policy* exists, just as the fact that there are many cases in which "people's policemen" abuse people in China does not necessarily mean that the government has a policy legitimating this practice. While official publications do not deny the existence of coerced abortion, they reject the notion that it forms part of national policy. The Chinese government has never explicitly advocated or justified coerced abortion. It has been emphasized that mandatory IUD insertions, compulsory sterilization, and coerced abortion originate not in central policy but in unauthorized local deviations.

As we have seen, the expression "remedial measure" is the standard Chinese euphemism for abortion—especially for late abortions and those performed as a result of pressure or persuasion. At the same time, this phrase contains some truth in that abortion is viewed by official documents and family planning physicians alike as a last resort in a comprehensive population control program in which the preferred means for birth control are marriage and delayed childbearing, the use of intrauterine devices (IUDs) and other various contraceptive methods, and surgical sterilization.

Here an important aspect of the Chinese birth control program that is often unacknowledged in the West should be noted: a justice and equality of sorts. In one of the best Western studies on the Chinese population program, H. Yuan Tien points out that:

> the country's policy of minimal reproduction observes the principle of equality— preventing any one couple from infringing on the well-being of others. The penalties are the same for all noncomplying couples. No social discrimination is involved; both social justice and social welfare are taken into consideration. (Tien 1991: 195)

The family planning policies have been implemented in a remarkably equal and just way compared to other areas of life, such as access to economic and educational opportunities. It seems that this is another major reason why many Chinese accept the birth control program and tolerate the use of coercion.

It has been argued in some semiofficial publications that, since family planning in China is compulsory, it should be enforced like any other law. This position has been argued by Ca Ruichuan, professor of population studies at Beijing University and a member of the National Commission for Family Planning:

> In order to safeguard the interests of society as a whole, including those of potential mothers and their children, the government and institutions that represent the people must stipulate rules of conduct that all citizens should follow. These rules are promulgated in the form of laws. *Since they are laws, they are of course coercive.* This is not to be seen as a violation of human rights. On the contrary, it guarantees the right of all citizens to a high quality of life. (Peng 1997: 627, emphasis added)

As we saw, the family planning program has been enshrined in law since 2002. It is thus not only legitimate but also necessary to enforce the laws whenever and wherever violation occurs.

Despite this, the realization of the government's plans faces some major obstacles. The preference of contemporary Chinese for two or more children has turned the overpopulation problem into a social crisis. Although the reproductive behavior of individual Chinese has always been limited by economic factors and cultural influence, as elsewhere, for centuries people were free to have as many children as they wished without the direct intervention of the state. In fact, under Confucianism, to be childless was considered the greatest violation of the principle of filial piety—having children was a fundamental duty of the individual. "More children, more happiness," as the ancient maxim runs. Some contemporary Chinese, perhaps especially those in rural areas, still hold this belief.

Confronted with a population crisis on the one hand and a cultural proclivity for many children on the other, the government seemed to have little choice in adopting both persuasion and compulsion to achieve its social aims. Coercive birth control, including forced abortion, while seen as undesirable in themselves, were deemed necessary for the good of society and the long-term interests of every citizen. Moreover, whether or not the policies are just, the program was to be implemented justly and equitably. As a result of the broad agreement among intellectuals and the public over the seriousness of the overpopulation crisis, Chinese came under sustained pressure to accept and even support the state's interference in reproductive matters and its use of coerced abortion in cases where the national family planning policy had been breached.

As an ethical strategy, the justification of coercion as a lesser or necessary evil is an approach that demands attention, although as far as I know there are no published materials in Chinese that have systematically explored the subject from this angle. A case of pressured or forced abortion reported by anthropologists Sulamith and Jack Potter (1990: 242) throws light on this implicit but important argument. The Potters were studying a couple who already had two daughters and a son. When the wife became pregnant again, she refused to have an abortion, despite the efforts of the women's leader of the local brigade, other brigade cadres, and even a county official to persuade her to do so. When the baby was nearly due, the couple left the area in an attempt to have their fourth child in seclusion. As soon as they left, the cadres sealed the couple's house, threatened the husband's brothers with the same penalty, and vowed that land allotted to the couple would be confiscated. The couple returned the next day, and a late-term abortion took place. Although the baby was born alive, it died a few hours later.

Special care is needed to make sense of this disturbing case of pressured late abortion, whose features are little different from infanticide. According to the Potters, "The women's leader could not tell this story without evident distress of her own, even after an interval of two years." The women's leader in charge of family planning work in the village, who played a crucial role in the event, justified the brigade's actions in the name of the social good and in the terms of collectivist ethics:

> In our opinion, abortion is not cruel. It would be much more cruel to let the population suffer. If we don't stop the population from growing, there will be what we call a human explosion calamity. People will be reduced to eating people. There will be no land and no houses. (Potter and Potter 1990: 242)

What are the sources of her "evident distress," which had persisted over at least two years? The Potters explained it by positing the existence of "another point of view, the family's point of view, existing simultaneously, and recognized as valuable" (242). In this case, "respect for the principles of the state conflicted with respect for the principles of the family, with the essentially tragic result" (243). The Potters framed the Chinese drama of family planning as a conflict between the state's determination to control the population and the villagers' desire to produce sons. The female cadre's "evident distress" was a powerful indication that she had made a difficult choice in the face of a genuine moral dilemma. To me, a further source of her distress lay in a concern for the life of the unborn child, a topic to be discussed in the next section. In sum, the cadre's distress reflects the fundamental moral conflict presented by the Chinese birth control program: the "human calamity" of overpopulation versus the interests of the individual and family and the life of the unborn child. If it is not always easy to seek the greater of two goods, it is even more difficult to pursue the lesser of two evils (the point of coerced abortion as a lesser evil will be further discussed in chapter 7).

THE ABORTED FETAL LIFE AS "SACRIFICE"

What is the official Chinese position—the Party line, so to speak—on the moral status of fetal life? Clearly, the fetus is invested with little or no moral significance, especially when its interests conflict with those of society, as in the need for population control. No laws or regulations protect fetal life. While the prohibition on selective abortion may protect some female fetuses, this measure was enacted to maintain long-term social stability and facilitate the implementation of birth control policies. Thus fetal life has little or no moral significance in the official discourse, and consequently abortion is not regarded as an ethical problem worthy of serious discussion.

Some Chinese, including some college students, share this official perspective. In order to preserve anonymity, the informants who consented to fill out my survey questionnaire were discouraged from adding personal comments. One of several exceptions was a biomedical student in a northern coastal city who expressed his strong support for abortion in a paragraph added at the end of the questionnaire. For him, abortion was appropriate as an adjunct to sexual pleasure:

> For some people, pregnancy is the purpose of sexual intercourse. But for others, pregnancy may be the incidental result of making love without taking contraceptive measures. In this case, the pregnancy should be terminated promptly. If pregnancy is not the purpose, the aim of making love is to seek pleasure. If

we cannot prevent the coming together of sperm and egg, it is completely legitimate to halt the development of the zygote or fetus.

What interests me here is not an argument that makes light of abortion, but the attitude behind the student's comment in which fetal life is given little attention and no moral significance. While the official discourse would certainly disapprove of his liberal attitudes to sex, his view of fetal life is in complete accord with the official line—that the interests of the fetus should be subordinated to those of society, the family, or the mother or parents (even, perhaps, in an extreme case, to the parents' sexual pleasure).

Despite this, a kind of ambivalence about fetal life prevails, if not in laws and regulations, at least in practice, especially when late abortion is involved. There are no doubt many high-level officials and local cadres who, like my biomedical student, consider it legitimate to terminate pregnancy at any stage as a means of birth control. But there is evidence that some sensitivity regarding the unborn life exists in official circles, as suggested by a case reported by the Chinese-American sociologist Huang Shu-min (1989). As the head (Party secretary) of a village in southeastern China, Mr. Ye was involved in birth control work and helped persuade women with unauthorized pregnancies to have abortions. But he did not treat all stages of pregnancy equally. In order to adhere to the very limited quota of births for the village, he gave first priority to women who were more than six months pregnant, whether their pregnancies were authorized or not. He argued that "it is too dangerous for women who are more than six months pregnant to have abortions." That year, the village exceeded its quota by four births. "Our village will pay the RMB$5,000 fine to the township government [for the excess births]," Mr. Ye told Huang, "but we saved four babies. I consider that a great achievement" (Huang 1989: 184–85). The female cadre whose case was discussed above suffered long-term distress because she felt partly responsible for the death of a baby as the result of "pressured" abortion. Mr. Ye expressed satisfaction in being able to save babies by paying a fine. However small the sample, these anecdotes show that sentiment for the unborn exists at the local level, though it may well be neither approved at higher levels nor shared by other local leaders. In chapter 5, we will meet some medical doctors who, although administratively classified as "cadres," have participated in performing abortions and yet share this sensitivity to and sentiment for fetal life.

According to the Potters, in the tragic case of later-term abortion reported by them, "no attention was paid to the child, nor were any measures taken to save it; the child died as a result of deliberate inattention to its prenatal distress" (Potter and Potter 1990: 242). What they called "the family's point of view" was the only factor that might have worked against full acceptance of the birth control program on the part of the villagers. Partly because the

Potters believed valuing the unborn life in and of itself was "alien and irrelevant" to Chinese, they excluded any moral significance for the unborn in this case or in China's birth control program in general. It may be true that no medical measures were taken to save the baby in this case. But it is very unlikely that no one, not even the parents, paid any attention to the newborn in the situation the Potters described. It is much more likely that those involved paid varying degrees of attention to the newborn, though not enough to save it. Whether or not she or others noticed it, the cadre's ongoing distress over the event might also be explained by her being continuously troubled or "haunted" by the dead infant (in the same way as a dying woman who had sold abortifacients felt haunted by the specter of aborted children, as recounted in an ancient Chinese medical ethics text discussed in chapter 3).

Nonetheless, the existence of such sentiments at the local level does nothing to change the official definition of fetal life—where the unborn child has no real moral significance. In Chinese public discourse, it is the *external* or *social* value of fetal life that is emphasized in discussing abortion, if it is discussed at all. The official view embodies a widely shared assumption that, although the fetus is a human life and although taking a human life is usually wrong, abortion is morally acceptable because the moral status of the fetus is always outweighed by the interests of the woman, the parents, the family, and especially society and the state. A number of Chinese scholars have articulated this assumption in their works. In order to examine this particularly Chinese way of reasoning, I quote at length three related passages from three different texts. In a medical ethics textbook written for medical professionals, the authors set out four ways of justifying abortion:

> The fetus has a right to be born. But this right is not absolute. When the interests of the fetus conflicts with the interests of society or the mother, depriving the fetus of the right to life is ethically permissible as long as there are sufficient reasons. . . . One should have a very cautious attitude toward induced abortion. Abortion can be performed only with sufficient moral justification. The purpose of abortion is first of all to protect the pregnant woman's health. When the fetus threatens the mother's life, abortion (killing the fetus) is morally acceptable in order to protect the mother's life. Second, abortion is intended to meet the needs of birth control. Family planning is a fundamental policy of our country. Population control is also a global task. The interests of a fetus are negligible in comparison with the interests of the whole of humanity. Abortion is thus morally permissible for the purpose of family planning. Third, abortion is intended to improve the quality of the population. "Limiting the quantity of population and improving the quality of the population" is the national policy of our country. Abortion is carried out for eugenic purposes, to avoid the birth of a fetus which may or certainly will be seriously deformed. This is permissible because the right of all humankind to health is doubtless higher than the right of

a fetus with a serious genetic disease or deformity. The ethical reason for abortion [in the case of eugenics] is thus sufficient. Fourth, abortion is intended to uphold the rights and interests of women. A woman has the right to control her own body. As long as the interests of society and the family receive sufficient attention, a woman should be permitted to freely choose abortion to protect her own interests, by terminating pregnancies resulting from premarital sex or rape, for example. The birth of such fetuses would cause permanent suffering and distress for the woman involved. In these conditions, the woman's right to happiness exceeds the right of the fetus [to life]. So abortion should be permissible. (Zhang and Zhang 1995: 191–92)

In his pioneering book *Bioethics*, leading Chinese bioethicist Qiu Renzong examines the ethical debate surrounding abortion in the West in the Chinese context:

On one side of the balance are the parents, family, and society, and on the other side is the fetus. Although the fetus is not a person, it is a human life after all and thus has a certain intrinsic value. But this value is not sufficient to attribute to the fetus the same rights as an adult or even an infant enjoys. Although the rights of the adult are never absolute, when the interests of the fetus are in conflict with those of the parents and society, they must be subordinated to the latter. This occurs independently of any person's will.

Thus, the fetus has mainly external value. When the population of a society is expanding at an excessive rate, as is the case in China, so that the social fabric and people's lives are impaired, it is necessary to loosen the restrictions on abortion and to allow it as a remedial measure of birth control after the failure of contraception. At the present time, the value of the fetus is greatly reduced due to social factors. In this situation, in spite of the fact that some fetuses are sacrificed, those that remain will receive much better care and have much brighter futures. On the other hand, in some developed countries in Europe the population shows zero growth or even a decline. Over a long period, these countries will be threatened by social problems brought about by manpower shortages and the aging of the population. In this situation, they will not only encourage reproduction but also restrict or even ban abortion in general by law, as they are doing at present. At such times, the value of the fetus is greatly enhanced for social reasons.

Yet the fetus is a human life after all and is directly connected with the later stages of human development. We thus should give it all necessary respect. Otherwise, harm will result to society and humankind. (Qiu 1987: 94–95)

It is worth noting that Qiu uses the term "sacrificed" (*xisheng*) to refer to fetuses aborted in the interests of population control.

Finally, Tang Kailin, a leading ethicist in contemporary China, justifies the use of selective abortion for eugenic purposes in a book on the ethics of population control (Tang and Long 1992: 125). His views on the ethical dimensions of eugenics in China were presented at a bioethics conference held in Dunedin, New Zealand, in 2001, and subsequently published in the *New Zealand Bioethics Journal*.

> Generally speaking, pregnant women with fetuses which have been diagnosed with serious genetic disease should follow the requirement of eugenics and have selected termination of those pregnancies to prevent the birth of babies with serious genetic disease. However, these fetuses are not simply human tissue, they have a special status amongst biological life. People thus face difficult conflicts when these sad situations develop and they are offered abortion services. On the one hand there are the demands of family and society to avoid the burden of a damaged child, the social demands of enhancing the genetic health of the population and the inability to provide the possibility of an independent and worthwhile life on the part of the child. On the other hand, is the value of the fetus. In choosing the former one will terminate the pregnancy and deny the value of life of the fetuses. In choosing the latter one will allow and even assist the birth of the fetuses. The second ethical approach should be to reject the latter and choose the former, for the value of family and society is higher than the value of the seriously impaired fetuses. The misfortunes which result from the birth of seriously impaired infants are greater than those associated with terminating the gestational process. Moreover, the misfortunes associated with terminating the gestational process are smaller than those the child would face after its birth. Therefore to carry out selective abortion of a fetus with serious deformities benefits family and society and avoids suffering of the disabled child. The opposite moral view is not sound and should be questioned. (Tang 2002: 14)

These perspectives offered by leading Chinese medical ethicists are far from personal views. They elaborate upon the officially sanctioned understandings of abortion and the moral-social status of fetal life in contemporary China. That is, the fetus is not important in and of itself; its importance is contingent on its external or social value. Fetal life has no significant moral weight, especially when it is in conflict with the interests of the pregnant woman, the couple, the family, the work unit, Party policy, the state, Chinese society, and even humankind. In this view, the interests of society should always be given first priority, followed by those of the woman and the family. High-sounding assertions such as "The fetus has a right to be born," "The fetus is a life after all," "Abortion can be performed only with sufficient moral justification," and "Fetuses have a special status" ring rather hollow in such a context. If contraception fails, the fetus will have to be sacrificed on the altar of the collective and social good.

CONCLUSION

According to the official ideology of the People's Republic of China, abortion is supposed to be merely a remedial measure; sex-selective abortion is prohibited by law; drowning and abandoning female infants are feudal evils that have nothing to do with the government's birth control policies; and forced abortion is not an inherent element of the program. A collectivist and statist morality is used to justify official perspectives on birth control, abortion, and fetal life. Laurence Tribe's generalization on abortion in China (1992: 63) cited in chapter 1—that "scant attention" is paid to the rights of women to choose and the right of the fetus to life, while great emphasis is placed on the interests of abstract collectives and the state—is an accurate summation of the official discourse.

It should be noted, however, that the official discourse on abortion and birth control is not fixed, coherent, and unified, but is always in flux. In the first decade of the People's Republic, the official standpoint was antithetical to that advanced today—induced abortion was legally prohibited to ensure "the life of the next generation," among other reasons. There are signs that birth control policies may be significantly modified in the near future, for example, allowing a second child to urban couples who are themselves single children. More importantly, diverse and even dissident views exist within the discourse, such as the moral sentiment favoring the interests of family and even the life of the unborn child among family-planning cadres at the local level. In addition, it would be a mistake to assume that those Chinese scholars cited here, who support some official perspectives, necessarily consider themselves party to the official discourse or uncritically accept its prescriptions.

The question I am most concerned with, nevertheless, is this: How representative of the views and experiences of ordinary Chinese is the current official discourse as presented in this chapter? Certainly, enforced by formidable state power, it is dominant and daunting. As a result, many people accept the official line, either consciously or unconsciously. However, as the following chapters will show, the official discourse on abortion and related issues, despite its power, is only one of many Chinese perspectives; in today's China there are voices that differ and run counter to the official line, just as diverse views on the subject have coexisted throughout history.

According to the official position, as expressed in a standard and influential textbook on ethics (Luo 2002 [1989]: preface), the socialist and collectivist or Marxist ethics promoted by the Party and the government represents the loftiest moral ideals achieved by humankind—although it is conceded that they are still in the process of development to meet new needs thrown up by socialist practice. Advanced science and technology, and even some ethical elements borrowed from the West, all have a place in constructing Chinese socialism, socialist ethical theories, and in particular, social practice. However, Western ethics and morality are officially regarded as being both decadent and moribund due to the "individualistic," "egoistical," "selfish," "materialist," and "utilitarian" features of capitalism. The same critique applies to the ethical ideals and moral norms associated with China's long history. Although some elements may be pertinent today, Chinese morality derived from the past is generally viewed as, in the official terms, "feudalistic," "backward," and a "massive obstacle" to advancing the socialist cause—"the greatest cause of humankind." On the subject of reproductive ethics, contemporary Chinese publications sharply criticize the Confucian regard for family and individual life as well as traditional customs and norms that directly or indirectly oppose the present policies. At the same time, other ancient values that happen to accord with current policies on family planning are praised as "excellent elements" of China's past (see Pan 2001).

Before discussing the plurality of voices emanating from contemporary China, we must attend to some long-forgotten and discarded stories from imperial China and draw our own conclusions on these "feudalistic pernicious vestiges" of the past.

3

The Forgotten Controversies: Heritage of Imperial Times

Forgetting the past means betrayal.

—Popular Communist slogan

"By using a mirror of brass one may see to adjust one's cap; by using history as a mirror, one may learn the rise and fall of empires." Originating in the earliest collection of Chinese poetry, *Shijing* (The Book of Songs or Classic of Odes), and popularized by the seventh-century emperor Tang Taizhong, this metaphor on history as a teacher of moral lessons has become a piece of household Chinese wisdom. While probably no other civilization prizes history and tradition so highly as China has, a historical peculiarity of twentieth-century China was "the emergence and persistence of profoundly iconoclastic attitudes to the cultural heritage of the Chinese past" (Lin 1979: 3). The radical antitraditionalism that first developed in the May Fourth era reached its peak in the "great" Cultural Revolution and still has echoes today. Negative attitudes to Chinese tradition, together with the myth of a unified and uniform Chinese culture, are manifest everywhere in China, in official and nonofficial discourses, and in intellectual and sociopolitical life. The past century witnessed an unprecedented level of destruction of traditional culture—of visible historical relics as well as many "invisible" values and institutions. In the relentless course of modernization and economic development, this destruction still continues. In the antitraditionalist and modernist context of contemporary China, the richness, diversity, and complexity of the Chinese past often remain deeply buried. Even a large part of the praise and pride for Chinese traditions is appealing only to the nationalist sentiment, with little concrete content. As a result of this historical amnesia resulting from peculiar

67

Chinese modernism and antitraditionalism, the abortion controversies of imperial China, and especially the "conservative" traditions, are largely unknown to contemporary Chinese. Regarding the abortion issue, the historical mirror has been discarded, as if it had never existed.

It is widely believed that abortion has never been a serious ethical issue throughout China's history (see Luk 1977; Qiu 1987, 1992; Qiu and Jonsen 2003). Commentators have repeatedly emphasized that most Chinese would agree with the great Confucian master Xun Zi (286–238 BCE) that "human life" begins at birth and ends with death. It has often been asserted that, due to the belief that the unborn fetus and even the newborn child do not constitute a human life, Chinese, followers of Confucianism in particular, not only permit almost any kind of abortion but even justify, or at least tolerate, infanticide. Accepting this common view, I myself once summarized the cultural characteristics of Chinese understandings of abortion from a Chinese-Western comparative perspective as follows:

> Among ancient Chinese philosophers, doctors, and lay people, the practice of abortion evoked little (if any) explicit discussion, not to mention public debate, as is still the case in contemporary China. Even though no ancient Chinese thinker explicitly advocated that both abortion and infanticide are justifiable on utilitarian grounds as did Plato and Aristotle, neither was there a Chinese "Pythagoras" to hold that abortion is killing because of the belief that human life begins at conception. The Chinese did not consider abortion morally objectionable mainly because they, like Jewish law and Platonists in ancient Greece, maintained that human life does not begin until birth. Confucians and Daoists rarely treated the fetus as a human being. So neither the "Absolute Sincerity of the Great Doctor" (the Chinese "Hippocratic Oath") by the "King of Medicine," Sun Simiao, nor any other pre-modern professional maxims written by medical doctors clearly claimed that the physician should "not give a woman an abortion remedy" as does the well-known Hippocratic Oath. (Nie 1999c: 469)

Despite the prohibition on abortion mandated by imported Buddhism, for a long time I believed that, in general, Chinese had taken a permissive attitude toward terminating pregnancy in the past and that this is equally true today.

Is it correct that Chinese have historically seen abortion as ethically permissible? Was my initial sweeping generalization about traditional Chinese standpoints on the subject mistaken? A systematic sociocultural history of abortion in China has yet to be written; to undertake such a project, one would need to explore an enormous range of materials, including the official histories of twenty-six dynasties and other classical works, medical manuals, as well as literary essays and fiction, unofficial histories, and local histories. This chapter is not intended to provide such a study. Rather, using a range of primary historical sources and the few modern studies available

(Bray 1997; Furth 1995, 1999), I will show that blanket generalizations supporting a permissive or "liberal" Chinese position on abortion are unfounded and that in imperial China there existed a wealth of conflicting moral perspectives on terminating pregnancy, fetal life, and related issues, as is the case today.

PRACTICE AND LAWS IN IMPERIAL AND REPUBLICAN TIMES

Abortion was certainly practiced in imperial China, as elsewhere, for a variety of reasons, including therapeutic purposes, concealing illicit sexual behavior, and birth control. It was undertaken among the populace and even in the palace as a tool in the endless power struggles that unfolded there, as a story about the emperor's concubines in the "Biography of the Empress Dowager Xiao Muji" in the *Mingshi* (Official History of the Ming Dynasty, 1368–1644) illustrates: "Concubine Wan, the emperor's favorite, was consumed by jealousy. She made all the other concubines, whenever they became pregnant, take drugs to induce abortion" (Chen 1982: 345).

Chinese physicians certainly prescribed abortifacients, taken mainly orally, and sometimes performed abortions by acupuncture and massage. The *Bencao Gangmu* (The Great Pharmacopoeia), compiled by the sixteenth-century Confucian physician, medical scholar, and scientist Li Shizhen, was the most systematic summary of *materia medica* literature that appeared in imperial China and is still the standard reference for Chinese pharmacology and medicine. In this well-known medical work, seventy-two agents are listed under the rubric of "drugs for dropping the living fetus" (*duo shengtai yao*) (Li 1988: vol. 4b). These abortifacients included accessory tuber of aconite (*fuzi*), claimed to be the first choice for abortion, roots of achyranthes (*niuxi*), pinellia tuber (*banxia*), arisaema root (*tiannanxing*), corydalis tuber (*xuanhusuo*), safflower or Tibetan crocus (*honghua*), leeches (*shuizhi*), sloughed snakeskin (*shetui*), lizard (*xiyi*), crab's claws (*xiazhao*), musk (*shexiang*), mercury (*shuiyin*), and benzoin (*anxixiang*), which was especially acclaimed for "bringing down the spectral fetus" (*xia guitai*). Li also recorded more than thirty drugs for evacuating the dead fetus and dozens of medical agents for hastening delivery in the face of difficult birth (Li 1988). According to traditional Chinese medicine, most of these drugs have the effect of "quickening the blood" and dispelling stasis.

It is, however, questionable whether these drugs were ever effective (for a review of the chemistry and bioactivity of some abortifacients used in traditional Chinese medicine, see Kong, Xie, and But 1986). While some ancient attempts at abortion were apparently successful, we cannot know whether these resulted from medical intervention or occurred simply by chance. In the *Nanshi* (Official History of the Southern Dynasties, 420–589

CE), we are told that an empress laid a wager with Xu Wenbei, a physician, about the effectiveness of his abortion techniques. Xu employed acupuncture on a pregnant woman, and the fetus was successfully aborted. Often, these attempts were not successful. Again, in the *Nanshi*, a story from the "Biography of Xu Xiaoci" records some desperate expedients:

> Xiaoci was still in his mother's womb when his father was murdered. His mother was still young and did not want to be pregnant as she hoped to remarry. So she took to jumping down from the bed hundreds of times and pounded her waist with the club used for washing clothes. She also took abortifacients. But the fetus proved immovable. At birth, he was given the nickname Yilu (Abandoned Slave). (Chen 1982: 135)

The belief that the power of life and death lies in the hands of Heaven or Fate, not human beings, is deeply rooted in Chinese history and still widely held in China today. In this story, the failure of the attempted abortion was attributed not to the ineffectiveness of the drugs and other methods employed, but to the supernatural intervention of the gods on behalf of the unborn child.

Besides medical and historical works, abortion is also described in classical literature. For instance, in the sixteenth-century realist novel *Jingpingmei* (The Golden Lotus), a women healer offers two "big black pills" to Moon Lady, first wife of the hero Ximen Qing, when she suffers stomach pain and bleeding—signs of a possible miscarriage. This medicine successfully aborts the fetus (cited in Furth 1999: 273).

However, the focus of this chapter is not the history of abortion in China or the effectiveness of the drugs and procedures used, but how ancient Chinese regarded it from an ethical perspective. Since the morality of any society or historical period is often expressed in the form of laws, these will be our first port of call.

According to the ground-breaking historical study of abortion law in China undertaken by Bernard Luk (1977), in imperial times there was no legal prohibition against deliberately terminating a pregnancy. Luk concluded that historically a Chinese woman

> had a far greater freedom than her Western sister to dispose of the contents of her womb—not because the fetus was considered a part of her body without its own soul or viability, but because its life in its organic unity was integrated with hers and derived from her. This did not however imply her absolute freedom to abort—the Chinese woman was subject to her husband and to her mother-in-law (if she was a concubine, then also to the wife), and she owed an obligation to her husband's ancestors to procreate—but it did mean a far more flexible and situational, and a far less moralistic, approach to the question of abortion. (Luk 1977: 384)

Procuring and performing abortion were not crimes in the imperial legal codes. Earlier Chinese law dealt with abortion only in two extreme situations: first, "abortion-through-assault," where abortion was induced as the result of an assault on a pregnant woman, and second, deliberately procured abortion resulting in the mother's death. Although it was a crime to induce abortion by assaulting a pregnant woman, abortion-through-assault was never legally classified as manslaughter or homicide. Therapeutic abortion could be recommended in the absence of pressing medical reasons.

According to Luk, comprehensive Chinese laws regulating the performance of and access to abortion did not exist until the nineteenth century (the late Qing Dynasty). The first legislation clearly prohibiting induced abortion was the *Daqing xin xinglu* (The New Criminal Code of the Great Qing), promulgated in 1910. The Criminal Code condemned abortion as "cruel to humanity, damaging to [social] order, and contrary to the public interest." It stipulated that any woman who procured an abortion using drugs or other means; anyone who caused a woman to have an abortion; and any physician, midwife, pharmacist, or herb dealer who assisted a woman to have an abortion would be liable for criminal prosecution.

Laws passed in the Republican period (1911–1949) continued to proscribe abortion. Sanctions directed at medical professionals who practiced abortion or assisted a woman in procuring a termination were more severe than in the late Qing. Publication of the methods and instruments of abortion was itself categorized as an offense. Nevertheless, therapeutic abortion in cases where the mother's life was at risk was legally permitted in 1935 for the first time, although pregnancy following rape was not included. Besides the drive to modernize China by following the example of the West, which had comprehensive antiabortion laws, legislators consistently appealed to concepts such as "the good of society," "maintaining good social practices," and "protecting the public interest." The nationalist government set out its objections to abortion and the reasons for prohibiting it in clear terms: "The objective of the nation is to multiply into strength. But multiplying and strengthening depends on the people. Unless abortion is severely prohibited, it runs counter to the national objective. Therefore, to say that abortion protects primarily the foetus is too restricted a view" (cited in Luk 1977: 388). As we saw in chapter 2, these same utilitarian concerns and "sacred" demographic goals—the good of society and the interests of the nation—were invoked as major reasons for relaxing the legal prohibition on abortion by the People's Republic in the early 1960s.

Luk argued that, from the early twentieth century, the flexibility of traditional abortion law and custom was "swept away" as a result of Western cultural impact on China. He pointed out that the 1910 New Criminal Code of the Great Qing was drafted by two Japanese advisers trained in German law, and its provisions closely paralleled contemporary European, American, and

Japanese law. For Luk, the cultural foundation for the historic legal shift from a permissive to a prohibitive emphasis in Chinese abortion law was laid by the acceptance of Western values such as the concepts of human equality (whether of infants, children, wives, or concubines) and the sanctity of human life.

The laws of imperial China might well have given "more freedom" to women to terminate unwanted pregnancies than those in force in the West. But does this mean that Chinese failed to see abortion as an issue that posed serious moral and ethical questions? Was the prohibitive legislation enacted in the late Qing Dynasty, the Republican period, and the first decade of People's Republic simply a consequence of Western influence, running totally counter to traditional Chinese norms?

BUDDHISM, CONFUCIANISM, AND THE MEDICAL PROFESSION

While the theory and techniques of Chinese medicine have been heavily influenced by Daoism throughout its history, from the moral and social perspectives health care in imperial China—its ethical framework and norms—was mainly defined by Confucianism and Buddhism. Buddhism, initially imported into China no later than the first century BCE and gradually acculturated ever since, teaches that taking a human life is morally wrong, that the fetus is a form of life, and that, therefore, abortion is morally questionable, if not necessarily always unacceptable. Terminating a pregnancy is clearly prohibited by the primary Buddhist precept against "depriving a human being of life." Although in its teachings and scriptures Buddhism appears straightforwardly opposed to abortion, it has been practiced in Buddhist societies from ancient to modern times. According to the pioneering work on Buddhism and bioethics by Damien Keown, although opinions on abortion in Buddhist Asia are characterized to a significant degree by divergence and variation, Buddhist condemnation of the practice has been interpreted with "remarkable consistency" (Keown 1995: 117). For Peter Harvey, although Buddhists hold a permissive view in practice and do not necessarily oppose its legalization, "the Buddhist scriptural tradition is clear in its opposition to abortion." Buddhism "considers abortion as worse when the foetus is older and when the reason for considering an abortion is weaker. It always considers it as worse than killing an animal in parallel circumstances" (Harvey 2000: 350).

In ancient China, at least some Buddhist physicians (and those influenced by Buddhism) took a conservative attitude. A story from Zhang Gao's *Yi Shuo* (Medical Compendium) written in the thirteenth century illustrates this ancient Chinese Buddhist viewpoint on abortion vividly. The section on medical ethics in Zhang's work is one of the most influential ethical texts in

Chinese medical literature. Through a series of twelve anecdotes, Zhang addresses crucial moral issues in medical practice. The abortion anecdote reads as follows:

> In the capital city lived a woman whose family name was Bai. She was good-looking and people called her "Bai Mudan" (The White Peony). She made a living by selling abortifacient drugs. One day, she started getting violent headaches: her head swelled up and increased in size day by day. All the prominent physicians treated her, but no one was able to cure her. After many days, an ulceration developed and the smell became unbearable. She cried every night and her crying could be heard near and far. Eventually, she gathered her family around her and begged them: "Burn all the prescriptions that I've kept." She also made her children swear not to pass on her trade. Bewildered, her son asked: "You have built yourself up through this work. Why do you want to give it all up?" His mother answered, "Every night I dream that hundreds of little children are sucking on my head. This is why I cry out in pain. All this is my retribution for selling drugs to damage fetuses." Right after saying this, she died. (Quoted in Ma 1994: 670; Lee 1943; Unschuld 1979: 48–49)

The moral of the anecdote is very clear: because the fetus is a human life and at least a potential child, abortion is tantamount to killing a child. The story gives no hint as to the gestational periods involved. Nevertheless, the author—who is best described as a Buddhist-Confucian physician—clearly maintains that abortion in general is morally indefensible regardless of its legal status, and believes that providing abortifacients, like being an accomplice to murder, will be punished by supernatural forces. For Zhang, a medical professional should refrain from performing abortions just as a good physician should never use fraudulent methods to bring himself fame and material gain.

Confucianism was the dominant moral-political philosophy and official ideology in China for more than two thousand years—from the time of the early Han Dynasty in the second century BCE to the May Fourth Movement in the early twentieth century and beyond. We begin our historical survey of Confucian attitudes to abortion with an anecdote that has been interpreted by contemporary Chinese scholars (see Ma 1994: 670–71) as evidence of ancient Chinese, especially Confucian, acceptance of abortion. The text comes from *Yuewei Caotang Biji* (Notes from the Hut of Subtle Reading), by Ji Jun (1726–1805), a celebrated prime minister and writer in the Qing Dynasty:

> Wu Huisu told [this story]. There was a physician who was well known for his prudence and kindness. One evening an old lady, carrying a golden bracelet, came to him to buy an abortion drug. The doctor was shocked and refused her request out of hand. The next evening she returned, with two pearl flowers as well as the bracelet. Exasperated, the doctor sent her away again. Six months later, he had a dream about being arrested by a police officer in the underworld.

He was told that someone had accused him of murder. As he arrived in the underworld, a woman with a long red towel wrapped tightly around her neck was complaining that the doctor had refused to supply her with drugs. The physician said: "Medicine is for saving life—how could I kill a human being for profit? Your adultery was brought to light—but that has nothing to do with me." The woman answered: "When I asked for medicine, the fetus had not yet formed. By aborting it, I could have survived. My life could have been saved by destroying an insensible blood clot. But since I couldn't get an abortion drug, the baby was born. The child endured his fill of suffering and in the end was killed. I was left no way out except to hang myself. You destroyed two lives in trying to save one. If *you* can't be prosecuted [for my death as well as my child's], who else should be?" The underworld judge sighed and said: "Your testimony takes real-life circumstances into account. He [the physician] on the other hand has stuck rigidly to *li* (ritual, order, reason, principle). Is he the only person since the Song Dynasty to cling stubbornly to *li* alone regardless of circumstances in the real world?" At that point, the judge rapped on the table. Filled with horror, the physician woke up. (Ji 1998 [1800]: 200)

The message of this story seems clear: the fetus, at least up to a certain developmental stage, is not a human being; abortion of the preformed fetus is no more than "destroying an insensible blood clot." The writer seems to have adopted the kind of pragmatic perspective taken by many in the West in the contemporary ethical debate to justify the choice of abortion. In this story, abortion seems to be seen as a moral necessity or at least as a lesser evil. For Ji Jun, along with the woman denied the abortion drug, the continued pregnancy destroyed two lives. Consequently, if a doctor fails to provide an abortifacient in such circumstances, he makes himself responsible for avoidable suffering and death and will have to give an account of his actions before the ultimate tribunal.

Since Ji Jun was the highest-ranking official and most distinguished Confucian scholar of his time, his views may be taken as representative of the standard Confucian position on abortion. Several caveats are in order, however. First, in this story Ji Jun does not deal directly with the issue of abortion. He uses the anecdote mainly to criticize the moral absolutism that had characterized Neo-Confucianism since the Song Dynasty (960–1279 CE) and to attack a rigid adherence to *li* (reason, principle) "regardless of circumstances in the real world." Second, the anecdote allows one to conclude no more than that, for the writer, as well as for the heroine of the tragedy and the underworld judge, abortion is morally permissible only at the early stage of pregnancy, when the fetus is no more than a "blood clot." The anecdote alone, unsupported by other evidence, does not allow the blanket conclusion that traditional Confucianism permitted abortion under all circumstances and at any stage of pregnancy. And it is totally another question how representative Ji Jun's views were of Confucian attitudes on the subject.

On the contrary, the anecdote suggests a "conservative" perspective that may have been widely held at the time. The doctor in the story, a Confucian most likely, makes a very strong ethical statement in reply to the woman's charges: *"Medicine is for saving life—how could I kill a human being for profit?"* The key term here is *sharen* (to kill a person, to commit murder). For the doctor, the fetus is a *ren* (a person, a human being), and providing an abortifacient is tantamount to committing manslaughter or murder. According to Confucian moral ideals and principles, since from an ethical viewpoint medicine is *renshu* (the art of humanity or humaneness), it is wrong to profit from the practice of medicine. To profit from providing materials that are intended to kill a human being is doubly inhumane, and thus even more reprehensible. The fictional physician's position probably represented that taken by many people in the author's own time—a standpoint that Ji Jun set himself to challenge.

As an attack on mainstream ethical beliefs, this moral story retold by Ji Jun has two serious flaws in its logic. First, justice, or *yi* (righteousness) to use the Confucian term, is ill-served here. The real cause of the deaths of both the woman and her child was not the doctor's action in refusing to give the requested drug, but the social environment that left them "no way out" except death. Although it was understandable for the woman to blame the doctor—for her, abortion was probably the easiest way out—he was not morally responsible for the tragedy that followed. Second, Ji Jun may well have believed that a medical practitioner is obliged to provide whatever service a patient requests; based on this premise, the doctor who stuck too rigidly to orthodox morality was responsible for the two deaths. But, even though traditional Chinese medical ethics might never make it clear whether a practitioner is justified in refusing to provide professional services that offend against his conscience and moral beliefs, physicians would always be discouraged from giving a patient toxic drugs such as arsenic if the intention to harm or murder was present.

Although further research is needed in this area, such stories show that the attitudes to abortion of premodern Chinese, Confucians included, were not as permissive as has been generally assumed. In Confucian eyes, while abortion may at times be morally permissible, this is not always the case, and it does not apply at any stage of pregnancy. As I show in the next section, Confucianism, in common with traditional Chinese medicine, holds that the fetus is already a human life and becomes a living human being at a certain stage of pregnancy. Ji Jun's story, together with Zhang Gao's moral fable against abortion, indicate in vivid terms that it remained highly controversial in imperial China whether the fetus is a person or "an insensible blood clot"; whether terminating pregnancy is killing or merely performing a medical service; and whether it is moral misconduct or sacred duty for a medical practitioner to perform abortion on demand.

It would be wrong, however, to conclude that medical practitioners in imperial China universally shared the belief of the doctor in Ji Jun's story that abortion is never justifiable. As mentioned above, the great physician Li Shizhen recorded a number of abortifacients in his monumental pharmacological treatise. Although his attitude toward abortion in general is unknown, he failed to raise any ethical concerns over the abortifacients listed in his text. Li's silence here forms an interesting contrast with his condemnation of the use of so-called human drugs (*renyao*), or drugs derived from human body parts (Li 1988: vol. 52). Here Li explicitly raises the ethical issues involved in employing human body parts as medicine, using Confucian ethical terms such as *ren* (humanity), *yi* (righteousness), *li* (ritual), and *li* (reason, principle). For Li, although the use of human material such as hair, fingernails, and urine may well be ethically justifiable, the employment of others such as blood, flesh, and bone is morally repugnant, "harmful to humanity," and "contradicting righteousness" (for a study of the Confucian critique of "human drugs" in traditional Chinese medicine, see Nie 1999a).

It is very likely that Li Shizhen, like many of his fellow physicians in late imperial China, considered terminating pregnancy, at least in some circumstances, to be morally acceptable. The following medical case reported by the orthodox physician Cheng Maoxian (1581–?), and involving his wife, expresses the permissive attitude of the time on terminating pregnancy.

> As she approached her fortieth year, suddenly her menses were one or two days late. [She] used medicines to move the menses [*tong jing*] for two or three doses, but when they produced no effect she did not dare take more. So she waited to see what the future would bring. . . . At three months her menses suddenly flowed, and [she] thought her week body, unable to carry another child, was about to abort; fearing the difficulty of labor and delivery, miscarriage seemed like a fortune misfortunate. As matters did not go smoothly, there was no alternative to using peach kernel [*taoren*], Tibeton crocus [*honghua*, "dark *hu* [*xuanhu*] and angelica root tail [*gui wei*] to break up Blood and abort. After one dose, the bleeding stopped. Greatly alarmed, I said, "If after these medicines the menstrual flow still stops, isn't it fated that his child should not perish?" She took ginseng and astragalus root and doses to stop bleeding. She bled again heavily. I said: "This [fetus] truly can't tranquilized," and again she took peach kernel and Tibetan crocus. But then the bleeding stopped. [I] had to go back to the method of supporting the centre. Blood still flowed out dripping. After five days I reflected: with this loss of Blood, how can the fetus be so rocklike? The pulse signifies pregnancy, while the symptoms suggest it can't be so. Whether she is pregnant or not, her disorder must be treated, and quickly. So I used a strong replenishing formula with ginseng and *baihu* to stabilize, and after half a month she was gradually calm. At ten full months she delivered a boy, my third son, Hanbiao [Banner of Han]. All my earlier sons and daughters were born prema-

turely; only this boy went to full term, and his constitution is extraordinary. If a mother's *qi* is depleted, her fetus ought to be weak, but here the child was full term and its body unlike the mother's. Didn't True Heaven intend this? When we doctors mistakenly use Blood-moving medicines, fetuses may perish and their families may blame the physician. From my wife's point of view this child's happy condition can't be the work of humans alone. I write this first that my fellow physicians may learn from it to avoid occasions for self-reproach, and second so that Hanbiao one day may fully know his mother's many-sided hardships, which were not only a burden of motherly toil [after birth]. (Quoted in Furth 1999: 252–55)

To make full sense of the medical aspects of this very detailed case report, one would need some basic knowledge of traditional Chinese medicine, an extremely complex healing system with distinctive conceptual foundations, physiological and pathological theories, methods of diagnosis and treatment, and thousands of *materia medica* derived from animals, vegetables, and minerals. But here we are concerned not with the medical dimensions of the case, but with the moral message it carries about early Chinese attitudes to abortion. Reading this case in the light of the extensive body of medical case reports that survive from late imperial China, the American sinologists Francesca Bray (1997) and Charlotte Furth (1999) have clarified our understanding of early medical practitioners' attitudes to abortion in their groundbreaking feminist studies of reproductive medicine and gender in China. Bray summarizes the issues at stake in Cheng's report:

In the late imperial period distaste for taking life, together with the theory that the interruption of a natural process can be harmful, combined to make many orthodox physicians reluctant to terminate a pregnancy if there was a chance of saving both mother and child. The mother's health, however, had clear priority over the life of the fetus. Furthermore, physicians would not hesitate to prescribe the same blood-moving drugs that were known to cause abortions if a women's health was threatened by menstrual irregularity or blockage. (Bray 1997: 325)

It is also noteworthy that here, as in the story from the "Biography of Xu Xiaoci" cited above, the life or death of the fetus was believed to be determined by Heaven or Fate, rather than by human intervention.

Although many physicians in imperial China gave the mother's health priority over the life and welfare of the fetus, the medical literature also indicates that, unless abortion was definitely seen as "the lesser of two evils" in a particular case, physicians "preferred to avoid it if they could" (Bray 1997: 322–23). In fact, the same reason given for justifying abortion—the mother's health—could be offered as an important reason for opposing it in principle. By definition, like premature birth, terminating pregnancy runs counter to natural processes and is potentially a threat to the mother's health. As the physician Xue Ji (1487–1559) put it:

> One should not underestimate premature births; one premature birth may be as exhausting as ten normal births. Premature birth is more serious than normal birth, for a normal birth is comparable to a ripe chestnut which falls from the tree by itself, while a premature birth is like plucking it unripe, rupturing the shell and breaking the stem. Yet most people take it lightly and so many women die. (Quoted in Bray 1997: 323)

For orthodox physicians, moreover, offering abortion drugs or services was seen as the domain of alternative healers, if not quacks, like the woman healer in the sixteenth-century novel *The Golden Lotus*.

While it is true that the early medical literature rarely if ever explicitly proscribes performing abortion, this should probably not be interpreted as representing a permissive attitude on the part of ancient doctors. Rather, the silence is likely to indicate that medical abortion was regarded as so obviously unethical that there was no need to include it in lists of professional precepts, just as medical ethics documents whether ancient or modern rarely explicitly state that physicians should not murder or kill. In imperial China, the first work to systematically deal with medical ethics was written by Sun Simiao (about 581–681), a physician whose works combined elements of Buddhism, Confucianism, and Daoism. The first chapter of his *Qianjin Yaofang* (Prescriptions Worth a Thousand Gold Pieces), titled "Dayi Jingcheng" (On the Consummate Skill and Absolute Sincerity of Good Physicians), is probably the most influential and important treatise on medical ethics in the history of China, enjoying a status similar to that of the Hippocratic oath in the West. Sun has been called "the King of Medicine," not only because his medical works summarize Chinese medical achievements prior to the seventh century, but also because his ethical precepts on the teaching and practice of medicine have become paradigmatic. Although Sun's work contains no explicit proscriptions against abortifacients, one of his basic principles of medical practice is summed up in the maxim "Whoever destroys life in order to save life places life at an even greater distance" (quoted in Chen 1962: 17; translation from Unschuld 1979: 31). Reflecting the influence of Buddhism, Sun believed that "Humans and animals are equal where love of life is concerned." Although drugs derived from animals have been widely used in Chinese medicine from ancient times to the present, Sun clearly opposed the practice. While the use of any living creature—from insects to large animals—was proscribed, the use of certain dead insects was deemed acceptable. Sun even considered it a "great wisdom" to avoid the use of hens' eggs, especially when their contents had hatched out. Although he never confirmed it explicitly, the attitude behind his exploitation of animals no doubt extended to opposition to abortion.

The ethical concerns about abortion held by Chinese physicians, as well as laypeople, may not have originated directly in Confucianism, but probably reflected the influence of imported Buddhism. Sun Simiao, the "King of Medicine" in China, is well known for being a follower of three major Chinese religions—Confucianism, Daoism, and Buddhism—at the same time. Zhang Gao, who as we have seen expressed a general opposition to abortion in his *Medical Compendium*, combined Confucian and Buddhist approaches to medicine. On the one hand, Zhang was well known as a Confucian physician. In the epilogue to Zhang's collected works, a contemporary scholar called him "a good example of the Confucian physician" not only because Zhang, against the mainstream Confucianism that devalued medicine as "a petty technique," practiced medicine himself, but also because he took a position with the civil service. On the other hand, Zhang's medical ethics were heavily influenced by Buddhism. As the medical historian Paul Unschuld has pointed out, Zhang "placed the practice of medicine in a striking relationship to Buddhist ideas of rewards and punishments by the powers of another world" (Unschuld 1979: 42–43). Zhang's story of the "haunting fetuses" shows that at least some ancient Confucian physicians subscribed to a conservative Buddhist view of abortion. While Confucianism did not oppose abortion as explicitly as Buddhism, it was not in conflict with Buddhism and on occasion even promoted the Buddhist case.

In the late Ming and early Qing periods (the sixteenth and seventeenth centuries), the popular morality books known as the "Ledgers of Merit and Demerit" (*gongguoge*) advocated preventing abortion as a moral good. According to this type of ethical manual, salvation after death was dependent on the accumulation by the individual of a substantial store of merits during life. The list of meritorious deeds included stopping someone from drowning a child or from having an abortion, both of which were worth one hundred merit points (cited in Bray 1997: 341). According to the pioneering study of the ledgers by Cynthia Brokaw (1991), the values embodied in these popular ethical guides not only reflected the teachings of Buddhism and Daoism but also were endorsed, with some reservations, by Confucianism.

In summary, both Buddhists and Confucians regarded abortion as an evil and opposed it in principle for ethical reasons that included the preservation of fetal life and respect for human life in general. Buddhist and Confucian physicians, such as Zhang Gao, Sun Simiao, and the doctor in Ji Jun's anecdote, condemned the practice of abortion precisely on the ethical grounds that it entailed the destruction of a human life. But this opposition was not absolute, especially for Confucianism. Both Buddhism and Confucianism seemed to tolerate abortion in practice, and many ancient physicians had no hesitation in terminating pregnancy where the mother's health was in danger, for example. In the next section, I show that Chinese

opposition to abortion was also based on a detailed and systematic knowledge of the physiology of fetal development.

FETAL DEVELOPMENT AND FETAL "SOULS"

Although physicians in imperial China lacked techniques, such as B-ultrasound, that allow us to monitor fetal development directly, this did not prevent both physicians and laypeople from knowing a great deal about what
happens in the womb after conception. By the time of the Sui Dynasty
(581–618), Chinese medicine, especially in the fields of gynecology and obstetrics, already possessed amazingly detailed knowledge of fetal development from conception to birth. Such knowledge may well have originated
from empirical observations of miscarried or aborted fetuses made by both
women and physicians (for some primary traditional Chinese medical works
on pregnancy, see Song 1991 and Wang 1995; for some excellent English-
language studies of gestation and birth in Chinese medicine and culture, see
Furth 1995, 1999: 101–16).

The earliest and most influential Chinese work on gynecology and obstet-
rics, *Furen dachuan liangfang* (The Compendium of Treatments for Women's
Diseases), was compiled by the Southern Song Dynasty physician Chen Zhim-
ing (ca. 1190–1272) and first published in 1237. In the section titled "General
Remarks on Pregnancy," Chen cites several theories recorded in earlier medical literature on fetal development—works with titles such as *Etiology and
Symptomatology of Diseases, Five Organs,* and *The Fontanelle Classic.* In
Zhubing Yuanhou Lun (Etiology and Symptomatology of Diseases), compiled
by Chao Yuanfang (550–630 CE)—an imperial physician to Emperor Yang of
the Sui Dynasty—and first published in 610 CE, we find a theory of fetal development based on the ten-month lunar cycle of pregnancy:

1st month: "The incipient embryo" (*yiyue ming shipei*)
2nd month: "The incipient fat" (*eryue shigao*)
3rd month: "The incipient fetus" (*sanyue ming shitai*)
4th month: The Water Essence (*shuijing*) activates the formation of blood
    and blood-vessels
5th month: The Fire Essence (*huojing*) activates the formation of *qi* [en-
    ergy]
6th month: The Essence (*jing*) activates the formation of sinews
7th month: The Wood Essence (*mujing*) activates the formation of bones
8th month: The Earth Essence (*tujing*) activates the formation of skin
9th month: The Stone Essence (*shijing*) activates the formation of hair
10th month: The organs, joints, body, and "spirits" (*sheng*) are fully formed.
    (Song 1991: 318; Furth 1999: 104; Furth's translation, with modifications)

In addition to this schema, Chao connected fetal development with the channel theory (or meridian system) of Chinese medicine, the theoretical basis of acupuncture. For Chao, the fetus was nourished by nine of the twelve major "channels" in different combinations, depending on the month involved.

Various alternative schemes were proposed by early physicians. According to *Wuzang Lun* (Five Organs), a work attributed to the "saint of medicine" Zhang Zhongjing (ca. second century, CE), the growth of the fetus in the womb during each of the ten lunar months of its development follows this sequence:

1st month: The fetus resembles "a pearl formed from dew"
2nd month: The fetus resembles "a peach flower"
3rd month: Male and female elements are differentiated
4th month: The fetus assumes recognizably human form
5th month: Sinews and bones are formed
6th month: Hair growth begins
7th month: The *hun* (a kind of soul) becomes active and the left hand becomes mobile
8th month: The *po* (another kind of soul) becomes active and the right hand becomes mobile
9th month: The "thrice-turning-body" moves about
10th month: *Qi* (energy) reaches its proper level. (Song 1991; Furth 1999; Furth's translation, with modifications)

In *Luxian Jing* (The Fontanelle Classic)—the earliest systematic work to deal with childhood diseases—fetal development follows yet another scheme:

1st month: The incipient fetus; essence and blood (*jing xue*) congeal; a pulse forms
2nd month: The fetus takes on a recognizable form
3rd month: The sun or male spirit (*yangshen*) forms the "three souls" (*sanhun*)
4th month: The moon spirit or anima (*yinling*) forms the seven *po* souls (*qipo*)
5th month: The Five Phases or Elements (*wuxing*) differentiate the five organ systems (*wuzang*)
6th month: The Six Musical Notes (*liuli*) establish the six organ systems (*liuhu*)
7th month: The Gate of Essence (*jingguan*) opens the apertures that circulate light through the body
8th month: The Primal Spirit (*yuanshen*) is formed; the True Anima (*zhenling*) descends
9th month: The "palace chamber" [of the fetus] is made ready for birth

10th month: *Qi* (energy) reaches a sufficient level; all the elements are now complete. (Song 1991; Furth 1999; Furth's translation, with modifications)

The embryological theories advanced in these ancient medical works reflect the general understanding of fetal development in ancient Chinese society, based on the concept of the unification of opposites. As early as the second century BCE, the Daoist classic *Huananzi* described the ten months of pregnancy in these terms:

> The spirit is received from Heaven but the physical is the endowment of Earth. So it is said that One creates Two, Two creates Three, and Three creates a myriad things. All things are *yin* behind and *yang* in front. With the effusion of *qi* they unite. So it is said that in the first month a blob of fat is formed, in the second sinews, in the sixth bone. In the seventh month [the fetus] is fully formed, in the eighth it is active, in the ninth it is boisterous, and in the tenth it is born. (Quoted in Furth 1999: 101, note)

Here the theory of fetal development is combined with the distinctive Daoist theory of nature.

The duration of pregnancy is often described as "ten months," as in the Chinese idiom *shiyue huaitai* (literally, embracing the fetus for ten months), which reflects the understanding of fetal development in traditional medicine in China. The notion of a ten-month pregnancy (each month with thirty or twenty-nine days, according to the traditional Chinese lunar calendar) is at odds with contemporary biomedicine, which sets the duration of pregnancy from conception to delivery at about 266 days (*Dorland's Illustrated Medical Dictionary* 2000: 1451). The Chinese concept no doubt refers not to the exact duration of pregnancy, but to the fact that a pregnancy normally spans a ten-month period. One fourteenth-century medical text divides the period of fetal development not into months but into periods of seven days' duration. It describes in detail the features of the fetus at the end of each weekly period: the "lotus root" look at the end of the first week, the appearance of hands and feet in the sixth, the formation of all the bones in the twentieth and of hair and nails in the twenty-seventh, and the arms stretching and the head upside down at the end of the thirty-eighth week. Reckoning by this theory, the entire life of the fetus in the mother's womb spans exactly 266 (38 x 7) days (Wang 1995: 2–3).

While this is not the place to explore traditional Chinese conceptions of fetal life in detail, some important characteristics should be pointed out. First, Chinese, and Chinese physicians in particular, were well informed about fetal development. Second, medical knowledge distinguished between the embryo, the unformed developing fetus, and the fully formed fetus. Third, Chinese medical beliefs about fetal life were a part of traditional knowledge about cosmology and human physiology. Fourth, it is clear that human life was regarded as beginning before birth, as early as the first month of pregnancy, and that the human being was seen as being physically formed at some time during pregnancy. Fifth, fetal development was seen as not merely a process of physical growth, but a spiritual component—named variously as "soul" or "spirit" (*hun, po, shen, ling*)—was added or "infused" at a particular time during pregnancy.

This last point, on fetal development and the soul, requires some explanation here, however preliminary. What concerns us here is the most complex and subtle part of fetal life, making its moral status correspondingly complex. In traditional Chinese culture, human existence is not only physical and social but also psychological and spiritual. A large number of terms, such as *hun, po, shen, ling, linghun, hunpo* (different types of soul), exist to denote the spiritual and psychological dimensions of human existence. Although the idea of soul was less important in ancient Chinese culture than it was in the West, terms for soul, such as *hun* and *po*, had already appeared as early as the "Axial Age" (800–200 BCE), to use Karl Jaspers's terminology. Classical Chinese thought distinguished between *hun*, the "spirit" within a human being that can exist independently of the body, and *po*, the spiritual component that coexists with the body. The material body cannot remain alive without the *hun* and *po*, which have separate functions in maintaining human life. Death occurs when the physical body, *hun*, and *po* are separated from one another. As we have seen, traditional Chinese teaching on fetal development held that the embryo and fetus develop separate souls (such as *hun* and *po*) at the various stages of pregnancy (the third and fourth lunar months according to one theory, the seventh and eighth according to another). In the West, the moment of "ensoulment" (the moment when the fetus receives a soul) was for centuries regarded as the most crucial factor in deciding the moral status of the fetus; "ensoulment" is in many ways the ancestor of the current term "viability," which still has special legal force. In the Chinese view of fetal life, the soul came into existence not at conception but in the later stages of pregnancy.

Based on its knowledge of fetal development, Chinese medicine developed a distinctive theory of fetal education (*taijiao*) at an early stage. According to this theory, the fetus in the womb is directly influenced by the mother's experiences. The food she ate during pregnancy, and the things she heard, saw, and read, were held to influence the physical, intellectual, and moral character of the fetus. Parents were encouraged to begin their children's education in the womb, and many early medical works contain special sections on the subject. For example, in the section on pregnancy in Chao's *Etiology and Symptomatology of Diseases* discussed above, he describes the state of the fetus in the third month:

> At this time, the blood is not yet circulating and the fetus begins to grow although lacking fixed form. It will change as it is influenced by external forces.

If the child is to be dignified, the mother should arrange to meet noble people rather than ugly and evil ones. If the parents prefer a boy, the mother should use a bow and arrow and ride mares. If a girl is wanted, the mother should wear plenty of jewelry. If the child is to be beautiful, the mother should handle objects made of white jade and observe peacocks. If the child is to be virtuous and capable, the mother should be reading poems and books [i.e., the Confucian classics]. (Chao, in Song 1991: 318)

The notion of fetal education derives from Confucian roots in two important respects. First, Confucianism holds that the common human nature shared by each person is initially identical and that individuals acquire differentiating characteristics in response to their particular environment and education. Second, in traditional China the materials for fetal education, including behavioral guidelines for pregnant women, were part of mainstream Confucian teaching. Fetal education as a social practice was popularized in late imperial and modern China; it has been revived in mainland China since the 1980s (see Dikötter 1998).

This is not the place for a detailed discussion of the subject of fetal education, which raises many complex sociocultural and ethical issues. The point I wish to make is that many Chinese, including Confucians and Confucian physicians throughout history, consider that a human being is formed sometime between conception and birth, if not at conception itself. Fetal education would make no sense unless the fetus was considered to constitute a real human life.

The Chinese conception of gestation emphasizes the gradual process of transformation from conception to birth and even beyond. Early Chinese, medical professionals included, rarely tried to define the precise stage at which human life begins—whether at conception, the appearance of a distinctive face or recognizable human form, the formation of the organ system, the activation of particular souls, or the birth itself. This lack of precision excludes an absolutist conservative position on abortion and leaves room for permitting it under certain conditions. Yet, despite such ambiguities, the material presented in this section has, I hope, been sufficient to refute the common claim that in imperial China human life was almost always considered to begin at birth.

THE ETHICAL FOUNDATIONS OF A "CONSERVATIVE" CONFUCIAN VIEW

Of course, it is well known that the abortion debate is concerned not so much with facts as with values. Knowledge about fetal development and even the belief that the fetus is a human life do not necessarily lead people to raise ethical questions about abortion and to assert that the unborn should be always morally and legally protected as a human being or person. Otherwise, by demonstrating the "facts" of fetal development, the physician in Ji Jun's story could easily have proven his innocence to the underworld judge. And the modern medical techniques that provide images of the developing fetus would have been sufficient for conservatives to win over those in the liberal camp. In other words, people can hold a permissive position on terminating pregnancy, especially under conditions such as danger to the mother's health, while at the same time acknowledging the fetus as a human being. In this case, abortion is treated as the lesser of two evils. Therefore, the aim of this section is to offer a normative Confucian account of abortion.

Little information has come to light on how Confucians and neo-Confucians in imperial China addressed the issue of abortion. The materials presented in the previous section indicate that, while Confucian physicians in late imperial China opposed abortion in principle, they had no moral problem with terminating a pregnancy in the interests of the mother's health. Thanks to William LaFleur's fascinating anthropological and historical study of abortion in Japan (1992), we have some knowledge of how Confucians and neo-Confucians there responded to the question of abortion as a means of birth control. During the late Edo period (between 1721 and 1846), despite rapid social development and modernization, Japan's population remained surprisingly stable—especially given periods of rapid growth before and after and the situation in neighboring China, where the population doubled between 1749 and 1819. Historians and demographers attribute this unexpected downturn to a combination of infanticide and abortion. The Japanese euphemism for the use of infanticide and abortion as birth control measures was *mabiki*, which literally means "the culling of seedlings," especially in rice fields. According to LaFleur, "a constant Confucian objection to mabiki" was heard in Edo Japan, and Confucian moralists "repeatedly tried to solicit the help of Buddhist priests in getting their anti-*mabiki* message across to common people" (LaFleur 1992: 106–7). In contrast to the Japanese government, which opposed the practice out of economic and utilitarian considerations, and neo-Shinto apologists who criticized it on religious grounds, Confucian moralists condemned *mabiki* on moral grounds and in terms of Confucian ethical concepts such as "true humanity" (103–18). It is a pity that in LaFleur's work, Confucianism, including its moral objection to *mabiki*, is reduced to the level of secular, pragmatic, and economic belief system—reflecting a long-rooted stereotype of Confucianism that strips it of its spiritual and transcendental elements.

To further establish why some Chinese—not only Buddhists but also Confucians—have historically opposed abortion on ethical grounds, a normative account of abortion ethics is needed. A normative Confucian account of abortion would be based on the ethical ideals and principles specific to Confucianism and would draw on wider medical, cultural, and religious understandings of fetal life. Confucianism contains a rich and complex array of ethical resources that provide an ethical basis for _restriction_ of abortion. For example, essential Confucian concepts and practices such as ancestor worship, _xiao_ (filial piety), _cheyin_ (empathy, compassion), _shengsheng_ (to preserve and nourish life), and the relational conception of personhood all act to undermine the moral legitimacy of abortion.

Rather than seeing human beings as created in the image of a supernatural and transcendent being, Confucianism stresses the social and relational nature of human existence and sees personhood as a continuing process. Confucianism actively professes this humanistic orientation, "not the humanism that denies or slights a Supreme Power, but one that professes the unity of man and Heaven" (Chan 1963: 1, 15). Although often characterized as a form of secular humanism, Confucianism has its potent spiritual dimensions. The Confucian vision of the spirituality and sacredness of human existence has two important aspects. First, the human body is seen as intimately interconnected with Heaven (_tian_), Earth, and indeed all that exists. The contemporary Confucian philosopher Tu Wei-ming sees the body as a "conduit" (Tu 1992: 98) that has the capacity to transform not only our own human nature but also the whole order of creation. Second, and related to this belief, human dignity is underscored by our participation in religious ritual. Confucius saw the human body as a holy vessel, made sacred through participation in ritual (_li_). When a disciple once asked him to define a human being, Confucius replied that a person was "a utensil . . . a sacrificial vase of jade." As the scholar Herbert Fingarette expressed this idea: "it is the ceremonial aspect of life that bestows sacredness upon persons, acts, and objects which have a role in the performance of ceremony" (Fingarette 1972: 75–76).

As Western moral philosophers have often invoked the concept of "personhood" in the context of the contemporary abortion debate, the Confucian concept of personhood calls for further discussion. According to the Chinese-Canadian theologian and philosopher Edwin Hui (2000), the foundational concept of _jen_ (= _ren_, a person, humanity) underlies the dynamic process of "person-making" or the relational basis of personhood in Confucianism. A "person-in-relation" has sacred and transcendent dimensions as well as social ones. Hui emphasizes the many dimensions of the concept and their complex interrelations:

> [I]n Confucius and later in Mencius, when ordinary people practice _jen_ through keeping _li_ (humanity's way), they are simultaneously fulfilling Heaven's way. Chinese personhood understood in the context of Confucian _jen_ implies relationality with fellow human beings as well as the heavenly deity. (2000: 115–16)

Hui acknowledges the similarities between the Confucian concept and the Christian theological understanding of personhood. Comparable implications for human rights, and particularly the rights of the unborn fetus, arise from both traditions: "The Confucian concept of *jen* and the Christian concept of *perichoresis* both have much to contribute to modify the narrowly psychological and individualistic understanding and the rights-based ethics derived from it currently prevalent in the West." Hui concludes: "A relational understanding of personhood would question whether it would be entirely a matter of a woman's right or autonomous choice to abort a fetus when the personhood of the fetus could very well have been established by the maternal-fetal relation" (Hui 2000).

Reverence for ancestors and the duties owed to parents by their children are particularly important Confucian concepts and have a direct bearing on the ethics of abortion. The extended family (*jia*) and descent through the male line or patrilineage (*zu*) were the key social institutions of traditional China. Ancestor worship was the most vital religious element in family life and held central importance in Chinese culture. Confucianism upheld the cult of ancestor worship for many reasons. The most fundamental was, in the words of the Confucian classic *Li Ji* (Records of Rites), to "express gratitude to the family's progenitors and recall one's origins." In a modern scholar's phrase, the ancestral cult is based on "the principle of the source of the water and the root of the tree" (Yang 1961: 44). It emphasizes one's physical, social, and spiritual connections with former generations.

For Confucianism, the cult of ancestor worship helped develop moral traits that were highly valued in Chinese culture, especially filial piety. As the *Xiaojing* (The Classic of Filial Piety) urged: "May you think of your ancestors, and so cultivate their virtues" (in Chai and Chai 1965: 303–22). In Confucian tradition, filial piety was not conceived as a merely domestic virtue. According to the *Classic of Filial Piety*, it is "the basic principle of Heaven, the ultimate standard of earth, and the norm of conduct for the people" as well as "the basis of all virtues and the source of culture." Among other duties, children are required to maintain the integrity of the body bequeathed to them by their parents. To quote the *Classic of Filial Piety* again, "The body and limbs, the hair and the skin, are given to one by one's parents, and to them no injury should come; this is where filial piety begins." Another moral duty is to continue one's family line. Confucianism considers having no heirs the most serious violation of filial piety.

An ethical system based on reverence for the family raises serious questions about induced abortion. Before the fetus is formed into a human being, it is seen as a part of the mother's body—which the demands of filial piety require should not be subject to self-harm. Furthermore, when the fetus eventually assumes human form, he or she becomes a member of the family and lineage, possessing a physical and spiritual connection with the ancestors. Induced abortion at this stage would constitute a serious violation of the ancestral cult and filial piety. Their sanctions would seem to make abortion

morally acceptable only if a continued pregnancy would severely damage
the mother's health or threaten her life. For some Chinese, if a choice must
be made between the lives of mother and child, it is morally acceptable to
save the child—particularly in the case of an only child (especially if male).

Other important features of Confucianism may be viewed as incompatible
with induced abortion, especially late abortion. Confucianism holds that the
whole basis of morality is the ability to show empathy or compassion (*cheyin*)
to others. This concept is related to humanity or humaneness (*ren*), which is
probably the most fundamental ethical concept of Confucian thought. For the
sage Mencius, compassion is the beginning of humanity (*ren zhi dan*). Those
lacking compassion were regarded as inhuman—Confucianism's most severe
ethical sanction. The taking of a life—even one in the womb—should clearly
invoke the universal human moral attribute of *cheyin*.

Another fundamental Confucian moral principle is to preserve and nourish life (*shengsheng*). Mencius expresses the concept in a well-known ax-
iom: "the humane approach lies in doing no harm" (*wu shang ye, shi nai
reshu ye*). In a recent study of Confucian ethics, He Huaihong, a leading
ethicist in contemporary China, has argued that this principle has both negative and positive aspects—to do no harm, as in Mencius's dictum, and positively, to nourish life (He 1998: 293–322). Life is like the flame of an oil
lamp: it would be equally harmful to damage the lamp wick or stop feeding
the lamp with oil. It is true that Confucianism does not hold that life should
be preserved at any cost: it is sometimes right to sacrifice one's life for the
sake of moral values such as *ren* and *yi* (righteousness). Nevertheless, Confucianism holds that life is intrinsically valuable, a philosophy reflected in
the popular Chinese saying, "A good death is not as good as a bad life."
Thus respect for life, including plants and animals as well as human beings,
is a central value in Confucianism. For leaders, cultivating compassion for
all living things was seen as the starting point of *ren* and humane governance. Neo-Confucian teachers of the Song Dynasty such as Zhou
Maoshou, Chen Daoming, and Chen Yichuang forbade the emperor to harm
even grass without good reason.

It might be that the Confucian silence on the subject does not mean that
Confucians had few concerns on the morality of abortion, but that destroying a life, though still in the mother's womb, was simply and obviously
wrong from the ethical viewpoint of Confucianism. Influenced by Confucian
principles as well as Buddhist ethics, the great physician Sun Simiao expressed this reverence for all life, but especially human life, in the Chinese
"Hippocratic Oath": "Whoever destroys life in order to save life places life
out of reach." At a conference on new technologies of generative medicine
and ethics held in Hong Kong in 2004, Jonathan Chan, a scholar of traditional
Chinese and Western analytical philosophies, commented on my presentation on the plurality of Chinese perspectives on abortion and fetal life: "Be-

cause abortion so clearly abrogated the basic Confucian principle of bringing life into being and nourishing life, there was little debate on the issue throughout the history of Confucianism."

Nevertheless, the issue may not be as straightforward as it appears. The evidence presented in this chapter will not allow us to conclude that abortion was so obviously wrong for Confucians that there was no need for ethical discussion. First, as we have seen, Confucian physicians in late imperial China had no hesitation in prescribing abortifacients. In general, medical professionals of the time gave priority to the mother's health over the life of the fetus. Second, as noted above, knowledge of fetal development does not necessarily result in a moral commitment to treat a fetus at any stage of pregnancy as a person. Third, Confucian ethical principles and practices do not proscribe abortion unequivocally. They thus leave space for a liberal interpretation of the issue.

However, the historical and normative approach taken above suggests that Confucianism, far from taking an uncomplicated "liberal" approach to abortion, places severe moral restriction on the taking of human life in general and fetal life in particular. This is so at least in theory. On the one hand, while the Confucian attitude to abortion is not as "absolute" as that held by the Roman Catholic Church (see Noonan 1970), Confucianism does not differ from the position taken by the other major world religions as much as is usually assumed. On the other hand, the ethical reasons advanced for the "conservative" Confucian view often differ sharply from those held by other religious-moral traditions. More systematic historical, theoretical, and comparative studies are needed to elucidate the distinctive Confucian perspectives on abortion and fetal life. My point here is that, even though Confucianism does not oppose abortion as strongly as Catholicism and even Buddhism, Confucian moral traditions certainly do not approve abortion as a blanket procedure. In the moral theory and historical practice of Confucianism, terminating pregnancy is in principle ethically wrong, impermissible without strong moral justification. It seems that the major question in Confucian thinking on abortion is not whether it is morally acceptable in general (which is out of question), but what conditions can justify it.

THE PRECIOUSNESS OF HUMAN LIFE

In the previous section, I discuss some of the reasons why Confucians place a high value on human life and their links with practices such as ancestor worship. In both Confucianism and Daoism, each individual's life from beginning to end is closely and mysteriously related to nature, both physically and spiritually. Both Confucianism and Daoism emphasize the importance of following the Dao (the way). For example, a popular ancient classic of

Daoist religion, *Taiping Jing* (The Classic of Peace), condemns female infanticide for the simple reason that this practice offends against the Heavenly Way:

> Man is to carry on the tradition of heaven and woman, the tradition of earth. Now people cut off the tradition of earth and thus make reproduction of life impossible. So people (who exercise female infanticide) are mostly deprived of their offspring. How heavy is the sin they commit! These people should all have offspring to propagate their species from generation to generation. But on account of their having cut off the tradition of earth and destroyed human beings, as a punishment Heaven takes away from them their posterity forever. (Quoted in Yü 1964: 86)

It is undeniable that, in many respects, traditional Chinese thought placed a higher value on human life than the contemporary official ideology. According to the Judeo-Christian tradition of the West, human life is precious and sacred because the first man was created in the image of God. Although Chinese and Western traditions may agree in principle that human life must be respected and valued, Chinese grounds for this notion are rather different. In Chinese culture, the preciousness and even sacredness of human life is often believed to originate in nature, from which human beings derive and on which human existence depends. It is on these grounds that the value of human life has been argued in numerous medical and philosophical works. As the *Suwen* of *Huandi Neijing* (The Yellow Emperor's Classic of Medicine), the classic work of traditional Chinese medicine, puts it in the twenty-fifth book, "Treasuring Life and Preserving Health": "Of all things in the universe, nothing is more precious than human beings," because human life "is born from the earth, depends on heaven, and begins with the intercourse of heavenly and earthly *qi*" (Nanjing College of Chinese Medicine 1981: 209).

Li Pengfei, a physician in the Yuan Dynasty (1271–1368), states that a human being is the most precious thing between heaven and earth, although few know the reason why. Li holds that human beings are not only an organic part of nature, but also have a remarkable correspondence with it:

> The roundness of the human head corresponds with that of heaven; the square shape of the human foot resembles that of the earth [The most popular cosmology in ancient China held that heaven is round and the earth is square]; human eyes the sun and the moon; the hair, flesh, and bone the mountains, forest, soil, and stones; exhaling the wind; inhaling the dew; joy the virtue star and the colorful (lucky) clouds; anger the powerful thunderbolt; the flow of blood the rivers and seas; the four limbs the four seasons and times [morning, evening, day, and night]; the five *viscera* [the heart, lung, spleen, liver, and kidney] the five elements [wood, fire, earth, metal, and water]; the six bowels [the stomach, small intestine, large intestine, bladder, gallbladder, and "triple burner"] the six

tones of sound. My body exists together and corresponds with heaven and earth. If this is so, isn't human life the most precious thing? (Li, in Wang 1995: 2)

Of course, it is far from clear to what extent this rather abstract notion of the preciousness of human life had a practical bearing on ancient abortion controversies. Nonetheless, these primary materials should form the basis for further studies of the various early Chinese traditions regarding abortion, the fetus, and the value of human life.

One of the most pervasive stereotypes about China is expressed in the phrase "Life is cheap there." It is widely accepted that the value of individual human life is less respected in Chinese culture than in the West, the United States included. As we saw in chapter 1, the apparent neglect of this issue in the Chinese public discourse on abortion has led Western observers, as well as many overseas Chinese in the pilot study, to the same conclusion. However, the prominent German historian of Chinese medicine and culture, Paul Unschuld, has questioned this assumption:

[F]rom studying the history of medicine and medical ethics in China it is obvious Chinese culture for at least two millennia has placed as much emphasis on the value of human individual life as has Western culture. Keeping in mind that in German history we have experienced only half a century ago a period where traditional cultural values were turned upside down, the findings by Dorothy Wertz [on the acceptance of eugenics by contemporary Chinese medical professionals; see Wertz 1998] and the medical media report on human rights violations in contemporary China may lead us to conclude that the phenomena described by these findings and reports have their origin in a difficult contemporary situation; they are definitely not intrinsic elements of Chinese culture. (Unschuld 2001)

Although Unschuld's conclusions need to be tested through further detailed and systematic comparative studies, the material presented both here and in the following chapters challenges the common wisdom about the value placed on individual human life in China and the West and supports Unschuld's general thesis.

CONCLUSION

As the French historian and philosopher Raymond Aron once said, "Man has in fact no past unless he is conscious of having one, for only such consciousness makes dialogue and choice possible. Without it, individuals and societies merely embody a past of which they are ignorant and to which they are passively subject" (Aron 1985: 153–54). History will speak to us powerfully and meaningfully only when we are willing to set aside our modern arrogance and conceit to dialogue with it. In other words, history, however long, is nothing unless we actively engage with it, just as a mirror is useless unless someone looks into it.

According to both the Chinese and Western consensus views, under the influence of Confucianism people in imperial China took a "liberal" attitude to abortion and did not consider it morally problematic, since they believed that human life begins at birth. Although further work is needed on ethical approaches to abortion in imperial China, the evidence presented in this chapter shows that the moral issues at stake had exercised Chinese for centuries and that "conservative" traditions regarding abortion were far from negligible. Traditional Chinese notions of fetal life emphasize that human life definitely begins before birth. Moreover, contrary to the common belief that Confucianism tolerates almost any kind of abortion and even infanticide, closer examination shows that a restrictive position is not only historically well attested but also theoretically consistent with Confucian moral traditions. In addition, as chapter 7 shows, while coerced abortion associated with the national birth control program might draw support from Chinese traditions such as "legalism," it can hardly be justified by appeals to the major Chinese moral-political traditions such as Confucianism.

Assumptions of a uniform Chinese attitude to abortion—a permissive one—are historically groundless: there has never been a single, univocal Chinese perspective on the subject. In this chapter, I have attempted to show the diversity of traditional Chinese viewpoints on abortion by disinterring forgotten controversies. It is crucial to counter the stereotypes of an unchanging, monolithic Chinese culture that are found widely in both China and the West and applied to China both past and present; these include, in the words of the distinguished French historian of Chinese civilization Jacques Gernet, "the repeated accusations of stagnation, periodical return to a previous condition, and permanence of the same social structure and the same political ideology" (Gernet 1996: 21). The great diversity of China and its history can hardly be overstated. Not only are Confucianism and Buddhism historically extremely complex, but medical philosophy and ethics have been just as diverse and complex throughout Chinese history (Unschuld 1985; Nie 2000, forthcoming-a). To ignore this great diversity both among and within each of these many traditions would undermine appreciation of the historical complexity of the abortion controversies and their sociocultural context in imperial China. This point is expanded in chapter 8.

The conclusions to be drawn from this historical survey have far-reaching implications. At the beginning of this chapter, I sketched the historical context—an antitraditionalist and modernist one—in which the current collective amnesia about the controversies of the past has arisen. There are other more specific reasons for this contemporary attitude. First, there is a tendency both in the West and in China to treat the official or dominant perspective on any issue as the representative view of Chinese. This intellectual habit has led both Chinese and Westerners to assume that, since "silence means consent," the official, permissive attitude to abortion represents Chinese views in general. Second, the Chinese authorities have a vested interest in promoting this liberal attitude as sanctioned by Chinese culture and history. Thus the legitimacy of the official standpoint is secured, and anyone daring to challenge it will be taking on the full weight of Chinese tradition.

But as we have seen, the public silence on abortion in contemporary China, together with the official line on the subject (permitting termination at any stage of pregnancy except in sex-selective abortion), does not necessarily accord with historical Chinese values and practices. The official standpoints discussed in the previous chapter constitute a historical and cultural aberration; they are not a product of Chinese traditions but a consequence of China's political environment over the past several decades. The official view, in which the fetus carries little moral weight in face of the demands of the national population program and the significant social good it is claimed to embody, latches on to the historical permissive tradition but stands in contrast to the opposing tradition whereby abortion is to be opposed because the fetus is *ren* (a person, a human being, a human life) and abortion involves *sharen* (killing a person, destroying a human life, murdering) and is thus morally reprehensible. Today, traditional Chinese culture is maintained more strongly in Taiwan, or even Hong Kong, than in mainland China. A recent anthropological study has shown that in Taiwan, as a result of Japanese influence as well as traditional Chinese ideas, there has been a resurgence of belief in fetal ghosts and demons, and aborted fetuses are often "memorialized" in Buddhist temples as a way of appeasing them (Moskowitz 2001). Although clearly at odds with official attitudes in contemporary China, such beliefs and practices fit comfortably with the traditional Chinese understandings of fetal life discussed in this chapter.

Moreover, these forgotten controversies exhumed from China's past suggest that the introduction of strict prohibitive laws on abortion in the late Qing Dynasty and the Republican and even early People's Republic periods should not be interpreted as the product of Western influence alone, but as having roots in the conservative Chinese traditions. Despite the radical antitraditionalism that has marked China throughout most of the twentieth century, the profound influence of Confucianism on many aspects of moral and sociocultural life in China is still widely recognized, especially in the countryside (see Madsen 1984).

Karl Marx, father of international communism and "the great teacher of Chinese revolution," to quote an official Chinese title bestowed on him, stated: "the tradition of all the dead generations weighs like a nightmare on the brain of the living" (Marx, in Tucker 1978: 595). The diverse attitudes to abortion of contemporary Chinese to be presented in the following chapters also have their historical roots, even if people are largely unaware of them. Humans are at the same time sociopolitical animals powerfully shaped by inherited historical circumstances and the makers of their own histories. The next three chapters illustrate this fundamental dialectic of human existence by showing the extent to which traditional Chinese beliefs weigh on the "brain of the living" as not only nightmare but also inspiration. They show how Chinese today are at the same time challenging the current political orthodoxy and developing the weighty legacy of their collective past.

4

Tidings from the Populace: Consensus and Contention in the Survey Results

> Blowing on the ten thousand things in a different way, so that each can be itself—all take what they want for themselves, but who does the sounding?
>
> —Zhuang Zi (Chuang Tzu), ancient Daoist philosopher

To discover the attitudes of a cross-section of people in today's China toward abortion and related issues, I conducted a survey during August and September 1997. The questionnaire was designed to obtain basic information on opinions on a number of issues, including the circumstances in which abortion is justifiable, the choice between abortion and continued pregnancy, the fetus as a human life and the question of when a human life begins, whether abortion is tantamount to murder, whether and in what circumstances abortion is morally problematic, what abortion means for women who have had it, the national population policy, "healthy birth" (eugenics), the optimal number of children, and infanticide. A total of 601 people participated, with 39% males and 61% females. Most (88%) were between the ages of twenty and fifty, with 46% in the twenty to thirty age group. Almost all of them (97%) were Han Chinese, the ethnic majority. Although most participants (80%) indicated no religious affiliation, the sample included twenty-seven Buddhists (5%), twenty-seven Catholics (5%), and fifty-two Protestants (9%). The survey respondents included twelve sample groups comprising three southern villages, a southern city, a northern city, Catholics, Protestants, university students, students of biomedicine, students of traditional Chinese medicine, and scholars of the medical humanities and medical ethics. Further information on this survey—the questionnaire and sample groups—is available in the appendix.

In the following presentation, the overall percentage is *not* the average of the percentages of different samples, but the percentage of *all respondents* who answered the particular item. In evaluating and discussing survey results, "an overwhelming or very large majority" means that 90% or more respondents shared that opinion or answer; "a large majority" refers to 67–89%; "a majority" means 51–61%; and "a significant proportion" (but not a majority) means 25–50%. The data were further analyzed by dividing the subjects using other criteria: residence (urban and rural), gender, membership of the Communist Party, and membership in the medical profession. In comparing and contrasting the twelve sample groups and interpreting the four variables, a difference of 15% or more between two groups was considered significantly meaningful.

INCIDENCE, SOCIAL VISIBILITY, AND ACCEPTANCE

Contemporary China has a very high abortion rate. Abortion at every stage of pregnancy has been carried out for reasons ranging from personal convenience and sex preference to the requirements of the national population policy. According to a 1992 United Nations publication, the rates of abortion per 1,000 women aged fifteen to forty-four in China in three selected years were 23.1 (1971), 44.8 (1980), and 38.8 (1987) (UN 1992, vol. 1: 86). In absolute terms, annual abortions exceeded ten million every year except one during the 1980s (Tien 1991: 178). A recent comprehensive study of birth control in China (Scharping 2003: 121) shows the pattern of abortion rates per 100 live births over four decades: 1.4 (1963), 13.3 (1971), 55.5 (1980), 49.6 (1985), 56.4 (1990), 36.2 (1995), 42.7 (1996), 32.3 (1997), 38.7 (1998), 35.4 (1999). The rates peaked in the 1980s and subsequently declined, although they still sustained high levels.

Nevertheless, the available data do not indicate that the Chinese abortion rate is excessively high compared with other countries: figures for countries such as Japan, Korea, and Russia are equally high or even higher than those in China. Moreover, abortion rates in Europe and the United States are not significantly lower than those in China. Scharping has pointed out that "a brief glance at the high abortion rates prevailing in other parts of the world will help to dispel some of the revulsion that reports on abortion in China provoke" (Scharping 2003: 123).

In my survey, female informants were asked whether and how many times they had had a termination. Of the 348 women who answered this question, 59% replied "Never," 25% replied "Once," 10% replied "Twice," and 6% replied "More than twice." This means that 41% of the women in the survey who responded to this question reported having had at least one abortion.

Of 166 women aged thirty and above, nearly two-thirds (61%) reported at least one abortion (of this number, 37% had had one abortion, and 24% two or more). The incidence of abortion among women in the survey increased with age and reached its peak in the forty to fifty age group. No woman below twenty (none in this group had married) reported an abortion. In the age groups twenty to thirty, thirty to forty, and forty to fifty, the numbers of respondents who had had one or more terminations were, respectively, 25%, 57%, and 67%.

My survey also clearly shows that abortion is socially quite visible in China. Sixty-three percent knew at least one close friend, family member, or relative who had had at least one abortion, and 37% of these knew of two or more such cases. In other words, only 37% of informants did not know of any friend, family member, or relative who had had a termination. Fifty percent of the respondents believed that "Most women have at least one abortion in their lives." This may suggest that information about personal experience with abortion is widely available and that there is little or no stigma about discussing abortion.

Abortion is not only a matter for women—men are often involved in decisions about abortion as well. Each male respondent in the questionnaire was asked whether and how many times he had requested his wife or girlfriend to terminate her pregnancy. Of the 198 men who responded to this question, 43 (22%) had made at least one such request, and the figure rose to 38% among men aged thirty to sixty (thirty-three of the eighty-eight questioned) and reached a peak (55%) in the forty to fifty age bracket.

To discern the degree of social acceptance of abortion among Chinese people, the interviewees were asked how they thought other Chinese, including family members and friends, might respond to women who have had abortions. Most respondents reported a lack of concern among their fellow Chinese with the morality of abortion per se. According to the informants, if a married woman voluntarily decides to abort a fetus and if her husband is the father, her situation poses no moral or social issue worthy of others' inquiry or even comment. Many informants indicated that premarital sexual activity is still not morally and socially acceptable in China, but for most this constituted no moral obstacle to abortion—indeed, conception out of wedlock was all the more reason for an abortion. One man said: "People don't care at all, or rarely care, if the woman is married. If the woman is not married, people may say something. People consider premarital sex unacceptable." Another man stated: "People have different views. . . . It all depends on how she gets pregnant." Yet another male informant articulated: "Everything depends on the reason [for the pregnancy and abortion]. If it's due to the family planning policy, no one comments. You're not allowed to comment. People may feel sorry for her. In the case of rape or a fetus with a genetic disease, people support her having an abortion. If she gets pregnant before marriage, it's OK and even necessary to have an abortion. But people usually don't think that it's OK to have sex before marriage." A fourth male informant responded: "If she's married, people have no comment, no criticism. But abortion damages a woman's physical health. If the woman is not married, people will talk. This will be a matter of whether her moral character is good or bad. China is a traditional society with traditional ideas, especially about sex. People will talk about the woman. Who got her pregnant? Is she a prostitute? Does she have sex to make money? Or did she have sex with an official to achieve some personal goal?"

Many informants suggested that others had no right to comment on a woman's actions, because the abortion was her personal affair. One woman said: "It's a rather common occurrence, [like eating] an ordinary kind of food. There's nothing worth talking about." Another woman commented: "It's got nothing to do with other people. No one would bother to comment on it." A third female informant also used the food comparison: "It's a very natural thing, like eating and drinking. It's not against the law. And it's quite safe to have an abortion."

In the pilot study, most of the overseas Chinese students and scholars questioned insisted that, while a woman has the right to abortion if she wants, she should avoid it if she can. They believed that abortion, especially if repeated, would damage the woman's health and even her reproductive capacity. For them, abortion was bad for the woman's health, but their concern did not extend to the fetus. After stating that a woman should have a termination in certain situations such as rape and compliance with the population policy, a male informant emphasized that abortion is likely to damage a woman's physical health. "Abortion must be permissible for women. But it's not good for the woman's health. It may cause sterility and other damage to the woman's body. Because of this, one should avoid abortion if there's no compelling reason to have one."

One male informant mentioned that, because of a preference for male children among Chinese, the gender of the aborted fetus may influence how others feel about the termination: "If the woman doesn't want the baby, people understand. But if she has to have an abortion because of the family planning policy, and especially if the aborted fetus is a male, family members may feel regret."

One woman made a comparison between China and America in the case of abortion involving an unmarried woman: "The family members support her; the mother usually accompanies the woman to the hospital. If she's unmarried, other people find it [terminating the pregnancy] understandable. But no one [in China] will say to her as some Americans do: 'Have the baby—we'll help you raise the child.'"

POSSIBLE REASONS FOR ABORTION

What are the reasons that Chinese women seek abortions? In the best review of abortion practice in China to appear so far, Susan Rigdon (1996: 549–52) lists the following: social taboos such as pregnancy caused by "demons," limiting family size and spacing children, preference for sons, compliance with the family planning policy, eugenic control, and contraceptive failure. In the pilot study, eighteen overseas students and scholars (eleven male and seven female) who had either just arrived in the United Sates or had left China several years before were asked to list as many circumstances as possible under which a Chinese woman might have an abortion.[1] A tabulation of their responses (with frequencies added, from highest to lowest) yields the following data:

- the requirements of the national family planning policy (13),
- as well as those of local policies and agencies (3);
- premarital pregnancy (13);
- inadequate economic and material circumstances (8);
- interference with the woman's education or career (7);
- contraceptive failure (6);
- fetal health issues, including some genetic diseases (6);
- instability of the marriage (6);
- sex preference, mainly preference for a son (6),
- preference for a daughter (1);
- extramarital pregnancy (5);
- the mother's health is not good enough to bear a child (4);
- the woman doesn't want the child (3);
- the couple lack sufficient mental preparation (2);
- the mother is too old (2);
- the couple wants to be free of caring for children (2);
- the pregnancy is the result of rape (2);
- the woman is a prostitute (2);
- the mother is advised by medical professionals to abort because the baby is defective (1);
- the couple does not want a child (1);
- the couple has several children already and does not want more (1);
- the husband and the wife disagree on whether to have children (1);
- the woman does not like children (1);
- the decision to have a child is the woman's alone (1);
- it is very easy to have an abortion (1);
- the pregnant woman has taken medication for an illness such as the flu or a cold, which may affect the development of the fetus (1).

This list indicates that a Chinese woman may have an abortion for a great variety of reasons that range from social policy, to the health of the fetus and mother, to personal career and life goals. It bears many similarities to the reasons given for seeking termination by Chinese women who had had abortions (see chapter 5).

Given the prominence of China's national population control program, it is not surprising that the social policy of birth control was mentioned most frequently by informants as the reason for undergoing abortion. More than two-thirds of the informants (thirteen out of eighteen) in the pilot study spoke of this, stating that "the family planning program doesn't permit" or "the policy doesn't allow" a couple more than one child (or in some cases two children). Two informants explicitly stated that many cases of abortion resulted from this constraint. One said: "The restriction of the policy is the most important condition. [If people] already have one child, [they] can't have more. The proportion of this kind of abortion is quite large compared to terminations undergone for other reasons."

On the question of whether this kind of termination was undertaken voluntarily or involuntarily, the overseas Chinese informants expressed a range of views. Most of those who mentioned social policy believed that "because people want more than one child, the government forces them to have abortions." This was seen as especially the case for rural people. One informant asserted: "People have no choice [if they already have a child]; but most women want the babies." Another informant stated:

> The family planning program forces people to have abortions. Some are voluntary, but most people have to [have an abortion]. Rural people hope to have more children. Most people in cities accept the family planning policy. Although some want to have more children, they may lose their job if they actually do so.

A third interviewee said:

> After contraceptive failure, state employees will go and have abortions because of the family planning policy. In the countryside, people want to have more children. But the policy requires them to have abortions. They especially want to have sons. If their attempts to have sons are discovered, they are forced into having terminations.

Most informants in the pilot study talked about the central government as the source of coercion. Some mentioned that local agencies and officials, acting in response to the national policy, played a significant role in forcing people to have abortions. According to one informant, "The 'work unit' has regulations about when to have a child." He pointed out that, in Shenzhen, the newly developed southern coastal city where he worked for several years before coming to study and live in the United States, some work units did not permit a female employee to have a child during her first year of work. If she did, she would lose her job. Such regulations did not necessarily have a mandate in national policy.

A minority of informants claimed that some women choose terminations voluntarily because they accept the national policy. One informant observed: "People know the national policy. They go and have abortions without being forced by the government because they accept the population policy." Another thought that although people might seek an abortion if they already have one child, this was not always done voluntarily: "In the positive sense, people have abortions in order to comply with the family planning policy. In the negative sense, the state's all-encompassing policy gives local officials no choice" but to enforce the policy. This last comment suggests that the very concept of "voluntary" is complex and reflects the tension between support for the national policy and personal preference.

Pregnancy resulting from premarital sex was the other situation most frequently mentioned by informants in the pilot study. Equal to the number of responses citing social policy, more than two-thirds (thirteen out of eighteen) of subjects believed that a woman would have an abortion if she became pregnant before marriage. According to them, the mother would encounter great "social pressure" since "traditional Chinese values don't sanction the pregnancy of an unmarried mother." Since premarital sex is widely considered shameful or immoral, a woman would probably "lose face" if her pregnancy became public knowledge. One female informant said:

> [Women] fear "losing face." Chinese culture is different [from the West on the issue of premarital sex]. Some of them are college or university students. Of course, they never reveal their identities. But we [doctors and nurses] can often figure out who they are. When I was working at a hospital, I lived in a student dormitory [as a single person]. I heard students gossiping about such-and-such students who got an abortion.

Another female informant commented on premarital pregnancies in the workplace:

> Because of the political atmosphere, people at the "work unit" will talk or gossip about the pregnancy. Most of them are willing to go and have an abortion. As an obstetrician and gynecologist, I know that this kind of abortion represents a high proportion.

But one female informant who had had a termination before her marriage disagreed that unmarried mothers were keen to have abortions. For her, "Most of these girls want their babies, but they have to have a termination because of social pressure. Society considers it immoral—'a bad way of living'— for a girl to get pregnant before marriage. If she doesn't marry her boyfriend, what will she do with the child when she gives birth?" For this female Ph.D. student, social and cultural pressure, rather than personal preference, forced unmarried women to have abortions.

Eight of the eighteen informants in the pilot study mentioned financial circumstances, including insufficient income to raise the child and lack of adequate "living quarters" (an apartment or house), as reasons for termination. Several pointed out that rural people especially often lack the financial resources to raise a child, even though they want many children. But one informant denied that finance was usually decisive for either rural or urban people when it came to starting a family.

Seven informants mentioned that a woman might have an abortion because an unplanned pregnancy would interfere with her career or education. A female who practiced obstetrics and gynecology in China described one such case: "I once performed an abortion on a *getihu* (freelance business agent). She was awfully busy selling clothes. In order to make money, she worked very hard. It was a very exhausting job. She had to have an abortion." Another female informant told of a colleague who had a termination so that she could keep "climbing the ladder" following her promotion as a university program director. One reason given for termination in this category was *xiahai* (literally, going to the sea). Originating in the mid-1980s, this expression refers to the attempt by people with academic or administrative careers, which were once very prestigious, to seek jobs in the previously despised business and commercial sectors, which had become potential sources not only of wealth but also of power and influence. Other reasons include going abroad for education and work pressures on people such as resident physicians.

The health of the fetus and genetic diseases of the embryo were listed by six out of eighteen of the overseas Chinese as possible reasons for a woman to terminate her pregnancy. Two or three explicitly pointed to situations where eugenics was a necessity. One informant stated: "Eugenics is necessary. One should have an abortion if the fetus has a genetic disease such as no-brain syndrome [anencephaly], just as pregnancy resulting from rape must be terminated."

A female informant who had studied and worked in the United States for four or five years was distressed at encountering a number of Americans—including a neighbor—who gave birth to seriously disabled children. Viewing this as a problem for both society and the family, she concluded: "About eugenics, China has done better than the U.S. For example, the congenital idiot will create difficulties for the family and will also be a burden to the country." Observing these children with serious physical and mental handicaps, she also felt that it was equally unfair to the child, who would suffer distress and be unable to live a normal and satisfying life.

The informants in the pilot study, like those in the survey, thought that medical doctors should play an active role in any decision to abort a fetus by diagnosing fetal defects. One informant said: "When something abnormal is found, the doctor usually persuades the woman to have an abortion. People usually accept the physician's opinion." A female biomedical scientist pointed out that, in China, genetic diseases of the fetus were usually discovered by modern technologies such as sonograms or amniocentesis. She mentioned specific examples of fetal defects such as Down's syndrome, Edward's syndrome, and anencephaly.

An unstable marriage was mentioned by six informants. For them, if the marriage was in trouble or on the verge of breaking up, a child could be a burden if the couple decided on divorce. In one male informant's words: "The couple has *maodun* ["spear and shield," or contradictions]. They fight—not about having a child, but other *maodun*. So the family lacks harmony—the emotional balance between husband and wife is not good. In this case, it's better to have an abortion."

Six overseas Chinese mentioned sex preference, especially preference for a son, as a condition under which a Chinese woman might have an abortion. In their view, many couples want a son and will abort a female fetus as soon as they know its sex. The majority believed that selective abortion for a son happens both in the cities and in the countryside, but mainly in rural and "backward" (*luohou*) areas. (Rather than merely preferring sons, people in rural areas *need* a son to take care of them in their old age, given the absence of any retirement or social security benefits in rural China and a family structure in which responsibility for parents usually rests exclusively with sons.) A male informant reported:

> I recently read a report that every couple in a particular village had a son. The village leader had bought an ultrasound machine; as a result, it was much easier for him to carry out the family planning policy. And people weren't complaining. Besides, the local authorities can make some money by using the machine for gender diagnosis.

One woman emphasized that intentionally aborting a female fetus rarely occurs in big cities. She commented that in cities girls are even preferred, because urban daughters are likely to take better care of elderly parents than are sons. But another informant pointed out that this was not really the case, arguing that, if other siblings in the extended family all have girls, strong family pressure is usually brought on the youngest couple to bear a son in order to continue the family bloodline.

Two men emphasized the importance of taking parenting seriously—not "just bringing a child into the world." They implied that a termination should be considered if the couple could not take adequate care of the child. One said: "A child is a burden because you have to take care of it. It's a big responsibility. So parents must think carefully about whether they're capable of raising a child. It's wrong to bring a child into the world and then fail to give it good care." For the other man, having an abortion could mean "taking social responsibility," whereas going ahead with the birth may be "irresponsible to society." He stressed that merely giving birth to children was insufficient in itself, and that people must have "the energy and ability to raise and educate children well."

TO CONTINUE OR NOT TO CONTINUE THE PREGNANCY

Based on the information gathered in the pilot study, the second part of the questionnaire (following the listing of demographic information) contained a list of thirty-six specific situations that might constitute grounds for termination. Respondents were asked to state whether a mother should continue her pregnancy or have an abortion under each of the conditions listed. Overall, respondents expressed a preference for termination in almost half (sixteen) of the thirty-six cases. An overwhelming majority (over 90%) agreed that abortion was acceptable and even necessary in the following eight situations:

- a genetic disease is diagnosed in the fetus (96%)
- the pregnancy results from incest (95%)
- a doctor concludes that the fetus is deformed or that its future physical/ mental development will be at risk (94%)
- the mother suffers from mental illness (93%)
- the mother is mentally retarded (91%)
- the pregnancy results from rape (91%)
- the mother is a prostitute (90%)
- the mother is an unmarried college or university student (90%)

A large majority (66%–90% overall) considered termination justified and even necessary in eight further situations:

- the couple already has one child and does not want more children (88%)
- the mother is an alcoholic (88%)
- the pregnancy resulted from an extramarital affair (86%)
- the mother is a heavy smoker (85%)
- the mother may possibly give birth to a defective baby (82%)
- the couple is seeking a divorce (76%)
- the mother wants to terminate her pregnancy (73%)
- the mother has taken medication that is said to harm fetal development (73%)

A significant majority (51%–66% overall) favored terminating pregnancy in the following six cases:

- the pregnancy will jeopardize the mother's opportunities for promotion or study abroad (64%)
- the pregnancy resulted from contraceptive failure (62%)
- the pregnancy will hinder the woman's career and work prospects (61%)
- the mother would experience problems and pressure at work (60%)
- neither partner wants a child (60%)
- the couple lacks sufficient income to raise a child (59%)

A significant proportion of informants favored termination under the following circumstances:

- the couple has an unhappy relationship (42%)
- the young couple is keen to "enjoy life" and wishes to postpone childbearing (40%)
- the pregnancy is ex-nuptial, although legally the mother and father are both of marriageable age (39%)
- the husband finds the pregnancy inconvenient and hopes that his wife will have an abortion (36%)
- the mother suffers from severe morning sickness (34%)
- continuing the pregnancy will impair the mother's looks (29%)
- the mother's waist or abdomen were injured (27%)

In the remaining seven scenarios, only a small proportion (less than 25%) of informants favored termination as an option:

- a close friend persuades the mother to postpone childbearing (24%)
- the mother sustains an injury to her limbs (23%)
- the mother has a very poor relationship with her mother-in-law (16%)
- the mother learns that the fetus is male, but the couple wants a girl (14%)
- the mother learns that the fetus is female, but the couple wants a boy (12%)
- the mother dreams that the fetus is abnormal (8%)
- a fortune-teller claims that the fetus is an "abnormal or monster fetus" (*guaitai*), although a doctor finds it perfectly normal (3%)

In the third part of the questionnaire, respondents were confronted with an old dilemma—whether to save the mother or the baby in a difficult birth. The response was overwhelming: overall, 93% privileged the mother's life over that of her unborn child. Although the more general question of whether termination is justified when pregnancy threatens the mother's life or health was inadvertently omitted from the questionnaire, this response strongly suggests that survey subjects would favor the mother in this more general situation, too.

To summarize. On the one hand, the findings reveal a high level of consensus across the sample on the legitimacy of abortion in a wide range of circumstances. On the other hand, there are significant group differences. Some of the sample groups were more inclined to choose abortion than others. The following breakdown shows the number of scenarios (out of thirty-six) in which more than 50% of respondents in a given sample group favored termination: Catholics (1), Protestants (16), Chinese medicine students (19), medical humanities scholars (20), university students (21), Buddhists (21), biomedical students (22), city (South) (22), city (North) (23), Village B (26), Village A (26), overall (22). The higher the number of the sample in this breakdown, the more often abortion was chosen. Clearly, the Catholic group strongly opposed abortion—much more so than the Protestants, who expressed the second lowest level of preference for terminations. The three village samples were slightly more permissive than the urban respondents. The following sections will further illustrate both the consensus and diversity of Chinese views of abortion and related issues.

WHEN A HUMAN LIFE BEGINS

Different societies use various criteria to determine the point at which human life begins. In ancient Greece and Rome as well as in Judeo-Christian tradition, "ensoulment"—the moment when the soul is infused into the body of the fetus—was regarded as critical. In the English common law tradition, "quickening"—the first recognizable movement of the fetus *in utero*—was at one time given great weight in deciding whether or not abortion was a crime. In the U.S. Supreme Court decision of *Roe v. Wade* (1973), viability was regarded as the "compelling" criterion with respect to the state's legitimate interest in protecting potential life. The ruling established that before viability (defined as twenty-four weeks of pregnancy) is attained, the mother's right to private choice overrides the fetus's right to life (Shapiro 1995: 46–70). As I indicate in chapter 2, contemporary Chinese law defines the starting point of human life as birth; so, although infanticide is proscribed, termination—with the exception of selective abortion for sex—is permitted at any stage of pregnancy.

It is often assumed that most Chinese accept the official position and consider abortion morally acceptable on the grounds that human life begins at birth. However, the survey results proved this assumption wrong. In fact, most informants believed that life begins at some point before birth and thus regarded the fetus as a human life. Overall, nearly half (48%) agreed that human life begins at conception; only slightly more than one-quarter (28%) of respondents considered that life begins at birth. A sizeable majority (72%, nearly three-quarters) of informants thought that life begins sometime before birth—whether at conception or when the mother feels the first movement of the fetus ("quickening"), or when the fetus is able to survive outside the mother's womb ("viability"). Table 4.1 lists the responses of different sample groups to the question about the starting point of human life.

Conception and birth were regarded as more significant criteria for judging when life begins than either "quickening" or "viability," each of which were favored by fewer than 20% of any group. This may reflect the fact that, historically, these two indicators were rarely treated as significant markers of fetal development. A large majority (76%) of responses settled on one of the two extremities of pregnancy—*either* conception *or* birth—with significantly more informants overall choosing conception (48%) over birth (28%). The twelve groups had diverse views. A large majority of Catholics believed that human life starts at conception, with much smaller numbers choosing viability and birth. And, while more than half of the Protestant, Buddhist, Chinese medical students, and respondents in northern city samples opted for conception, medical humanities scholars and Village B residents were more inclined to see birth as the starting point. Most informants believed that a human life starts sometime before birth, rather than at birth itself. In only two sample groups—Village B and medical humanities scholars—did fewer than half the subjects hold that human life begins sometime before birth.

Questions about the status of the fetus in the third part of the questionnaire provoked responses that support the above findings. Confronted with the statement "A fetus is a life," overall 84% of respondents agreed. Most groups strongly supported the proposition: Catholics (96%), Village B (96%), Protestants (95%), Buddhists (92%), Chinese medical students (89%), city

Table 4.1.   Responses to the Question, "When Does a Human Life Begin?" (number of respondents in parenthesis)

Sample Groups	Conception	"Quickening"	"Viability"	Birth
Catholics (23)	87% (20)	9% (2)	—	4% (1)
Buddhists (26)	62% (16)	19% (5)	8% (2)	12% (3)
Chinese Medical Students (57)	65% (37)	12% (7)	4% (2)	19% (11)
Protestants (39)	64% (25)	15% (6)	—	21% (8)
City (South) (105)	47% (49)	18% (19)	14%(15)	21% (22)
University Students (43)	42% (18)	19% (8)	16% (7)	23% (10)
City (North) (45)	53% (24)	18% (8)	4% (2)	24% (11)
Biomedical Students (26)	42% (11)	12% (3)	19% (5)	27% (7)
Village C (84)	36% (30)	18% (15)	10% (8)	37% (31)
Village A (50)	40% (20)	18% (9)	—	42% (21)
Village B (43)	37% (16)	12% (5)	—	51% (22)
Med. Humanities Scholar (17)	19% (3)	6% (1)	12% (2)	64% (11)
Overall (558)	48% (269)	16% (88)	8% (43)	28% (158)

Note: The order of the samples is arranged by the lowest to highest percentage which agrees that a human life begins at birth.

(South) (86%), university students (83%), Village A (81%), city (North) (78%), Village C (78%), medical humanities scholars (74%), and biomedical students (71%). But when asked to comment on the proposition that "The fetus does not become a human being until it has left the mother's womb," overall support for the fetus as a human being fell to 46%, less than half. The figures for those *disagreeing* with the statement, that is, agreeing that the fetus is a human being, were: overall (46%), Catholics (85%), Protestants (62%), Chinese medical students (59%), Buddhists (54%), university students (50%), medical humanities scholars (47%), Village C (42%), city (South) (41%), biomedical students (41%), city (North) (32%), Village A (31%), and Village B (31%). The large discrepancy in the responses to these two questions probably reflects the ambiguity and uncertainty of Chinese views on the status of the fetus. The strong agreement that the fetus constitutes a life versus the divided opinions on its precise status at birth may reflect Chinese beliefs about the development of a "life" into a "human being."

The diversity of opinions on this issue was reinforced by the findings of the pilot study, where interviewees were likewise asked about the inception of human life. The question seemed to confuse several informants—although not those who were converts to Christianity. A few informants had difficulty understanding what the question meant. Nevertheless, the answers given show a striking multiplicity of viewpoints. Responses to the question "When does a human life start?" in the pilot study were marked by four characteristics. First, most participants acknowledged the difficulty of the question and several began their answer with the phrase: "I don't know." One male informant simply stated: "I don't know. Any cell is a life." Second, as in the main survey, understandings of when human life begins varied. Third, and most important, most informants did not believe that abortion involves killing a human being, regardless of their views about the fetus. Fourth, conversion to Christianity (after having no particular religious commitment) signaled a radical change in attitudes toward the fetus and thus toward abortion.

Two informants in the pilot study admitted the difficulty of determining when human life begins. One man stated: "I've never thought about this. There may be different possibilities. From a scientific perspective . . . life should have various definitions. I really can't say clearly." A woman, formerly an obstetrics and gynecology doctor in China, said: "It's really very hard to say. Does life begin at the fortieth day or so of pregnancy? The fetus is starting to breathe in the fourth month. At seven months [28 weeks], the fetus can live outside the mother's womb."

One female informant regarded the status of the fetus as merely a medical question that called for no further discussion. She said: "I don't know. It's not necessary to discuss whether the fetus is a human being or not. It's up to medicine to make the decision. Abortion and murder are two totally different things."

Despite these indecisive responses, most informants had their own ideas about the inception of life, although no obvious consensus was forthcoming. Some considered birth as the starting point. One woman said: "The human being is a person from the moment of birth. The fetus doesn't have the same significance as a human being." Some saw biological viability as the starting point of life; as one woman stated: "Viability should be the most important factor. In the first trimester, the fetus isn't a human being."

But even those with an opinion on the issue were far from sure about the exact moment at which life begins. One male informant decided first for birth and then for viability: "The human being starts at birth. The fetus is not a human. . . . If the fetus can live outside the mother's womb, it can be seen as a human being." Similar uncertainty was expressed by a woman who, as an obstetrics and gynecology doctor, performed abortions in China and was now a biomedical researcher:

> It isn't clear when the fetus becomes a human being. This is not just a medical but also an ethical and social question. Medicine has no clear-cut answer. Personally, I believe that the standard should be when the fetus starts to "think." So the electrical pulse from the fetus's brain could be used as a measurement to decide.

In summary, a large majority of informants believed that the fetus was a human life and that human life starts, if not at conception, then at some time before birth. There was a strong consensus among the various sample groups, with only the medical humanities scholars and one of the village groups showing majorities (albeit small ones) in favor of birth. Their views differ markedly from the official discourse, which defines birth as the legal starting point of human life. Of course, from the historical point of view, this equation of the fetus with human life is not surprising, since knowledge of fetal life has long been a part of Chinese culture, as we saw in chapter 3. However, informants were probably unaware of both this historical connection and their disagreement with the official view.

IS ABORTION EQUIVALENT TO KILLING A HUMAN BEING?

Although most respondents considered that human life begins before birth, and regarded the fetus as a human life, only about one-third regarded abortion as taking a life or "killing." Again, the sample groups differed on the question, as table 4.2 shows. Here, the three religious groups—Catholics, Buddhists, and Protestants—stood out, with strong support for the propositions that abortion is equivalent to taking a life, killing an infant, and killing a human being. Approximately one-tenth to one-third of respondents in other groups regarded abortion as tantamount to manslaughter.

Table 4.2.   Percentages of Respondents Who Agreed That Abortion Was Equivalent to Taking a Life, Killing an Infant, or Killing a Human Being

Equivalent to . . .	Taking a Life	Killing an Infant	Killing a Human Being
Catholic	92	96	88
Buddhist	54	58	59
Protestant	64	60	57
Chinese Med. Student	38	23	30
Village B	37	36	25
Village C	36	36	25
University Student	32	26	24
Village A	30	31	23
City (South)	21	19	19
City (North)	23	14	18
Med. Humanities Scholar	37	11	11
Biomedical Student	22	19	8
Overall	36	31	27

Note: The order of the samples is arranged by the highest to lowest percentage who agreed that abortion was equivalent to killing a human being.

As many Western visitors and scholars have observed, abortion appears not to be morally problematic in China as it is in the West (see chapter 1). In the survey, overall a large majority (71%) of informants agreed with the statement that "Abortion in itself has nothing to do with ethics or morality." Those *disagreeing* with the statement broke down as follows: Catholics (77%), Buddhists (65%), Protestants (56%), medical humanities scholars (42%), Chinese medical students (38%), university students (30%), Village B (29%), Village C (22%), biomedical students (22%), Village A (21%), city (South) (16%), and city (North) (11%). Once again, in contrast with the other sample groups, most of those in the three religious groups considered abortion an ethical issue. Conversely, a large majority of the two urban and three rural samples, and the biomedical students, disagreed that abortion per se had any ethical dimension.

For the informants, the *circumstances* of pregnancy, rather than abortion per se, were the focus of ethical concern. Comments were not solicited in the questionnaire in order to preserve anonymity. Yet five informants provided unsolicited comments on this question; all considered that the status of abortion as a moral issue depended on such contingent factors as how the mother became pregnant.

A woman's marital status was regarded as a crucial factor in assessing the morality of abortion. Only a tiny minority (8%) agreed with the statement that "It is shameful (*choushi*) for a married woman to have an abortion." In Chinese, the phrase *choushi* is often applied to socially unacceptable or immoral behavior. The respondents who agreed with the proposition ran as follows: Catholics (31%), Village C (21%), Village B (15%), Buddhists

(15%), Village A (14%), Protestants (7%), biomedical students (4%), Chinese medical students (2%), university students (2%), city (South) (1%), city (North) (0%), and medical humanities scholars (0%). Significantly, two-thirds of the Catholics saw no shame involved in a married woman having an abortion.

For a single woman to terminate pregnancy is quite a different matter, and nearly half (46%) of the respondents agreed that "It is shameful for an unmarried woman to have an abortion." The sample groups responded as follows: Protestants (70%), Catholics (65%), Village A (60%), city (South) (51%), Village B (48%), city (North) (44%), biomedical students (37%), Chinese medical students (36%), Buddhists (35%), Village C (34%), university students (33%), and medical humanities scholars (26%). The proposition was most strongly supported by the two Christian groups, followed by the Village A and southern city samples. However, majorities in the other groups rejected this view, with medical humanities scholars and university students showing strong disagreement. Here it should be noted that, for those who agreed with the statement, it was not abortion per se but premarital intercourse and pregnancy that was seen as morally unacceptable, since only a tiny minority (8%) also supported the proposition that "It is shameful for a married woman to have an abortion." The fact that the Protestants surpassed even the Catholics in support for the proposition may reinforce the view that this question is more about premarital sex than abortion as such. As we have seen, a very large majority (90%) of respondents thought that an unmarried college student should have an abortion if she became pregnant.

In summary, the responses presented here and in the previous two sections suggest that a significant proportion of Chinese (about one-third) hold, in contradiction of the official discourse, that abortion constitutes the taking of a human life and thus becomes an ethical problem. Once again, there is ample historical precedent for this attitude, even though the informants were probably unaware of it. Moreover, these responses also indicated the moral uncertainty and ambivalence of Chinese toward fetal life and abortion. For around one-third of respondents—and presumably of the wider population—even though the fetus is seen as a human life, abortion is not necessarily equivalent to killing. In other words, a significant proportion of Chinese may believe that abortion is morally acceptable if there exists a legitimate reason, such as genetic disease, premarital (especially if the woman is young) or extramarital pregnancy, or rape.

In the survey, a majority considered a legitimate reason to be important for having an abortion. This was indicated in responses to the statement "A woman should be able to have an abortion for any reason." Given the wide sociopolitical acceptance of abortion in China, it was perhaps surprising that overall only 35% of informants agreed with the statement. Support ran as follows: Village A (56%), Village C (51%), city (South) (44%), medical humanities scholars (42%), city (North) (36%), Protestants (36%), Village B (35%), Buddhists (35%), biomedical students (22%), university students (15%), Chinese medical students (11%), and Catholics (8%). These figures demonstrate a low level of support for terminating pregnancy without a valid reason.

A TRAUMATIC EXPERIENCE

As we saw in chapter 1, the participants in the pilot study believed that Chinese would not normally bother to comment on a woman who has had an abortion, especially if she is married and if the pregnancy resulted from marital relations. Yet most respondents in the survey believed that abortion was a traumatic and painful (*kuse*) experience—involving emotional or psychological distress as well as physical pain—for the woman involved, irrespective of her marital status.

Opinions varied about the extent of the harm suffered. On the one hand, there was no consensus about whether termination could damage the mother's physical and reproductive health. Almost three-fifths (58%) agreed with the statement that "It is impossible for an abortion to impair a woman's health and reproductive capacity." *Disagreement* with the proposition was as follows: Chinese medical students (67%), university students (57%), Buddhists (46%), Village B (45%), biomedical students (44%), medical humanities scholars (42%), Catholics (40%), Village C (38%), city (North) (38%), Protestants (37%), Village A (33%), and city (South) (28%). While the traditional medical students believed strongly that there were potential risks to the woman's health, the southern city and Village A samples downplayed such risks. The other groups lacked strong agreement on the issue.

There was substantial agreement, on the other hand, about the risk of psychological harm; overall, 62% agreed with the statement that "After abortion, a woman always has emotional and psychological difficulties." Opinion varied among the sample groups, with northern city dwellers and medical humanities scholars recording the strongest dissent. The results were: Chinese medical students (82%), Catholics (81%), Buddhists (77%), Protestants (77%), Village B (73%), university students (70%), Village C (69%), Village A (59%), biomedical students (56%), city (South) (47%), medical humanities scholars (37%), and city (North) (36%).

A more general statement about the effects of abortion elicited a clear consensus. Overall, a large majority (83%) agreed with the proposition that "To a woman, abortion is always a traumatic experience." The breakdown was as follows: Buddhists (96%), Protestants (93%), city (South) (91%), city (North) (89%), Village B (88%), Catholics (88%), Village A (83%), biomedical students (81%), university students (81%), Chinese medical students (77%), Village C (71%), and medical humanities scholars (67%).

Another major source of the trauma of abortion for women was the aborted fetus. Confronted with the proposition "After abortion, a woman often mourns (*aishang*) the aborted fetus," overall a small majority (53%) of informants agreed, although that is significantly fewer than the number who equated abortion with generalized trauma. Here, the phrase *aishang* in Chinese usually refers to feelings associated with the death of a loved one. Strong consensus was lacking in the sample groups, with the medical humanities scholars once again showing the highest degree of skepticism. Still, at least a majority of respondents in most sample groups agreed that a woman often mourns her aborted fetus, with the Buddhists scoring highest: Buddhists (80%), Chinese medical students (74%), biomedical students (63%), Catholics (62%), university students (59%), Protestants (59%), Village A (56%), Village C (54%), city (North) (53%), Village B (47%), city (South) (42%), and medical humanities scholars (32%).

In summary, there seem to be several reasons for the high level of consensus on this proposition. One is the association of abortion not only with physical pain but also with potential damage to the mother's physical and psychological health. Another reason relates to the snuffing out of a human life. The stories presented in chapter 5 give real-life examples of the trauma suffered by Chinese women who have had to experience abortion for whatever reasons.

SUPPORT FOR THE BIRTH CONTROL POLICIES

As presented in chapter 1, many Westerners (e.g., Aird 1990; Mosher 1993) consider the population control policy a violation of human rights because of its compulsory and coercive character. Although the Chinese government has repeatedly claimed that the population control program enjoys widespread popular support, such assurances have met with considerable skepticism, if not total rejection, in the West. My findings—in the interviews with women and doctors presented in chapters 5 and 6 as well as in the survey—offer evidence to modify this Western view. While confirming the use of coercive measures in implementing the policy, my results challenge the assumption widely held in the West that the Chinese family planning program has little support among those affected by it. Although a number of previous surveys (discussed below) have shown that both rural and urban residents would prefer more than one child, people in China nevertheless strongly support the national birth control policies, as the Chinese government has claimed.

The Ideal Number of Children

When respondents were asked the number of children they would prefer in the absence of any restrictive social policy, 41% answered one, 54%

answered two, 3% answered three, and 2% answered more than three. The overwhelming majority (95%) stated that one or two children would be sufficient, while 59% preferred more than one child.

The findings presented in table 4.3 elicit some answers that run counter to the accepted wisdom. First, the rural samples were no more likely to favor having more than one child than the urban and other groups; in fact, their expressed preference for only one child was quite marked. Second, most of the groups who disagreed strongly with the one-child option preferred two children as optimal. Third, only a very small proportion of respondents (5%) preferred three or more children, with the two Christian groups, followed by the medical humanities scholars and university students, showing the strongest support for large families.

Although the option of having no children was inadvertently omitted from the questionnaire, five informants (two young women, one middle-aged woman, and two young men) noted their preference for no children. In the course of my fieldwork, I was often told that a growing number of urban young people (although still a small percentage), especially the well educated, did not want children. One respondent, a nurse in her fifties, said that she had had a child—now a university student—only because of pressure from her husband and his family. After this child, she had had two abortions. She observed that, although few couples of her generation had chosen to be childless, more and more of the younger generation were choosing this option. It remains to be seen whether such couples can withstand the strong social pressures exerted by Chinese notions of family and marriage to have at least one child.

The survey results were consistent with the findings of other surveys of family-size preference conducted in China in the late 1990s. Three surveys

Table 4.3.   Ideal Number of Children by Sample Groups (percent)

Sample Group	One	Two	Three and More
Chinese Med. Students	58	40	2
Village B	51	43	6
City (South)	47	51	2
City (North)	39	59	2
Protestants	38	46	15
Village A	36	62	2
Village C	34	65	1
Catholics	32	50	18
Buddhists	30	67	4
Biomedical Students	30	63	7
University Students	30	61	10
Med. Humanities Scholars	22	67	11
Overall	41	54	5

carried out in 1997 recorded preferences of 29%, 25%, and 42% for one child and 59%, 55%, 52% for two children (cited in Scharping 2003: 215–16). (These surveys also inadvertently omitted the no-child option.) It seems that, while increasing numbers are opting for one (or no) child, most couples would still prefer two children. The 1997 surveys also showed significant rural-urban differences, with 25% opting for one child and 62% for two children in rural and/or suburban areas, and corresponding figures for urban areas of 42% and 52%, respectively (cited in Scharping 2003: 215–16). In addition, one of the 1997 surveys revealed a smaller preferred family size than was found in similar surveys conducted in 1985 and 1988 (cited in Aird 1990).[2] The earlier surveys also showed a much more significant preference for two children among rural people.

In contrast to all these previous studies, my survey showed no significant difference between rural and urban populations on this question. This rural-urban consensus may mean that more rural Chinese are coming to prefer fewer children than before—or perhaps the three village samples in my survey were not taken from sufficiently remote areas. The perception that peasants prefer large families is merely one of many stereotypes of rural people, and it has been used to justify coercive measures in implementing the birth control program in the countryside.

Strong Support for the "One-Child" Policy

My survey results support the official claim that the national family planning program is endorsed by the great majority of Chinese. A large majority of respondents considered overpopulation to be a serious social problem, approved social and/or government intervention in population control and reproduction, and favored the current family planning program—the "one-child" policy.

Overall, a large majority (88%) of informants agreed that "Overpopulation and rapid population growth will hinder the social and economic development of our country." There was strong agreement on this issue across all twelve sample groups: university students (98%), Chinese medical students (95%), medical humanities scholars (94%), city (South) (95%), biomedical students (93%), city (North) (89%), Village B (88%), Buddhists (85%), Village C (84%), Protestants (83%), Village A (79%), and Catholics (60%). Although the Catholic group offered less support for the proposition than the other groups, a majority of Catholics still agreed with it.

Overall, an overwhelming majority—a massive 94%—agreed with the statement that "Our country must carry out the family planning policy strictly in order to control population growth." All groups showed strong agreement here: city (North) (98%), university students (98%), Chinese medical students (98%), Village B (96%), Village C (96%), city (South) (96%), Village A (95%),

Buddhists (92%), biomedical students (89%), medical humanities scholars (89%), Protestants (83%), and Catholics (72%). Given their milder support for the previous statement, it is interesting that almost three-quarters of the Catholics agreed with this one.

The strong response to the previous question was reinforced by the very large majority (92%) who opposed the proposition that "Couples should be able to have as many children as they want." Those *in favor* of the proposition responded as follows: Catholics (42%), Protestants (26%), Village B (13%), medical humanities scholars (11%), Village C (8%), Buddhists (8%), biomedical students (7%), university students (5%), Village A (4%), city (South) (2%), city (North) (0%), and Chinese medical students (0%). Again, Catholics, and to a lesser extent Protestants, stood out.

Respondents showed strong support for the government's "one-child-per-couple" policy, which was the subject of the following two questions. Overall, a very strong majority (94%) agreed with the statement that "'The one-child-per-couple' policy is beneficial to the country." The breakdown was: Village C (99%), city (South) (98%), Village A (97%), Chinese medical students (97%), Village B (96%), Buddhists (96%), biomedical students (96%), university students (93%), city (North) (89%), Protestants (88%), Catholics (84%), and medical humanities scholars (68%). Overall, four-fifths of respondents (82%) agreed with the next statement, that "'The one-child-per-couple' policy is beneficial to the individual and the family." The groups responded as follows: Village B (94%), Village C (94%), Chinese medical students (92%), Village A (89%), city (South) (81%), Buddhists (78%), biomedical students (74%), university students (73%), city (North) (73%), Protestants (63%), Catholics (60%), and medical humanities scholars (58%). As with the previous question, Christians and medical humanities scholars were more reluctant to support the "one-child" policy than were the other groups, just as they showed the least support (although still registering very high levels) for population control in general.

Strong Support for Eugenics

As we saw in chapter 2, the state family planning program is partly aimed at improving the quality of the population. The concept and practice of eugenics (*yousheng*, healthy or superior birth; literally, "excellent birth") was very strongly supported by informants. Overall an overwhelming majority (95%) agreed with the statement that "It is necessary to take eugenic measures to improve the quality of our country's population." There was strong agreement across all sample groups: Village B (100%), university students (100%), city (South) (99%), city (North) (98%), Chinese medical students (97%), Buddhists (96%), biomedical students (96%), Village A (93%), Protestants (93%), Village C (90%), medical humanities scholars (84%), and

Catholics (80%). As we saw above, eugenics was considered one of the most legitimate reasons for an abortion. Overall, 96% of informants favored terminating pregnancy if the fetus showed genetic abnormality—90% if it was deformed or its mental or physical development would be impaired. Most respondents were unwilling to take any chances: 82% thought that a woman should have an abortion if there was any risk of a defective baby. Moreover, 73% agreed that the mother should terminate her pregnancy if she had taken medication that might harm the fetus.

Medical research has shown that a pregnant woman's personal habits—such as heavy drinking and smoking—may result in cognitive impairment, low birth weight, and other problems for the newborn. Information of this kind has been widely disseminated in China as a part of family planning education. In the survey, 88% of informants agreed that a woman should not continue her pregnancy if she was alcoholic, and 85% considered heavy smoking a reason for termination.

Overall, a very large majority (93%) favored procuring an abortion if the mother suffered from mental illness, and a similar high number (91%) agreed that a mentally retarded mother should also have an abortion. Informants may have considered mental illness and retardation to be hereditary or that children by these mothers would be a burden on society.

Who should decide whether a fetus is normal or abnormal? The survey shows that, in China, medical professionals are widely regarded as the authorities in this matter. While only 3% agreed that a woman should terminate her pregnancy when a fortune-teller foretold an abnormality, overall 96% said they would follow this course on a doctor's advice. And while 82% thought that a woman should terminate her pregnancy on suspicion of abnormality, only 7% agreed that a woman should do so if she merely dreamed that the fetus was abnormal.

Approval for Coerced Abortion

A strong majority in almost all groups agreed that coerced abortion was sometimes necessary; 75% agreed that "Under some situations, it is necessary to force a woman to have an abortion." The breakdown was: medical humanities scholars (84%), Chinese medical students (84%), city (North) (80%), Village B (79%), university students, 78%, Village A (76%), city (South) (76%), Village C (75%), biomedical students (75%), Protestants (74%), Buddhists (68%), and Catholics (25%). Only the Catholics strongly opposed coerced abortion—although a quarter still supported it. This evident support for coerced abortion, at least under some circumstances, together with the overwhelming support for the national family planning program, suggests that coerced terminations may be accepted by a large majority of Chinese as a legitimate means of implementing the population policy.

As noted above, a legitimate reason is important for having an abortion. Overall, only 35% of informants agreed that "A woman should be able to have an abortion for any reason." The response to this question implied support for pressuring a mother to continue her pregnancy in some circumstances, even against her will. Yet, when the question was put directly, 66% agreed that "A woman should never be forced to continue her pregnancy if she has decided to have an abortion." Approval for this proposition ran as follows: city (North) (84%), medical humanities scholars (83%), biomedical students (81%), university students (78%), city (South) (75%), Chinese medical students (70%), Village B (64%), Village A (60%), Buddhists (59%), Protestants (56%), Catholics (50%), and Village C (42%). Half the sample groups strongly opposed forcing a woman to continue her pregnancy, although support from the village groups was relatively low. Even the Catholic sample was evenly divided on this issue.

The responses to these statements present a complex picture. On the one hand, they suggest that, for many Chinese, reproductive issues, far from being private or personal matters, affect the interests of the family, the community, and the nation and thus can be legitimately subject to social intervention. On the other hand, two-thirds of respondents opposed forcing a mother to continue her pregnancy against her will, more than one-third (35%) favored termination for any reason, and a quarter were opposed to coerced abortion. These figures suggest that a significant proportion of informants did in fact consider abortion and reproduction as matters that should be determined by the mother. However, for Chinese, "the woman's right to choose" is more likely to be based on the Chinese understanding of reproduction and womanhood rather than derived from the moral principles of Western liberalism.

Support and Reservations from the Overseas Chinese

This acceptance of and support for the national population policy was evident even in the pilot study, where only two out of eighteen informants expressed criticism of the population control program. In unsolicited comments, over half the interviewees expressed their support for a national birth control policy and stated that it was morally acceptable to use abortion for this purpose. Two informants expressed strong support for coercion; one man stated:

The family planning policy must be carried out. Overpopulation is a big problem. Abortion should be used for population control—but not as a primary measure. The emphasis should be on contraception. It's important to improve people's cultural and educational levels [so that they can appreciate social problems such as overpopulation]. Because of the situation in China, the government ought to use compulsory measures. Circumstances in China and the United States are quite different. I read a news item some time ago saying that peasants and government officials had a serious clash [over family planning]. Since I come from the countryside, I'm aware that many rural people have very low educational standards and are pretty ignorant. It's all right to use compulsory measures in these conditions. In the future, everyone will have a better life. The final outcome will be good, so the use of force is acceptable at times.

He went on to explain the lack of debate over abortion in China on the grounds that human life is not valued in China as highly as in the United States.

Some who supported the national birth control policy in general expressed concerns and even criticism about the methods used in implementing the policy. A male informant, whose wife had given birth to two additional children in the United States, stated that, while he supported the population policy, some of the methods adopted in the current program were "too cruel" (*tai canren*). On one hand, he agreed that the "national reality" (*guoqing*) of China was very different from that of the United States. The United States, he stated, a vast landmass supporting relatively few people, was in no way comparable with China, where population pressure was enormous. He claimed that, without the birth control program, China would have had 1.5 billion people by 1997. On the other hand, he believed that the implementation of the population policy was seriously flawed. There were many late abortions, and sometimes infanticide was practiced. He considered termination within the first trimester acceptable, unacceptable thereafter, and absolutely wrong when performed after six months. But he also agreed that forced termination was acceptable in the first trimester. If a woman refused to terminate an unauthorized pregnancy, it would be legitimate to punish her financially or even send her to prison.

OPPOSITION TO INFANTICIDE

As people in many other societies, Chinese people, together with the official discourse in China, draw a clear line between inducing abortion and killing the newborn. In contrast with the widespread social acceptance of abortion, the survey suggested that infanticide was not acceptable to most Chinese. While 90% agreed that an unmarried student should terminate a pregnancy, only 7% agreed that she should kill the infant following a clandestine birth. Support for infanticide ran as follows: Village B (22%), biomedical students (11%), Village A (9%), Village C (9%), city (North) (7%), city (South) (6%), Protestants (5%), university students (4%), Chinese medical students (3%), Buddhists (0%), Catholics (0%), and medical humanities scholars (0%).

However, infanticide was not seen as equivalent to manslaughter or murder. Despite this clear rejection of infanticide, only 63% overall agreed with the proposition that "Causing the death of a newborn is equal to killing an adult." The strongest support for equating infanticide with homicide was shown by the three religious groups, as the breakdown shows: Catholics (80%), Buddhists (77%), Protestants (74%), city (North) (72%), Chinese medical students (67%), Village A (65%), city (South) (59%), Village C (59%), Village B (58%), biomedical students (54%), university students (50%), and medical humanities scholars (47%).

Neither did respondents show particular anxiety over the fate of a late-term fetus. In situations where the lives of mother and baby were equally at risk, 93% placed the priority on the mother's life. In circumstances where it was impossible to save both, the sample groups all placed lower priority on the baby's life: Catholics (32%), Village C (11%), Village B (8%), Protestants (8%), Buddhists (7%), city (South) (6%), university students (5%), city (North) (4%), Village A (4%), Chinese medical students (2%), medical humanities scholars (0%), and biomedical students (0%). Although the Catholic sample registered the highest support, most Catholics still privileged the mother's life.

To summarize, in contrast to their generally permissive attitude toward abortion, respondents very strongly opposed infanticide. Despite this, most did not equate infanticide with homicide and privileged the mother's life over that of a very late-term fetus. The fetus, the newborn, and the adult each seemed to have distinctive moral status for Chinese respondents.

A RELIGIOUS ISSUE AND THE QUESTION OF A SOUL

The role of institutionalized religion is much less important in China than in Western societies. The majority of Chinese, especially people of the Han nationality, have no explicit affiliation with institutionalized religions. In this survey, 80% of informants reported no particular religious affiliation, 5% were Buddhists, 5% were Catholics, and 9% were Protestants. However, the fact that most contemporary mainland Chinese have no particular religious connections does not mean that they reject the existence of supernatural beings such as gods, goddesses, and ghosts. Confucianism is basically a social-political-moral system with some religious elements, rather than an organized religion in the Western sense. Although Confucianism has developed many rituals, such as the worship of ancestors, it lacks religious institutions or places of worship such as temples. Daoism (Taoism), which distinguishes between "*Daojiao*" (Daoism as a religion) and "*Daojia*" (Daoism as a philosophy), is more institutionalized than Confucianism and has its temples and priests. But few Chinese claim to be "believers" in Daoism, even though many visit Daoist temples to worship various gods.

The three largest institutionalized religions in contemporary China—Buddhism, Islam, and Christianity—originated from outside China. Buddhism, first imported into China around the second century, has had the largest following, both historically and in contemporary China. Islam has many followers, too, especially in Northwest China. Christianity, which was first introduced into China in the sixteenth and seventeenth centuries, constitutes the third biggest religion in China. While these three faiths, along with Confucianism and Daoism, have experienced great difficulties since the establishment of the PRC, since the 1980s religion has assumed a more prominent role in people's lives (for a recent review on religions in China today, see Overmyer 2003).

While it would be misleading to claim that abortion is primarily a religious issue, the abortion debate in the West is rooted in Christian tradition to a significant degree. In spite of the recent revival, religion, and Christianity in particular, plays a minor part in Chinese sociocultural life. Nevertheless, the influence of religious beliefs on attitudes to abortion is evident in China. In the main survey, the three religious groups—Catholic, Protestant, and Buddhist—often stood apart from the other sample groups in their responses. The former consistently affirmed that human life begins before birth, notably at conception, and that the fetus is a life. And much higher percentages of Catholics, Protestants, and Buddhists believed that abortion was equivalent to killing than did those in the other sample groups.

Catholics stood out as the most conservative of the three religious groups. This was particularly evident in their responses to the thirty-six scenarios in which abortion might be considered. In thirty-one of the thirty-six scenarios, a large majority (75%) of Catholics preferred continuing the pregnancy. The only circumstance in which a majority of the Catholic respondents (60% vs. overall 96%) considered that abortion was justified was when the fetus was diagnosed with a genetic disease. A substantial minority of Catholics also supported termination in cases where the fetus was known to be defective (46% vs. overall 96%), the mother suffered from mental illness (46% vs. 93%) or was mentally retarded (44% vs. 91%), or the pregnancy was the result of incest (33% vs. 95%) or rape (25% vs. 91%).

In the pilot study, the influence of Christianity on the views of overseas Chinese students and scholars was also marked. If the notion that abortion means taking a life is foreign to most Chinese, this was not the case for the Chinese Christians who participated in the pilot study. One informant who had already obtained a master's degree in social sciences before coming to the United States and was a practicing nurse told me about her radical change of beliefs after becoming a Christian (a Baptist in Texas):

> I used to think that abortion was a way of correcting a mistake [contraceptive failure]. I wasn't concerned about the fetus. After becoming a Christian, I realized

that life comes from God. The fetus is a life—this is what the Bible says. God has arranged everything well. In my study of physiology, I found it a real miracle that, among so many sperm, only one meets the egg and a new life begins. I now believe that abortion is tantamount to killing and even murder. But the woman has a right to make a choice in situations such as rape.

Questioned further about the respective roles played by her religious beliefs and her knowledge of human embryology in changing her views, she replied: "Both of them contributed to the shift in my opinions about the fetus and abortion. Religion gives me a point of view, and the physiological evidence confirms it."

A male biomedical scientist also reversed his opinions after becoming a Baptist:

Before becoming a Christian, I didn't consider termination a problem—it was just getting rid of a fetus. I knew that it would influence the woman's health. With regard to abortion itself, I didn't see it as a problem. But now I believe that the fetus is a life. Human beings shouldn't be the masters of life. A child is a gift from God—as the Old Testament says, "a bounty from Jehovah." A Christian shouldn't choose to have an abortion.

He was disturbed by the widespread availability of abortion in China: "It's very easy to have an abortion. Society encourages that. People will get into trouble if they don't terminate the pregnancy." His views on abortion in America were very different (if inaccurate):

Public hospitals aren't allowed to perform terminations. No Christian will have an abortion. Because of people's religious beliefs, abortion is viewed as murder here. I think there are more people against abortion than for it—let's say 6:4. And there are differences between conservative and liberal Christians on the issue.

He went on to express his disagreement with those he called "liberal" Christians on issues such as prayer in schools as well as abortion.

Two items in the questionnaire refer to the possession of a soul (*linghun*) by a human being or a fetus. The concept of a soul is deeply embedded in Western culture, especially in ancient Greek philosophy and the Judeo-Christian tradition. But the theory of ensoulment—devised by Aristotle and widely held in the Middle Ages—is not explicitly linked to the contemporary abortion debate in the West. In chapter 3, we saw that the notion of a soul is also an important part of Chinese culture, including Chinese understandings of fetal development. The communist atheist dogma that has dominated China for more than half a century treats all such concepts as nonscientific "feudal superstition," to be rooted out as thoroughly as possible.

A large majority of respondents (74%) in the main survey maintained their belief in a human soul. The three religious groups held this unanimously. It is perhaps surprising that the Buddhist informants supported this view so strongly, as the concept of the soul is a minor doctrine in Buddhism. In the other groups, rural residents were more inclined to believe in the soul than were urban and better-educated people. Biomedical students and medical humanities scholars were the most agnostic. Detailed results were: Buddhists (100%), Catholics (100%), Protestants (100%), Village A (91%), Village B (80%), Village C (78%), city (North) (70%), university students (69%), Chinese medical students (64%), city (South) (62%), medical humanities scholars (47%), and biomedical students (37%).

Support for the concept of a fetal soul was much lower, but still significant, at 36% overall. A very large majority (96%) of the Catholics and a large majority (75%) of the Protestants believed that the fetus has a soul, compared with a minority of the Buddhists (42%). The other groups supported the proposition as follows: Village B (49%), Village A (43%), Village C (42%), Chinese medical students (34%), city (South) (21%), university students (20%), city (North) (16%), biomedical students (12%), and medical humanities scholars (5%). Again, rural residents were more inclined to believe in a fetal soul than urban and better-educated groups.

Of course, the concept of *linghun*, or "soul," may have meant different things to different informants. In chapter 3, I have presented different terminology to refer to different kinds of souls in human beings, including fetus—*hun, po, ling*, and so forth—in imperial China. The contemporary Chinese usage of the term emphasizes primarily a nonmaterial, supernatural element that inhabits the human body while living and leaves it at death. But this is not the only meaning of the term in the modern Chinese context. Metaphorically, the term *linghun* is sometimes used to refer to consciousness or personality, rather like "spirit" in English. It also metaphorically means something of crucial importance for the existence any being or realization of human projects. Therefore, informants did not necessarily understand the term in a religious sense. For instance, after completing her questionnaire, a middle-aged woman remarked that, for her, the word *linghun* referred only to a kind of spiritual power (*jingshen liliang*). To probe this issue more deeply, the questionnaire contained the statement, "The concept of a human soul is a religious idea." Overall, less than half (46%) of informants agreed: medical humanities scholars (58%), city (North) (57%), city (South) (50%), Village B (46%), Village A (45%), biomedical students (44%), Village C (42%), Buddhists (42%), Catholics (42%), and Protestants (27%).

These responses are difficult to interpret, and the statement may be ambiguous to contemporary Chinese. Many informants may have taken it to mean that "the concept of a human soul is a *merely* religious idea"—that the soul is not real, but only a religious concept. This may explain why in some groups a higher percentage believed in the human and fetal soul than believed that the concept was a religious one. For them, the existence of the soul was not merely a notion based on outmoded superstition, but an ontological reality. Whatever the term may have meant to the respondents, the historical tradition affirming the existence of a fetal soul continues in contemporary China—among religious people as well those having no particular religious commitment—regardless of their awareness of this historical continuity.

OTHER SOCIAL VARIABLES

This section explores the relationship between a number of social variables—gender, membership of the medical profession, place of residence (rural vs. urban), and membership of the Chinese Communist Party (CCP)—and respondents' views on abortion and related issues. The numbers involved were: 231 males versus 366 females; 58 physicians and nurses versus 404 in nonmedical occupational groups; 202 villagers versus 150 city dwellers; and 110 CCP members versus 182 informants with no party affiliation or membership in "democratic parties."

In general, respondents' opinions bore only a slight relationship to their membership in a particular grouping. On the question of when human life begins, for example, the only significant differences were between rural people and city dwellers: more rural subjects considered that human life begins at birth than believed it begins at conception (42% vs. 22%), whereas slightly more urban residents viewed conception as the starting point (49% vs. 37% who located it at birth).

Male versus Female

Surprisingly, gender did not prove to be a significant variable in determining informants' responses. A high level of agreement was shown in answers to the thirty-six hypothetical abortion scenarios listed in the questionnaire. Only proposition 31—"the mother has a poor relationship with her husband"—elicited a significant gender difference. Here, 49% of women favored termination compared to 32% of men. There was very strong agreement about the thirty statements in the third part of the questionnaire, which dealt with state birth control policy, the status of the fetus, the morality of abortion, and related issues such as the existence of a soul. Male and female respondents showed near unanimity on all thirty questions—the largest differential was only 6%.

Rural versus Urban (Agricultural vs. Nonagricultural)

In China, the question of residency—rural or urban—is a very significant social determinant. Just as it would be difficult to understand U.S. society without the interpretative lenses of race, gender, and even class, it would be impossible to make sense of Chinese society without considering the social and legal category of residency (*hukou*, registered permanent residency). The *hukou* system creates a caste-like social stratification that divides all citizens into two civil groups with membership ascribed from birth: rural and urban. Partly as a consequence of the system, more than 0.8 billion rural Chinese—the majority of the population—suffer serious inequalities in health care, education, social welfare, and general living standards. Although rural residents have been legally permitted to work and live in the cities since the 1980s, urban residents are heavily subsidized by the state and rural residents continue to face severe discrimination. For example, rural migrants to the cities pay much higher school fees than urban residents.

There are clear fertility differences between the rural and urban populations. Although rural fertility rates have fallen sharply over the past two decades, they are still considerably higher than urban rates (e.g., 1949: 5.54/5.51; 1965: 6.53/3.78; 1970: 6.31/3.22; 1985: 2.35/1.27; 1990: 2.32/1.21; 1995: 2.00/1.48; Scharping 2003: 273). And, as various surveys have indicated, rural people are more likely to prefer two children to one. These differences, together with the rural preference for sons, are dictated not by personal choice but also by practical necessity—in China's rural areas, in the absence of any effective social security or welfare system, basic support and care of the elderly still fall on male children.

Despite these major social differences, the responses to the questionnaire—including the statement on family-size preference—by rural and urban residents did not diverge markedly. Among the thirty-six scenarios for possible abortion, rural and urban respondents differed in their assessments in only five: cosmetic reasons (53% rural vs. 20% urban); severe morning sickness (49% vs. 34%); termination advised by the mother's best friend (45% vs. 15%); injury to the limbs (38% vs. 23%); and objection by the husband to the pregnancy (54% vs. 35%).

In the third part of the questionnaire, only seven of the thirty statements elicited significantly different responses. Rural people were more inclined to see abortion as the taking of a human life. They also believed more strongly in the existence of a human soul (82% vs. 65%). Belief in a fetal soul was not strongly held by either group, although the proportion of rural people who held it was more than double that of city dwellers (44% vs. 20%). Furthermore, more villagers than city dwellers considered that aborting a fetus was tantamount to killing an infant (35% vs. 17%).

Through their responses, city dwellers expressed greater familiarity with and acceptance of abortion. A significant majority of urban people (72%) believed that most women had at least one abortion at some time in their lives, as against only 42% of rural residents. More urban residents agreed that a mother should never be forced to continue her pregnancy (78% vs. 53%), and city dwellers were less inclined to believe that a woman always had emotional and psychological difficulties following termination of pregnancy (44% vs. 67%). A tiny handful of urban residents—1% of the two city sample groups—considered it shameful for a married woman to have an abortion, while 18% of rural residents thought it was shameful.

Although social stratification based on residency is presumed to have profound implications for people's views about children, family, and reproduction, this was not reflected in the survey. The similarities between the responses of rural and urban groups suggested the influence of broader factors such as economic development and official propaganda. This may, once again, reflect one of the limitations of the survey—the three village groups were located close to the capital city of an inland province (although not in the suburbs). In addition, the rural participants in this survey were better educated than most rural people—as their ability to fill out the questionnaire indicated.

Medical Professionals versus Laypersons

Likewise, the responses of the medical professionals in the sample—practicing physicians (78%) and nurses (22%)—were not markedly different from those of laypersons. Significant differences were apparent in only eight of sixty questions. First, fewer medical professionals saw abortion as tantamount to killing, medical professionals disagreeing with laypersons over whether aborting a fetus is equivalent to taking a life (19% vs. 40%), killing a newborn (14% vs. 37%), or killing a human being (7% vs. 32%).

Second, medical professionals showed a greater skepticism about the soul's existence. Even though a majority of both medical staff and laypersons professed belief in a human soul, medical professionals held less strong views (63% vs. 80%). And although fewer than half in both groups believed in the existence of a fetal soul, fewer medical professionals shared this belief (14% vs. 41%).

Third, although a majority of both medical professionals (86%) and laypersons (84%) considered abortion a traumatic experience for a woman, only about one-third (32%) of the medical group considered emotional and psychological problems likely, against two-thirds (65%) of laypersons. Medical professionals were also slightly less inclined to believe that abortion would impair a woman's health and reproductive capacity (30% vs. 41%), and they dismissed the notion of injury to the mother's waist or abdomen as grounds for abortion (91% vs. 69%). And a much larger proportion of the medical group believed that most women would have at least one abortion (74% vs. 49%).

Party Members versus Others

In China, membership in the CCP is not only politically significant, but also bestows social and economic advantages. But CCP membership seems to have exercised only a modicum of influence on subjects' opinions on abortion and related issues. With several exceptions, Party members' responses both to questions on policy and to statements about the grounds for abortion did not differ significantly from those of nonmembers. Most Party members rejected the equation of abortion with killing, as did most nonmembers. The proportion of Party members who considered terminating pregnancy as killing was consistently lower, but not significantly lower, than the proportion of other respondents—27%, 24%, and 19% equated aborting a fetus with taking a life, killing an infant, and killing a human being, respectively, as opposed to 38%, 34%, and 28% of non-Party members.

In China, Party members are officially obliged to renounce belief in "religion and superstition" (*zongjiao mixin*), whether presented as gods, spirits, or the soul. It is not surprising, then, that more Party members (but not many more) agreed that the existence of the soul is a superstitious concept (38% vs. 23%). More significantly, 61% of Party members indicated belief in the concept of a human soul, as opposed to 83% of other respondents. And 20% (vs. 44%) expressed belief in a fetal soul. In interpreting the data, it should be remembered that the term "soul" may have held ambiguities for Party members despite its primary religious reference.

Fewer Party members agreed that emotional or psychological difficulties always follow an abortion (42% vs. 59%), and that an abortion should be performed for any reason (43% vs. 59%). A few more Party members opposed continuation of an unwanted pregnancy (76% vs. 61%). On the supposed grounds for abortion, Party members opposed termination on cosmetic grounds more strongly than did nonmembers (76% vs. 60%).

THE POSITION OF THE INTELLIGENTSIA

As in other societies, intellectuals have long played a crucial role in Chinese political and sociocultural life. Just as freedom of thought, expression, and association are written into the Chinese constitution but scarcely protected in practice, there exists no institutionally protected independent intelligentsia in the contemporary Chinese political system. Nevertheless, in every society there are individuals and intellectuals who are prepared to pursue independent judgments and critical engagement with their environment despite adverse political conditions. One of the twelve sample groups, which I have referred to throughout as "medical humanities scholars," was drawn from participants at a national conference on medical ethics and humanistic medicine held in Dalian. The viewpoints expressed by this group constitute a window into the current status of the intelligentsia in China.

Due not only to the advanced education they had received but also to the fact that most were teachers at medical schools or universities, members of this group were typical "intellectuals" (*zhishifenzhi*) and perceived as such by society. Administratively, they were categorized as "state cadres" (*guojia ganbu*). Their routine teaching work is officially considered a part of the "political and ideological education" (*zhengzhi sixiang jiaoyu*) undergone by university and medical students, a practice that is often regarded as "brain-washing" in the West. The courses they were teaching and their research specialties included Marxist philosophy, political economy, scientific socialism, and "natural and medical dialectics" (the philosophy of science and medicine, and medical ethics). Formerly attached to "departments of Marxism," since the late 1980s these scholars have worked in institutions with more politically neutral titles such as "humanities and social sciences."

Although the sample size (only nineteen respondents) was too small for substantial comparisons, some general trends can be noted. While the medical humanities scholars showed broad consensus among themselves and supported a number of wider trends evident in the survey, they also showed strong dissent from aspects of the official discourse as well as some popular attitudes.

The reported incidence of abortion was rather higher in this group than for others, and indeed abortion was a common event for these scholars. Of seven female informants, five (71%) had had at least one abortion. A large majority (82%) knew friends, family members, or relatives who had had abortions. A majority (65%) knew two to five women close to them who had undergone the procedure, and 17% knew one person. A large majority (74%) agreed that "Most women have at least one abortion at some time in their lives." When compared to the overall results, fewer informants in this group viewed abortion as a traumatic experience for a woman. Only a significant proportion (37%) rather than a majority, in contrast to 62% overall, agreed that abortion leads to emotional and psychological difficulties.

The questions about the specific grounds for abortion elicited responses from the medical humanities scholars similar to those of other sample groups. Nevertheless, there were a few significant differences. For example, the medical humanities scholars were more inclined to support continuing pregnancies resulting from premarital and extramarital sex than the overall sample, although the majority still considered that these pregnancies should be terminated. Sixteen percent of the academics, in contrast with 38% overall, thought that an unmarried woman who got pregnant by her fiancé should terminate her pregnancy. And 68% (vs. 84% overall) thought that a pregnancy resulting from an extramarital affair should be aborted. Moreover, the medical humanities scholars were less inclined to favor termination for minor problems such as minor injuries or morning sickness. In fact, no academic, in contrast with 22% overall, considered injury to the limbs as sufficient grounds for abortion. And only 18% and 11% (vs. 33% and 28% overall) considered serious morning sickness or cosmetic considerations, respectively, as such grounds.

Although many medical humanities scholars considered abortion to be a serious ethical problem, to them it was not comparable with taking a life or murder. In fact, no one in this group agreed that it was shameful or unethical for a married woman to terminate a pregnancy, and 74% disagreed that it was shameful for an unmarried woman to do so. Only 11% (vs. 31% and 27%, respectively, overall) agreed that aborting a fetus is equivalent to intentionally causing the death of an infant or killing a human being. Similar to the overall trend (36%), only seven (37%) of the nineteen academics agreed that abortion involved destroying a human life. But only 58% of respondents agreed, in contrast with 71% overall, that abortion per se had nothing to do with ethics and morality. Of all the groups, only Catholics and Protestants were firmer in their perception of abortion as a moral issue—a view no doubt influenced by the academics' professional familiarity with the Western abortion debate.

In contrast to the majority view, most of the scholars considered that human life begins at birth, with only a very few opting for conception. Of the seventeen who answered this question, three (19%) chose conception, one (6%) "quickening," two (12%) viability, and eleven (65%) birth. Although a majority (53%) agreed that the fetus does not become a human being until it has left the womb, fourteen (74%) agreed that the fetus was a life. Just 32% of the scholars, in contrast with 52% overall, agreed that mothers often mourned the aborted fetus. Since no one in this group expressed a religious affiliation, it was perhaps not surprising that only one informant (5%)—the lowest proportion of all twelve sample groups and in contrast with 32% overall—believed in a fetal soul, although nearly half (47%) indicated belief in a human soul.

The relationship of intellectuals with the official discourse is both cooperative and ambivalent. One the one hand, their views on population control, abortion, fetal life, and state power support the official position. The survey results have reinforced that, as the previous paragraph shows, in disagreeing with the populace, the medical humanities scholars tended to agree with the official discourse on the fetus *not* as a human life. In line with both the official discourse and the overall trend of the survey, the overwhelming majority of medical humanities scholars supported the national population control program and official claims about related issues. A very large majority (94%) agreed that overpopulation and rapid population growth would hinder China's social and economic development. A large majority (89%) supported strict enforcement of the family planning policy to control population growth. Only 11% of this group favored unlimited family size. A large majority (84%)—the highest of any group and on a par with Chinese medical students—supported the use of coerced abortion, a position with significant ethical implications.

On the other hand, medical humanities scholars gave a relatively low level of approval to the "one-child" policy—the lowest of any group, including the Catholics—although over half thought it would benefit the country (68% vs. 94% overall) as well as the individual and the family (58% vs. 82% overall). This relatively low level of support for the "one-child" policy might have stemmed from their knowledge of the psychological and social problems of single children, especially the phenomenon of the "little emperor"—the single child who grows up self-centered and lacking in cooperative skills. They would also have been aware of the difficulties involved in single children having to take care of elderly parents. Other factors include female infanticide and gender imbalance as a consequence of the "one-child" policy, even in modified form. In addition, although a large majority (84%) of academics supported eugenic measures, they produced the second lowest figure of all the sample groups, slightly higher than the Catholics alone. In fact, some Chinese demographers have expressed serious reservations about eugenics (Dai 1992: 310–15).

Despite registering broad agreement with both the official discourse and popular attitudes as expressed in the survey, the medical humanities scholars showed evidence of dissident views. This trend was most notably expressed by a conspicuous dissident in the medical humanities group, although he had a background very similar to his peers. A married man in his thirties with one child, he was a university graduate and a CCP member with no religious affiliation. He listed his occupation as "medical teaching/research," suggesting that he worked in the social sciences and humanities department of a medical school. His views on abortion and related issues ran strongly counter to those of his peers, the majority of people in the survey, and most official perspectives. Of the thirty-six grounds for abortion listed in the questionnaire, he approved only of those cases where the fetus has some genetic disease or is defective, when the mother is mentally ill or retarded, or when she is a chronic smoker. He did not respond to the statements about alcoholism or pregnancy resulting from incest and rape. He agreed that the fetus was already human before leaving the mother's womb. Indeed, he held that a fetus is a life and that human life starts at conception. The fetus has a soul just like all human beings. While denying that it is shameful for women to have terminations, regardless of marital status, he believed that abortion has a direct bearing on ethics and morality. For him, aborting a fetus is tantamount to killing, however it is defined. He agreed that, after a termination, women not only experience emotional and psychological difficulties, but also often mourn the aborted fetus. He opposed the strict imposition of the national family planning program and supported the notion of unrestricted family size—he himself wanted more than three children. He rejected the supposed benefits of the "one-child" policy and opposed coerced abortion. He left unanswered the question about the effects of overpopulation and rapid population growth.

Chinese intellectuals (called *shi* in premodern China) suffered greatly in the second half of the twentieth century. Together with the Chinese people as a whole, from the 1950s onward intellectuals as a group suffered profound trauma on an unprecedented scale during the notorious "Antirightist Movement" and the Cultural Revolution. Chinese intellectuals, like everyone else, have their weaknesses, and many actively participated in the disastrous history of the People's Republic, including by persecuting their peers. Nevertheless, facing the reality of persecution, including imprisonment and even execution on the one hand and the temptation to engage in various forms of political and economic collaboration on the other, Chinese intellectuals have continued to rise up to fulfill their collective function as the conscience of society through both active resistance and remaining silent under pressure to conform. It is not yet clear whether China will develop a truly independent intelligentsia, or whether the dissident views presented in this book will ever be aired publicly. But it is certain that dissident views exist in China, among both intellectuals and the populace at large.

CONCLUSION

As we saw in chapter 1, many Western observers and even some Chinese have concluded that, in contemporary China, the prevailing attitude toward abortion is one of "no questions asked" (to quote an article in *Time* magazine) (Drake 2001), that abortion is regarded as merely a medical procedure, and that Chinese have decided that human life begins at birth. The survey data provide compelling evidence of how misleading these conclusions are, based as they are on deep-rooted stereotypes of Chinese people and their beliefs. Despite the sociocultural acceptance of abortion in contemporary China, the responses of 601 Chinese to the questionnaire powerfully underline the many questions, concerns, and feelings about abortion that lie just beneath the surface. These concerns reflect not only the widely acknowledged traumatic impact that abortion has on women, but a respect for the life of the unborn child as well. Overall, nearly three-quarters of the sample (72%) believed that human life begins at some time before birth, while almost half (48%) believed that life begins at conception. Moreover, although most respondents did not consider abortion itself to be on an ethical par with taking a human life or killing an infant, still about one-third believed it was.

Among the social variables taken into account, religion was the most significant factor in influencing Chinese people's views on abortion and related issues, while gender, perhaps surprisingly, had no significant influence.

The survey's conclusions about Chinese attitudes toward the official population control policy runs totally contrary to the common wisdom in the West on this issue. The survey overwhelmingly suggests that, despite their personal preference for two children, Chinese—irrespective of residence, profession, Party membership, or even religious belief—strongly believe in the necessity of controlling the nation's rapid population growth and support the family planning program in general and the "one-child" policy in particular. Respondents in all the sample groups very strongly supported the necessity of implementing eugenic measures to "improve the quality" of the population. Forced abortion was also accepted by a majority of respondents as justified in certain circumstances. These are the issues that show the strongest consensus. As for the reasons and the Chinese logic behind this consensus, while the official discourse goes some way to explaining it (as we saw in chapter 2), I return to this question when exploring the sociocultural and ethical issues attached to coerced abortion in chapter 7.

Although the survey has considerable strengths, it also has its limitations—particularly given the sensitive nature of the issues broached. The various sample groups and the informants within each group were chosen for convenience rather than on a random basis. The three village groups were all located close to the capital city of an inland province (although not in the suburbs), and the members of the two city groups were selected by staff at two family planning institutes where abortion services were provided. Ethnic minorities are underrepresented, and the sample overrepresents highly educated people and professional health specialists. Nevertheless, despite all these limitations, the survey offers the first systematic quantitative analysis of the attitudes of Chinese from many walks of life to abortion and related issues and reflects both the consensus and diversity of their beliefs.

For besides consensus, Chinese people also exhibit great diversity, ambivalence, uncertainty, and inconsistency regarding the moral status of the fetus and the moral nature of abortion. This is bound to be the case with such a sensitive topic. The intimate experiences of women who have undergone terminations and the physicians who routinely perform them confirm this mix of consensus and dissent in a most dramatic fashion, and especially underline the trauma of abortion for Chinese people.

NOTES

1. Here I have used the "free-listing" method of collecting data. According to Susan Weller and A. Kimball Romney, the advantages of this method include: "to ensure

that one is dealing with culturally relevant items and to delineate the boundaries of a semantic or cultural domain" and "to study or make inferences about informants' cognitive structure from the order of recall, the frequency of recall, and the use of modifiers" (Weller and Romney 1988: 10). For more information on the pilot study, see the appendix.

2. A 1985 survey of one-child households in the rural suburbs of Tianjin Municipality found that about 80% hoped to have two children and that some had accepted one-child certificates only because they felt they "had no choice." In the 1988 survey, the State Family Planning Commission found that 72% of all couples, and 90% of rural couples, wanted more than one child; and a demographic journal reported other survey results showing that 88% of Chinese couples wanted both a boy and a girl. Even in Beijing, a survey found that fewer than 20% of a sample of 7,622 married women wanted only one child; 79.7% wanted two or more. These data are quoted in Aird (1990: 54, 84). Aird also cites an unpublished survey conducted by the Chinese Society for Sociology in 1979 that showed that a considerable proportion of city dwellers (between 19.44% and 30.95%) and the majority of peasants (between 51.34% and 79.53%) preferred two or more children.

5

Bitterness beyond Words: Women's Narratives

another infant girl
breaking the net
born at the boat's hold across the river
the ancestors' blood pouring into
the sound like thirst
going through inside her body . . . wa . . . wa

—Hai Zi, "But Water, Water"

"So painful as to not want to live" (*tongbu yusheng*), "so bitter that no words can describe it" (*kubu kangyang*), and "that feeling, that scene will always remain fresh in memory" (*ciqing cijing, jiyi youxin*): these are three phrases Ms. Lin used to describe her abortion experience. The abortion this success-ful and fashionable businesswoman in her early thirties was referring to hap-pened eight years ago, after contraception failed. The interview occurred in the well-decorated office of her own company, affiliated with a university in Guangzhou, one of the most developed coastal cities. Surely, not all Chinese women interviewed experienced abortion as bitterly as Ms. Lin did. Yet her phrases, especially "so bitter that no words can describe it," as the personal accounts of Ms. Li and Ms. Liu presented in the prologue of this book have hinted and this chapter will demonstrate, well summarize the most salient common feature of Chinese women's experiences: immediate physical pain, long-term emotional distress, and the unforgettable nature of the event in their lives. A strong dislike of abortion, together with a feeling of utter pow-erlessness, helplessness, and hopelessness was so widely shared by them that, in telling their stories to me, quite a few used the same phrases "no way out" (*meiyou banfa*) or "no alternative" (*meiyou biede banfa*) again and

135

again. Note that, as will become clear soon, all these are true not only in the cases of abortion pressured or coerced by the birth control policy, but also in the cases of those "freely chosen" by women. In fact, the abortion Ms. Lin referred to was not due to the policy but done for the sake of her career.

The bitterness, nevertheless, varies for individual Chinese women. To paraphrase Tolstoy, each bitter case of abortion is bitter in its own way. This chapter constitutes my effort to listen to and interpret what Chinese women have said about their abortion experiences, that is, the complexity of the physiological, psychological, sociological, and even existential meanings of their narratives, at both collective and personal levels. This chapter draws on semistructured interviews with thirty women in three cities—the first on the Northern coast, the second inland, the third on the Southern coast—and three villages in an inland province. Further information about the interviews is available in the appendix.

Almost all the women interviewed were excellent narrators, although many claimed that they were not good at speaking. The following case is rather typical. A woman in her early thirties was visiting a doctor at a family planning clinic for a pregnancy test. Her doctor, who once performed an abortion on her, suggested that I interview her. She seemed to be very shy. At first, she strongly refused her doctor's suggestion and my request. She insisted that she was not well educated (*meiyou wenhua*), that she did not know how to speak well (*buhui shuohua*), and that she had nothing to say on the topic (*meiyou shenme huaoshuo de*). I told her that all these things did not matter, that what I was interested in was her own feelings and life stories, and that I believed she would have something to say. She still was unsure. But her doctor had already seated her on a chair across from the desk where I was sitting. It turned out that she had much to say and that she vividly described her experience and articulated her opinions. One unique point she made was that every woman should experience as much as a woman could possibly experience, even including abortion.

A TURNING POINT TOWARD WOMANHOOD

Abortion as a life event was never light. For the heroin of the story to be presented in this section, terminating a pregnancy was one of the few most significant incidents in her life, and it indicated the completion of her transformation from girlhood to womanhood. Although for most Chinese women abortion may not be such a turning point in life as for Ms. Zhou, it is surely unforgettable, with multiple meanings and far-reaching implications.

A friend of mine and his colleague ushered Ms. Zhou into a medical school office, which three faculty members shared, for her interview with me. About twenty-five years old, she had received higher education and worked as an administrator and school teacher. Her voice was pleasing to the ear and had a soothing effect. After listening to her talk for a few minutes, I could tell that she, like many other Chinese women, had a great talent for oral narration. As soon as my friend's colleague introduced Ms. Zhou to me, she and my friend signaled that they were about to leave the office. But Ms. Zhou stopped them and said, "It would be no problem at all for me if you want to stay. Actually, I welcome listeners." So they stayed, and their occasional encouraging comments and light jokes helped make the process of interviewing more like a chat among three or four old friends.

Ms. Zhou began her story by telling how things had gone wrong with her pregnancy several years before:

> It was early April. I was just married. We used the safe period and condoms for contraception. I was very healthy before. But that month I felt a bit unwell all the time, so I took various kinds of medicine. Soon, I realized that I was pregnant. From magazines and books, I knew some medicines should not be used during pregnancy for the sake of the fetus's health. I went to the hospital to consult a doctor at the department of obstetrics and gynecology. The physician told me that the medicine I had taken might have some harmful effects on the fetus. If the doctor had said, "no problem," we would have had the child. Because the policy allows one child only per couple, we must think about eugenics (*yousheng*). We of course want to have a healthy child.

With thoughts of good birth or eugenics in her head, Ms. Zhou started to fear giving birth to an unhealthy or impaired child, pondering how sad it would be if her only child was unhealthy. She discussed the issue of abortion many times with her husband and her parents-in-law. She consulted not only doctors, but also friends and colleagues. Finally, she and her family reached a decision to terminate the pregnancy. The decision was not easy, of course. In Ms. Zhou's own words,

> This was a very difficult decision for me, for my family. First, abortion might result in a series of consequences including infertility. A friend of mine is no longer able to become pregnant after an abortion. Second, the children some mothers had, even after taking the same or similar medicine, were born healthy and are all right. As a result, we hesitated for quite a while. We went to the hospital for consultation two or three more times. I raised this issue with my friends. I even discussed it with colleagues in the office. My husband and I had even discussed what we would do if I were not able to bear a child after the abortion. At first, my parents-in-law really wanted the child. But they supported me in having an abortion when they knew I had taken medicine.

For Ms. Zhou, like almost every other Chinese woman who has had an abortion, the experience can be characterized by the Chinese phrase "engraved on one's bones and heart" (*kegu mingxin*).

I can talk about my abortion experience now, but I could not do so before. Whenever I told it before, my eyes were always full of tears. I remember it as though it happened this morning. I will remember it for good. While I was waiting for the abortion, my mind was in a state of great turmoil (*maodun*, literally, contradictions or opposing feelings). I worried I would become infertile. I worried my health would be damaged. During the operation, I realized that it was really not easy to be a woman. It is painful, very painful. Since I work in this medical school, the doctor was very friendly to me. But the dilatation and curettage were not performed successfully. The embryonic tissues were not sucked out completely. Consequently, I had to have a second one to clear it up.

Ms. Zhou referred to the aborted fetus as "my son" (*wode erzhi*), noting that she often thought about the fetus after the abortion.

When the abortion was nearly done, it was so painful that I was almost in shock. The doctor let me see the bloody tissue. I watched the aborted fetus. It looked like a roll of fine hair. All I could do was sigh: "Oh, my poor son. How miserable you are!" I described what I saw to my husband several times. When our mood was not too bad, we occasionally cracked a joke about it. How miserable my son's fate! Sometimes I thought that he might have been the smartest child I could ever bear. But he was gone.

Asked why she used the term "my son" and not "my child" or "my daughter," she replied that "son" was just a general word for the fetus or child: "I do not regard men as superior to women. Personally, I would prefer to have a girl." But she acknowledged that despite her own preference, she had actually wanted to have a boy for the sake of her parents-in-law as well as her husband. Although Ms. Zhou grieved and mourned her aborted fetus as though she had lost something extremely special and precious, she said that she would probably feel much worse had she lost a child.

At this moment, my friend's colleague, who had also had an abortion and did not yet have a child, told us that she shared this with Ms. Zhou—the feeling of having lost something very precious, but not exactly a child. She too referred to the aborted fetus as "my son."

For Ms. Zhou, abortion constituted a turning point in her life. After the abortion, she felt her girlhood was gone—that she was now a woman. She was somehow sad about this. In many ways, she regretted the sudden imposition of "womanhood" upon her, with all its heavy responsibilities.

After the abortion, I became much more mature than before. I started to worry about a lot of things. When I was a girl, I was a naïve fool. I had no anxiety, no worries. I could wear all kinds of beautiful dresses. There were always boys after me. They gave me a lot of attention. When I had my boyfriend and especially when I got married with him, I was even happier than before. My husband, who is eight years older than I am, took good care of every aspect of my life. Life seemed to be always good—from the fun and joys of being a child to the happiness after marriage. Every day was full of sunlight. But the abortion made me lose a lot of my joyfulness.

Stressing how fortunate and grateful she was for the care and love her husband had given her during the abortion process and in everyday life, she still deeply felt the loss of her happy girlhood and the anxiety about the coming of her womanhood.

Ms. Zhou told me that the most significant source of her new anxieties was her fear that she will be unable to bear a healthy child. Facing increased pressure for a healthy child from her husband and her parents-in-law, Ms. Zhou expressed her worry about meeting the expectations of society as well as pleasing her loved ones:

My husband was the only child in his family. We lived with my parents-in-law. You know, Northern people want to have children. They want "three generations in one house" (*sandai tongtang*) or even "four generations living together in a house" (*sidai tongtang*). Everything seems to be perfect in my family and in my life except that we need a child. I really worry that I may be not able to give birth to a healthy child for my family.

She was concerned that unless she got pregnant soon people would say that she was a failure as a woman, that is, a woman unable "to bear a healthy child."

As a result, Ms. Zhou felt that she needed to attend to her health, which became worse and worse after the abortion. She felt she had to get physically and psychologically stronger in order to produce a healthy child. In her own words: "To be ready for the next pregnancy, after the abortion I just wanted to recover as soon as I could. I eat and drink a lot. I even force myself to eat. I encourage myself to eat meat, including fat meat. I really do not know what I am going to do if I can't give birth to a healthy child." Also, she felt that she had to avoid future abortions if at all possible. She said: "Abortion is not like having a cold. In the future, I will be very, very careful about contraception. You really can't be too careful about this."

Ms. Zhou made it clear that, if she could help it, she would never have an abortion again. Once again, she emphasized: "The love of my husband was indispensable. He was so caring that he even washed my underwear after I had the abortion. Without his love, I might not have been able to bear it." "However," she added, "no matter how much your husband and family members love you, no one can experience the pain *for* you. I must suffer it by myself."

The personal story of Ms. Zhou in particular and Chinese women's abortion experiences in general cannot be properly understood and interpreted without addressing the mainstream Chinese definition of womanhood—the customary, social, political, historical, and cultural requirements in China on what a woman should be. The character of *"fu"* (woman) in the traditional way of writing, which has been used for more than several thousand years, consists of two parts: *"nü"* (female) on the left and *"zhou"* (broom) on the right. It thus means that the woman's role is domestic, to submit to and serve men. The traditional term for a woman to address herself to the other is *"lu"* (slave). For centuries, the dominant ideology had promoted an ideal of womanhood that included "three obediences" (to father before marriage, to husband after marriage, to son after the death of husband) and "four virtues" (women's morality, proper speech, modest manner, and diligent work). Chinese women not only had been spirituality and morally fettered, but they had also been physically bound through such notorious practices as foot binding. The social role and economic position of Chinese women have undergone many dramatic and positive changes in the past century. Chinese women's feet have been liberated, and the Confucian notions of the "three obediences and four virtues" have been seriously criticized. They are playing a more active role in every aspect of social, economic, political, cultural, and public life. Generally speaking, their performance in Olympic and other international sports games has been better than Chinese men's.

Yet Chinese girls and women continue to experience gender inequality and discrimination in not only interpersonal but also structural levels in various areas, including education and employment. The dominant understanding of womanhood in contemporary China is still suppressive. It requires that the individual woman, like the individual man, must subordinate herself to state, society, country, and collective. It defines the ideal woman as "a virtuous wife and good mother" (*xianqi liangmu*). The characteristics of a good woman include being considerate, kind, good-tempered, physically beautiful, and so on. But the most important requirement for a woman is still to bear and raise two healthy children (in the countryside) or one healthy child (in the city). Consequently, Chinese women who do not have the requisite number of healthy children view abortion as a risk factor—something that might damage their status as women as well as their reproductive capacity. As a result, for most Chinese women who have had abortions, abortion is a bitter experience because they fear they might be jeopardizing their reproductive health and, therefore, their ability to fulfill what they view as their essential womanly duties.

PHYSICAL PAIN, EMOTIONAL DISTRESS, AND ADVERSE IMPACTS ON HEALTH

Because most induced abortions, especially in the early stages, are almost always carried out without anesthesia, nearly all patients suffer physical pain—

enormous pain in some cases. In addition to being physically painful, in spite of the strong political and some sociocultural acceptance of abortion in China, terminating pregnancy is usually vested with immediate and long-term psychological trauma, and even existential and spiritual distress. Moreover, Chinese women reported that, as a result of abortion, they often suffer from the long-term negative impacts over their general health. The abortion experience was a profoundly memorable event for most of the women. But the reasons for their bitterness varied.

For some women, the worst part was the procedure itself. This is clear from the remarks of Ms. Min, a very shy thirty-year-old woman whom I interviewed at her doctor's office. She was initially reluctant to speak. But after her doctor encouraged her to try to answer my questions and pressed her to sit down in a friendly way, she started to talk. It turned out she had quite a lot to say. Ms. Min told me that after having a son, she had had two abortions. Because she did not want a large family to support and educate, she went to the clinic willingly for an abortion each time she knew she was pregnant. For her, the worst part of both abortions, particularly the second one, was the intense physical pain: "My heart was sinking. My *qi* could not come up." She said that, since then, whenever she heard the sounds of medical instruments, she became scared. For her, both abortions were "unforgettable."

Ms. Wang's two abortions led her to reflect on the fate of being a woman. For her, the two abortions she had had to go through simply and intimately confirmed what she knew well: "to be a woman is really miserable." Ms. Wang further expressed sadness that her daughter would have to share her sorry lot in life, stating that when she had given birth to her she had felt "really sad, terrible," because, in her own words, "my daughter would have to suffer the various pains and bitterness I do." Ms. Wang, the mother of one female child, was a biomedical research technician at a medical school. The interview was conducted at her lab. She had had the first abortion due to the abnormality of the fetus and the second due to the "one-child" population policy. The first time, she went to the hospital with her husband, the second time, with her mother. She described her first abortion, which had been a surgical one, as painful and bitter: "The medical examination found out that the fetus was not normal. I had to have an abortion. How could I feel anything but pain and bitterness? Since I wanted that child, my mood was definitely bad. It was really painful. When I could not bear it anymore, it was finally over. Thank heaven." Ms. Wang tried a chemical abortion drug the second time in hope of avoiding the pain of surgical abortion. However, the drug was ineffective, and once again, she had to submit to a surgical abortion:

> When my daughter was one year old, I became pregnant again. Because the policy allows only one child, I had no choice but to have an abortion again. Since I

experienced great pain last time, this time I chose to use the drug. Half an hour later, as I took the second dose of medicine, the fetus was expelled. I bled a lot. I continued bleeding for many days, at least a month. Then I took some Chinese herbal medicine for bleeding. The bleeding stopped. The B-ultrasound indicated that the fetus was aborted completely. But bleeding started again a few days later. The doctor had to perform a dilatation and curettage on me.

Ms. Wang, like many other women, believed that the two abortions had damaged her health. "After the abortions, my health was not as good as before. My constitution became weak and fragile. I now often catch colds. Whenever my daughter has a cold, I have one, too. I coughed for an entire summer the year following the second abortion."

Ms. Gao, a resident of a big city and a university graduate in her early twenties, vividly described the pain that accompanies an abortion, and how desperately she needed the presence of her husband or any family member during the process. She strongly opposed the hospital policy that bans support people from the operating room, insisting that women need as many comforting caresses and words as possible during the abortion procedure:

> I didn't have the abortion here in this big city but in a smaller town, because a friend of my husband was an obstetrics and gynecology doctor there. My physical reactions to early pregnancy were very severe. My mind was relatively peaceful before going on the operating table because other people told me, "No problem, not too much pain." But it was extremely painful for me. I never had much bleeding. But my belly was bloated and hurt. Fifteen minutes felt like a long, long time. I was totally helpless. I held up my hand, but none of my loved ones was there. The hospital's policy didn't allow them in. I just wanted it to end as quickly as possible. I just wanted to say to the physician: "Stop." The hospital should allow the woman's husband or mother to be in the operating room.

While in general being discontented and angry with the indifference of medical professionals, like "butchers," to patients' pain and suffering, she was moved by the empathetic gesture of an intern—intended or nor. In Ms. Gao's own words, "The doctors were all like butchers. A female doctor was also working around the bed. I really hoped that she would give me a touch and some comfort. Unintentionally, one of my feet touched an intern and I felt much better. Then I kept my foot in that position. I was and still am grateful to that intern for not moving himself away from me."

For Ms. Fang, a village woman, her two abortions were extraordinarily painful. The horror of her experience could be easily perceived from her tone and facial expression:

> Before the abortion, I was very nervous. I worried whether a medical accident would occur, like the tearing of the womb and heavy bleeding. My physical reactions to the abortion were very serious. I constantly vomited. My body was

cold, and I broke out in a cold sweat. My entire body was trembling. It was extremely uncomfortable, very painful, and bloated. Since then, whenever I see a medical instrument, I am scared. Even the physician was scared to death, too. After the abortion, she said to me, "I will never perform an abortion on you again." When I came out, I could barely stand on my own two feet. The second time was even worse. I hear now there are abortions by drug. I hope that it is a better method of inducing abortion.

Because a different doctor performed each of her two abortions, Ms. Fang was well aware of how much difference it makes for a woman to have an empathetic rather than an unkind, even cruel doctor:

Some doctors are good; some are very bad. I had my first abortion at the People's Hospital [a Western, biomedical-style institution] in this city. Because the machine had some problems, the doctors got angry at me. When they performed the abortion, they said some very bad words about me, such as my getting pregnant due to an affair or extramarital sex (*bu zhengjing*, literally "not right" or "not normal"). They implied that I deserved all the pain. The second time, I had the abortion at a much smaller clinic. The doctor was very polite. Before, during, and after performing the abortion, she asked many questions with deep concern and sincere care. I felt much less pain.

In addition, expressing considerable unhappiness with her husband, who refused to accompany her for her abortion, Ms. Fang commented that if a husband does not stand by his wife when she really needs his support, the couple's relationship will be in trouble.

Abortion is very painful. Every time, I went to the hospital alone. I really wanted my husband to accompany me. But he didn't. On one hand, he was very busy at work. On the other hand, he was too shy. He considered abortion shameful. He felt embarrassed. He was afraid of being teased by his male coworkers. But I didn't think that abortion was shameful. If a man doesn't give his partner (*airen*, literally "lover") care and warmth when she really needs it, the couple's emotional relationship will be harmed and become strained. Every woman wants her man to be at her side when she is suffering. If he isn't, the family may break up.

If a loving husband or boyfriend can greatly comfort a woman in going through all the pain, frustration, and distress brought about by abortion, not doing so can worsen her bitterness. One woman complained that her husband did not care about her abortion: "People say that abortion is like 'sitting a small month' [after giving a natural birth]. But my husband even did not accompany me for my abortion. It was my lover who went with me [to the hospital]. Abortion was so painful that it had nearly taken away of my life (*tongde yaoming*)" (quoted in Li 1998: 140). Some women became angry with unwanted pregnancy, especially if they felt no love with their husbands.

A bad relationship often makes women feel more pain and wronged (Li 1998: 139).

One woman described her gloomy mood and many concerns when going to have an abortion. For her, abortion might bring her a bad name.

> It was the third day after my period. He [her husband] was very excited and I thus became pregnant. I felt angry, and my mood was terribly bad. Firstly, there were too many troubles [with this unwanted pregnancy]. Besides, I am a traditional person and felt embarrassed. I am afraid that other people will gossip about me as having too strong a sexual desire and being not disciplined. As for sexual desire, I believe that both man and woman should be rational and be able to control it. Abortion is not a good deed; it brings about a bad reputation for the woman. Only those people with the low social status (*di chengci*) often have this kind of problem [abortion]. It sounds as if someone has a low educational level. She will be seen by other people as being unable to control and restrain herself. (Li 1998: 139–40)

The main concerns expressed by the women interviewed included physical pain, safety of abortion, the desire for a quick recovery, and possible short-term and long-term negative effects on their health and reproductive capability. A woman who was waiting for an abortion commented in the following words about her concerns:

> I am most concerned about the safety of the abortion operation. I chose to come to this big hospital solely out of considerations of safety. I hope there won't be any incomplete abortion (*buwanchuan liuchan*). I really worry that it will be very painful. I also worry that it will influence my bearing another child in the future, that it will affect my health, and that I may not recover from the operation soon. I will have two weeks' leave from work. I've obtained some medical knowledge by reading. After the operation, I hope the physician will guide me and tell me how to take care of myself, what kind of diet to follow.

Over and above the fear of pain, one of the major concerns of Chinese women was that the abortion procedure might damage their reproductive or general health, even make them infertile. One woman described her feelings in these words: "I am quite scared. I am afraid of pain. I am especially afraid of whether the abortion will damage my future reproductive capacity. It is said that abortion makes many women barren. In the school where I teach, a woman became sterile because of abortion." Another woman found that her physical health was actually damaged by abortion. She reported that she recently had been suffering from "anemia, dizziness, bad appetite, and chills." She attributed all these health problems to the abortion three months previously. She emphasized that a woman should do her utmost to avoid abortion because it is not good for her health.

The findings from an independent study conducted by a group of Chinese scholars in the early 1990s through group discussion with 140 women in Shanghai support what I have presented in this section. According to the study, a rare one that focuses on the women's personal abortion experiences and perspectives, "In all sessions, there were women who thought they would be apprehensive, nervous and anxious if they discovered they had an unwanted pregnancy. A very significant finding is that there was tremendous fear—indeed terror—of the pain of the procedure, which had been unbearable for most of the women who had an abortion" (Zhou et al. 1999: 231). Moreover, "The reactions of dread and agony were much greater among the women who had already had at least one induced abortion than among the women with no abortion history" (240). In addition, many women in the study mentioned subsequent psychological anxiety toward coitus. A thirty-five-year-old textile worker informed that abortion was perceived as such an agonizing experience in a woman' life that her coworkers usually said that "to go to the operating room for an induced abortion is just like to go to an execution ground" (Zhou et al. 1999: 231). Another woman, a thirty-year-old assembly line worker, reported:

> An induced abortion involves surgery on the human body. It will disturb a woman's normal internal functions and possibly injure her uterus, especially if she has more than one. It can result in secondary infertility, irregular menses and spontaneous abortion. My sister-in-law was ill with secondary infertility after her induced abortion. Since then, she has not had a pregnancy. (Zhou et al. 1999: 233)

As shown in chapter 4, abortion is widely believed by medical professionals and laypersons to weaken the body and its constitution, similar to the results of a natural birth. Here, one can only speculate whether their physical health problems stemmed directly from two abortions, they were somatized symptoms originating from their own experience of psychological trauma of abortion, or both. The psychiatrist and medical anthropologist Arthur Kleinman (1986) has documented and analyzed the somatizing process in China—how culturally shaped psychological mechanisms lead Chinese to suppress distressing emotions. An important issue that needs further exploration concerns how the physical complaints of Chinese women have disguised or disclosed the emotional distresses following abortion.

While most women experienced pain during the procedure, not every woman did. In fact, two women explicitly said that they never suffered any physical pain in their abortion operations. Still, even without immediate pain, a Chinese woman might suffer from emotional distress for various reasons. This is powerfully illustrated in the case of Ms. Deng. Ms. Deng had three abortions after giving birth to a girl. On the one hand, she did not feel much physical pain in the process of the suction curettage.

Each time, my husband accompanied me to the hospital. The husband should take responsibility together with the wife. But I am very unusual and different from other women. My tolerance for pain is extremely great. Other people all say that it is difficult and painful to bear it [abortion]; I do not feel that way. They praised me because I am brave. But I just did not feel much pain. As soon as the operation was done, I stood up, left, and went to work. Whenever a woman who is going to have an abortion asks me about it, I always tell her: "No pain at all."

Ms. Deng was satisfied with the medical service she received. She stressed that she had felt no pain at all during her abortions, partly as a result of her doctors' kindness:

Since the doctors were my friends or acquaintances, they were very caring. They talked with me about various light topics. Their manner was very good. An affable manner can help the woman to feel better in having an abortion. It's horrible if the doctor's manner is bad. The doctor should be kind. They should be especially caring if the woman came to have an abortion not of her own will, but rather due to the "one-child" policy.

On the other hand, in spite of all those positive elements of her abortion experience, Ms. Deng was still suffering, for the sake of the aborted fetuses. All three of Ms. Deng's abortions were performed when the fetus was about fifty days old. Ms. Deng said that she had four children—the living daughter and the three aborted fetuses. She called each of her fetuses the little child (*xiao wawa*), observing that she often thought about "how old they would now be if they had lived":

Three times I saw rolls of fine hair (*rongmao*, i.e., the aborted tissues, which resemble such rolls). After seeing them, I felt the little child (*xiao wawa*) was really pitiful. If the policy [had] allowed, they would have been born. They were very little. If they were bigger, I would feel much worse. Everyone has emotion, right? I often think of them. I often imagine how old they would be if they had been born. If they had been born, one of them would have been in senior high school now.

Later in this chapter, we will give closer attention to Chinese women's feelings and views on the fetus.

Although abortion causes suffering and may damage the woman's health, at least one woman took a rather positive attitude toward it. In her own words, "As a woman, I should try everything" a woman could possibly experience. She believed that abortion was bad for her health, especially that "the injury to the womb was very difficult to heal." But she still did not consider her abortion experience completely negative. For her, a woman should have an abortion in her life just as she should give birth to a child. Otherwise, she would never know what being a woman really means.

ACTUAL REASONS FOR ABORTION

Abortions, even repeated abortions, are common among Chinese women. As shown in the previous chapter, 41% of the 348 female subjects in the survey had already had an abortion. Among the women who had had an abortion, 37% had had two or more terminations. Here, of the thirty women interviewed, not including women who were waiting for an abortion or who had spontaneous abortions, 42% had already had two or more induced abortions.

Thirty women whom I interviewed expressed many reasons for their decision to have an abortion. Listed in order of frequency, their reasons included:

1. State policy does not allow the pregnancy to continue (13). Specific reasons include:
   - insufficient time has elapsed following a previous birth (five years required) (3)
   - the mother has not reached the required age (twenty-three and a half years old for women with urban registration) (2)
   - no birth permit has been issued because the mother has already had one or two children (2)
   - the mother is not married (1)
2. Living conditions do not allow support of a child (8), including
   - the family economy is unstable, income is insufficient (4)
   - the family situation is not good (2)
   - the family lacks decent housing (2)
3. The mother does not want the child (8)
4. Failed contraception (6)
5. The mother thinks she is still young and wants to enjoy life (*wan*) for a few more years (3)
6. Problems with the fetus (3)
7. Fears that medicine taken during early pregnancy might result in fetal defects (3)
8. Current work is too demanding (3)
9. The mother wants to bear a child later (3)
   - at age twenty-six or twenty-seven (2)
   - at nearly thirty (1)
10. The mother wishes to heed the government's call [to have one child only] (2)
11. The mother is not yet married (2)
12. Bearing a child is considered a burden (1)

Sometimes, the reason for a woman's having an abortion is very simple. For instance, she may really want the child but is unable to obtain a birth permit. However, in most situations, the reasons for a woman's decision to terminate her pregnancy are far from simple. In general, the women I interviewed offered several reasons for their decision. For example, one university graduate gave at least three reasons for her abortion:

> I had several reasons for deciding to have an abortion. I do not want to have a child too early. I want to wait a couple of years more. I prefer having a child at twenty-six or twenty-seven. I want to relax, be free (*qinsong*) for a few more years. More importantly, I took many medicines before I knew I was pregnant; I even received a fluid injection. Those medicines might have a bad impact on fetal development.

Another young woman who had also received a university education said she became pregnant because contraception—the rhythm method and condoms—had failed. For her, abortion was the elimination of a child that neither she nor her husband wanted.

> We have been married for less than a year. We could have gotten a permit, but we really don't want to have a child right away. We're too young. But age is just a minor problem. Mainly, our living and economic conditions are not good enough. We want to be free of the burden of caring for a child for a while longer. I'd prefer to have a child when I'm nearer thirty. Although my husband wanted this child, and although he was concerned that the abortion procedure would damage my health, I persuaded him that abortion was in our best interests. He accompanied me here for the abortion on his own initiative.

Another young woman, working at a medical university in a coastal city, was interviewed at her home, a single room in an apartment building. The room contained a queen-sized bed, a wardrobe, a desk, and a small table. When I sat down on a folding chair, I seemed to occupy most of remaining space. She sat on the edge of the bed. Each of the eight or ten rooms on the same floor of the dormitory contained a single person or newly wed couple. She had had an abortion a few weeks earlier:

> I didn't have a birth permit at the time, but I was able to get one since I was above the required age for bearing a child. My living conditions aren't good enough for having a child, either. We have only one room. Moreover, the B-ultrasound suggested that the fetus might have some problems. So I had to have an abortion. But, if our living conditions were better, we probably would want it. Besides, I wanted to change my current job—college administration. As a matter of fact, it is better to do the job [bearing a child] soon. But having a child right now would be too soon. Having the abortion will help my future career.

Ms. Fang had had two abortions because she wanted only one child. She lived in a village in a suburban county near the capital of Hunan, an inland province. She explained that if she had two children, she would have to "split my heart into two parts," a state of affairs she could not abide. In other words, she wanted to devote herself to providing the child she had with the best care possible:

> As soon as I had a girl, I got an IUD. But I became pregnant again. Even though I am now living in this village, my registered permanent residence is in the capital city of this province, so I can have one child only. But even if the policy allowed it, I don't want more than one child. Now the economy is developing and the cost of raising a child has become a big burden. Everything is expensive. If I had two children, I would have to split my heart into two parts.

All the above circumstances can be considered socially acceptable reasons for a woman to have an abortion in China. In comparing the reasons listed above for abortion to those given by overseas Chinese students and scholars in the first section of chapter 4, some trends become clear. Reasons given by overseas Chinese students and scholars included pregnancies resulting from premarital sex, extramarital sex, and sex for money. But those who actually had abortions and whom I interviewed in China mentioned only premarital sex of these three. Of course, it is understandable that a woman might not tell a stranger that she had terminated a pregnancy resulting from an extramarital affair or from prostitution. One woman's narrative invited speculation that she had had an abortion while pregnant by an extramarital lover. Two young women said straightforwardly that they were not married and did not want the child because of both the official social policy and their own preference. Yet each of these two women had a fiancée.

Furthermore, no woman said gender preference, especially preference for a boy, was her reason for having an abortion. This may be mainly due to official prohibition of the practice. Selective abortion for sex preference is not only banned by policy, but is also opposed by most people. As indicated in chapter 5, my survey shows that 86% of subjects thought a woman should not have an abortion if she "knows that the fetus is male, but she and her husband want to have a girl baby." Eighty-eight percent of respondents agreed that a woman should not terminate her pregnancy if she "knows that the fetus is female, but she and her husband want to have a boy." Conversely, the survey results indicate that selective abortion was acceptable for some informants (12% to 14%). This does not, of course, mean that those who oppose sex-selective abortion in theory would not do so themselves in practice.

Compared with the reasons given by overseas students and scholars in chapter 4, it is significant that eight out of twenty-seven Chinese women who had actually had abortions (nearly one third) said that they had done so because they "did not want the child" themselves. This may suggest that the personal wishes of women are playing a more important role in whether pregnancy is continued, although the importance of the woman's choice is rarely recognized by other people.

In their decision making on the issue, Chinese women usually consulted with their husbands or boyfriends. Some discussed the matter with their mothers or mothers-in-law, friends, or colleagues. One woman who preferred having a child later, both for her career and to be free from the burden of children for a few more years, told me whom she had consulted and whom she would tell in the future about her decision.

> I discussed this matter with my husband only. I did not dare tell my mother and my mother-in-law. They want me to have a child, the sooner the better. I will tell them after I have had an abortion. Then, it's a reality. They can't really do anything. They probably won't understand me at first. But I will tell them my situation. I believe that eventually they will understand me.

FEELINGS ON THE FETUS AND (IR)RELEVANCE OF RELIGIOUS BELIEFS

To ask about their feelings about the fetus was one of the most difficult tasks in interviewing women, due to the nature of the question, which could imply a kind of moral criticism on abortion in general. For me, it was a great relief that the women interviewed showed that they understood well my intention, that is, knowing what they personally felt, rather than making a moral judgment. Their way of responding to this challenging question made me feel that this question should be asked.

There existed a radical disagreement in women's feelings on the fetus in general and the aborted one in particular. On the one hand, the majority of the women interviewed did not report that they had ever given much thought to their aborted fetuses. On the other hand, some had very strong feelings about the fetus (the unborn child, in their term) and this feeling constitutes another significant source of the bitterness of their abortion experiences.

Understandably, few women initially mentioned their feelings about the aborted fetus. Of the nineteen women who responded to the question whether they thought of the aborted fetus after termination, fourteen (74%, a large majority) said that they never gave it any thought. One woman asked me: "Why should I think of it?" She further stated that "there is no use in struggling to let the fetus go." Another woman who had had a termination very early in the first trimester said she rarely thought of the aborted fetus, since "it was not formed yet [like a human being]. If I'd had to experience induced birth [late abortion], my feelings would be very different."

Ms. Xue was a young woman working and living in a northern coastal city. She had had two abortions—one before marriage and the other after having a child. Responding to the question about the aborted fetuses, she gave me a very sweet smile and replied: "No, I never thought about them. Should I?" Her tone was calm and confident, the charm of her smile brought out by two deep dimples. From their provoking responses, I sensed that my question might be a misleading and wrong one.

As presented in the second section of this chapter, Ms. Wang had two painful abortions that she believed damaged her general health afterward. It seemed that her bitterness associated with abortions had nothing to do with the fetal life. On being asked about her feelings toward the aborted fetuses, Ms. Wang responded: "I have no particular feelings. Anyhow, you are not able to have these children [because of the policy]. I never think of the aborted fetus." She seemed to realize she differed from some other women and added, "A colleague of mine aborted a son and cried in great grief. But I was fine [about the aborted fetus]."

However, some women did think of the aborted fetus afterward, as revealed in several of the personal accounts that have been presented in this book. In fact, five out of nineteen women interviewed who explicitly responded to the question whether they thought about the aborted fetus (26%, a significant portion) clearly answered "yes." Their feelings about the aborted fetus (or the unborn child, in their term) certainly contributed to their emotional distress, which some found that they could never fully recover from. In the West, the argument that the fetus is a part of the pregnant woman's body has been used to support the woman's right to decide whether to terminate her pregnancy. In the Chinese context, to say that the fetus is a part of the woman's flesh and blood is to emphasize that one should not choose to have an abortion easily because of the preciousness of the fetus.

Ms. Jiang and her husband found it particularly difficult to make the decision to terminate the pregnancy. In the woman's view, the fetus was "a growing life" inside her. But she had to abort it because she had taken a lot of medicine before realizing it could harm the fetus. She noted, however, that she would have continued the pregnancy if the population policy had permitted them to have more than one child. To have an unhealthy child as one's only child would be very difficult—indeed a tragedy.

Both my husband and I hesitated greatly at first. My husband told me, "We should keep this child since we already have it." It was difficult for me to make the decision. I was hardly willing to part with it. After all, it is a little life. I was pregnant for a month and a half. It was a life, a growing life in me. I'm really very sorry for it. But the external circumstances (*keguan huanjing*) didn't allow me to keep it, mainly because I took a lot of medicine. It wasn't certain whether the fetus would have problems. But I really worried that my baby would have serious diseases in the future. I can't bet on this, can I? But the policy permits only one child. We must do our best to guarantee that this only child will be completely healthy. Along with my husband, I want from my heart to have two children. If the policy allowed us to have two, I would have liked to keep this child.

Ms. Fang, the village woman, described her two abortions as extraordinarily emotional experiences. She found it difficult to part with her aborted fetuses because she, like several other women, viewed the fetal life as *maomao*—a phrase used for the fetus, infants, and very young children:

> The two fetuses (*maomao*) were forty to fifty days old [this gestational age was probably estimated by the doctor according to the time elapsed since her last menstrual period]. The doctor let me see them. I saw them. I was scared and overcome by nausea. It was a mound of bloody flesh, all ground up (*rudandan*). Of course, I could not bear to part with it [the fetus] (*heng kexi*). After all, it is a piece of flesh from my own body. I told myself that I should be more careful in the future in order to avoid this kind of pain and suffering.

As noticed in chapter 4, numbers of people with certain religious commitments, such as Buddhist or Christian, are growing dramatically. However, people's reservations on abortion and strong feelings about the fetus are not necessarily based on religious beliefs. Although I did not ask about their religious beliefs in interviewing the women in China, I am certain that most women who expressed uneasiness about abortion and especially the aborted fetus have no particular religious commitment. In the pilot study, I interviewed a female student in her late twenties who had arrived in the United States for only a couple of years. She told me that she had already had three abortions. Although there was little emotion associated with her first abortion, she was very miserable after the second and third terminations. She referred to the fetus as her child, and found the procedure morally flawed: "After several abortions, I really think that abortion is wrong in some way. Everyone says abortion isn't a big deal. Some people look as though nothing has happened after having a termination. The older I got, the more terrible I felt within myself about the abortions I'd had. I'd destroyed my children, my *own* children, by that." When asked whether her feelings had anything to do with her religious beliefs, she replied that she did not have any particular religious commitment, at least not yet. She could not identify any particular reason for feeling so bad about her terminations: "Maybe they're due to a woman's and mother's natural instincts (*yuxing he muqing de tianxing*)." She added that, although she sometimes attended church since arriving in the United States, she was not sure whether she would become a Christian. In any case, her feelings about abortion and the fetus had taken shape much earlier than her contact with Christianity.

Nevertheless, how does the woman who, mainly based on religious reasons, believes that abortion is morally wrong face the dilemma in which she is not allowed to continue her pregnancy due to reasons such as the national birth control policy? There seem to be two choices only: to have the abortion against her religious belief or to accept the harsh punishment by continuing her pregnancy. I did not interview any Chinese woman who was in this kind of difficult situation.

Yet I heard of a case in field research in which the couple chose to be loyal to their Christian belief. The couple lived in the capital city of a southern inland province. After having had a child, the wife was pregnant again. The couple refused to terminate the pregnancy as required by the authorities of the work unit. I was told that their refusal to have an abortion was based mainly, if not solely, on their Christian faith. Finally, the wife gave birth to a second child. As punishment, both of them were recently discharged from their state jobs, which meant that they would lose housing, pension, healthcare coverage, and many other benefits, even their residence cards permitting them to live in the city. I attempted to obtain an interview with the couple through a relative who was a friend and coworker of the husband. At first, they agreed, but they later changed their minds. On the phone, the man explained to me in an apologetic and regretful tone: "We very much appreciate your interest in our hard lot. But we really prefer not to talk to you. Not right now. It is not that we do not trust you. We just do not want to talk, now. Sometimes, maybe years later, I may talk to you in great detail. I hope you will understand."

WAS SHE FORCED BY THE POLICY?

The previous section shows that the most frequently mentioned reason for Chinese women to have abortions was that "State policy does not allow the pregnancy to continue." For the Westerners, that someone, indeed anyone, has terminated her pregnancy due to a social policy directly means that she was forced in one way or the other. But in the context of China, it may be true, but it is far from necessarily so. The more I talked to Chinese women, the more I realized that they meant very different things when they said that they had an abortion because the policy did not permit them to have a child. Some women meant that they would have carried the pregnancy to term had it not been for the policy. Others meant that they agreed with and supported the policy and that they had not really meant to get pregnant. In this situation, many of these women referred interchangeably to the disapproval of the policy and the failure of contraceptive methods. It is also possible that some, though it is hard to know how many, used the state policy as an excuse to hide the fact that the pregnancy was the result of illicit sex or an accident and they wanted to terminate it, anyway. Most important, in the context of China, it is much more difficult than usually imagined to determine whether a case of abortion is voluntary or involuntary.

Some women who had abortions because of the state policy concerning the number and timing of bearing children accepted or even supported the policy. They had abortions in order to "heed the call of the country" to have one child only. Two women claimed that they had their abortions in order to meet the call of the state's family planning program. While most Chinese women may just passively accept the national population policy, some voluntarily participated in it and actively supported it.

Contrary to widely held Western perceptions, my survey indicated that most Chinese women, like Chinese men, support the government's population policy (see chapter 4). What is more, most women I interviewed, like most people in my survey, did not want large families. Most of them thought that two children were ideal. Unable to obtain a birth permit for a second child, one woman said this about her abortion:

> If I had been able to get a birth permit, I would not have aborted the child. I like the idea that every family should have two children. In that way, each has company. They can help each other. If we parents need their help, they can discuss with each other how to resolve any problems. Although three or four children in each family are too many, I don't think that two are too many. I don't think that most families would want more than two children.

Although this woman and most of the women I interviewed expressed a preference for two children rather than one child, it seems that even in the countryside an increasing number of people want only one child. Of course, the total number of such people is still small.

A village woman in her middle twenties preferred one child, mainly in order to provide it with a better education. Since the 1990s, education costs have increased rapidly.

> I have a girl. Although the policy permits me to have one more child, I am not so sure I will actually have another one. For me, one child is sufficient. In the countryside, raising a child is a heavy burden. It's not easy to take good care of a child. It's even more difficult to nurture and educate (*peiyang*) a child well. The schools are a long way from home. Therefore, the first priority is to raise the family's living standards. If the parents don't take responsibility, they may end up having many children. But now, more and more people are paying attention to educating their child into a person of ability (*rencai*). If you want your child to graduate from college or university, this is a rather difficult task for rural parents.

Nevertheless, whether this young woman will actually have only one child is far from a foregone conclusion. She may face great pressure from her husband, her parents, her in-laws, and her peers to have two or more children, a son in particular.

A village woman in her late forties had four abortions in the late 1970s, two after having her first child and two after the second. According to her, state policy was quite permissive at that time. But she and her husband found two children were sufficient for them. She remarked: "Why do people want many children? Other people might need ideological education or thought reform (*sixiang gonguo*) [to ensure that they adhere to the policy]. But I never needed that at all." Her tone and gesture indicated feelings of pride that she, unlike her fellow villagers, was an enlightened woman who could recognize that it is in people's best interests to have small rather than large families.

In the context of China, even if one can distinguish voluntary abortions from involuntary ones, it is even more challenging to differentiate whether a case has resulted from persuasion, pressure, or coercion. In the following two cases, especially the second one, both women clearly felt pressured or even forced to terminate their pregnancies, but neither considered herself to have done so involuntarily.

Ms. Deng was in her forties and had had three abortions after giving birth to a girl. All the medical costs were reimbursed by her work unit (*danwei*). She told me the reasons for the abortions: the first time, no birth permit; the second and third times, contraceptive failure. But having no birth permit was the real reason for all three abortions. Although she and her husband wanted to have at least one more child, and although they toyed with the idea of violating the state policy, they concluded that the negative consequences of defying the policy were too great:

> To speak from my heart, if the policy permitted, I certainly would have at least one more child. One child is too lonely. However, as the policy permits one child only, what could we do? We have no choice (*meiyou banfa*). One of my colleagues always says that the more children the better. My husband is the only child in his family, the only son. As you know, Cantonese people like male children. It would be wonderful if I could have another child, a son. Nevertheless, I never hesitated to have an abortion and voluntarily went to the hospital whenever I was pregnant after having my daughter. I know there is a national policy. No one can escape it.

Ms. Wen lived in a village in Hunan and was interviewed at her home. She had two children, a daughter and a son. She had had an abortion seven years earlier after giving birth to her first child. The birth policy requires that a rural woman delay her second child until five years after the first. She really wanted to have the child, but could not get a birth permit. The township ordered every woman to have a medical examination four times each year. Every married woman of childbearing age had to go to the health clinic at the township to receive a B-ultrasound examination. This was still being practiced when my field research was conducted in 1997, and I suppose it still is. The major purpose of the procedure was to discover unauthorized pregnancies.

When Ms. Wen became pregnant, she was working in a business selling snakes in Guangzhou, the capital of the province near her own, where, according to her, people especially prize snake dishes. Since she really wanted to have the child, she hid at a relative's house for almost a fortnight in the hope that she would be able to give birth. She soon found out that the fine for giving birth to a child without a permit was severe—three or four thousand *yuan* (four to five hundred U.S. dollars, more than one year's income for an ordinary villager in her area). She also realized that other women with unauthorized pregnancies were brought to the clinic for abortion no matter how late in the pregnancy they were. She knew that she could not escape the punishment, that she could not afford to pay the fine, and that the later the abortion the more physically difficult it would be. So Ms. Wen came home from Guangzhou city and went to the township clinic to induce the birth of a fetus already five months in gestation.

Despite all this, Ms. Wen did not see herself as having been forced to have the abortion:

> Induced birth—late abortion—is of course very painful. It was terrible. When the baby was born, it was dead. The doctors did their best to make sure that the baby was born dead; it was not able to cry. But I was willing to do it by myself (*xingan qingyuan*). I was not caught and sent to the clinic. I went to the clinic on my own. So I did not suffer much pain. The doctor who performed the abortion was an acquaintance. She did it very well. I appreciate this. After the abortion, I had no feeling. I did not feel sad or regretful.

The reasons Ms. Wen gave for not considering her abortion a forced one included: first, she was not caught by the family planning authorities and sent by physical force to the clinic; second, she gave up because the fine was too harsh for her and her family; third, she was somehow satisfied with having a daughter only, and she did not want the second child that much anyway. Therefore, she considered that she had the late abortion because she was willing to do it herself.

After the abortion, Ms. Wen and her husband considered accepting the fact that they would have only a girl. But later, the local family planning official issued a birth permit to her without her requesting one. "Since no fine would be imposed on me, since there was no necessity to hide the pregnancy from anybody, I gave birth to another child," she said.

The provoking case of Ms. Wen raises many thorny questions on the administration of China's birth control program and especially the ethics of late/forced abortion in the context of population policy. One of them is whether Ms. Wen was coerced by the state policy to have the late abortion. For Westerners, it may be obvious that she was. But she herself did not think so, at least not consciously. She seemed to agree with the Chinese authorities that physical force is the only genuine type of coercion and that the population policy is necessary and legitimate. Problems are: Is a conscious acknowledgment of being forced an essential prerequisite for any case of coerced abortion? Does Ms. Wen's conscious denial of being forced simply indicate a false consciousness? How important is the individual's self-consciousness for adequately dealing with moral and political dimensions of coerced abortion? Voluntary or not, is this kind of late abortion morally justifiable? In chapter 7, I will further address the difficulties of defining coercion and discuss a series of related sociological and ethical issues of coerced abortion.

DESPERATE CASES

For socially marginalized, economically underprivileged, politically deprived, and culturally prejudiced women, abortion can be even more bitter. Among desperate and life-or-death cases are the following three that were witnessed and recounted by Dr. Zhang, an OB/GYN physician who despaired of her professional work and was extremely sensitive to her patients' sufferings (see the next chapter for more information on Dr. Zhang).

A Rural Girl Who Died from Abortion

The countryside and the city are two different worlds in China. National health insurance covers the majority of urban residents but only a very small percentage of rural people. In the past, with limited exceptions and without special permission, rural people are not allowed to work and live in the city. Following the economic reforms begun in the 1980s, many young women joined the stream of rural residents pouring into the cities to seek better lives. Young country women constitute a most vulnerable group—they are not only exploited by officials and emerging capitalists, but they also run the risk of being cheated, assaulted, and raped. Some of them join the growing sex trade. They may even lose their young lives in the city—far away from home and family members. In the following story told by Dr. Zhang, no one came up to claim the body of a young rural girl who died from an abortion:

> It was several years ago. A nineteen-year-old girl came to me for an abortion. She came from the countryside to this city to work as an unskilled construction worker. She came to the clinic with a young man. She was a typical patient. There was nothing special in her medical history. She didn't answer the question about who her boyfriend was. She told me the man was her "older brother."

Regardless of who accompanied her, I would perform the abortion if she requested. The abortion operation was very smooth. As it ended, she almost jumped out of bed. Then, she walked to the next room for a rest.

All of a sudden, some other patients yelled: "Someone's fainted and fallen on the floor." I found her cyanotic [bluish in the skin due to deficient oxygenation of the blood] and having difficulty breathing. Obviously, all this was caused by the convulsion of blood vessels in the brain resulting from the abortion having stimulated the vagus nerve system. Usually, this problem goes away quickly. But this case was very unusual. We resuscitated the girl for three days and three nights. But in the end, we failed to save her.

During that period, the male who accompanied the girl went away and never showed up again. We never saw him again. No family member was there to care for her. All her care was handled by physicians and nurses. All the costs were paid by the hospital. We believed that the man was not her older brother at all. If he was her brother, he would not just have left. He would not have left even if he had to pay the hospital bill.

After she died, no one came to claim her body. Later, the hospital disposed of the body according to regulations. This was an exception. Such a case is very rare.

Dr. Zhang said that more and more young rural women were coming to her for abortions. Most were not married, so they usually did not let the doctor know their real names and addresses. In order to avoid the social discrimination directed by many urban residents against rural people, they often concealed their rural origins. Two or three other doctors made similar comments. In Dr. Zhang's experience, many of these young women were not under the protection of the law:

When these girls come from other places—small towns or small cities or the countryside—to this big city, they usually work in the service trades, such as hotels and restaurants. The people they come into contact with and are serving everyday are usually men. If they cannot look after themselves properly (*ziji bawo buju*), they can be easily taken advantage of. Some of them are willing to have [sexual] relationships with their customers to achieve their own ends. Some are not. Some of them are even raped. The most serious danger usually comes from their bosses, who have almost total control over these girls. They can give them raises or lay them off. Some of those bosses still have a bit of humanity (*youdian renxin*). They sometimes accompany the girls to the clinic, pay medical costs and food bills, and take a bit of care of them. But some bosses just leave the girls alone and don't take any responsibility.

A Rural Woman Who Almost Died to Have a Son

Giving birth to a boy is not merely culturally preferred in China for the sake of continuing the family bloodline; but in the countryside a son is essential for the well-being of the aged because of the lack of basic social security. Rural residents usually have neither medical insurance nor welfare of any kind. In the following story, a peasant woman almost died in an illicit attempt to have a third child she was hoping would be a son. Here is Dr. Zhang's account:

> I was on duty during an evening shift. It was after midnight. I was in the delivery room. A group of people came in howling. They shouted: "Help! Help!" Except for one person, you could easily see that they were all peasants because they had bare feet. The patient was wearing ragged clothes that were too dirty to look at. I learned that she had been trying to give birth to a child at home for more than two hours. The baby had come out. But the placenta was just not dropping off.
>
> Then, her husband and a few of their neighbors had put the woman in a wheelbarrow. She was covered by a tattered quilt that could not have been dirtier. On their way to the hospital, a truck driver kindly stopped and brought them in. We used all possible measures, including blood transfusion, to save the woman.
>
> The couple had had two children, both girls. In order to have a son, the couple left their home village, because the local officials would not have allowed her to give birth to a third child. They would have required the woman to have an abortion, even a partial-birth abortion. In order to escape the local family planning officials, they took their two children and went to a suburb of this city. They rented a room there. Because she wanted so much to have a boy, the woman almost lost her life.
>
> The living conditions of this woman were really very bad. Four people—two adults and two children—shared one quilt, one bed. This kind of situation is now quite rare in China.
>
> The hospital must take care of all the medical costs. It was impossible to collect fees from the family, since they could not even afford food. How could they pay the medical bill? We doctors and nurses felt very sorry for this family's misery. We either bought food or brought it from home for them. After three days, the patient was discharged from the hospital. When she left the hospital, her body was very weak and her anemia was rather serious. Under normal circumstances, she would have stayed in the hospital for two weeks. But in this case, the hospital saved the woman's life. After that, how the woman recovered was her own and her husband's business as far as the hospital was concerned.

Seeing that the family was in abject poverty, Dr. Zhang and other doctors and nurses suggested that the woman and her husband give the third daughter to someone else. The woman would obtain some payment, which could be used to buy food and medicine to help her recover. At first, the couple agreed, but after further arrangements were made through the hospital, they changed their minds. Later, they changed their minds again and wanted to offer their third child up for adoption. The hospital decided not to do anything more about the matter. Dr. Zhang told me that she couldn't understand the couple still wanting the child, despite the obvious fact that the child herself would suffer from the family's poor living conditions.

A College Student Who Carried Her Pregnancy to Term

Partly due to the Chinese sexual revolution since the 1980s, youth and teen pregnancies are becoming a more and more serious social issue in China (see, e.g., Xu, Liu, and Lou 1996; Luo et al. 1999). Several doctors interviewed expressed their concerns about the growing number of unmarried young women, especially college students and even teenage girls, who demanded abortions. In the following story told by Dr. Zhang, the student carried her pregnancy to term.

> It was at noon. I was ready to go home for lunch. Several people carried a girl into the examining room of the obstetrics and gynecology department. She was transferred from the emergency room. At that time, the head of the baby had already come out from the opening of the womb. The girl, nineteen years old, was terrified. She told us that she didn't know she was pregnant. She didn't know she was going to give birth to a child. She had no brothers and sisters. We delivered the baby and wrapped it well.
>
> The girl had not passed the national exam for admission to universities and colleges [for free higher education]. So she was studying at a college where her parents paid her tuition fees. One of her companions—a female classmate and roommate of the patient—said that they had carried her here because she was in such pain. The doctor in the emergency room found out she was pregnant. The patient replied, "I'm not married yet." We asked the girl who the baby's father was. She did not say.
>
> What concerned us most was what to do with the baby. Obviously, she did not want the child. She kept saying: "I can't have this child. I can't have this child." She wouldn't allow us to contact her family, because she was afraid that her parents would beat her to death. Since the parents had given her money to go to college, they would care very much about "face" (*gu mianzi*). They would be desperate to save face. Later, the child was given to a couple who had been married for many years but had not been able to have a child of their own. The doctors arranged for the couple to offer the girl one thousand *yuan* as a nutrition fee.

Dr. Zhang felt very sorry that the young girl had to "sit out the month" in the student dormitory, where she could hardly expect to receive any special care after giving birth.

CONCLUSION

The survey results presented in chapter 4 indicate that a great majority in all survey samples, including both female and male participants, agreed that abortion is always a bitter experience for a woman. In other words, Chinese believed that for women abortion is normally *kuse* (bitter and astringent, pained, agonized, or anguished), something more than an issue of physical pain, something that also affects emotional or even spiritual well-being. Chinese women's experiences and narratives presented in this chapter do far more than validate this point of view. The narratives forcefully demonstrate that, although terminating pregnancy is indeed a fundamentally personal matter, abortion in China is far beyond a mere medical procedure or a personal issue, but has complex political, social, cultural, moral, and interpersonal meanings. For Chinese women, abortion is indeed "so bitter that no words can describe it." But compelling evidence also illustrates how misleading it would be if we treat Chinese women's experiences in any overarching category. Every case of abortion is bitter in its own way. The sources of this bitterness include the physical pain immediately caused by the abortion procedure, various anxieties, long-term emotional distress, perceived negative impacts over general health and especially the productive capacities, the feeling of the aborted fetus as a child, being compelled or forced to have an abortion due to the state population policy and other reasons, the incompetence of medical professionals in caring, a bad relationship with the husband or boyfriend, abortion as a reminder of the miserable fate of women, and so on.

It is thus not a surprise that a deep feeling of powerlessness prevails in Chinese women and that the phrases "no way out" or "no alternative available" were frequently used by them. As a matter of fact, not only "abortion patients" but also those doctors who routinely perform abortions frequently used these phrases and shared this powerless feeling. To present experiences and narratives of doctors will be the task of next chapter.

6

Fulfilling Discordant Duties: Doctors' Narratives

> Heal the wounded, rescue the dying, practice revolutionary humanitarianism.
>
> —The Motto of Chinese socialist medical ethics

The story of abortion in China is not solely the stories of women. A woman's decision to terminate or continue her pregnancy has often been shaped by social policies or other interests. Yet, in another sense, abortion in contemporary China is very much a woman's story because almost all abortions are performed by female doctors. All thirty OB/GYN doctors I interviewed throughout China—urban and rural, northern and southern—were female, with one exception. This chapter presents the narratives of those doctors, revealing how they feel and think about their work, the national birth control program, and the aborted fetus, and how they deal with discordant professional obligations, those toward the patients and those toward the state. Further information about how the interviews with doctors were conducted is presented in the appendix.

They are not "abortionists," although their professional routine consists mainly in performing abortions and providing the medical service of family planning. With systematic medical training, they are qualified OB/GYN doctors. People treat them so, and they see themselves in this way. Together with surgeons and other medical professionals, they are usually called "angels in white coats" (*baiyi tianshi*). Those who must have forced abortions or sterilization hardly see them this way, yet even these unfortunate women very often understand that performing the unwanted service is the doctors' *job*, not their *fault*. Dr. Ying, whose story I related at the beginning of this book, is one of them. Many doctors interviewed cannot say that they chose the job they are doing, because they started their careers at a time when almost all positions—medical and nonmedical—were assigned to individuals according to the needs of the state and the Party (*guojia he dong de xuyao*), not their personal choices (*geren zhiyuan*). In general, the doctors' economic and social position is not nearly as high as that of physicians in the West, especially the United States, but medical professionals, like teachers, are usually economically secure and well respected. Administratively, they, at least most of them, belong to the politically privileged category of "state cadres" (*guojia ganbu*). Basically, they work at state- or collective-owned hospitals, clinics for children and maternal health, or institutes of family planning (*jihua shengyu yanjiusuo*). Since the middle and late 1980s, more and more physicians, though still a very small portion of the whole profession, have started their own private medical practices in order to make more money and have more freedom. I did not interview any of the private doctors (*geti yisheng*), partly because they have not yet played any significant role in providing abortions and other family planning medical services.

TWO PHYSICIANS: ONE RURAL, ONE URBAN

A Country Doctor: Bitterness and Sweetness of Her Work

Dr. Li, in her early forties, had been working as an OB/GYN doctor in the township since the mid-1970s. The township had fourteen villages and a population of nearly 21,000. A typical village in her township has about 1,700 people with more than 500 families whose main means was planting rice year in and year out. After graduating from junior middle school, Dr. Li was sent by the township to a hygiene school (*wensheng xuexiao*) in the only city in the county to which her township belonged. There she received two years' medical training. As with all other physicians interviewed, her routine work included two principal functions, maternal and infant health care (*fuyo baojiang*), such as delivering children, prenatal care, and taking care of common female diseases, and the medical service of family planning (*jihua shengyu*), such as inserting and removing IUDs and performing abortions and sterilization on women by ligation of the oviducts. According to Dr. Li, sterilization of men (vasoligation) was usually performed by male doctors. Some abortions were performed by family planning nurses rather than by doctors.

Dr. Li's way of dressing and her manner made her stand out from most other villagers. An elegant and quiet woman, she rarely initiated conversation and always spoke in a soft voice. She accompanied me on a visit to a well-known Buddhist temple located on the top of the highest nearby hill.

She informed me that many women and men came there from cities and villages to worship Buddha as a cure for their infertility. Unlike most medical professionals, Dr. Li seemed to respect what those people were doing there, although she personally did not believe in any religion. On the way there, we bumped into several people, each of whom greeted her warmly and respectfully. She said that she had delivered two of them—a teenager and a younger child.

Dr. Li believed that helping women and relieving their pain and suffering were the basic duties of a female OB/GYN. She performed every abortion as carefully as though she were doing her first one. She indicated that, if she could choose, she would prefer maternal and infant care to family planning work. But she had to do the work associated with the family planning, anyway, whether she liked it or not.

Dr. Li used four words about taste—sweet, sour, bitter, and spicy (*tian xuan ku lua*)—to describe her experiences as a country OB/GYN doctor. There was sweetness in her work because the Party and the government backed up the family planning service she was doing. She said that the medical workers in family planning were given high political positions by the Party and the government. For instance, she had been selected to participate in the meeting of the representatives of the excellent workers and the convention of the Party representatives. Obviously, she was proud of these honors.

The sourness in her work came from the difficulties of being both a good wife and mother and a good physician. She felt that other people rarely understood the nature and pressure of being an OB/GYN doctor. "If you are good at your work, you cannot take good care of your family. Career and family are often in conflict," she said.

The bitterness came mainly from the fact that family planning work was difficult. Dr. Li and the family planning official had to carry the medical instruments to every village in the township to perform abortions. She was called up in the dead of night to conduct sterilization on people because the family planning officials were afraid that if they delayed, they might miss the opportunity—that is, "a long night is fraught with dreams" (*yechang mengduo*). One of those "dreams" might cause the woman who had agreed to comply with the policy to change her mind and decide not to be sterilized. The village people sometimes blamed doctors and vented their anger on them. They called out the doctor's name and even spat on the doctor's face. Moreover, the OB/GYN doctor's pay was low, while her work was always hard and dirty.

The spiciness came from the fact that her work was always challenging, partly, she felt, because she had not received sufficient medical training. For example, she did not learn much about internal medicine at the hygiene school. While practicing OB/GYN in her township for more than two decades, she had had only one opportunity to study medicine further, at a county hospital. Moreover, medical appliances were not good, and technical conditions were rather bad.

According to Dr. Li's estimate, forced abortions and sterilizations were frequent. Most women did not tell about being forced to have abortions and did not talk about their pains. Performing abortions and sterilizations on these unwilling women was the most difficult part of Dr. Li's work. According to Dr. Li, because Chinese women must have four B-ultrasound exams yearly to discover whether they are pregnant, cases of forced abortion and sterilization were becoming fewer and fewer. More people were starting to accept the family planning policy.

Dr. Li said she sometimes felt pity (kexi) for the fetuses after late abortions, but in most cases, she did not have much feeling. "After all, family planning is a fundamental national policy. After all, you as an OB/GYN doctor should help the women," she said with a soft sigh.

A City Doctor, One with Limited International Experience

Dr. Wang, in her early or middle thirties, had worked as an OB/GYN physician at the hospital affiliated with a biomedical school for nearly ten years. The city she lived in, a middle-sized one according to Chinese standard, had a population of three or four million. She graduated with a bachelor of medicine degree (equivalent to an M.D. degree in the United States) after having received five years' training at a biomedical school. Dr. Wang described her job as including three areas: gynecology, obstetrics, and the medical service of family planning. She loved her work and loved being a physician. As a child, she had enjoyed wearing a white mask on her mouth and had dreamed of becoming a doctor. She said that, if she had the opportunity to choose her career again, she would choose OB/GYN. Although she liked performing abortions, her favorite task was delivering babies. The most enjoyable moment in her work was when the patient recovered and said "Thank you, doctor." After asking me to stop taping the interview, she told me that it was not uncommon for the patient to give her a "red envelop" (hongbao) (in which some money would be enclosed) before or after the treatment, but she never accepted such gifts.

Dr. Wang estimated that 80–85% of abortions were due to the national population control policy. But she said that she never met any patient who was forced to have an abortion—no case in which the patient was brought in to see her by the family planning official. According to her, late abortions were few because people knew that a late abortion was not good—it could damage the woman's health. More and more people wanted to have one child only, she believed, even when they could get permits for a second one.

Dr. Wang knew very well that abortion was not socially acceptable in some countries, because she once spent a year as a member of a medical team in Tanzania, where abortion was illegal. Doctors in the medical team were ordered not to perform any abortions, however strongly a native Tanzanian woman might request one. But, according to her observation, abortion was practiced there, even though it was illegal. In her view, abortion should be legal; every woman has a right to decide whether to bear a child or not. If a woman decided not to continue her pregnancy, society should allow her to terminate it. For Dr. Wang, this was especially true for Chinese women, since China has so large a population.

The most important reasons for Dr. Wang's belief that abortion should be legal were medical—the safety of proper medical abortions and concern for women's health:

> I think that the woman's demand for an abortion should be respected. If you prohibit abortion, she will go to see the underground abortion doctor. But performing abortion demands certain medical training. If the doctor's medical technique is not good enough, it will bring about many health problems for the patients— various complications, postabortion infections, abnormal menstruation, and menopause. Thus I feel the abortion law in a country such as Tanzania should be loosened. No matter what the law says, the woman usually has an abortion, anyway. Societies should make abortion legal. Then the medical quality of abortion can be improved.

Dr. Wang knew that many people in Tanzania and the West opposed abortion and considered it the same as killing or murdering. She attributed this view to religious beliefs that regarded the fetus as a human being. She disagreed with this belief and was convinced that abortion was not killing because a fetus was not a human being. "I do not have any religious belief. I am a member of the Communist Party. My opinion on this issue may be wrong, but I think that a fetus is not a human being, not a living individual, until it is born." she said.

One aspect of her work that Dr. Wang disliked was the fact that more and more abortions were being sought to terminate pregnancies that resulted from what she called "improper interactions" (*buzhendang jiaowang*), such as premarital or extramarital relationships.

> Now even the young university or college students come to have abortions. Some young unmarried women become pregnant with men who are much older. They have relations with these older men just for money or other favors. I really do not like this. I am not discriminating against them. But I really think their actions are wrong. Some women have had their own families and children, but they still go into affairs with men who are often married and have their own families and children, too. In these situations, I often say something [critical] to the patient.

Dr. Wang dreamed about getting further OB/GYN training in the not-too-distant future at a hospital in a Western country such as the United States. She was making a plan and taking steps such as locating a setting and contacting foreign physicians by mail or e-mail to achieve this goal. Her dream was shared by young doctors in other cities, especially big cities. The dream of going abroad would never occur to a country doctor like Dr. Li, and even if it did, it would almost never be realized.

HELPING THE PATIENT AND SERVING THE COUNTRY

The doctors I interviewed were, first and foremost, physicians. Almost everyone believed that her work, including performing abortions, helped women—her patients—resolve their problems (*bangzhu bingren jiejue wendi*) and relieved their pain and suffering (*jiechu tongku*). One doctor said the following about the nature of her job:

> At the beginning, I did not like the department of OB/GYN a bit. I did not like performing abortions and delivering babies. My favorite specialty is pediatrics. I started to like OB/GYN, including performing abortions, when I realized that the society needs family planning. Although I perform abortions every day, I believe that the main, and more important, responsibility of a doctor is to help the patient reduce the possibility of needing an abortion. Moreover, as an OB/GYN doctor, you can help to relieve the pain and suffering of the woman. The part of my work I favor most is that I can help the woman. Actually, whatever work you are doing, you should always do it as well as you can. If a woman wants to have an abortion, you should perform it. If a woman wants to use a contraceptive [such as an IUD], you should help her with the most appropriate method.

For many doctors, the primary task and most satisfying part of the job were clearly helping women. Quite a few of them compared performing abortion to curing patients or even to delivering babies in the sense that all these services helped women. As one doctor said,

> Whenever I cure disease and the patient recovers, I am very satisfied. I have the same feeling about abortion. The most exciting and happy (*kaixin*) moment is when you successfully deliver a child. At that time, you feel very warmhearted. Sometimes the patient says to me before an abortion: "Doctor, I have put everything in your hands." Pain is sometimes severe, sometimes less so. Some patients are very nervous. One time, the patient even stood up from the bed and told me that it was too painful. Recently, we have started to employ anesthetic. This is good.

Dr. Qin, the only male doctor interviewed in my field research, worked at the hospital of traditional Chinese medicine. He observed that the major reason women sought abortions was that more and more people wanted only one child or none. People know they must take care of the baby if it is born, and some did not want that responsibility. The second most common reason for abortions was that more and more unmarried women were getting pregnant. Yet, in Dr. Qin's words, "the system (*tizhi*) of China has determined that unmarried motherhood is not a possibility." Other reasons observed by Dr. Qin for women to desire abortion included failure of contraception and the possibility of defects in the fetus due to medicine. In all cases, performing abortions helped the woman. As he said, "If an unmarried woman is pregnant or if the fetus is defective, how can I not help the woman? Performing abortions usually helps the patient solve her problems." As a male OB/GYN doctor, Dr. Qin felt strange at first because male OB/GYN doctors are so rare in China. Later, he realized that whatever a doctor does helps patients and relieves their pain and suffering. He also realized that one can find enjoyment and satisfaction whatever one's job is. Dr. Qin said the most enjoyable aspect of his work was curing infertility. He believed that curing infertility constituted one of the strengths of traditional Chinese medicine.

Mainly due to their concern for women's health, it was not uncommon for doctors to persuade the patient who sought an abortion *not* to have it. The previous chapter indicates that Chinese women sometimes have abortions due to eugenic reasons, such as fearing the fetus might be ill as a result of medication taken during the early pregnancy. A fifty-five-year-old female professor in family planning research, who participated in a research project conducted by a group of Chinese scholars on client and provider perspectives on abortion, stated:

> I oppose induced abortion strongly, except when needed for medical reasons. If a married woman is pregnant, I hope the woman can deliver the baby. In the outpatient family planning clinic, there are many reasons given for having an induced abortion: 1) to work, study, or travel abroad; or 2) concern for possible genetic weakness in the foetus. In Shanghai city proper, pregnant women will terminate their pregnancy for eugenic reasons if they are ill with some minor diseases or if they take some medicine for these diseases during the early gestational period that they think will affect the foetus. Our ob-gyn doctors try to persuade them not to have induced abortion, because most these induced abortions for so-called eugenic reasons are not necessary. . . . The possibility of complication from prior abortion is not high for most women, but it is really sad for the women who do experience them. So our ob-gyn doctors and family planning staff should prevent excessive pregnancy termination for eugenic reasons. (Quoted in Zhou et al. 1999: 237–38)

For many of the thirty doctors interviewed, another major source of joy from their professional work constituted direct participation in the national birth control program. They, like Dr. Ying, about whom I write in the introduction, were proud of providing the medical service on which the national birth control program depends. They believed that, in doing so, they were contributing greatly to Chinese society. They seemed to support the population control policy from their hearts. One city doctor stated: "One of the greatest satisfactions in my work is that I am able to help the national family planning, which is a fundamental policy of our country. The program is beneficial not only to the society and the whole country but also to the family and the individual woman." In other words, many doctors believed that, in doing their jobs, including performing of abortions, they were serving both the individual patient and the whole county.

Because of the political sensitivity of the topic, I tried at first to focus on Chinese attitudes toward abortion per se and to avoid directly studying people's opinions about and experiences of birth control policies. At that time, I believed the sensitive, respectful thing to do in the course of field research was to avoid asking anyone about his or her view or experiences with the population policy and family planning program unless she or he introduced the topic. Yet, on their own initiative, several doctors expressed strong support for the national family planning program. For whatever reasons, not one of the thirty doctors raised any doubt about the necessity for population control and the family planning policy.

Like Dr. Ying, quite a few doctors strongly agreed with the official point of view that Western countries, especially the United States, had interfered too much in Chinese birth control policies. The following quotation from Dr. Dang, an official physician (she was both a practicing OB/GYN doctor and a Party officer—the director of a clinic for child and maternal health in a county town), is representative:

The American view that abortion is killing is based on religious beliefs. It is wrong. The United States has interfered too much in Chinese internal affairs. It interferes too much in the issues of human rights in China. It interferes with almost everything in China. As for the United States, the wise action would be not to interfere in any Chinese internal affairs. Overpopulation, a poor foundation to start with, an undeveloped economy, and the poor health and genetic quality of the population—these are realities in China. Therefore, bearing many children is disadvantageous not only to the country, but also to the family.

Her opinion about this matter, far from original, restated the official standpoint that appeared repeatedly in internal Party documents and government-controlled mass media. Yet, in my judgment, this officer–physician believed what she was saying. In fact, she asked me to do something to change the Westerners' negative attitudes toward the Chinese family planning program. Dr. Dang said to me sincerely and seriously: "You should do your best to let the outside world know the Chinese reality. Let the Westerners know that they should not interfere with the internal affairs of China, including the family planning policy."

Dr. Dang further asserted that the family planning program was based on voluntarism, as the official documents have claimed, and not on force. She also pointed out that family planning work was less and less difficult. Her county's population growth registered a decrease in 1996. She predicted that in five to ten years, family planning would no longer be a problem because the desire to bear many children was growing weaker and weaker among people under forty years old. Even in the countryside, the old belief of passing on one's bloodline was becoming less and less popular.

Dr. Tian, a country doctor, felt that the foreign criticism of China's family planning had caused China to lose face and dignity. She viewed China and the United States as though the two states were two individuals. She stated: "The United States alleges that the Chinese practice of abortion is a violation of human rights. As a result, China loses its dignity (*zuobuqi ren,* cannot be respected like a decent person). The United States attacks us, but we are not able to say anything about the United States."

As a consequence of their strong and genuine support for the principle behind the population control policies, most doctors seemed to be very happy and satisfied with their work. They believed not only that they were helping women by resolving their problems and relieving their pain and suffering, but also that they were serving society by making the national family planning program possible and by actually participating in the good cause of slowing the rapid population growth. They viewed these ends as necessary social goods for China as a country and for the overwhelming majority of individual Chinese. Rarely did they report any moral conflict about what they did every day.

However, several OB/GYN physicians expressed that sometimes they could not serve the individual patient and the country at the same time. In other words, they felt that these two duties were not always in harmony. It was this disharmony that led Dr. Li, the country doctor whose personal story has been presented in the previous section, to use the four words about taste—sweet, sour, bitter, and spicy—to describe and summarize her experiences.

The doctors addressed the possible and actual moral conflicts they faced in different ways. One approach that doctors adopted was to ignore that there were any real conflicts and to believe that they could always serve the interests of both the country and the individual women. They did so by accepting and internalizing the official reasoning that the interests of the country were always much more important than those of individuals. According to this dominant ideology, the individual was defined as "the little me" (*xiaowo*) and the country as "the big me" (*dawo*). The interests of individuals should be always subject to the interests of the country (*xiaowo fucong dawo*). Whenever the interests of the individual patient and the country were in conflict, it was obvious to which the priority should be given. To understand properly this communitarian or holistic or even totalitarian way of thinking in contemporary China, it is important to know that, as pointed out in chapter 2, the terms "country," "people," and "society" are never clearly distinguished from the entities "state," "government," and "the Party" in the ordinary Chinese language or even in the intellectual circles. The official propaganda always insists that the latter represent the fundamental interests of the former. Like many other Chinese, the doctors I interviewed very often used all these terms interchangeably. For the OB/GYN doctors, to serve the country thus meant to actively participate in implementing the national birth control policy without questioning it.

"Not questioning, just doing it" seemed to be the most common attitude the doctors adopted to cope with their uneasy feelings when conflicts arose between the duty to the birth control policy and the duty to the individual patient. It seemed that in general most OB/GYN doctors did not reflect critically on their medical practices, including performing abortions. Rather, they treated performing abortion as nothing more than just a routine part of their professional job.

However, there were a few doctors, unlike Drs. Ying, Wang, and Dang, for whom performing abortions was not simply a good thing to do for the individual women and the aborted fetus. Nevertheless, though they had uneasy feelings at first, they finally reconciled their feelings to their acts by saying to themselves something such as "it is a good job, one should just do it and be happy with it." One urban physician described her experience in these words:

> When I performed an abortion for the first time, I felt pity or something like it for the aborted fetus. Later on, as I performed more and more abortions, I started to believe that what I was doing was helping the woman resolve problems. If a doctor does not help her, who else will do so? China has so many people, and the economy and living conditions such as housing are so bad. A doctor should treat it [abortion] as a regular [medical] operation. [If you see the woman] as a person who is sick, it will be very natural [for a doctor to help]. Just as when someone is ill, I help her to resolve her [health] problem. In this way, your mind will be very much in peace; you will not think about other things.

For a few other doctors, like Dr. Zhang, whose personal story will be presented later in detail, the conflict between professional duties to the state and to individual patients can be so intense that they simply cannot "just do it" and be happy with it. Since rebellion or even resistance was often too risky to be an option, they therefore felt there is no better alternative (*meiyou biede banfa*) to complying with the requirements of the state policy and accepting the reality.

Whether or not doctors felt the moral conflict, whether or not they could genuinely reconcile some of their uneasy feelings, all the doctors interviewed performed abortions as a routine part of their professional work.

Some are truly proud of what they were doing, while most just did it without questioning. A few felt that they were forced to perform abortion, but that there was no way out. Even this last group seemed to believe that the pregnant woman was better off if they, as trained OB/GYN doctors, performed the abortions.

FEELINGS OR LACK OF FEELING ABOUT THE FETUS

Like the situation of asking women about their feelings on the fetus, it was not easy for me to raise this issue to the doctors, since the question itself could suggest a kind of moral criticism on abortion and their professional work in general. In fact, one urban physician responded to the question in a defensive and indirect way, that is, by explicitly opposing the view of treating abortion as killing or murdering. Abortion was emphasized to have nothing to do with killing a human being, especially if it is performed before the twenty-eighth week of pregnancy: "Seeing abortion as equal to killing or murdering is too one-sided. We must first of all control the rapid growth of population. If survival is impossible, how can we talk about anything else. Besides, most abortions are performed before the twenty-eighth week. It is not killing a human to perform an abortion before the twenty-eighth week." Fortunately, almost all doctors interviewed, except for a couple, had shown to me that they knew my motivation—interest in what they personally felt, rather than wanting to make any moral judgment. Doctors in cities and countryside responded to this hard question in a very friendly manner, that is, straightforwardly, telling me what they felt about the topic.

As among people surveyed and women interviewed, there were different attitudes toward fetal life among doctors. On the one hand, the majority of them reported little feeling about the fetus in general and about an aborted fetus in particular. On the other hand, some doctors did express concerns, even serious ones, on the moral status of the fetus.

Obviously, a kind of silence or lack of feelings existed among many physicians. Once, I interviewed two doctors together. Upon being asked about their feelings toward the aborted fetus, one of them laughed: "Nothing (*meiyou shenmo*). [I] have already become accustomed to this (*xiyi weichang la*). I have never thought about it [the aborted fetus]." I turned to the other doctor, who smiled and nodded to express agreement with what the first had said.

Dr. Liu's was another "silent" situation. Dr. Liu had been an OB/GYN doctor for two decades and performed hundreds of abortions—dozens of them at the middle or late stage. She practiced medicine mainly in the city. Several times, she had been sent to the countryside as a member of a family planning work team—sterilizing men and women, inserting IUDs, and performing abortions. Asked how she felt about the fetuses she had aborted, she replied with a calm and certain tone: "I do not have any feeling. Should I feel something?"

The following is a portion of an interview with a city doctor. What struck me was not so much the content itself but the doctor's comfortable and easy tone in speaking:

Q: What does the aborted material look like?

A: Usually, it is just a mound of fine hair. To find something that has been formed [into human shape] is comparatively rare.

Q: What do you feel when you see [the aborted material]?

A: I do not have any feeling. If I perform the abortion successfully, I do not have any feeling such as "Oh, how is the child?" Everything is fine as long as the pregnant woman's health is satisfactory.

Q: How is the aborted fetus treated [after abortion]?

A: It is thrown into the trash can.

According to several physicians, the related regulations required that the aborted fetuses should finally be burned in the hospital's incinerator.

Of course, there were doctors who had feelings, sometimes rather strong ones, about the fetus. They felt pity (*kexi*) toward the aborted fetus because it was potentially a child, a human being. One city doctor said: "Sometimes I feel it is a pity. I know a doctor who once had an abortion herself. She often talks about how old and how big the child would be had it not been for the abortion."

One doctor said that how she felt about the fetus depended on whether abortion was early or late and why the woman had it. In other words, she did not want to answer the question generally, without discrimination. She put it this way:

How do I feel about the aborted fetus? That depends on what kind of abortion. I, of course, feel it is a pity in the case of a delivered abortion. It also depends on what reasons led the women to have the delivered abortion [delivery of a live fetus]. Some have it because of the family planning policy, some because of the bad relationship of the couple, and some because of their personal preference.

Many doctors felt differently when the abortion was late. Although many had not much feeling for the fetus aborted at the early stage of pregnancy, quite a few felt uneasy or sorry for the fetus aborted at the middle or late stage. It was perceived that the fetus at the early stage, unlike that at the later stages, was not yet a "formed" human being. Dr. Jiang, a city doctor, stated this thoughtfully:

The fetus has not formed into a human shape when early abortion is performed. You cannot see anything but a piece of tissue. I usually do not have much feeling if the abortion is early. But the fetus (baby) is complete when coming out through partial-birth abortion at the middle or late pregnancy. In this case, I do not feel comfortable. The pregnant woman does not feel comfortable, either. If one has to have an abortion, the sooner, the better. It is better not to have partial-birth abortion. I always feel uneasy with this. One should not have late abortion without strong reasons. I do not know why and I do not know how to say it. A piece of tissue and a formed fetus [baby] are very different after all. The fetus at the middle and late stage of pregnancy has been formed [into a complete human shape].

Dr. Jiang further distinguished between the fetal tissue, the formed fetus, the baby at birth, and the child one would raise. Thus, she disagreed that abortion is killing a human life:

The child knows how to cry, how to laugh, and how to respond to you. But what is the early fetus? It is nothing but a piece of tissue. From a newspaper article I once read, I know that some view abortion as taking a human life. I rarely hear my patient say so. No one else told me that abortion is like taking a life and killing a human being. Anyway, I do not agree with this view.

Some cases of middle- or late-stage abortions affected the doctors dramatically because the aborted fetus was in the "lively shape of a human being." Dr. Liu, a country doctor, told of her own experience:

I was on duty for an absent doctor. It was in July, the season of rush harvesting and rush planting (*shuangquan*). Her pregnancy was already four months, but she did not want the child because she believed that she had had enough children. When she came, the fetus was already dead. I used the forceps to grip the fetus. It took me quite a while. I really felt very bad about this. That big, a human being! A lively shape of a human being (*huoshengsheng de yige renyang*). I was very scared.

Dr. Yao, another country doctor, told about not feeling sorry for the aborted fetus, especially if the abortion was performed for the sake of the family planning program, because population control was a fundamental and strategic national policy. "I have got used to it. I do not feel sorry. The fetus is dead, but I am not scared of it a bit. A doctor should not feel anything else if the abortion, even late abortion, is for carrying out the family planning policy." Naturally, she did not have any feeling about the aborted material at the early stage.[1]

Some doctors who felt sorry about aborted fetuses at the beginning of their careers gradually lost the sense of pity upon getting used to performing abortions. A doctor told me that she had become a "machine": "At first, I was sometimes curious and often felt sorry. But now, I have become a machine. Nothing will be strange to you if you have continually seen one strange thing after another." From what she said and from her gestures as she was speaking, I could sense that she was not as comfortable as she wanted to be.

Some doctors interviewed seemed to be ambivalent on the moral status of the fetus. As indicated in the survey results presented in chapter 4, the responses of the medical professionals to most items in the questionnaire were not markedly different from those of laypersons. But in general, fewer medical professionals than laypersons believe in the existence of a fetal soul (14% vs. 41%) and saw abortion as tantamount to taking a life (19% vs. 40%), killing a newborn (14% vs. 37%), and killing a human being (7% vs. 32%). According to a research conducted by a group of Chinese scholars who surveyed 250 physicians—general practitioners, surgeons, gynecologists, pediatricians— working in eight different hospitals in Shanghai and Xi'an on stem-cell and other fetal research (Qiu et al. 2003), the portion who showed concerns on fetal life seemed to be much higher. In that study, 50.8% of respondents disagreed with the statement "The embryo is not a person so that one needs not to worry about whether it is dead or not," with 35.6% agreeing; 28.0% disagreed that "The embryo within 14 days is not a human but a common biological cell," with 58.4% agreeing. At the same time, 24.4% agreed that "Life begins from embryo so that the fetal experiment is murdering," with 60.4 agreeing. Among many other things, these differences shown in different surveys might suggest that a significant portion of medical professionals are uncertain on the moral status of fetal life.

Several Chinese physicians from the pilot study conducted in Texas insisted that there are situations in which abortion is permissible and even necessary, even when they believed that human life begins at conception. One male doctor who practiced medicine in China said:

> From the perspective of human biology, human life starts at conception. Fertilization is the starting point of life. A zygote is a life. But a zygote doesn't have the same value as a child. It really doesn't make any difference *when* the fetus is aborted—it's impossible to say that *this* month we'd be killing the fetus, but last month we wouldn't be. Killing a person is too sweeping a concept. One kills people in battle and executes criminals. Aborting a fetus is not the same as a murder committed by a criminal. It's not easy, actually it's very difficult, to say whether aborting an unborn "infant" is killing or not. The woman should have the right to make the decision whether she wants the baby or not.

Another male doctor working in China had a similarly nuanced view:

> The fetus can be seen as a human being even before birth. Physiology and ethics may have different perspectives. Medical doctors have different opinions. As far as I know, in Hong Kong as well as Shenzhen, the fetus is counted as a

human being at the sixteenth week of pregnancy. The zygote is the starting point of human life. But whether abortion is killing depends on circumstances. One shouldn't sever everything with one cut.

For one female informant from the pilot study with a medical background, however, the physiological development of the fetus was the crucial factor:

Human life starts sometime during pregnancy. The view that the fetus is not a human life may provide a pretext for someone who is determined to take a life. And the woman has her own right to make a choice. Nevertheless, one shouldn't abort the fetus too late, no later than the twenty-eighth week—when the fetus can live independently from the mother's womb. Aborting the fetus after the twenty-eighth week is inhumane.

Similar uncertainty was expressed by a woman who, as an OB/GYN doctor, performed abortions in China and is now a biomedical researcher:

It isn't clear when the fetus becomes a human being. This is not just a medical but also an ethical and social question. Medicine has no clear-cut answer. Personally, I believe that the standard should be when the fetus starts to "think." So the electrical pulse from the fetus's brain could be used as a measurement to decide.

AN EXTRAORDINARY BUT LOST DOCTOR

In their professional lives, most doctors interviewed seemed either to feel no moral conflicts in performing abortion or to maintain a satisfactory feeling in balancing their different duties. However, this was not always the case. There was at least one doctor, Dr. Zhang Hua, who was not just doing her job as her profession and the state or society required. Rather, she admitted that she felt "lost" as she reflected on her routine work in general and the task of performing abortions in particular.

Among thirty intensive interviews with doctors, this one with Dr. Zhang was the longest—it lasted more than three hours. Moreover, she was the most quick-spoken and eloquent narrator. It was a hot summer afternoon, and there was no air conditioner in her office (or anywhere in the building), only an electric fan. With beads of sweat on her forehead, she told her own stories and her patients' stories, recounted her experiences, and gave her opinions.

Dr. Zhang, in her middle or late thirties, had been an OB/GYN doctor for sixteen years. She first worked at a clinic for maternal and infant care for several years. Then she was transferred to the Institute for the Science and Technology of Family Planning in a southern coastal city. She was recently promoted to be a president of a general hospital. Besides some administrative work, she saw patients every day and conducted research projects. At the time of the interview, she had just started to conduct a research project, sponsored by a national governmental agency and a provincial committee, on the contraceptive behaviors of the people in the city. She had become a Party member when she was a medical student. She was married and had a child. In the eyes of others, Dr. Zhang was a very successful professional woman.

Like some other doctors, she had not chosen OB/GYN at first. She loved general surgery, but her medical teachers had told her that surgery was too physically exhausting for her. They had suggested that OB/GYN was best, for OB/GYN practice was not too tiring, yet still provided the opportunity to perform surgical operations. Unlike most other doctors, who basically enjoyed their specialty and were satisfied with their work even though they had not chosen OB/GYN themselves, Dr. Zhang felt that she was in the wrong specialty. Although she had many reasons to be satisfied with her career, she described herself as "lost." "Now I sometimes tell my former classmates and friends that I feel that I have chosen the wrong specialty. I tell them that I am lost and cannot find myself. I do not know what I am doing every day or what I should do. I just feel that I should not be an OB/GYN doctor. But now it is too late for me to change it." Dr. Zhang did not directly address why she felt lost about her work and career in the interview. From the stories, experiences, and views she shared, her feelings appeared to come from three sources. First, she had witnessed so much suffering in her patients in her clinical work and seemed to be much more sensitive to this suffering than many of her peers. Second, even though she never questioned the necessity of population control in China and the national family planning program, she did not support the program without reservation, as most of the other doctors interviewed did, especially the measures employed in carrying out this policy. Third, she believed that the fetus was "a lively life," and she displayed more sentiment toward the aborted fetus (or baby, in her view) than many other doctors did.

I will begin with the last of these three factors—her feelings about and attitude toward the fetus. Dr. Zhang believed that a fetus was a life, a lively life, an unmatured human being, and that it became a human being when it formed into a human shape. Visual perception played a crucial role in her judging when a fetus was a human being. For her, early and late abortions were totally different. She was the only doctor who used the term "morality" or "justice" (*daoyi*) in talking about abortion and the fetus.

> Before it has been formed, [the material that comes out in an abortion] is just a roll of ground meat (*ruo tantan*). After it has been formed, when you can see the fetus's nose, eyes, arms, and legs, the fetus becomes a human being. It just has not grown up yet. From the angle of morality and justice (*daoyi*), the fetus

is a life, a formed life, a lively life. After the ten months' pregnancy, it will be complete [a human being]. Through abortion, you abort it alive at its early stage [of development]. I always felt that to have an abortion after the formation of the fetus is a pity.

Yet, regardless of what she felt about the fetus, Dr. Zhang had to perform abortions at all stages because this was a part of her job. "No matter how much pity you feel for the poor fetus, sometimes you have to perform the abortion. There is no way out (*meiyou banfa*). It is much better to have an abortion before the fetus has a human shape. Every day, we see these materials [aborted fetuses]. It is a sight we do not like to see. If someone has to have an abortion, the sooner, the better." Here, the plural pronoun "we" in the Chinese context means "I," partly because people in contemporary China do not like to say "I," even in expressing their own individual opinions. They are accustomed to using "we," even when it actually refers to "I."

Dr. Zhang usually lets the abortion patient see the aborted materials. She does this to warn her patients that abortion is bad because of the possible negative influence on the patient's physical health. Moreover, although she did not clearly state it, she shows her patients the aborted materials for the sake of the fetus. Actually, in talking about the fetus, Dr. Zhang frequently used the term child (*xiaohai*), and always did so when talking about middle- or late-stage abortions, rather than the general medical term fetus (*taier*). She said:

> Just the day before yesterday, I showed the hands of an aborted fetus to the patient. I said to her: "You see, the hands are this big now." Several days ago, I performed an abortion of an eighty- to ninety-day fetus using an abortion drug. The aborted fetus looked well like a human being. Some days ago at noon, I performed another abortion, the child (*xiaohai*) was probably fifteen centimeters long. It was complete, and the human body had all formed. The eyes, nose, hand, legs, and sex all could be seen. When seeing these . . . I really cannot explain why I did what I did [showed the aborted materials to the patient]. I just wanted to show it [aborted fetus] to her. This was a warning. If you cannot carry your pregnancy to term, you should come sooner. I wanted to remind her of the importance of contraception. She should see a doctor as soon as her period does not come and she suspects she may be pregnant. Postponing too long is not good for her health. The risk associated with the abortion becomes higher, too.

Dr. Zhang hardly considered abortion, especially late abortion, an acceptable method of birth control. She preferred contraception for this purpose. "Whenever a woman comes to request an abortion, I always ask her why she did not take contraceptive measures," she said. She could not understand why so many women do not take these measures, since many contraceptive methods are available to them. She commented critically that the current practice in China is "not good enough on this issue." She suggested that the authorities should take more effective steps to make sure every woman of childbearing age uses contraceptive measures.

Dr. Zhang disapproved of the practice of throwing aborted fetuses into trash cans. Asked how the aborted fetuses were treated, she said: "They should be sent to the burn oven. But sometimes they are just thrown into the trash cans. Sometimes they are running away in the sewer."

Dr. Zhang had experienced two events that still filled her with horror—being asked to cut off the heads of several aborted "children" for scientific research and witnessing an infanticide. She narrated what happened in the first event and how she felt about it.

Soon after I started to work at the general hospital as an OB/GYN doctor, a good friend and classmate of mine asked me to get several heads of children—the heads of children after delivered abortion—for scientific research. At first, I did not think anything about it and said "yes" without any hesitation. After all, there were many late abortions then. The classmate needed the heads of children aborted at six months or later. Since there were many delivered abortions, I took two children's heads to give them to her/him (*ta*).[2] I have a very deep impression about this event. Sometimes I feel what I did was not moral. You see this child . . . a good . . . you cannot say a good child since it had no life anymore. But I felt great pain in my heart (*feizhang xingtong*). After that, I had nightmares for several nights. I am not sure what the nightmares were, something like the ghosts (*gui*) coming to grasp me or something else. They were frightening nightmares.

Later, the classmate told me that two were not enough and two more were needed. I remember that I got one more for her/him. I remember clearly that several aborted children were all put into buckets to be sent to the burning oven of the hospital. I got one head for her/him and put it aside. I felt that I had conducted a deed that would weigh on my conscience (*kuixishi*). I did have this feeling. I did not dare to tell anybody. But a second thought told me that my classmate/friend needed these for the scientific experiments, not for something else. This comforted me a little bit. As time passed, I felt a bit better gradually. But it was always there, in my mind. I have always remembered it. I always felt it seems. . . .

Now that event has passed for fourteen or fifteen years. I was very young then and like a newborn calf who is not afraid of the tiger (*chusheng zhidu bu pa fu*). If now you asked me to do the same thing—cutting the head off an aborted child with scissors and knife—I would not dare to put my hands on it, even though I once dissected corpses and even though I am not afraid to use a knife on living human bodies for surgical operations. But now, I would not say "yes." After all these years' experience and from the outrage of morality and justice [*daoyi*], I. . . .

Two common circumstances led to late-month abortions, Dr. Zhang said. First, there were the unmarried teenage girls who did not know they were pregnant, thinking instead they had a tumor or something like that, until the doctor discovered the truth. The second common occurrence was women who knew they were pregnant but wanted to have the children, and hid their pregnancies intentionally. It seemed to Dr. Zhang that middle- or late-stage abortions—abortions after the fetus was formed into a human shape—usually had a very negative influence on the pregnant woman, including great psychological pain. Dr. Zhang always tried to avoid performing late abortions, but sometimes she had to do them.

> Some women come to the clinic for an abortion with a pregnancy of eight or nine months. If she does not come with the family planning official, we [I] usually do not perform a delivered [live-birth] abortion. If she comes with the family planning official, we have no way out but performing the operation. In most situations of late abortion, the aborted babies are alive. We have to employ medical measures. We just wait for the appearance of the baby's head [at the opening of womb], then inject some medicine into the skull. We really cannot bear to see these children, but we have to do what is required. Otherwise, we will break the rule and be punished. From the humane perspective, we are unwilling to do what we have to do. But we are not allowed to have a live baby after an abortion. [Another doctor who was in the interviewing room interrupted at this moment and said, "By all means, it cannot be alive."] But, sometimes the baby is alive despite all the injected medicine. It seems that the child (*haizi*) of a late abortion has great vitality. It was not unusual for a child after a regular delivery to not survive despite medical rescue measures. But the life force of these children [undergoing delivered abortion] is very strong. I have a true story.

At this point, Dr. Zhang went on to tell about the second event that still fills her with horror.

> It was an abortion of late stage. The child was alive after the abortion. The child burst out crying, making the sound "wa-wa." The lying-in woman raised her head: "Doctor, the child is alive?" I could not tell her the truth and just asked her to lie down on the bed without moving. I told her this had nothing to do with her. But the lying-in woman sat up desperately and begged me. "Doctor, the child is alive. Please leave it alone." I replied to her, "You lie down." Then I told the nurse on duty to fetch Dr. Guang, the supervisor of the department. I knew how to kill the child, but I just could not put my hand on it.
>
> Soon the nurse came in with Dr. Guang. Dr. Guang was a senior doctor. As soon as I saw Dr. Guang, I said to her, "I will leave this to you." She replied, "You cannot do it in this way. The child was delivered by you. You cannot deliver it at this moment and then be out of charge of the mess. I will get a bucket and fill it with water. We drown the child to death by putting her head down into the water first." She got a bucket of water and put the child into it.
>
> After about half an hour, Dr. Guang drew the child out of the bucket and wanted to send it to the burning oven of the hospital. But the child got back its breath again and burst into crying. The life force of the child was too indomitable.

Even being submerged in the water for half an hour could not kill her. I really felt
that there was something very strange here. I said to Dr. Guang that I had to leave.
But she did not allow me. She said to me, "I still need to do something." She then
filled the washing basin in the room, which was bigger than the bucket, and put
the child into the water again for another half an hour.

After all this, I did not use the washing basin for a long time. For a long time,
I felt terrible.

Immediately after telling this story, she made the statement about her feeling
of being lost that is quoted above.

What should be emphasized here is that Dr. Zhang's sympathetic feelings
and high sensitivity to the fetus, especially aborted ones, were expressed in
secular terms—sense perception or human sensation. She had been a member of the Communist Party for years and had no particular religious belief.
Furthermore, she did not reveal any belief in the supernatural, such as the
spirit of the aborted fetus. Although she mentioned the word "ghost" (*gui*)
when asked about her nightmare following the cutting of heads from the
aborted fetuses for her friend, she emphatically did not believe that the fetuses would become ghosts after being aborted. (I do not think Dr. Zhang
knew the ancient story presented in chapter 3, in which the woman who had
sold abortion drugs for a living had a deathbed nightmare that the ghosts of
the unborn children were attacking her.)

The second source of Dr. Zhang's feeling "lost" in her career appeared to
be her reservations about the means used in the state family planning program. Like almost all doctors I interviewed, she realized that the size of
China's population needed to be controlled if China was to prosper. But, like
quite a few of them, she had serious reservations about the *means* government authorities used to achieve this goal. Dr. Zhang was outspoken on this
issue. She admitted to me that she had had second thoughts about some of
the "family planning" operations she had performed in the past. She did not
question the necessity of controlling China's population or the legitimacy of
the state family planning program. In fact, she considered limitations on people's procreative choices the business of the state and not, in her own terms,
that of an "ordinary OB/GYN doctor" such as herself. Nevertheless, she was
not entirely comfortable with the methods the state employed to achieve its
goals. In particular, she was uncomfortable with the role she had played and
was asked to play in controlling other women's bodies. As an example, she
related the following situation to me.

Something happened, and I do not know whether it was right or wrong. Some
time ago, women in the countryside were compelled to go group by group by
automobile to the hospital in the city for IUD insertion, abortion, and sterilization. The family planning cadres surrounded them. They guarded the gate out
of the ward. They even watched the women when they went to the bathroom

because they were afraid [the] women would run away. Then, I performed many "family planning" operations [that is, abortions and sterilizations].

In retrospect, what bothered Dr. Zhang most about the operations she performed was that no attempt was made to secure the women's informed consent for sterilization or abortion. She was particularly troubled by her participation in a coercive late abortion in which the pregnant woman had no say, commenting that:

> The reality is that the pregnant woman has no rights if the family planning official requires her to have a late abortion. The woman cannot say whether she wants it or not. She cannot do anything but accept. However, I felt, . . . I do not know how to say it. In present and new-fashioned terms, you should at least get consent from the woman herself (*zhengde benren tongyi*), let her know beforehand (*geita dage zhaohu*). Yet, in that situation [in which the pregnant woman was required by the family planning official to have the abortion], no one got consent from her.

Fortunately for Dr. Zhang, for the women on whom she performs abortions and sterilizations, and for Chinese women in general, local and state authorities have begun to give Chinese women more say in the kind of birth control methods they use. Since the 1990s, some social experiments have been carried out giving rural women more freedom to choose the method of birth control most congenial to them. The experiment is called "the village of informed choice" (*zhiqing xuanze cun*). Dr. Zhang applauded these experiments, hoping to see them expanded.

> Now there have been some experiments regarding informed choice in some villages where people choose their methods of birth control. After bearing a [first] child, people are allowed to choose for themselves what they think is the best method. Even after the second child, sterilization is not forced on people. This practice gives people some degree of freedom of choice (*yiding de xuanze ziyou*). While some experiments have been conducted in some villages, unfortunately, this practice is not fully under way yet.

Although Chinese women still do not have much choice about participating in the effort to control China's population, it is encouraging to know that local and state authorities are beginning to recognize people's need to have as much freedom as the constraints of necessity permit.

The third probable reason for Dr. Zhang's feeling lost was that she had witnessed so much suffering in her patients. Medical professionals deal with disease, illness, dying, and death every day. In their routine work, they always encounter and witness suffering—physical, psychological, and social. Some professionals are more sensitive to their patients' suffering and life stories than are others. Dr. Zhang was extremely sensitive to her patients' suffering and told me several tragic stories of her patients. Three are reported in the last chapter. Described as "softhearted" or "kindhearted" (*xinchanghuo*) by her colleague who was present during portions of the interview, Dr. Zhang tried her best to reduce the physical pain of her patients.

As a doctor, you must be responsible for yourself, your duty, and for your patient in every operation. In proceeding with an abortion operation, you should do your best to calm your patient. You should chat (*lalagua*, an idiom in the area that refers to informal talking) with her and ask her something about her family and her work. The purpose of this is to distract the patient's attention from the operation. In this way, the operation often ends with the patient feeling no pain.

Dr. Zhang also tried her utmost to alleviate the psychological pain her patients might have. She used the term *tianzi* (the heavenly duty) in her narrative.

To their patients, some older doctors and nurses are likely to ask, "Are you married? If not, what happened?" Along with the openness of the society, there are more and more of these cases. We doctors and nurses are not surprised any more after we see many strange things. Most of them come to see the doctor for an abortion operation after they have already endured a lot of pressures. According to my view, one should avoid any improper words. This is wrong according to the ethics of the medical profession.

If a woman comes for an operation, it is the heavenly duty (*tianzi*) of the doctor to do a safe one. As a result, we [I] usually do not ask the patient this kind of question. If they talk on their own initiative, we just listen carefully. It is a psychological vent for her if the patient talks about it. As her physician, a doctor should give her patient some comfort through words and gestures. If the patient has something that would be awkward or embarrassing to mention to other people, the doctor should not ask.

The old generation of doctors and nurses are often harsh to unmarried women. They would be even harsher to them if they were their own children. Even though the way those doctors and nurses admonish and warn the unmarried young women is harsh, their intention is good. They do so for the good of the patient, the patient herself. But all this just increases the psychological pain of the patient.

Dr. Zhang sensed that the term "patient" (*binren*) was not a very appropriate word to refer to the woman who comes to her for matters of family planning: "We are doing a profession or a specialty called 'family planning.' Almost all the people we contact every day are those who need abortions, IUDs, or other services of family planning. We may be able to call them the 'patients' only from the angle of medicine."

In the following case recounted by Dr. Zhang, a young woman could not get a permit to bear a child because she had married a middle-age widower who already had one. While deeply sympathetic to the woman and believing that she should be allowed to continue her pregnancy, Dr. Zhang performed an abortion on her, anyway.

This happened last week. A young woman who looked to be in her early twenties told us that she was twenty-nine. We felt she was not telling the truth about her age. The man who accompanied her to the clinic was in his middle forties. We thought the man was not her husband. We did not ask more questions. We knew we should perform the abortion. The girl was far from calm. She was not willing to have the abortion. She was not even willing to answer questions such as when her last menstrual period was. Then the man came and answered questions about her medical history for her. When the man took a note from us to the cashier to pay, I asked her who this man was. The girl cried at once and told me he was her *duixiang* (husband or boyfriend). I said to her: "The ages of you two are rather different." She replied: "He has remarried, but I am married for the first time. His wife died a couple of years ago." I guessed the girl might come from a small town or from the countryside to work in this city. But she said that was not so. The present policy is that a couple cannot have a second child if one of them has already had a child. The girl was really miserable and very unhappy. When she had first come to schedule an abortion several days before, she had been drinking very much.

Dr. Zhang was sympathetic to her and tried to comfort her. But all she could do as a doctor was persuade her to accept the misery.

She cried badly. I told her that she should not be like this. I said something to her like this: "Since you have married him, you must accept everything about him. He has had a child and you thus cannot have your own. You also must accept this." Sometimes, we will let the woman go home if we feel it is possible for her to continue the pregnancy. But in this case, it was impossible. If he had divorced and the court had given the child to his ex-wife, the man could father another child. But the situation now was that his wife had died. Therefore, the girl had to have an abortion, no matter how unwilling she was. Since it was impossible for her to carry the pregnancy to term, the sooner she had the abortion, the better. A late abortion would be more damaging for her. All we could do was persuade her to accept the fact. Actually, we could see that the man was very good and caring toward her. Even though we sympathized with her, we as doctors could not do anything. We had no other alternative (*meiyou biede banfa*). We could only persuade her, try to comfort her, and be more careful in the abortion operation. She chose to use the abortion drug. But the drug abortion was not complete. Then we had to perform vacuum suction.

In this case, the doctor experienced a difficult moral conflict—between her deep sympathy for her patient and her obligation to carry out what the population policy required. Both the patient and the doctor experienced helplessness—the feeling of having no way out except by complying and accepting the reality.

In sum, although Dr. Zhang said she did not know why she felt lost in her professional life, her stories clearly pointed to three sources for her discomfort: her sympathy for the fetus, her reservation about some methods employed in the population control program, and her high sensitivity to her patients' suffering. I do not intend to suggest that these thoughts and emotions constitute a sufficient explanation for the lost feeling of a doctor in her middle or late thirties and in the middle of her career. A psychologist or psychiatrist might consider a general theory of midlife crisis or phases in the development of an individual's personality as an important tool for making sense of Dr. Zhang's feeling lost. It is impossible for anyone to give a sufficient explanation for another person's deep feeling about her or his career and life. Nevertheless, the three factors discussed above can be interpreted as significant "moral" values that had contributed to the doctor's deep perplexity about her own work and her feeling of having lost herself. In other words, Dr. Zhang felt lost because she could not find a satisfactory balance between the different duties in her professional life.

CONCLUSION

Many doctors interviewed felt very satisfied and even proud about their work because they believed that they were not only helping other women—assisting their patients in solving their problems and relieving their pain and suffering—but also serving the whole society by providing medical services that made the national birth control program possible. An attitude of quite a few doctors toward performing abortions can be summarized as "just doing it"; that is, performing abortions was nothing more than a routine part of their professional life. Although some felt sorrow or pity at times about the aborted fetus, most did not think much about the fetus at all. Some considered that late abortion was totally different from the early because in their perception the fetus is a human being in the former case. Dr. Zhang offered a dramatic case in which an extraordinary professional had become lost within her professional work because she considered the fetus an unborn child, had strong reservation on many methods employed in implementing the birth control polices, and deeply sympathized with her patients' various sufferings.

In the introduction to the book, I stress that Chinese views and experiences of abortion are so diverse, complicated, intriguing, and different from one another that any interpretation and overarching generalization will inevitably distort their profound humanity, individuality, and sophistication.

Because these voices come directly from real Chinese life, I often hesitate to offer interpretations beyond telling what they said in their own words. I fear that my generalizations will fail to grasp the full and often contradictory sociocultural, interpersonal and personal, political, and moral dimensions, and even the crises behind those voices. I also fear that my interpretations will fail to capture the unimaginable hardship and admirable struggles, the courage and weakness, the complexity of local texture and general social-political context, the great diversity, the individual uniqueness and universal appealing, as well as the hopes these voices embody. All these issues become even more salient as I present the personal narratives of thirty women and thirty doctors in this and previous chapters.

Nevertheless, we must try our best to understand these voices, however insufficiently we are able to. Before ending this chapter, let me mention a piece of information that in my view is essential for making better sense of doctors' views and experiences in general. Like the official ideology, the socialist discourse of medical ethics in the People's Republic of China is statist and collectivist, emphasizing the almost absolute primacy of the interests of the state, the country, and the collective over those of individuals. As a result, medical professionals are morally obliged to be loyal to not only the individual patient but also the state. Historically speaking, however, this statist and collectivist element in contemporary Chinese socialist medical morality is unprecedented, because for centuries major Chinese medical ethics traditions rooted in Confucianism, Daoism, and Buddhism have always advocated that the primary duty of healers is to the individual patient (Nie forthcoming-a, forthcoming-c). Moreover, while some doctors interviewed apparently accepted and believed in the basic principles of socialist medical morality, especially that on the primacy of collective interests, in their hearts, some seemed not to accept it, as in the case of Dr. Zhang. In addition, even when people agree in principle with the primacy of collective interests in the professional duties of medicine, doctors still may disagree on how to interpret the principle and on the best measures to achieve the collective good. This has also been illustrated in Dr. Zhang's narratives.

As a part of my attempt to better understand Chinese perspectives on abortion, in the next two chapters I will explore the major sociological and ethical issues related to the problem of coerced abortion and undertake a preliminary comparative study with the U.S. abortion debate.

NOTES

1. There are rumors or reports saying that aborted fetuses and even the babies from later abortions are used by some Chinese to make tonics. In a way, Dr. Yao

confirmed the existence of this disturbing practice: "These materials [the aborted fetuses] are somehow in great demand. No one throws them away. It is said that one can build up one's health after eating them. People first let a chicken eat them, then kill the chicken several days later and eat the chicken. Some people directly consume them by cooking them with pork, chicken, goose meat, or pork stomach."

2. In oral Chinese, "he," "she," "him," "her," and "it" are not distinctive.

7

An Inquiry into Coerced Abortion: Sociocultural and Ethical Issues

Land embracing lambs to villages that slaughter lambs,
Suddenly they bleat innocent words

—Hai Zhi, "The Natural Desire and Death of Earth"

A woman, Chinese or not, may be forced by many different agents to have an abortion for a variety of reasons. Since the 1980s, thousands upon thousands of Chinese women have been pressured and coerced to terminate their pregnancies in accordance with national population policies. Coerced abortion in China's birth control program is a tragedy. It is a tragedy not in the ancient Greek sense, in which terrible outcomes, predetermined by fate and supernatural force, are unavoidable. It is a tragedy in the common sense of the term, that is, something that causes a number of unhappy endings, great suffering, and much distress. As shown in chapter 5, the practice of coerced abortion makes termination of the pregnancy, a bitter experience even for women who have voluntarily chosen it, much more bitter. The coercive element in China's birth control program, including pressuring and forcing women to have abortions against their wishes, often at the late stage of their pregnancies, has brought about devastating consequences, such as damage to the physical health of women, emotional and psychological injuries to women and their family members, disproportionate abortions of female fetuses, and an increase in the killing and abandoning of female infants. Coerced abortion is a tragedy in the sense that, although it is human made, that is, a direct result of birth control policy, policy makers never meant to produce this consequence. It is certain that neither the coerced women nor the top national leaders, neither the local cadres nor the medical professionals

189

involved, really desire this outcome. Coerced abortion is a tragedy in the sense that no actor in this drama has really won. The state appears to have won. But the victory is pyrrhic, achieved at extremely high cost. The state's preferred outcome is, of course, compliance with the birth control policy through delayed marriage and contraception. Lastly and most importantly, coerced abortion is a tragedy in the sense that it is against not only Western but also Chinese moral-political traditions. As will become clear soon, the presumed argument of regarding coerced abortion as a lesser but necessary evil—a tragic choice—for achieving some essential social good faces serious theoretical difficulties.

For Westerners, notably Americans, the most troubling and angering aspect of abortion in China centers on the fact that coerced abortion is used to implement the national population control policy and apparently ignores the interests and wishes of individuals. Coerced abortion as an aspect of China's birth control program has been documented in numerous media reports, scholarly works, and even congressional hearings (see chapter 1). The Chinese government insists that the birth control program is based on state guidance combined with public education and voluntary participation, not on commands and coercion. According to official statements, coerced abortion, when it occurs, is due to the failure of local cadres; it has nothing to do with the national family planning policy (see chapter 2). Actually, Chinese authorities have admitted to the occurrence of coerced abortion while denying the direct causal relationship between national population policy and coerced termination. This book, not only the story of Li Xiaohua but also the narratives of women (chapter 5) and physicians (chapter 6), further confirms that Chinese mothers are not only persuaded but actually pressured and even coerced to have abortions.

At the beginning of this book, I recount the case of Li Xiaohua, who had to terminate her five-month pregnancy because she was one year younger than the local policy required—twenty-three-and-a-half years old. In her sad, frustrated, and angry voice, she asked: "Shouldn't this [forced termination] be regarded as murder?" Though her voice was extremely soft and barely audible when posing this question, it was a cri de coeur—a heartfelt cry. After eight years, the question Li Xiaohua asked about the nature of her abortion still echoes in my ears, although her question was not directed to me. I can still clearly see the helpless, frustrated, and angry expression on her pale face.

The tragedy of coerced abortion raises a number of ethical challenges and sociocultural issues. I embark in this chapter on a sociological and ethical inquiry into the problem of coerced abortion by focusing on two questions:

1. How does the tragedy of coerced abortion occur in reality? Or what roles do the state, local agents, and views of the general public on the birth control program play in allowing coerced abortion to take place?

2. Why is coerced abortion not a straightforward moral evil in the context of China? What are the strengths and difficulties of "a lesser but necessary evil" argument? In what senses does this practice violate not only Western but also Chinese moral-political traditions?

THE STATE POWER AND CONTROL

Sociologically and politically speaking, three elements are essential for the existence of forced termination: (1) the determination of the state to control the rapid population growth; (2) the widely shared experience and view among Chinese that overpopulation is a serious problem and, thus, the wide acceptance of a national birth control program; and (3) the complexity of the local world in which resistance, compliance, acceptance, and support coexist and influence behaviors. To a great degree, understanding the social and political mechanism through which the birth control program operates and coerced abortion occurs can be an excellent vehicle to make a better sense of the dynamics of contemporary Chinese society—how the state, the state will, the state bureaucracy from highest level to the local institution, the family, and the individuals and their interests all interact with each other.

The relationship between the individual and the state is one of the crucial dimensions of human life and has significant ethical and political implications. One of the most important and salient features of any society is how the state exercises its power over individuals and where the reach and limits of the state power are located. There are two tendencies in describing the role of the state in Chinese society. One emphasizes what the state can do and the other focuses on what the state cannot do. In the former approach, China is portrayed as a typical case of "oriental despotism," in which the state—either the emperor during the imperial periods or the central government in twentieth century—has absolute, totalitarian, and never-truly-beneficent power and the individual is subject to "total terror," "total submission," and "total loneliness" (Wittfogel 1957). A soft version of this classic theory of Chinese authoritarian state power still exists but gives more attention to the benevolent, idealized, and father-like side of the authorities, with both authoritarian and benevolent sides rooted in traditional political culture (Pye 1992 [1968], 1985). Critics of this theory, both strong and soft versions, claim that it errs in saying that "there is practically nothing the Chinese state could not do" and, more vividly, that officials can "pick up the phone in Beijing and make any decision stick down in the village" (Shue 1988: 76). Against this description of an omniscient and omnipotent state, the alternative approach, focusing on what the state "was (and is) *unable* to do, and why," and on "everyday Chinese politics," tends to stress the interactions, negotiation, and bargaining among the central state, the local world such as villages and individuals (Shue 1988).

My task in this and the next two sections is not to use China's birth control program and its implementation as support for one or the other of these two views of the relationship between the state, the local world, and the individual in contemporary China (for two outstanding ethnographical accounts on this in the rural context, see Mueggler 2001 and Yan 2003). Rather, I will briefly describe the three sociopolitical elements essential for the practice of coerced abortion and use the birth control program to illustrate some aspects of today's Chinese society, including the scope and limits of state power, the dynamics between the central and the local, and the relationship between the state policy and the individual.

Generally speaking, the power of the state or the Party–state has been much weakened and challenged by a variety of social forces since the late 1970s. Scholars have used the phrase "dynamic economy, declining party–state" to describe this general tendency of the Chinese history in the past two and half decades (Goldman and MacFarquhar 1999: 3–29). However, in some areas of life, the Party–state has gained much stronger control than in Mao Ze-dong's era. Birth control is one of these areas. While the state control over production—planned economy—has been greatly lessened, its control over reproduction has dramatically increased. This control is achieved by a number of means, from voluntariness to persuasion, from public education to economic and administrative penalty, from administrative and legal coercion to physical force. Due to the rapid transformation of contemporary Chinese society, especially in the economic sphere, and also due to the intellectual inadequacy of the notion of "oriental despotism," a number of new terms or labels have been invented by scholars since the 1980s to characterize the changing Chinese state, including "nomenclature capitalism," "bureaucratic capitalism," "capitalism with Chinese characteristics," "capital socialism," "incomplete state socialism," "local market socialism," "*danwei* socialism," "socialist corporatism," corporatism Chinese style," "local state corporatism," "state–socialist corporatism," "symbolic clientelism," "Confucian Leninism," "Leninist patrimonialism," "market-preserving federalism," "institutional amphibiousness," and "bureaupreneurialism" (Baum and Shevchenko 1999). Whatever phrases or labels are used to articulate the characteristics of the contemporary Chinese state, one fact that should never be ignored is the strong state control in the sphere of human reproduction. If strong state control over material production and ideologies is characteristic of China in Mao's era, then strong state control over human reproduction is a salient feature of Chinese society in the post-Mao era.

State control over family planning in contemporary China is not only strong and basically successful but unique, both historically and worldwide. For Thomas Scharping, "Later historians may evaluate it [the Chinese birth control program] as the last mass campaign and the last large-scale attempt at social engineering in China" (Scharping 2003: 6). Unfortunately, I am not sure that this program will be the last large-scale, state-controlled project of social engineering. Yet it is certain that the Chinese birth control project is unprecedented in the history of China. Moreover, the program is unique worldwide. No other state, even that of Nazi Germany, regarded as the archetype of totalitarianism, has ever exercised such a strong and successful control over reproduction as the contemporary Chinese state has done.

It would be impossible to mobilize people in a country as large as China to comply with the birth control policies without an effective bureaucracy. Rarely does the state exercise its power over the individual directly. Rather, this power is usually realized via the bureaucracy. In fact, China is well known for its long history of complicated systems of bureaucracy. A nationwide and complicated bureaucracy for regulating population and family planning has been well established since the early 1980s. It consists of an administrative system, a supporting system, and the mass organization system (see Editorial Committee 1996: 398–414; also Scharping 2003: 159–96). The administrative system operates at three levels: the high, middle, and local. The highest level is the State Family Planning Commission, which belongs directly to the State Council and is the national administrative body. At midlevel are the provincial, county, and city family planning commissions, each with its own administrative organization in charge of the work of birth control. The local administrative organ, which exists in every township, village, factory, or work unit, is directly responsible for implementing the policies and thus is crucial for the success of the birth control program. The supporting system comprises, at the state and provincial levels, institutes for science and technology of family planning, centers of public education (propaganda) on birth control, and institutions for training family planning cadres; support systems at the county and local level include stations for the family planning service and stations for public education. The mass organization system comprises such organizations as the Chinese Society of Family Planning and the Chinese Association of Population.

As presented in chapter 2, the Chinese government has stated categorically and repeatedly that family planning is practiced in China on a voluntary basis. When cases of forced sterilization or abortion are admitted, they are regarded as the shortcomings and mistakes of local cadres rather than consequences of central policies. Unfortunately, overwhelming evidence leads to the opposite conclusion. Based on a great number of official and semiofficial Chinese publications that include national, provincial, and local materials, John Aird concludes his monograph on Chinese family planning policy in the 1980s by saying: "Despite official denials and intermittent efforts to discourage some of the more extreme manifestations, since the early 1970s if not before, coercion has been an integral part of the program" (Aird 1990: 88). The Chinese program "remains highly coercive, not because of local deviations from central policies but as a direct, inevitable, and intentional consequence of those policies" (89). The central and provincial policies have permitted and assured, at least indirectly, that local cadres can and sometimes must use coercion in their work. In *China's Changing Population*, Judith Banister also concludes that the Chinese policy "makes extensive use of compulsory family planning, compulsory limitation of the total number of children to one child, required signing of double contracts and pledges to stop at one child, forced sterilization, compulsory IUD acceptance, forced IUD retention, and forced abortion" (Banister 1987: 216). Like Aird, Banister argues that "although the problem is seen at the grassroots level, its roots lay with the upper level" (209). In other words, the Chinese family planning program remains highly coercive at all levels. It is the central policies that lie behind forced abortions and other forceful activities carried out at the local level.

The official excuse or argument on the cause of coerced abortion as local deviations becomes questionable when "real action," "effective measures," and "practical results" are emphasized by the central policy makers. In order to carry out the family planning program "strictly," "firmly," "resolutely," and "effectively," local cadres have to choose between losing their positions and using coercion against the strong will of many people to have more than one child, and especially of countryside people to have a male child. Many tactics and concrete methods are employed to persuade or compel people to submit to family planning demands against their will, including the following: officials go to the houses of women with unplanned pregnancies again and again to have "heart-to-heart talks" with the family; women pregnant without permission are required to attend "study classes"; the government initiates mass "movements" or "mobilizations" for contraception, sterilization, and abortion; penalties for resisting policies are issued, including measures that threaten family subsistence, such as loss of employment for urban residents or destroying the houses of rural people; collective punishments and rewards are designed to involve the entire membership of a factory, an institution, or a rural political unit, so that peers will participate in persuading and compelling the women with unauthorized pregnancies and their families to follow the policies (Aird 1990: 16–17). While persuasion is involved in some of the above measures (for instance, "heart-to-heart talks" and "study classes"), local cadres often cross the line between persuasion and coercion.

State control takes many different forms that fulfill different functions. An important but often-ignored aspect of the family planning program in China is what Danish sociologist Cecilia Milwertz has called "control as care" (Milwertz 1997: 110–14). The functions of birth planning institutions and workers are not only to implement the policies but also to provide women with a variety of services related to contraception, childbearing, and childrearing. Urban women perceive and experience the control implemented to prevent the birth of a second child not only as control but also as care and concern. In the words of a Beijing woman:

> When you become pregnant, you cannot have the child and must have an abortion. Many abortions are not good for women's health. The birth planning workers are caring (*zhaogu*) for women by applying a method of supervision and urging. They supervise and urge you to use a certain contraceptive method to avoid injuring your health. They are showing concern (*guanxin*) for women by continuous urging. When you have one child and have a one-child certificate, they help you to find a safe contraceptive method to save you from enduring hardship. (Quoted in Milwertz 1997: 110)

Here, in the form of control as care or care as control, coercion has merged with concern; ideological education has merged with service.

Another form of control is the suppression and silencing of different, especially critical, opinions on birth control policies and related issues. The birth control program remains a politically sensitive topic in China; political repression and the nameless fear among people constitute one of the direct causes for the Chinese silence on abortion in the public discourse (see chapter 1). From ancient times to the present, the state, the emperor, or the Party has controlled Chinese people, not only by means of explicit rules issued by the state and such state institutions as the police system and prisons, but also by the widespread fear of the state and the resulting self-censorship among ordinary people. The state exercises its power and control on people's behaviors, speech, and thoughts in many ways—some direct, many very subtle. The fears of Dr. Wei and her husband, and other interviewees presented in chapter 1, raise a series of questions that beg for answers: Why are so many people so fearful and cautious in their speech? What political, social, and cultural factors have left them in such fear? Why do so many people still prefer being silent, even though governmental agencies have not set forth direct limits on speech? What can ordinary Chinese people do to build (or rebuild) a social-political environment in which every citizen feels less fearful and is even free of fear about the government and the state when talking about social policies? To address these questions adequately, one must consider the entire history of Chinese politics and polity, especially political life in China in the second half of the twentieth century.

The successive states in twentieth-century China enjoyed much stronger control over the citizens in many areas of life than those in imperial China. As the renowned sinologist John Fairbank has summarized, "One great difference between China before and after 1949 would be that material means such as radio, other communications, and police firepower could be combined with ideological sanctions in the Soviet totalitarian form" (Fairbank 1987: 47). This combination makes it possible for the state to "penetrate Chinese society as never before." It is naïve to think that modern technologies such as the Internet will automatically undermine a totalitarian state or dictatorship and thus result in democracy. In the case of China's birth control program, to gain support from the people for the national policy and promote public education on the issue of population control, the Chinese government and its bureaucracy have mobilized a number of modern communication technologies, including newspapers, radio, television, print publications, and most recently, the Internet. With advanced modern technologies and multilevel bureaucracy, the will of the Chinese Party–state to control the population can reach almost every corner of China.

RESISTANCE AND DRAMA IN THE LOCAL WORLD

No matter how powerful an authoritarian or totalitarian state, it cannot do whatever it wants without recognizing the importance of the local worlds in making and implementing policies. From the very beginning, the birth control policies have confronted persistent resistance in the local level in a great variety of forms. Resistance was especially strong in the 1980s. American sociologists and sinologists Elizabeth Perry and Mark Selden summed up the resistance:

> The single-child policy is fraught with profound implications and complications for a society whose core cultural values are based largely on kinship relations and an emphasis on the filial obligation to assure family continuity through future generations, an act that requires a male offspring. The single-child policy achieved considerable success in the cities where most families could rely on state or collective welfare to provide for them in retirement. But in the countryside, where no such welfare regime existed, the one-child policy posed agonizing choices for households, generating fierce resistance that took such forms as flight to give birth to a second child, female infanticide and, at times, murder of cadres or family members of cadres who had imposed forced abortion or sterilizations. (Perry and Selden 2000: 5)

Due to persistent resistance, the work of birth control has been called in China "the Hardship Number One under Heaven."

Grassroots resistance to the national birth control policy is overwhelming. As sinologist Tyrene White points out, "the tens of millions of such births [in violation of the policy] that have occurred over the past two decades are a living testament to just how widespread and sustained the resistance has been" (White 2000: 106). Furthermore, violations of the birth plan are by no means the only form of resistance. White has classified various strategies of resistance into three basic patterns: (1) direct confrontation between policy enforcers and targets, such as violence and the threat of violence against family planning officials and workers; (2) evasion of enforcement, either through deceiving rural cadres or colluding with sympathetic ones; and (3) the middle ground of accommodation (102–19). Here, accommodation means that desperate people resort to female infanticide, female infant abandonment, and sex-selective abortion while they comply with the number requirement of the policies.

Even though the central government exercises almost unlimited power, especially as applied to the individual, it is a mistake to think that the local world and its inhabitants are totally powerless and helpless in the face of the policies from the highest level. All national policies in China must be interpreted and implemented at the local level and in everyday social practice (see Mueggler 2001 and Yan 2003). Thus, many policies, the national family planning program included, are often moderated or revised or resisted according to the local conditions. After studying a village in the Guangdong province, anthropologists Sulamith and Jack Potter warned that, regarding Chinese birth planning, "Any preconception of Chinese society as a series of subordinate levels carrying out with unthinking obedience the fiats they receive from above is a considerable distortion of Chinese political process" (Potter and Potter 1990: 241).

Western literature about the subject, especially mass media reports, usually depict Chinese women (or more exactly, couples) who have been forced to terminate their pregnancies either as victims of the totalitarian political system or as fighters for the rights of reproduction. In reality, however, there is much more going on than the conflict between the central government and the individual. In other words, the conflict between the national policy and the individual plays out at the local level in a complicated way. To demonstrate the role of the state and complexities of the local world in the practice of forced abortion, I will start with a case reported by an American medical anthropologist and psychiatrist. Arthur Kleinman (1995: 183–86) has used the example of forced abortion to illustrate the complex relationship between political violence and the local setting of social experience. Mrs. Fang, who lived in a rural county town, told how she was forced by the cadres of her work unit to have three abortions within four years; the third was a late-term abortion. While this story can be interpreted as a typical example of human rights abuse in China, it has another side. The small factory in which Mrs. Fang worked was "repeatedly criticized by the local population control authority for failing to assiduously enforce the one-child policy" (184). When the population campaign reached its height, people in the factory agreed collectively to avoid pregnancy for a while. It was at that time that Mrs. Fang revealed her pregnancy. "The entire work unit—workers and leaders—were deeply angered" (184). The members of the work unit collectively demanded abortion. The dramatic consequences included the forced abortion, a suicide attempt by Mrs. Fang's husband, and a series of stress-based symptoms, such as suicidal behavior on the part of Mrs. Fang herself.

Kleinman points out that one must enter Mrs. Fang's world and "attend to its complex array of discourses, sensibilities, and competing demands" to understand her suffering. He continues:

> That world is not a passive recipient or vector of macrosocial forces, such as the one-child-per-family national policy, any more than is Mrs. Fang. Rather, the local world actively mediates the effect of political pressure on persons. In the interactions between positioned participants that make up that world, the dynamics between victims and victimizers turn on what is locally at stake. (185)

Kleinman has firmly established how medicalizing the suffering and trauma of political violence has distorted the personal experience of the individuals involved. His emphasis on the local setting and the need for an ethnography of political violence yields insights for a penetrating analysis of the sociocultural and ethical issues related to the problem of coerced abortion.

Besides the national policy and the will of the state, a number of agents from different institutions are involved in forcing a woman to have an abortion, including people at the work units where the woman and her husband are working, as Kleinman's case has powerfully shown. Among other agents are the local cadres of family planning and the Women's Federation, the physicians who provide medical service, and the strong will of women and their families to have children without permits. Absence of participation, active or passive, from any of these agents would render forced abortion impossible. For example, if the medical professionals resisted and refused to provide the service women were forced to receive, coerced abortion would not be carried out, even after women were already in the clinics. The following late abortion case—a case in which coerced abortion succeeded and failed at the same time—reported by Chinese scholars sheds light on the roles of multiple agents in realizing coerced abortions.

> [Mrs. C] is a 40-year-old worker in a state-owned factory, with two daughters and one son from five pregnancies. She wanted more children. When she conceived the sixth time, she succeeded in covering the truth till seven months later, when the cadres of her factory discovered her condition. The cadres asked her to give up the fetus, but she refused, because she believed the Chinese maxim "More children, more happiness." She said she did not care if she was fined. One month later she was persuaded to undergo an abortion, but the physician refused to perform the operation. The cadres of her factory complained that if she gave birth to a fourth child, the rewards of all of the workers would be diminished, because they had broken the birth quota assigned to the factory. Finally the physician was convinced, and he performed the abortion with an intraamniotic injection of Huangyan Flower. The next day a 3000 g. live baby was born, and later adopted by an infertile couple. (Qiu, Wang, and Gu 1989: 343–45)

The following case reported by two American anthropologists illustrates the impact of the national-level campaign and especially the role of the Women's Federation cadre in persuading people to comply with the policy. The peasant woman narrated her story in these words:

> I preferred to have two sons and one daughter, and I was trying for a second son. Well, actually, I was using an I.U.D., but it failed. I chose to be fined and have the third child. But then the campaign started at the upper level, and the local-level cadres had to follow. The women's leader said, "Now the campaign has come. You have one son and one daughter, you must go get an abortion." At first, I refused her request. Later, the head of the Women's Federation at the commune level came to see me. She told me not to give birth. She said it was unfair of me to try to have more children than other people. She said "You must carry out the abortion. If you refuse to do so, and try to give birth, cadres of higher and higher levels will come to educate you, and you will be fined." I didn't want to be fined 400 yuan [about $50] for the third child, so I got an abortion. (Potter and Potter 1990: 232)

The family members, especially the husband, may play the crucial role in persuading or pressuring a woman to have an abortion, as the following case shows:

> [Mrs. B] is a thirty-year-old accountant, the wife of an army officer. She has been pregnant two times, but only gave birth once, to a girl, and was given a "One Child" certificate [for obtaining favored treatment]. When she became aware of being pregnant the third time, she felt a physical difference, and she inferred that the fetus might possibly be a boy. Her husband was performing his duty outside Beijing at that time. She made every effort to hide the truth for seven months. During this period she economized on food and clothing, and she worked very hard to save money for the penalty fine; both courses of action jeopardized her health. When her husband came home to visit, he persuaded her to give up the fetus in the interests of their family and country. [It is not clear whether the husband voluntarily obeyed the policy or feared harsh punishment such as being dismissed from the army, or both.] Mrs. B agreed . . . to undergo an abortion. . . . A 1800 g. dead baby was born the next day. (Qiu, Wang, and Gu 1989: 343–45)

On the one hand, all the cases of forced abortion reported in this book show that forced abortion is beyond doubt a tragedy resulting from the inevitable conflict between the strict population policy of the central government and the individuals' interests in having as many children as they want. On the other hand, as presented above, coerced abortion is a tragic drama involving more actors than simply the national policy and the individual woman. Members of community, local cadres, OB/GYN doctors, and the interpersonal relationship of the woman with people in the local world also play significant roles. These local complexities are difficult to decipher. In the practice of coerced abortion, not only the woman but also her husband, her coworkers in her work unit, and even the physicians are ultimately forced to do something all would rather not do.

The cases of coerced abortion constitute an indicator of how much control the state has over the individual in contemporary China. Yet the active role of the local worlds in the family planning program is evident in the fact that the "one-child" policy has been moderated by several structural exceptions to such a degree that the term "one-child policy" becomes misleading (see chapter 2). For example, in rural and ethnic minority areas, couples usually have more than one child. Although the policy is national, it is satisfactorily carried out mainly in the cities, rather than in rural areas, where the great majority of the population resides. These exceptions are possible due, not to the mercy of the state power, but to the resistance and struggle of the local world and ordinary people and to the government's awareness of and adjustment to local resistance and struggle. This suggests that the hope and force for improving and, if needed, changing the current policy and practice come not only from the Party–state and high-level governmental officials but also from the local communities and ordinary people.

PEOPLE'S SUPPORT FOR THE
POPULATION POLICIES: AN ANALYSIS

The Chinese birth control program is, by and large, successful; the population growth rate in China has been reduced to below 2% within two decades. The arrival of the day when China's population reaches 1.2 billion has been postponed by about a decade. This remarkable achievement would be unimaginable without the strong will and control by the state and the efficiency of its bureaucracy in implementing the state policies. It would also be impossible without the popular consensus that rapid population growth and overpopulation constitute such a serious social problem in China that strict state intervention is necessary.

A number of paradoxes exist in China's birth control program. One of the most striking is the coexistence of the wide acceptance and even strong support on one side and the persistent and even violent resistance on the other side. Without making some sense of these paradoxes, it would be impossible to understand the sociocultural dimensions of coerced abortion in particular and contemporary China in general.

Over and over again, the Chinese government has claimed that the national birth control policy has won and is enjoying the wide support of the people. The results of my survey presented in chapter 4 confirm this claim; that is, the national birth control policy is endorsed by a great majority of people. Chinese participants in the survey—no matter where they resided or their profession, Party membership, education level, gender, or even religious beliefs—overwhelmingly believed in the necessity of controlling the rapid population growth in China and supported the national family planning program in general and the "one-child" policy in particular. In fact, this was the area with the strongest consensus among all the participants surveyed and interviewed. Even Catholics, who clearly oppose abortion in general, were somehow more cautious about population control and the "one-child" policy than participants from other groups, but still were considerably supportive. Ninety-four percent of the participants in the survey agreed that the one-child-per-couple policy is beneficial to the country; 82% agreed that the policy is beneficial to the individual and the family. Moreover, Chinese participants in all samples supported "very strongly" the necessity of taking eugenic (*yousheng*) measures to improve the quality of China's population. In other words, the national family planning program, whose main task is not only to control the rapid increase of population but also to improve the quality of the population, was highly supported by all groups, including rural people, urban residents, intellectuals, university students, doctors, overseas students and scholars, and even Catholics.

The interviews with physicians who provided family planning medical service and with women who had abortions further confirmed this wide acceptance and strong support of the Chinese people for the birth control policy. Almost all of the thirty doctors whose interviews are summarized in chapter 6 were proud of directly participating in the family planning program—a good and great cause—because they believed they were serving the whole society by helping slow the rapid population growth. The most frequent reason mentioned for their abortions by the thirty women who had had them was that the policy did not allow the pregnancy to continue. But, as stated in chapter 5, it is incorrect to interpret this to mean that they disagreed with the population policy. On the contrary, most women supported and accepted the birth control program, though they were less supportive than the doctors.

In my fieldwork, I encountered people from all walks of life—peasants, urban residents, medical professionals, university professors, hotel workers, taxi drivers—who were forthright in expressing their concerns about overpopulation and voicing their approval for the national population policy. An official at a provincial institution said to me on his own initiative: "Even though I am a member of the Communist Party and a governmental official, I oppose many policies of the Party and the state. But I support the family planning policy from my heart."[1]

There were reservations and criticisms regarding the national birth control policy, most notably among overseas Chinese and doctors. But, as presented in chapters 4 and 6, these reservations and criticisms targeted not so much the population policy as the methods of implementing this policy. In other words, the necessity of a national birth control policy was rarely questioned.

No item in the questionnaire is directly about coerced abortion caused by the birth control policies or about the morality of coerced abortion. But the survey results do indicate that most survey respondents, with the Catholic sample as the only exception, agreed with the statement that it is sometimes necessary to force a woman to have an abortion. As stated in chapter 4, the evident support for coerced abortion, at least under some circumstances, together with the overwhelmingly strong support for the national family planning program, suggest that coerced terminations *may* be approved and accepted by a large majority of Chinese as one legitimate means of implementing the population policy.

While Chinese support for the national family planning program is widespread and there is general approval for employing coerced abortion to effectively implement the national policy, crucial questions are raised: How genuine, if genuine at all, is this strong consensus among Chinese people, or the agreement between the Party–state and the people? If the data are reliable, then why do the overwhelming majority of Chinese accept and support the national birth control program? One can explain all this consensus away by saying that Chinese people were either simply afraid of saying what they really believed or merely giving lip service to the birth control policies, or both. In other words, the consensus or agreement was a result of political repression and enforced silence and thus said nothing about the genuine views of Chinese people. However, according to my judgments and observations, this factor is far from the most significant because the survey and interviewing results in general are reliable (see the appendix), because participants in the survey disagreed with several other officially approved statements (see chapter 4), and because different and dissenting views on other issues were often expressed. That is to say, I believe that Chinese participants' expressed opinions on population control—accepting and supporting the birth control program—are basically genuine.

It is important to understand that overpopulation is an obvious and serious social problem for Chinese people. People living in China, especially in cities, readily perceive and suffer the consequences of overpopulation, every day and everywhere. As a result, Chinese have reached a "conscientious acceptance" of the need to limit family size. The phrase "conscientious acceptance" was used by Cecilia N. Milwertz (1997) to account for the fact that most urban women, despite their clearly stated preference for two children, accept the "one-child" family policy. Milwertz (1997) has convincingly shown that city district women widely accept a policy that does not necessarily correspond to their own fertility preference—more than one child. In other words, it is incorrect to take the preference for two children as an accurate measure of nonacceptance of the policy. For "acceptance transcends individual and family fertility preference" and "compliance is not necessarily perceived as something negative." Among reasons urban women give for accepting the policy are (1) given the present demographic and economic situation in China, they agree with the official rationale for the necessity of a national population control program; (2) they have neither the funds nor the energy to support more than one child, in spite of their personal preference for two or more children; and (3) they want to respond to the call of the state. According to Milwertz, "conscientious acceptance" (*zijue jieshou*) "connotes the exercise of self-control and is related to the political consciousness in terms of acting according to the prescribed norm without having to be persuaded." The logic or "cultural meaning" of conscientious acceptance, compliance, self-control, or self-sacrifice is not necessarily perceived as something negative. Milwertz, by focusing on the nondemographic consequences of the "one-child" family policy—how women handle it "in their everyday life context"—has indicated the subtlety of coercion in the Chinese sociocultural context.

However, that Chinese people were expressing their true feelings and opinions does not necessarily mean that their agreement with the official policies is genuine in the sense that it is ethically valid. Or it must be emphasized that it is a mistake to see the extremely strong consensus as an agreement reached after sufficient public discussions. In fact, to a great degree the consensus is not a genuine but a forced one, created by continuous governmental propaganda and powerful public education. Since the late 1970s, the state-run media have hammered home the dual message that overpopulation is a grave social problem in itself and that many other problems such as food shortages and deficits in housing and education have resulted from uncontrolled population growth. Meanwhile, different or opposing views are hardly heard in public and official discourse. Scant literature, if any at all, argues that population is not a severe social problem and that, if it is, strict national policies do not necessarily constitute the best solution. The dissident voices are usually, if not always, repressed even before they are fully developed. Not informed by different perspectives, Chinese people are left no choice but to accept the government views that overpopulation is one of the biggest social problems, if not the biggest, in China and that the only way out is through direct and strict state interference. Hence, strong propaganda on the one hand and the suppression of dissident perspectives on the other hand have actually forced Chinese people to believe that, in the face of the serious condition of overpopulation, there is no way out but the present national policies.

Consequently, the strong acceptance of and support for the national birth control policy is itself a paradox. It is based on Chinese people's awareness of the problem of overpopulation, but the nature of this problem and the best social policies for addressing it are far from sufficiently deliberated and discussed by the public. Even if the Chinese strong consensus on the population problem and the birth control program is a "conscientious acceptance," it is a misinformed or, at best, an insufficiently informed one. From the angle of the efficiency, the state can exercise much better control over people by controlling and manipulating information available to them, rather than directly suppressing their thought and speech.

NOT A STRAIGHTFORWARD MORAL EVIL

Through analyzing the roles the state, local agents, and the consensus of the general public on the birth control program play in the practice of coerced abortion, so far I have tried to give a sociological explanation of how the tragedy of pressuring and forcing women to terminate their pregnancies can occur in the first place. Yet the reality is not necessarily what it ought to be. In other words, even if everyone in China approves of and accepts coerced abortion in China for implementing the national birth control policy, even if this consensus is not misinformed or insufficiently informed but a valid result of full public discussions, this still cannot establish that the practice of coerced abortion is morally right or justifiable. If whatever exists is necessarily morally justifiable and right, then slavery, various forms of gender and racial discrimination once and still legal and socially accepted, the old Chinese imperial political system, the foot binding widely practiced in China for nearly a millennium, and the registration institution (*fukou*) that legally discriminates against rural people in contemporary China would all be morally justifiable and right. Therefore, it is necessary to shift the focus of our inquiry into the problem of coerced abortion from a sociological analysis to an ethical examination.

Women who want to continue their unapproved pregnancies and who hope to give birth eventually usually make every effort to hide their pregnancies from others. When they eventually give up under various kinds of social and political pressure, their pregnancies have often progressed into the second or third trimester. As a result, most persuaded or coerced abortions are also late abortions. So there are, among others, two closely related moral problems involved in the thorny issue of coerced abortion: (1) Can late abortion be ethically justified? (2) Is coerced abortion morally acceptable or unacceptable? Some Chinese scholars have attempted to address the first question. Their conclusion is that it is justifiable under some conditions:

[L]ate abortion can be justified ethically in China: 1) if the "one couple, one child" policy is justifiable; 2) if the couple and the physician take the social good into account; 3) if the mother expresses her voluntary consent, no matter whether the decision is made on the basis of her own original desire or after persuasion by others that is not coercive; and 4) if the late abortion will entail only a low risk to the mother's health or life. (Qiu, Wang, and Gu 1989: 349)

Can coerced abortion associated with the birth control policy be morally justified? For many Westerners, the answer is decidedly no. But the case is not that straightforward in the Chinese context. Part of the difficulty in discussing the ethical issues of coerced abortion lies in the definitions of the terms "coercion" or "compulsion" and the related concept "persuasion." Even more difficult than drawing a clear line between the *definitions* of persuasion and coercion is drawing a line between persuasive and coercive *practices*. The Chinese government and some family planning advocates limit the term "coercion" to the use of physical force. Although physical force is sometimes used by local officials, the Chinese government never openly approves or formally legitimizes such action in any official directive. Understanding coercion in this narrow sense, Chinese policy makers are able to deny the existence of coercion in the family planning program. For them, all cases of coerced abortion mentioned are the results of either women's voluntary choices or persuasion and education, rather than compulsion or coercion.

Many people question this narrow definition. For Aird, if a method is powerful enough to compel many people to act in ways contrary to their wishes, that method is coercive. He states: "People who practice family planning out of fear of public humiliation; strong peer pressures; such penalties as loss of food, housing, employment, possessions, or essential services; or simply because of threats and intimidation are acting under compulsion even if no overt force is in evidence" (Aird 1995: 2023). Even though this definition grasps the ordinary meaning of the term "coercion," it does not distinguish the strategies of persuasion and strong persuasion from the category of coercion or compulsion.

The dictionary definition of "coerce" given by *Merriam–Webster's Collegiate Dictionary* (10th edition) is: "to restrain or dominate by force"; "to compel to an act or choice"; "to bring about by force or threat." The word "persuade" means "to move by argument, entreaty, or expostulation to a belief, position, or course of action." Although these dictionary definitions are of little help for moral exploration of coercive activities of Chinese birth control and abortion policies, they provide a starting point.

American philosopher–bioethicists Tom Beauchamp and James Childress claim that coercion "occurs if and only if one person intentionally uses a credible and severe threat of harm or force to control another." They further point out: "For a threat to be credible, both parties must believe that the person making the threat can effect it, or the one making the threat must successfully deceive the person threatened into so believing." For Beauchamp and Childress there is a distinct line between coercion and persuasion, since in the latter, "a person must be convinced to believe in something through the merit of reasons advanced by another person" (Beauchamp and Childress 2001: 94). They thus deny that there exists such a measure as "forceful persuasion."

Two points require attention here. First, the determination that an act is the result of coercion or compulsion is never value free. Some may think that whether or not a person is coerced into doing something is a fact claim, an empirical matter. But to others, as Alan Wertheimer has argued, "coercion claims are moralized" and "they involve moral judgments at their core" (Wertheimer 1990: xi). In fact, different people may have very different responses to the same pressure or threat or force. And certainly different cultures have different understandings of and attitudes toward coercion.

Second, and more importantly, coercion itself is not necessarily unacceptable morally. For Aird (1990), coercive birth control in China is simply "slaughter of the innocents." Since China's use of coercion in family planning obviously violates human rights to reproduction, he perceives that the Chinese family planning program is morally evil, because it is highly coercive. Aird's argument seems to represent the first response of many Westerners to the practice of coerced abortion and sterilization in China. Yet Beauchamp and Childress give two justifiable examples of coercion: the threat of force or punishment used by police, courts, and hospitals in acts of involuntary commitment for psychiatric treatment and society's use of compulsory vaccination laws. In discussing the normative, remunerative, and administrative coercion of the Chinese birth control program, Thomas Scharping mentions that Westerners normally "accept fines and sentences if, for instance, they serve to punish non-compliance with state schooling or quarantine regulations" (Scharping 2003: 8). In these cases, coercion does not make involuntary civil commitment, compulsory vaccination, or state schooling morally unacceptable just because of the employment of force.

It may even be morally required in some circumstances for certain people or institutions to control others by coercive or other manipulative means. Red B. Edwards and Edmund L. Erde (1995) offer as morally justifiable the examples of parental coercion of children at times, good laws and penalties for noncompliance, and proper enforcement mechanisms such as the police, the courts, and the prisons for coercing lawless persons to behaving themselves. They conclude, "using coercion is often, but not always, the morally right thing to do. Other human values besides freedom must be protected coercively" (Edwards and Erde 1995: 886). The crucial question is not whether coercion can be morally justified, but, as Wertheimer poses, "what constitutes the coercion or duress that violates the voluntariness principle?" (Wertheimer 1990: 4). Or, in the words of Edwards and Erde, "when is coercion morally unacceptable? And how can we tell when it places morally unjustifiable limits on freedom?" (Edwards and Erde 1995: 886).

These examples indicate that moral exploration is needed to answer the question of why and how coercive birth control programs in general and forced abortion in particular are ethically wrong. What moral principles does the practice of coerced abortion violate? Can compulsory abortion be morally defended for protecting other human values—for instance, the social good? Is coerced abortion always evil? Can it be a lesser but necessary evil in preference to a greater evil at present and in the future? The following sections examine these ethical questions.

FOR THE SOCIAL GOOD: AN ANALOGY WITH TAXATION

In the official discourse on birth control and abortion, as illustrated in chapter 2, a collectivist and statistical ethics constitutes the core of the morality to justify the related polices. The rationale is obvious and simple: the extant overpopulation and the population's continuing rapid growth in China threaten the whole society, the future generations, and even the world, so that individual Chinese must make sacrifices for the sake of the eventual common good. From official perspectives, abortion is always treated to be a remedial rather than a primary measure of birth control. Being confronted with overpopulation on one hand and the strong will of people to have many children on the other, the government seems to have no choice except adopting both persuasion and compulsion for achieving a decrease in the rate of population growth and thereby a rise in people's standard of living. Therefore, coercive birth control, forced abortion included, is bad and undesirable, but necessary for the good of society and eventually the long-term interests of every member. As a result, Chinese people seem to be forced to allow, tolerate, accept, and support state interference in human reproduction and coercion of some women into having abortions if they violate the national family planning policy.

In chapter 2, I also point out that in the official Chinese discourse there are two approaches to addressing the Western criticisms on the coercive nature of China's birth control program. The first and explicit approach is to deny the existence of coercion as an essential element of the policies or regard coercion as a consequence of the bad working style of local cadres. The second and implicit one, existing not so much in published materials as in practice, is to justify coercion, forced abortion included, as the lesser of two evils. In the chapter, I furthermore try to bring this implicit but important argument out through citing a case of forced live-birth abortion and analyzing the justifications of the local female leader. In the face of the fundamental moral dilemma originating in the inevitable conflict between the calamity of population explosion on one side and the interests of the individual, the family, and the unborn on the other, coerced abortion can be seen as a lesser but necessary evil for some important common good.

It is not always easy for Westerners, especially people in North America, Australia, and New Zealand, to appreciate fully the seriousness of overpopulation in China. The concrete numbers—now more than 1.2 billion, more than one-fifth of the world's population, living in China—may not make real sense to many people. To grasp this, imagine that all Canadians lived in two cities, since the combined population of the two biggest cities in China, Beijing, and Shanghai, is close to the total population of Canada. Wherever you are in the United States, multiply the number of people you meet daily by five or six. While the total areas of the United States and China are almost same, the population of China is five times that of the United States. Furthermore, China has far fewer natural resources and less inhabitable area than the United States.

To better understand the official moral grounds of birth control policies and the logic of Chinese people's conscientious acceptance of these policies, I offer an analogy that compares limiting family size to paying taxes. The existence and operation of every society depend on taxation, labor, materials, services, and so forth collected or contributed by individuals. As a result, those in the United States have a saying that goes: only two things are inevitable—death and taxes. In addition to the taxes on goods and labor just mentioned, every American is taxed on his or her earnings or income. In China, everyone must pay taxes to the state, too—directly and indirectly—although most people, especially those in the countryside, do not have to pay income tax per se. But limiting family size is almost as inevitable as death for contemporary Chinese people. For urban residents, one couple can have one child only.

Even though being required to pay taxes and to limit childbearing appear to be vastly different, there are some surprising similarities between these two methods for satisfying the common needs of the populace. To grasp these similarities, let us first assume that population is a serious social problem in China and that the national birth control program in general and the one-child-per-family policy in particular are necessary, or even the best solution to the problem. On the basis of these assumptions, which are matters of facts in the official discourse, several similarities between paying taxes and limiting family size become apparent.

First, both paying taxes and limiting the number of offspring are regarded as necessary governmental intrusions for the sake of social good. People in the West pay taxes to finance highways, railroads, public education, health care, public libraries, national defense, and so forth. People in China pay taxes and limit the family size for similar reasons. According to the official view, overpopulation and rapid population growth have resulted in a series of difficulties in providing food, clothing, housing, transportation, education, public health care, and employment.

Second, an argument can be made that limiting family size serves not only the social good but also, ultimately, individual interests. Chinese official documents stress again and again that having fewer children improve the quality of life for the individual, his or her family, and the child. In other words, the more food and resources are available for the country, the more each individual family will have.

Third, limiting family size and paying taxes share the immediate conflict between self-interest and desire for the general good of society. In one case, the couple wishes to have as many children as they want while others limit fertility. In the other case, the individual wishes to avoid paying taxes while others pay theirs. Both responses ignore the point made prior to this one—that more tax revenues and lower population growth actually benefit the person who is paying taxes or restricting his or her family size. Putting this aspect positively, just as Americans are willing to pay taxes, Chinese people conscientiously accept and support the birth control policies, both for the common good.

If the analogy between limiting family size and paying taxes makes sense, then coercion in China's birth control program, forced abortion included, might be justified as a necessary evil for achieving some essential social good. Just as the U.S. state, any state, morally and legally uses forceful measures against those who violate tax law, the state in China can morally and legally utilize forcible measures against individuals who have violated the birth control policy. Since paying taxes is a legally defined obligation of the individual to the society, the state can legitimately and does force the individual to fulfill this duty. The birth control policy in China has the effect of law and is actually written into laws, including the constitution (see chapter 2). Based on this analogy, the state could employ coercion—fine, penalty, even physical force or imprisonment—to guarantee the smooth implementation of this law or policy.

For Chinese policy makers, officials, and many scholars, the dilemma can be seen in terms of either adopting the coercive measures or failing in the objectives of the birth control program. The moral issues at stake in Chinese population control are, therefore, in the words of Spinoza, to seek "the lesser of two evils," "a lesser evil in the present in preference to a greater evil in the future" (*Ethics*, Props. LXV and LXVI). One may cite plenty of reasons why the greater evil involved here is not as great as assumed and that the lesser evil is much greater than acknowledged. But all should agree with the moral principle of seeking the lesser of two evils, and it would be inappropriate to deny there is no genuine moral dilemma here. In other words, China's birth control program and coercive measures employed may well be what two U.S. legal scholars, Cuido Calabresi and Philip Bobbitt (1978), have called the "tragic choice" every society has to make in confronting scarcity—a "fundamental fact of existence"—and allocating tragically scarce resources. Actually, Clabresi and Bobbitt consider a population-restrictive policy that sets acceptable rates of procreation in a society to be one of the typically tragic, not merely difficult, choices within the large context of natural and social scarcities.

The justification of coerced abortion as a necessary evil for the sake of some important social good becomes even more powerful if Chinese, as often assumed, find nothing morally wrong with abortion itself. But these chapters have proven this assumption is incorrect. Furthermore, using the social good as a theoretical way to justify restrictive birth control policies and coerced abortion has to address some further questions.

- Is there really a serious population problem? Is controlling the population growth rigorously really a social good? In fact, there is controversy about this issue, and some thinkers and scholars, even including the founders of communism, Marx and Engels, refute altogether the claim that overpopulation is a real social problem.
- Has overpopulation been used by the government as an excuse for other social problems resulting from its misgoverning? Is promoting family planning policy just an integral part of retaining and enforcing the extant structure of power?
- If controlling population increase is indeed a social good in today's China, does that good confer equal advantage to every member in the society? If not, who benefits most from the social good? Who least? Might some even be harmed?
- If population control is a social good overall, why must the interests, rights, or freedom of individuals be subordinated to the social good of the whole nation and even all of humanity? The individual may disagree that population control is a social good and believe that having more children contributes more to the society than having just one. Why should this individual's freedom be restrained?
- If the one-child policy is a social good to which everyone should be committed, does that justify using coerced abortion, especially late abortion or induced birth, as a means of birth control? Is there a better way than this? Can the fertility control program be built on voluntariness, as the government says it is, rather than on coercion or force?

Most notably, the necessity of controlling overpopulation and using forced and late abortions as means of achieving the goal are significantly different, though closely related, issues. The moral legitimacy of the former does not necessarily lead to the moral legitimacy of the latter, just as the moral justifiability of population control would not justify reducing overpopulation by killing all the old, the sick, the physically handicapped, and the mentally retarded in the society. Unfortunately, in the official discourse of China and among Chinese people, it is often assumed that the need to control the rapid growth of population straightforwardly justifies coerced abortion and other forceful measures. Ethically, these are two different issues. Coerced abortion demands more strict and specific moral justifications than those on population control in general.

VIOLATING REPRODUCTIVE RIGHTS

For many Westerners, as Geoffrey McNicoll has put it, "Browbeating a woman to have an abortion, a practice reported in some studies of China's antinatalist program, would *of course* be found to be highly objectionable" (McNicoll 1995: 2021; italics added). This view of coerced abortion as always evil derives from the concept of individual rights and freedom that constitutes a cornerstone within Western political, legal, and moral thought. Promoting the birth control program by coercion conflicts with and challenges fundamental values and moral principles such as the right to reproductive decision making and women's right to personal privacy. So it is not surprising that the Chinese fertility-control programs have raised serious criticisms and strong objections for as long as the use of coercion has been known in the West.

The distinction between the public and the private has its origins in Greco-Roman political and ethical theory and practice and is crucial to preventing the unlimited intervention of the state or community into the life of the individual in the Western democracy. The English political philosopher James F. Stephen wrote in 1873 that "conduct which can be described as indecent is always in one way or another violation of privacy" (Stephen 1967: 160). Even though the U.S. Constitution does not explicitly mention a right to personal privacy, the U.S. Supreme Court has derived from constitutional language and intent a right of personal privacy that protects a woman's decision about whether or not to terminate a pregnancy. Feminists expressed this rationale in the popular phrase "a woman's right to control her own body."

In the well-known essay *On Liberty*, British philosopher John Stuart Mill argued powerfully that civil or social liberty concerns mainly "the nature and limits of the power which can be legitimately exercised by society over the individuals." For him, liberty meant protection not only "against the tyranny of the political rulers" but also "against the tyranny of the prevailing opinion and feeling; against the tendency of society to impose, by other means than civil penalties, its own ideas and practices as rules of conduct on those who dissent from them." Mill pointed out that, "The only purpose for which power can rightfully be exercised over any member of a civilized community, against his will, is to prevent harm to others. His own good, either physical and moral, is not a sufficient warrant." On Mill's view of liberty, then, adopting coerced abortion to promote the "one-child" family planning program must first of all satisfy the condition that having many children really constitutes harm to others. Only then would state intervention in enforcing one-child-per-couple be morally and politically justified.

Opposing coercive measures of birth control from the angle of individual freedom of reproduction is not as straightforward as it may appear, but has its own problems. For instance, one could argue that, since overpopulation constitutes a serious obstacle for social and economic development, letting individuals bear as many children as they like would harm others and the common good of the society. More seriously, is the right to reproduction a fundamental human right? The Universal Declaration of Human Rights classifies the following rights as in the first tier of human rights: life, liberty, and the security of person; freedom from arbitrary arrest, detention, or exile; right to impartial tribunal; freedom of thought and religion; freedom of opinion and expression; freedom of peaceful assembly and association. The right to decide on issues of one's own fertility and reproduction is not, at least not explicitly, included as a fundamental right. And the U.S. Constitution does not claim the right to reproduction as a constitutional right, either, at least not explicitly. One way to overcome this theoretical difficulty is to argue that the practice of coerced abortion doubtlessly violates the personal security of women (to use the language of the Universal Declaration of Human Rights) and, using the legal terminology of the United States, the personal privacy of women derived, as just mentioned, from the U.S. Constitution. Still, the question whether or not the right to reproduction is fundamental might result in many further questions: Why and how is the right to reproduction a fundamental or secondary human right? Must reproductive behavior, like sexual behavior, be completely free from state intervention? When the right conflicts with some kinds of common good, such as controlling the rapid growth of population, to which should priority be given? Obviously, I am not able to answer any of these questions here.

JUSTIFICATION AND CRITIQUE FROM
CHINESE MORAL-POLITICAL TRADITIONS

The unique existence of forced abortion in contemporary China has led Westerners and many Chinese as well to conclude that it must have something directly to do with Chinese culture. Coerced abortion in contemporary China is seen as evidence of the historical acceptance of abortion and lack of reverence for human life in Chinese culture on the one hand and the authoritarian or despotic feature of Chinese political-moral traditions on the other. In chapter 3, I argue that, historically speaking, the first part of this assumption—blanket assumptions of a permissive or "liberal" attitude to abortion in the history of China—is far from sound. Among a great number of "conservative" perspectives is Buddhism, which disapproves of abortion in principle. Against the common impressions, a conservative or restrictive position in Confucianism is not only historically evident but also theoretically consistent with the ideas, ideals, and principles in Confucian moral traditions. Also against common wisdom, a more typical traditional Chinese notion of fetal life is that human life has clearly started before birth. In this section, I will explore whether the use of force in the case of forced abortion can be justified by Chinese moral-political traditions.

China seems to possess a long-standing and well-established authoritarian or totalitarian tradition, both in practice and in theory. Not only is the dominant ideology—Confucianism—authoritarian in essence, but Legalism, originated in the Warring States period (480–221 BCE.), explicitly advocates a totalitarian political system—the absolute power of a central authority and harsh punishment—to rule and control the people. The name "Legalism" is somewhat misleading because the scholars and administrators who can be classified in this school never stood for jurisdiction and laws that protect individuals from the abuse of power by a single authority. They contributed no ideas like those expressed in C. L. Montesquieu's foundational legal and political work *The Spirit of the Laws*. Chinese Legalists were so labeled because they believed in draconian laws and promoted even the extensive use of force in governing. Han Fei, the most important Legalist thinker and a founder of the school, once said:

> The empire can be ruled only by utilizing human nature. Men have likes and dislikes; thus they can be controlled by means of rewards and punishments. On this basis prohibitions and commands can be put in operation, and a complete system of government set up. The ruler need only hold these handles [rewards and punishments] firmly, in order to maintain his supremacy. . . . These handles are the power of life and death. Force is the stuff that keeps the masses in subjection. (Quoted in Greel 1953: 149)

According to the logic of legalist tradition, coerced abortion can hardly be regarded as a serious moral problem. In imperial China, political operations were somehow framed by Legalism, to some extent, even more than by Confucianism. Legalist political thought has also greatly influenced contemporary China. Like the notorious dictator Shi Huang-di (the First Emperor of the Qin Dynasty, in the third century BCE), Mao Zedong favored Legalism greatly, even though he proclaimed himself a Marxist and Communist. In the 1970s, Mao initiated a national political and cultural movement to commend Legalism and condemn Confucianism, partly because Confucianism rarely condoned a ruler's (or central authority's) governing by tyranny, extensive coercion, and draconian laws.

However, Legalism is just one of a variety of Chinese political and moral traditions. A critique of forced abortion can be given from Confucianism, the most influential political-moral tradition. Confucianism requires the individual to have male offspring to continue the family line and promotes the idea of a large family. It considers a large and growing population as an auspicious sign of a good society. Because of all these social values, Confucianism has usually been viewed as a force acting against population control. But it is superficial to argue that Confucianism straightforwardly disapproves the Chinese birth control program in general. Here one needs to make a distinction between what can be called "primary" and "secondary" values or norms in any moral tradition. According to the primary Confucian moral values, it is more likely that Confucians would endorse the social program due to its emphasis on the primacy of society and social good.

Nevertheless, Confucian moral support of population control does not mean support for forced abortion as morally justifiable. While Confucianism gives great importance to the community, the power of the ruler, and the merit of obeying the authorities in human life, it never approves governing by coercion rather than by persuasion. Confucius and his followers defined a good government as one that loves its people and makes them happy and held that the highest technique of governing is teaching or education. Mencius, the Confucian master second only to Confucius, once distinguished two kinds of government—*wang* (kingly) and *ba* (forceful). He exalted the former and rebuked the latter. In contrast to *ba*, who governs by the means of coercion, *wang*, the leader of kingly government, is a sage. On behalf of the people, the sage–king administers through moral instruction and virtues, and he practices *ren* (humanity, humaneness). In fact, *ren*, translated as benevolence, human-heartedness, goodness, is a, if not *the*, core concept of Confucianism. Mencius's ideal of *renzheng* (government of humanity, humanely governing) has been the heart of Confucian political thought (see Mencius 1970, Hsiao 1979: 148–66). In the long history of traditional Chinese thought, only the totalitarian thinkers of Legalism advocate the absolute power of strong centralized government, draconian law, and harsh punishment.

Furthermore, according to the Confucian views of abortion presented in chapter 3, late abortion would be considered killing a human being and, hence, a form of manslaughter. Based on traditional medical literature, there is no doubt that the fetus at the late, if not early, stage of pregnancy has already been a member of the family, the patrilineage, the country, and the human community, with a physical and spiritual connection to heaven, earth, and ancestors. Using late abortion as a measure of birth control is thus equal to killing another living human being for the purpose of decreasing the population.

In conclusion, Confucianism may support the birth control policy but clearly condemn or at least question the practice of coerced abortion. Another reason for this limited support for current policies is that, in general, Confucianism opposes taking economic and material development as the most important goal of the society and calls for establishing a people-centered governance or state, a polity of humanity (*renzheng*), a harmonious and righteous society (Nie 2004c).

SUPPRESSED PUBLIC DISCOURSE

In the previous two sections I argue that forced abortion is morally unjustifiable not only because it is counter to the mainstream Western liberal notion of reproductive rights but also because it goes against Confucian moral and political ideals. In this section, I argue that, due to suppressed public discourse, coerced termination associated with birth control policies lacks moral legitimacy, even if coerced abortion could be ethically justifiable as a lesser and necessary evil.

The Party line may claim that the public discourse in contemporary China has not been suppressed or silenced, but Chinese voices on abortion heard in this book indicate that public discussions on birth control are far from sufficient. As demonstrated above, control of information and public discourse is a major method of state control in contemporary China. The Chinese Party–state does not allow people to discuss most social issues and policies, including the population problem and the national family planning program, *freely and publicly*. Concerns, complaints, and dissident opinions are often, if not always, suppressed and even silenced through depriving citizens of the freedoms of expression and association, as well as through citizens' self-censorship due to the fear. In fact, as analyzed above, a significant reason for the overwhelming Chinese support and acceptance for the current birth control lies in the fact that the government has both strongly propagated the official views and desperately suppressed different voices so that people have no information to think otherwise.

In the section called "For the Social Good," I offer an analogy between paying taxes and limiting family size. On one hand, the analogy could be used to justify the state's use of force whenever and wherever violation occurs. On the other hand, the analogy uncovers a serious criticism of the current Chinese practice of planned childbearing: that people are not allowed to discuss the subject and related issues freely and publicly. If someone in any country strongly opposed his or her present government's engagement in a war against another country for the manufacture of weapons of mass destruction or whatever reasons, he or she could refuse to pay one or several years' income tax in protest. At the same time, the state has a legal as well as moral right to respond to this act of civil disobedience by putting the individual in jail, forcing him or her to do public service, or confiscating appropriate properties of the individual. As it now stands, the state in China can legitimately do the same thing to an individual if he or she violates the birth control policy, which, like a citizen's obligation to pay taxes, has been legally approved. But it would be morally wrong for the state to prohibit the individual's making a public speech, writing an article or book, or conducting research that criticizes and opposes the birth control policy and to punish the individual who actually does so.

This may sound like the reasoning of a typical Western libertarian. What about traditional Chinese perspectives? Do Chinese political and moral traditions contain the notion of liberty of thought and speech? Since China has been a typical example of "oriental despotism" or "authoritarian society," are liberalism in general and freedom of thought and speech in particular commensurable with Chinese culture? Since the general issues on human rights in the Chinese context are discussed in the next chapter, on Chinese-Western crosscultural dialogue, here I will illustrate only that the practice of suppressing public discourse on birth control is unjustifiable according to Chinese political-moral perspectives.

Until the early twentieth century, it appears that China had never developed a political-moral doctrine similar to Western liberalism. No single thinker or writer in imperial China seemed to have written anything like poet John Milton's speech for the liberty of unlicensed printing to the Parliament of England in 1644 or John Stuart Mill's systematic defense of the liberty of thought and discussion in the second chapter of *On Liberty*. On the contrary, with a long tradition of censorship and literary inquisition from ancient times to the present, Chinese history is full of stories of imprisonment or execution of authors for writing or even just speaking against officially approved views (*wenzi yu*). As early as 213 BCE, the First Emperor ordered the notorious event called "burning the books and executing intellectuals" (*fenshu kengru*), in which all banned books were destroyed and hundreds of dissidents killed. In the twentieth century, millions of Chinese were persecuted and executed simply for what they said and wrote. Among those martyrs was a frail daughter of China, Zhang Zhixin, whose throat was cut on the eve of her execution lest she speak out in the public "trial," whose only purpose was to humiliate the accused "antirevolutionary" and intimidate and warn the others. The case happened in the 1970s, more than two thousand years after the empire of the First Emperor collapsed in 221 BCE, and in a place where the "highest form of democracy" was in action.

Nevertheless, it is wrong to assert that freedom of speech has never been valued by the Chinese, just as it is ridiculous to claim that freedom of speech is not valued in the West on the basis of the execution of Socrates and Jesus Christ and the occurrence of the Inquisition. As a result of his fifty years of studying Confucianism and Asian civilization, Wm. Theodore de Bary concludes that "one can call freedom of discussion and association a value recognized in Confucian tradition, however qualified its practice may have been by limiting circumstances in dynastic situations" (de Bary 1998: 108). De Bary deliberates:

[P]ublic discussion (*gongyi*) was a recognized value, both in terms of the responsibility Confucian scholars felt to speak out against the abuse of power, and in terms of the increasing recognition by Neo-Confucians, culminating in the advocacy by Huang Zongxi, Lu Sheyi, Lü Liuliang, and Tang Zhen in the seventeenth century, of duly constituted institutions to protect this public discussion (described by Huang in terms of laws and by Lü in terms of rites). One cannot, of course, claim this as a dominant political tradition in China; it does, however, constitute a significant line of Confucian thought from Confucius and Mencius down through Ouyang Xiu, the Cheng brothers, and Zhu Xi in the Song, as well as a number of Ming scholars from Fang Xiaoru down to the Donglin scholars of the sixteenth century and Huang Zongxi in the seventeenth century. (de Bary 1998)

Freedom of speech in the particular context of the ruler/minister relationship has been often emphasized in Confucianism. For de Bary, "by logical and natural extension" this could become applicable to anybody's participation in the political process (de Bary 1998: 21).

Long before Confucius and the First Emperor, the practice of silencing people vied with beliefs in the importance of allowing people to speak out freely, as the familiar household story of the minister Duke Zhao and his ruthless and tyrannical King Li indicates. Hating criticism and complaints from people, the king killed those who dared to criticize and complain. Soon, no one criticized anymore, and the king was happy. When he boasted of this silent condition of no criticism, Duke Zhao, the wise minister, gave a long reply. The minister developed his central idea around the well-known metaphor in which dealing with people's expressions was compared to dealing with water. To block either is useless, wrong, harmful, and dangerous. The right and natural way to deal with them is to direct them. Knowing that people have minds and can speak is as important for the governing of a country as mountains and rivers are for the earth. It is thus beneficial for the country for a ruler to allow and encourage all subjects, including officials, intellectuals, professionals, and common people, to speak what is in their minds. King Li did not listen to Duke Zhao. And his kingdom, as the story goes, fell into serious crisis within three years as a result of his silencing people's criticism and would have collapsed without a reformed governance led by Dukes Zhao and Zhou. All this has been narrated in the volume "Chronicle of Zhou Dynasty" of *Records of the Grand Historian* (*Shiji*), by Sima Qian (145–86? BCE), the Herodotus and Thucydides of China.

According to volume thirteen of the monumental history, *Complete Mirror for the Illustration of Government (Zizhi Tongjian)*, finished in 1084 by Sima Guang (China's Edward Gibbon) and his colleagues, freedom of speech was institutionalized in some dynasties at least, by the wise rulers who, afraid of mistakes and ignorance in governing, established channels called "the Wood for Criticism and the Drum for Remonstrance" (*she feipang zhi mu, zhi gangjian zhi gu).* Through this institution, people, especially intellectuals, were able to express publicly their concerns and opinions about social policies. The Tang was probably the most glorious dynasty in Chinese history, comparable to the Roman Empire, and its best moment was the Zhenguan period (627–649). A cornerstone, a sign of this glory, was that officials and people were free to speak out—at least they were not punished or executed for doing so. The practices of seeking remonstrance (*qiujian*) and accepting remonstrance (*najian*) constituted a foremost element of the good governance according to the *Essential Political Experience of the Zhenguan Period (Zhenguan Zhengya)*, written in the early eighth century and one of the most important political works in China. In this tradition, critical engagements, especially officials and intellectuals, with a regime's policies were considered to be an indication, if not requirement, of genuine loyalty to the emperor and the empire. It is historically evident that the importance of free speech and public discussion for the prosperity and harmony of the whole society, if not for the sake of freedom itself, has long been a tradition in China.

Therefore, the suppressed public discourse on the birth control policies in contemporary China is not morally justifiable according to not only Western liberalism but also traditional Chinese values. It is as legally wrong also since the current Chinese Constitution stipulates that every citizen has the fundamental rights of free speech and free association. In the Chinese political tradition, the ruler who allows and encourages his officials and subjects to speak freely is called "enlightened ruler" (*mingjun*), in contrast to the "fatuous and self-indulgent ruler" (*hunjun*), who refuses to listen to criticism or listens only to what he wants to hear. Moreover, the tradition encourages, if not requires, the officials, scholars, and subjects, scholar–officials in particular, to speak out, especially if they perceive problems and dangers that social policies may bring about. Those who do not speak truth for self-interested reasons can become "unruly officials and betraying subjects" (*luanchen zeizi*).

Putting Chinese and Western political-moral traditions aside, common sense tells us that it is not prudent to carry out such a massive project of social engineering without sufficient public debate through which most, if not all, possible problems and negative impacts can be adequately addressed. Chapter 2 illustrates that, if Mao Zedong and the Party–state had not silenced the dissident view led by Ma Yinchu on the importance of birth control in the 1950s, the population problem in today's China would not be so severe. Even official discourse has acknowledged this mistake. It would be simply stupid to make the same mistake again, this time by silencing the dissident views that question the severity of overpopulation and the necessity of forceful measures to control population and explore alternative or better social policies for dealing with the population problem. As the famous remark goes, those who do not learn from history are condemned to repeat it. If we make the same mistake again, we will become the people condemned by history (*lishi de zuiren*).

CONCLUSION

In spite of official denials, coerced abortion has been carried out in China in the name of social good and the long-term interests of individuals. Confronted with overpopulation and many people's desires to have two or more children, coercion is employed as the last resort to limit rapid growth in population. Coerced abortion is a tragedy in the common sense of the term. In the first part of this chapter, I discussed three crucial sociological factors that have led to the practice of coerced abortion: the strong state will and control, the complexity of social relationship and pressures in the local world, and conscientious (but far from well-informed) acceptance and support of the birth control program by the Chinese populace.

Ethically speaking, coerced abortion is highly objectionable, yet it is not impossible to make a moral argument for the practice on the grounds that it is part of a program that is assumed to produce a greater good for society. I put forward paying taxes as an analogy for limiting family size to test the possibility that governmental employment of coercive measures in implementing the family planning policy could be morally and legally justified on the same basis on which any state justifies use of coercive measures in implementing its tax laws. In other words, taking the serious problem of overpopulation in China into account and assuming the necessity of a national family planning policy, forced abortion might be seen as a lesser and necessary evil for some essential social good, or as a tragic choice or genuine ethical dilemma rather than an outright moral evil as it first appears. But this argument turned out to have serious problems; for example, it confuses the necessity of the population control policies with the justification of coerced abortion as a means for implementing the polices. Even though coercion itself is morally justified, and even required under some circumstances, from the Western perspective coerced abortion and other compulsory fertility control mechanisms violate an individual's right to reproduction and a woman's right to personal privacy, as seen through the lens of liberal democracy. Since what we are discussing here are matters in China, I turned to Chinese history and traditions to seek possible justification for the use of coercion, coerced abortion included, in controlling reproduction. Legalism may be able to fill this role, but other moral-political traditions, such as the most influential, Confucianism, may not. While Confucianism gives priority to the common good of society, it is against Confucian moral-political values to use coercion, especially coerced and late abortion, in pursuit of that good. Finally, then, I argue that, even if coerced abortion could be morally justified in the service of some important social good, the suppressed public discourse on birth control poses another, even more serious, ethical problem according to not only Western but also Chinese political-moral traditions. That is, the absence of a fully informed consensus among people strips the program of legitimacy, whereas attempts to justify coercive measures can begin only *after* the ends have been legitimated.

This last statement raises another ethical issue. The practice of forced termination of pregnancy sets up an example in which the state can employ any means for pursuing good causes. This way of thinking about moral issues—justifying the means by the ends—can seriously undermine the moral foundation of the whole society and thus become dangerous to the long-term stability and development of China. Legitimate ends are only starting points for testing the morality of means. End-justifying-means thinking has further alienated Chinese people from the government and aggravated the conflicts between people and the state. In fact, Confucianism has repeatedly stated that moral ends do not justify immoral means.

In this chapter and throughout the book, I discuss China's birth control program as part of the coerced abortion topic. Very surprisingly and worrisomely, no work up to now that at the same time critically and systematically examines the moral issues related to the program appears to have done this. I must admit that what I have to say about the ethical issues of the program is preliminary. There are a great number of complicated ethical issues involved in such a massive project of social mobilization as China's birth control program. For example, what are the normative Confucian, Daoist, and even Marxist positions regarding the setting of policies concerning population or overpopulation and national birth control? What is the relationship between economic and social development on the one hand and human dignity and freedom on the other in controlling overpopulation in China? What is the proper role of the state in regulating the personal interests in balance with the social good? Is the Chinese birth control program based on sound ethical justification? Is it a moral practice? If yes, how and in what ways? If not always, what aspects are wrong and in what sense? All in all, what are the moral issues at stake in making and implementing population policies in China? A systematic ethical and critical inquiry into China's birth control program remains long overdue (for results of my own initial effort on this important subject, see Nie 2003, 2004a, 2004b, 2005).

This chapter raises far more questions on coerced abortion associated with Chinese family planning policies than it resolves. More ethical, sociological, and historical exploration into the practice is greatly needed, and more important, a free public discussion on coerced abortion, population, and the birth control policies among Chinese people is desperately needed. Sadly, it seems unlikely this latter necessity can become a reality in the not-too-distant future. Moreover, Marx once remarked somewhere that the aim of philosophy is not merely to interpret this world but to change it. Confucianism would agree with this ideal; that is, the mission of moral exploration should not be limited to theoretical meditation in the ivory tower but should include engagement with the social practice of people. If the theoretical exercise determines that coerced abortion cannot be morally justified, then the most daunting challenge would be to face the tragedy and change what is morally wrong through the guidance of human moral wisdom, ideas, ideals, and principles regardless of where they originated—in the East or West.

NOTE

1. Another policy he completely agreed with was that of *andin tanjie* (maintaining stability and unity of the society). This policy became the number one national guiding principle after the democratic movement of 1989. The government has spared no pains to propagate the principle that any demonstration or protest similar to those that occurred in 1989 will cause great social turbulence and disaster, especially holding up the economic construction and development of China. It is obvious that the real purpose of the policy is to prevent and repress any direct or indirect challenge to the current political-social order, that is, to maintain the absolute leadership of the Party and the current government in the name of social stability and unity.

8

The Challenge of Cross-Cultural Dialogue: Taking Seriously China's Internal Plurality

So vast is our land that no fable could do justice to its vastness, the heavens can scarcely span it—and Peking is only a dot in it and the Imperial palace less than a dot.

—Franz Kafka, "The Great Wall of China"

"Taking cultural differences seriously" has become a resounding slogan in this age of globalization and multiculturalism, or "the clash of civilizations." While differences among cultures are often highlighted, differences or diversity within other cultures, particularly non-Western ones, are often downplayed. So much is made of American pluralism and diversity that it is easy to overlook the fact that, throughout its history, China has been socially and culturally as diverse as the United States, if not more so. Contemporary Western China scholarship, as well as that in Taiwan, Hong Kong, and Singapore, has been revealing and documenting the great diversity of Chinese history and culture. But, as will become clear soon, the conventional modernist or colonist way of thinking dies hard among the general public, policy makers, and scholars in the fields outside of China studies. While the United States is said to represent the modern, multiracial, multicultural, plural society, China has long been treated as essentially homogeneous. Still, the obvious and profound plurality of Chinese culture has never been taken as seriously as it deserves outside and, to a lesser extent, inside China. Rather, as the common wisdom on abortion in China indicates, a modern myth on China has been created and spread worldwide that characterizes Chinese society and culture as united and communitarian, in striking contrast with the plural and individualistic West, the United States in particular.

This chapter will examine the roots and popularity of this conventional way of thinking and make a plea for taking cultural diversity seriously—not cross-cultural differences so much as the differences that exist *within* each and every culture. Using Chinese perspectives on abortion as an example, I will argue that taking seriously the various kinds of internal plurality within China constitutes the critical step to developing an adequate cross-cultural dialogue with Chinese people. First, I will show the problems generated by the underlying myth of a communitarian and monolithic China, a myth shared by two popular approaches to cross-cultural differences—one can be called "modernist" or ethnocentric and the other "postmodernist" or relativist—and explore the elements of a more effective, what can be called "interpretative," approach toward cultures and the diversity within them. Then, in a preliminary comparison with the U.S. abortion debate, I will illustrate my argument by revisiting the major findings of this study on Chinese views and experiences of abortion.

TWO DIFFERENT APPROACHES, ONE SHARED MYTH

For U.S. constitutional authority Laurence Tribe, as cited in chapter 1, the Chinese understanding of abortion "is structured almost wholly in terms of corporate groups, like the state and the family, and centers on the needs of and the duties owed to such groups" (Tribe 1992: 63). It thus differs in nature from the U.S. abortion debate, in which the issue is characteristically defined in the language of individual rights, women's rights to choose, and the fetuses' rights to life. For Tribe, together with John Aird (1990), Steven Mosher (1983, 1993), and many others, it is obvious which framing of the subject is right and which is wrong, and they have had no hesitation in condemning China's totalitarian and statist perspective.

Tribe's comments on abortion in China display what I call the "modernist" or ethnocentric way of thinking about cultures. The modernist way of generalizing and appraising Occidental and Oriental cultures was vividly described by the German author Thomas Mann through the character of Herr Settembrini. Settembrini, an inmate in a tuberculosis sanatorium in Switzerland, was the intellectual guide of Hans Castorp, the questing young hero in *The Magic Mountain*. According to the "Settembrinian cosmogony," Mann wrote, two incompatible principles, one Asiatic and the other European,

> were in perpetual conflict for possession of the world: force and justice, tyranny and freedom, superstition and knowledge; the law of permanence and the law of change, of ceaseless fermentation ensuing in progress. One might call the first the Asiatic, the second the European principle; for Europe was the theatre of rebellion, the sphere of intellectual discrimination and transforming activity,

whereas the East embodied the conception of quiescence and immobility. There was no doubt as to which of the two would finally triumph: it would be the power of enlightenment, the power that made for rational advance and development. (Mann 1969: 157)

For Settembrini, an Italian humanist zealot, the Asiatic principle has to be "crushed" for the sake of progress, science, and human reason. With "his suave smile," he foresaw that, in fulfilling this task and other "sublime exertions," the blessings of enlightenment would soon come to all of Europe and the whole of humankind, "if not on the wings of doves, then on the pinions of eagles" (157).

In the past several decades, a different approach to understanding cross-cultural differences—one that can be called "postmodernist" or relativist—has been developing. Countering the negative view of the East, the "postmodernist" standpoint takes a positive attitude toward non-Western cultures. One of the many historical forces that has contributed to this postmodern turn is the radical criticism of modernity and such modern values as rationalism, universalism, liberalism, and scientism. The postmodern way of thinking about cultures criticizes judging the values and norms in one cultural system, the non-Western culture in particular, from the standpoint of Western culture.

The anthropological accounts of birth control in rural China from 1949 to the mid-1980s by Sulamith and Jack Potter (1990) well display this postmodernist approach. The Potters stress that it is important to understand Chinese people "in their own terms" and that "anthropological understanding is based on the development of empathy with what is initially perceived as alien, rather than on taking an ethnocentric or adversarial position" (Potter and Potter 1990: xiii). Their account on the birth planning at the village in southeastern China constitutes an indirect response to the criticism of Tribe, Aird, and Mosher on the Chinese practice of abortion. For the Potters, the common Western criticism of abortion in China is ethnocentric and too harsh, or at least not culturally sensitive.

However, like the modernist discourse, the postmodernist viewpoint emphasizes the radical differences and incommensurability of different worldviews, discourses, paradigms, and cultures. Although the rise of the postmodern discourse challenges the modernist or ethnocentric evaluations of the Eastern "principle," it nevertheless still views the East and the West as two different worlds inscrutable to each other. In spite of their commitment to an empathetic approach to what is alien, the Potters describe the culturally specific assumptions of the Chinese villagers by contrasting them with those of Americans. In other words, though opposing the ethical evaluation by Tribe, Aird, and Mosher of the Chinese norms and practice of birth planning, the Potters agree with them that fundamental differences exist between

American and Chinese understandings of related issues. Like Tribe, the Potters conclude that the Chinese way of thinking about and dealing with birth and abortion is collective or communitarian and statist. In the Potters' own words, the Chinese birth planning system

> does not respect the essentially un-Chinese idea that the individual has exclusive rights over his or her reproductive capacity. Instead it is a system in which a birth is seen as appropriately the concern of the state and the concern of the family; because a birth is important to these levels, its importance to the individual is superseded. It is a culturally specific Chinese way of understanding the meaning of birth, and birth prevention, and in order to be understood at all, it must be understood in its own terms. (Potter and Potter 1990: 231)

A series of Chinese versus American contrasts follow from the Potters' China-oriented anthropological account of birth planning in China. For instance, he contends that though care is needed in childhood as well as in old age, "in the West, the moral emphasis is on the importance of caring for the children, and in China, the moral emphasis is on the importance of caring for the old" (228–29). In the West, an unborn life is valued in and of itself, but this idea is "alien and irrelevant" in Chinese social thinking, which defines a birth in a "purely instrumental term" (231). In the United States, the concept of privacy has become crucial for the abortion debate, and the Chinese practice of making birth control a "subject of public record" is "invasion of privacy." Since this concept of privacy "does not exist" in China and "is not present in people's thinking," behaving according to the notion of personal privacy could be "antisocial" in a Chinese cultural setting (235–36).

Two seemingly reasonable conclusions or assumptions exist here. First, there are fundamental differences between American and Chinese perspectives of abortion. Second, these differences can be defined in the typical series of U.S.–China dichotomies—individualistic versus communitarian, individual rights versus primacy of the state and family, privacy versus social relationship, the unborn life valued in and of itself versus in instrumental terms.

Twentieth-century people in both the East and the West are accustomed to thinking of and talking about the Oriental and Occidental civilizations in the contrasting and very general terms reminiscent of Settembrini's categories: individualism versus communitarianism; autonomy versus family decisions; individual liberty versus social or common good; the individual versus the collective or community; individual rights versus personal virtues; individual development and perfection versus family and filial piety; contract versus trust; self-determination versus self-examination; freedom versus the concept of duty and obligation; and so on. The most widely accepted generalization is that Western and Chinese cultures are dominated by individualism and authoritarianism, respectively, the latter thought of as totalitarianism by its opponents and communitarianism by its empathizers. In his book, *Americans and Chinese*, the Chinese-American scholar Francis Hsu (1970 [1953]) argued that the American way of life is "individual-centered" (emphasizing the predilections of the individual), in contrast to the "situation-centered" Chinese way of life (emphasizing an individual's appropriate place and behavior among his or her fellow human beings). Most recently, eminent social psychologist Richard Nisbett (2003) tried to show how East Asians, Chinese included, and Westerners or Anglo-Americans think and see differently and why. Nisbett argues that East Asian thought contrasts strikingly with Western thought: the former holistic, dialectic, seeking a middle way between opposing thoughts, and focusing on the perceptual field as a whole and relations among the objects and events within that field; the latter analytic, applying rules of formal logic, focusing on salient objects or people. The differences in the modes of reasoning and thinking, observable in medicine, law, science, human rights, and international relations, are due to different ecologies, social structures, philosophers, and educational systems that date back to ancient Greece and China and that have survived into the modern world. For Nisbett, collectivist Asians and individualistic Westerners have maintained very different systems of thought for thousands of years.

China's twentieth-century intellectuals, regardless of their positions on Chinese and Western cultures, begin their arguments with the assumption that *the* Western individualistic way of living and thinking contrasts with *the* Chinese authoritarian or collectivist way of living and thinking. Some, such as Hu Shi, are advocates of antitraditionalism and wholesale Westernization who radically criticize Chinese Confucian values and promote Western democracy and science. Some, such as Liang Shuming, are advocates of cultural conservatism who criticize Western materialism and individualism and promote sociocultural construction on a Chinese basis. But, whichever attitudes they take about Chinese and Western cultures, almost all of twentieth-century Chinese commentators agree that there is a fundamental difference between the two cultures and that this difference can be summarized as "collectivist China versus individualistic West." This is true not only of the New Culture Movement in the first decades of the twentieth century and the Cultural Revolution in the 1960s and 1970s, but also of the post-Mao reform era starting with the "Cultural Craze" (*wenhua re*) in the 1980s (see de Bary and Lufrano 2003).

Underlying this dichotomous way of approaching Chinese and Western cultures is a myth about China. The myth of a unified and homogeneous Chinese culture has been created and accepted in an attempt to understand what has united the entire Chinese civilization. The myth assumes two "matters of fact": first, Chinese society and culture are basically or at least by and large homogeneous, and second, something essential distinguishes China from the West (in this case, communitarianism vs. individualism).

The myth has power because it offers simple and clear-cut explanations of why Chinese and Westerners are different. As a result, outside and inside of China, it still persists in casual conversations and serious discussions among general public as well as scholars. It still dominates, often in an unconscious manner, how Chinese and Westerners perceive and interpret China and Chinese culture, especially in comparison with the West. For example, this myth constitutes such a fundamental assumption and conclusion in the Chinese official ideology when characterizing Chinese and Western cultures that Chinese ethicists define Chinese and Western morality in this fashion (e.g., Luo, Ma, and Yu 2004 [1986]). It manifests abundantly in the general image of Chinese and Westerners of the "Chineseness" of Chinese medical ethics, which is seen as collectivist and familistic in contrast with the individualistic Western one (e.g., Fox and Swazey 1984; Fan 1997). Surely, since 1980, more and more contemporary scholarly works in China studies have powerfully demonstrated, mostly in an indirect way, inadequacy, superficiality, simplicity, limits, wrongness, problems, and even absurdity of the myth. Yet, these fruits from China studies as an academic discipline have so far exerted little significant influence over the public life and other intellectual areas.

It is simply common sense to recognize that China has always been pluralistic, given its wide geographical area; long history of disunity interrupted by unity; large number of dialects or languages; enormous economic variation; various current political systems (in mainland China, Hong Kong, and Taiwan); rich and varied social customs and cultural norms; ethnic diversity of the population (there are more than fifty nationalities in China); great local complexity; and vast silent majority. In fact, it is difficult, if not impossible, to define the fundamental terms "China" and "Chinese." In other words, it is essential to make sure "whose China" and "which Chinese" whenever thinking and talking about China and Chinese. Then, the question can be raised: Why was the modern myth of China bred in the first place and why has it become widely and persistently accepted?

As for any myth, there are obviously complicated political and intellectual reasons for the birth and persistence of this one on China. First, politically speaking, the West at one time needed a primitive or backward "Other" to extol by contrast its own modernity, enlightenment, progress, and realization of a universal history. More recently, the West has sought a radical, different Other to lend support to the cultural factions within any Western country that emphasize religious, racial, cultural, gender, sexual preference, and other differences. The myth is also politically useful internally in China. The ruling ideology promotes the belief of a single and unified Chinese culture or China in order to legitimate its universal dominance and to maintain its own interests and power. Taking the plurality of China seriously has the potential to undermine the current power structure. Second, the modern myth of China arises from certain intellectual and academic traditions. Just as early anthropology focused on the radical difference of other cultures in comparison with the West, modern scholarship in Chinese studies has taken as its primary goal the discovery of a unique Chinese way of seeing, thinking, and acting. Ironically, though understandably, while emphasizing the radical differences between non-Western and Western cultures, influential anthropological works have often minimized, if not totally ignored, both the great internal plurality *within* every non-Western society or culture and the common humanity shared by all societies and cultures. Following the lead of first-generation anthropologists such as Lucien Levy-Bruhl, who aimed to discover the particular mentality of primitive societies and peoples, twentieth-century sinologists and scholars in other disciplines have attempted to find the unique ways of seeing and acting in Chinese civilization. Quite a few theories have been put forward in defense of the notion of Chinese uniqueness. They include holism, collectivism, categorical thinking, the system of correspondence, the organic worldview (correlative thinking), the philosophy of organism, or synchronicity (*Synchroniziät*), and so on. But is there really a unique and uniform Chinese mentality? If there is, does that mentality truly characterize each individual Chinese and pervade every aspect of Chinese life? For me, the answer to both these question is "no."

Actually, the Greeks and Romans of antiquity were already inclined to think that foreign cultures were by and large homogeneous, in contrast with the plurality of their own. In *Politics*, probably the most influential work in Western political thought, Aristotle compared the people of the colder region of Europe, the people of Asia, and the people of Greece (1327b18–35, Aristotle 1995: 266–67). The peoples of northern Europe, he said, "are full of spirit, but deficient in skill and intelligence." The peoples of Asia are "peoples of subjects and slaves" because they "are endowed with skill and intelligence, but are deficient in spirit." However,

> The Greek stock, intermediate in geographical position, unites the qualities of both sets of peoples. It possesses both spirit and intelligence, for which reason it continues to be free, to have the highest political development, and to be capable of governing every other people—if only it could once achieve political unity. The same sort of difference is found among the Greek peoples themselves. Some of them are of a one-sided nature: others show a happy mixture of spirit and intelligence. (1327b18–35, Aristotle 1995: 266–67)

Implied here is that the non-Greek peoples are one-sided in nature and that any diversity among them can, by and large, be ignored. In relating cultures different from one's own, this Aristotelian mode of thinking was popular among Westerners and Chinese in the twentieth century, and it continues to be alive and well even in the new millennium.

The problems of the modern but long-rooted myth about China lie exactly in its apparent strength of offering a simple but grand and black-and-white generalization. That is to say, it is too simplistic. Among the flaws of the myth is what has been called by the American philosopher Richard Bernstein "false essentialism" in thinking about different cultures, especially non-Western ones. False essentialism and its popular dichotomous classification about Eastern and Western cultures seduce discussants "into thinking there are essential determinate characteristics that distinguish the Western and Eastern 'mind'" (Bernstein 1992: 66). Consequently, false essentialism "violently distorts the sheer complexity of overlapping traditions that cut across these artificial, simplistic global notions" (Bernstein 1992: 66).

To repeat, with the modern myth about China, the other side of China—the ever-changing China and, most notably, the great diversity of China—has been downplayed and even ignored. With regard to the issue of abortion, as will be shown below, an unfortunate consequence of characterizing the American and Chinese cultures as individualistic versus communitarian is that the great variations within the two cultures, and the amazing similarities between the Chinese and American perspectives, have been downplayed, even ignored. It is time now to lay the myth to rest by taking seriously the internal plurality of thoughts and values in China. Or, put more exactly, it is time now to realize the overgeneralizing the myth has caused and put it in its appropriate position, since it, like any other myth, is not totally groundless and useless.

THE INTERPRETATIVE APPROACH TO CULTURE

The mutual understanding constitutes a major dimension of human interactions and communications, whether cross culturally or within any particular culture. Understanding is not possible without interpretation or recognition of meanings. One of the significant developments in social science and the humanities in the second half of the twentieth century was a turning toward hermeneutics and interpretative approaches. For the founder of contemporary interpretative anthropology, Clifford Geertz (1973, 1983), the central methodology for the interpretation of culture is a process he called "thick description" or "thick narrative." American medical humanist Ronald Carson, German philosopher–sinologist Ole Döring, and I have separately argued that bioethics or medical ethics, cross-cultural bioethics in particular, are fundamentally interpretative enterprises (Carson 1990, 1999, forthcoming; Döring 2002b; Nie 1999a, 2000). This present study of abortion in China has taken an interpretative approach as its general methodology.

An interpretative approach recognizes, applauds, and promotes the conception of the internal complexity of each and every culture. American philosopher Martha C. Nussbaum has observed an increasingly new trend in the study of non-Western cultures in the United States that stresses the following points: (1) real cultures are plural, not single; (2) real cultures contain argument, resistance, and contestation of norms; (3) in real cultures, what most people think is likely to be is different from what the most famous artists and intellectuals think; (4) real culture has varied domains of thought and activity; and (5) real cultures have a present as well as a past. All cultures—non-Western and Western alike—are a "complex mixture, often incorporating elements originally foreign" (Nussbaum 1997: 127–28; 117). The variety of Chinese perspectives on abortion presented in this book proves that Chinese culture is no exception to this "new" notion of culture.

The interpretative approach has a number of features. First and foremost, it resists false essentialism on cultures and deconstructs a series of extant stereotypes on Chinese culture and Chinese. Most notably, it distrusts the popular way of generalizing everything, explaining all differences in China and the United States by the global and dichotomous terms of collectivism versus individualism (Nie 1999b, 2000).

The communitarian way of thinking is not as alien to Americans as it appears. For example, the collectivist rationale behind the wide acceptance and strong support of Chinese people for the birth control program is, as I argue in the previous chapter, very much parallel with that of U.S. citizens' support for the state's taxation program. I noted in chapter 1 that the official Chinese discourse prohibited abortion in the 1950s and legalized it in the early 1960s for the good of society and the interests of the nation. The major reason given by the nationalist government in the first half of the twentieth century for prohibiting abortion was also communitarian, for strengthening the nation. This might sound very Chinese and alien to the United States. Yet, according to the authoritative historical study on abortion in America by James Mohr (1978), a major rationale proposed as part of the successful crusade against abortion (except for therapeutic purposes) conducted by the medical establishment in the nineteenth century was societal. For American doctors of the period, the two most significant factors in support of a prohibitive abortion policy were a perceived racial imbalance in the population and the primacy of the woman's health over fetal life. In fact, a survey conducted in the late 1980s by a group of American and Chinese scholars on people's values in the two countries indicates that a large number of American respondents, more than contemporary Chinese, held traditional Confucian values and that there are more similarities between the two cultures than often perceived (Pan et al. 1994.)

It is obvious that the myth of the "individualistic United States" distorts the complexity of American culture, just as the communitarian myth distorts the complexity of Chinese culture. The persistent awareness and constant criticism of various actual and possible problems of extreme individualism show that the United States is not as individualistic as usually assumed. Besides the first language of individualism, there is always a "second language" in American "habits of the hearts," the language of community, of deeply rooted biblical and republican traditions (Bellah et al. 1985). My experience of living in the United States tells me that Americans' pursuit of the common good, concerns for the community, and love for the country are no less strong than those of Chinese people—perhaps even stronger. In fact, if the wide acceptance of the birth control program in China indicates the communitarian mores in Chinese habits of the hearts, then the nationwide hot debate on abortion in the United States, especially the activities of both pro-choice and pro-life activists in the local communities, illustrates powerfully that Americans deeply and genuinely care about their country and communities, from both of which they derive, in large part, their individuality. While the American abortion controversy is often simplified as a debate over the woman's right to choice and the fetus's right to life, fascinating sociological and ethnographic studies on grassroots activists by Kristin Luker (1984) and Faye Ginsburg (1989) have proven beyond doubt that, in reality, abortion itself is the "tip of the iceberg," reflecting people's different worldviews, religious beliefs, and views on womanhood, life, individual liberty, and the state. As I see it, the American abortion debate demonstrates not only the "clash of absolutes, of life against liberty" but also *the shared concerns and efforts on how to develop and sustain a good community and a good society in the face of the fundamental fact of unavoidable plurality and individuality.*

The dichotomous way of characterizing the difference of Chinese and American perspectives on abortion distorts the complexity of China and simplifies its plurality even more. As the medical anthropologist and psychiatrist Arthur Kleinman commented on the early version of this work, a Ph.D. dissertation, the study of abortion in China "demonstrates that, *pace* the claims of China experts on behalf of the Chinese—which assert a cultural master narrative supposed to represent China's 1.26 billion people uniformly— there is no master narrative, no uniform cultural position on abortion" (Kleinman 1999: 86). Indeed. No such thing exists as *the* master narrative, *the* single position, or *the* uniform perspective on the issues of abortion in China. While the official state position approves almost any kind of abortion at any stage except sex-selection abortion, there are unofficial voices as well. While some Chinese people, especially many well-educated intellectuals, often show no significant moral concerns about abortion, a large number among the silent majority think that abortion is morally problematic or wrong. Despite its wide social acceptance, some Chinese explicitly oppose abortion in general. Most notably in my studies, three religious groups—Catholics, Protestants, and Buddhists—demonstrated a more conservative position about abortion than did urban and village people, university and medical students, and the medical ethics/humanities scholars. Actually, though not at all surprisingly, Catholics strongly opposed abortion—most strongly of all the population groups surveyed and much more strongly than Protestants and Buddhists. The great majority of Catholics and the majority in Protestant and Buddhist samples agreed that abortion was a serious moral problem and believed that abortion was equal to killing a human being. Furthermore, a large number of people with no particular religious commitment—for example, one-fourth of subjects in three village samples and nearly one-fifth in two urban population groups—also considered abortion the same as killing a human being. In a word, contrary to the common wisdom on Chinese perspectives on abortion, just as the recent studies of social psychology on people's values in China have illustrated, "there is no identifiable constellation of values common to all Chinese," and "there is little justification for continuing the descriptive tradition of [Chinese-Western] bicultural comparisons of values" (Bond 1996: 226).

Second, taking seriously the plurality within every society or culture, an interpretative approach pays special attention to the commonplace experiences, life stories, and voices of local worlds. It centers on and is oriented to ordinary, underprivileged, marginalized, and deprived groups and individuals, to nonofficial, nonmainstream, or nonlegitimate discourses and practices, to minority, silenced, and dissident voices. As a result, it is clearly against the tendency of treating the contemporary official or mainstream discourse as representative of the whole culture. The brief historical study, the survey results, and personal narratives by women and doctors presented in previous chapters illustrate how mistaken it is to view contemporary official Chinese discourse on abortion as *the representative, even the only legitimate discourse* in China.

Decades ago, Franz Kafka made these points powerfully. Written in the typical symbolic and surreal style of Kafka, "The Great Wall of China" (1970: 83–97) should be read not as a story about the Great Wall of China per se, but as a parable about the conditions of human existence in general, about authority and the individual, about how one tries to make sense of the absurdity of life and the ambiguity of the local world, the society, the history, and the culture one is living in. At the same time, "The Great Wall of China" *is* a realistic story constructed by a brilliant Western artist *about China* as symbolized in the Great Wall, about the challenging, puzzling, alienating, fascinating, mystifying, and inspiring power China has imposed on people living outside as well as inside its borders. Taking the persona of a knowledgeable and contemplative Chinese, a southerner living "almost on the borders of Tibetan Highlands" who participated in building the wall located thousands of miles away in the north, Kafka has produced one of the most insightful works ever written on Chinese society and culture. If we interpret the parable as a story about China, Kafka's "points" should be remembered as a means for better understanding China and promoting a genuine cross-cultural dialogue with Chinese people. These points include: *never forget the local world; pay attention to the China experienced by the individual*

Chinese watch out for generalizations; and always remember the vastness of China. Although Kafka never visited China, "The Great Wall of China" demonstrates through a series of ironic contradictions the difficulty of understanding and the elusive cultural characteristics of such a vast land with such a long history. In general, although written in the early twentieth century, Kafka's story urges that, without taking seriously the great internal diversity, especially those local and marginal voices, one can never have a decent understanding of China or any society.

Kafka's most insightful point is that the emperor—the symbol of the ruling authority of China—is not as powerful as often perceived. The mini parable in "The Great Wall of China" tells that an emperor from his deathbed commanded the messenger to send a message to "you," the humble subject alone. But the messenger was barely able to get through all the gates of the palace, stairs, and courtyards, one after another. The ruling authority might be not as powerless as Kafka has described. After all, in spite of the deeply rooted "no emperor" mentality among common people, the Great Wall was successfully built. It is true that, sometimes for good and often for bad, the modern central state of China has been much more powerful and forceful than the emperor in Kafka's story was, as the Chinese birth control program, along with the whole of twentieth-century's Chinese history, has demonstrated. This has much to do with modern developments in communication technologies and organizational methods, including radio, newspapers, telephone, nation-state, and party politics. However, what Kafka has depicted about the impassable gulf between the central power and local worlds is critical to understanding not only imperial but also contemporary China. Kafka's points are worthwhile bearing in mind when attempting to understand China: no matter how powerful and totalitarian the modern Chinese state is, it cannot do everything as it likes; taking the official perspective as *the* representative Chinese view is misleading and wrong.

I do not want to be misunderstood to be saying that nothing unites and unifies China and Chinese culture. There must be something there. But that something cannot be reduced to a simple characterization of China as collectivist, communitarian, or whatever contemporary official or mainstream discourse promotes. That something, that unifying power or magic, must be characterized as embodying much flux, complexity, and great diversity as Chinese views and experiences of abortion have suggested.

Third, an interpretative approach focuses on not only differences between cultures but also similarities, more exactly, on *difference as well as similarities, the similarities in differences, and the differences in similarities* (Nie 2000). Cultural differences and common human values—whatever they are—are emphasized. Unlike the modernist approach to cross-cultural differences, the interpretative one values the diversity of cultures. Unlike the postmodernist approach, which doubts the possibility for the mutual understanding between cultures, the interpretative one holds that a genuine cross-cultural dialogue is possible. The theoretical orientations in different cultures often appear incommensurable. But through thick description and interpretation, comparability and similarities will emerge. Since all the cultures are plural, it is insufficient to compare them by means of highly abstract and contrasting generalizations. The interpretative approach makes cross-cultural discussions more fruitful, for example, by comparing differences and similarities between Chinese and American expressions of individualism on the one hand and the differences and similarities between Chinese and American expressions of communitarianism on the other.

The interpretative approach promotes a deeper and richer dialogue by treating the "other" as a partner of dialogue. The "other" place is neither a paradise nor a hell, its people neither gods nor inferior beings. The primary goal is to know oneself better and to understand the other better through constant conversations. By promoting long-term coexistence, continuous dialogue, reciprocal learning and criticism, ongoing negotiation, and mutual flourishing, as well as reasonable ways of dealing with dissimilarities and tensions between different cultures, the interpretative approach cultivates rather than destroys the diversity of perspectives within and between different medical moralities. Of course, sustaining the dialogue among different traditions is not an easy task. In order to encourage efficient and productive conversations, tolerance of, respect for, and curiosity about differences are always necessary.

Last, but not least important, unlike the relativist, postmodernist way of thinking about cultures, the interpretative approach to culture does not rule out the necessity and possibility of normative judgments (Nie 2000). It simply says that understanding and interpretation must precede those judgments. The interpretative approach works from the bottom up. The first and most important question to ask about the perspectives and practices in other cultures, especially those that appear strange and ethically problematic, is how they have come into existence. At the same time, one must ask how they contribute to or are supported by other cultural practices. Only then can an informed ethical judgment begin. In this sense, engaged interpretations are essential or foundational for a normative judgment. The interpretative approach thus complements the normative examination. It helps normative criticism to be culturally relevant, both by discovering moral norms similar to one's own in the culture being studied and by encouraging and empowering critical voices indigenous to that culture. My exploration of coerced abortion, reported in the last chapter, constitutes an attempt at making critical moral judgments via an interpretative approach.

Paying attention to the importance of cultural difference never means simply justifying everything that transpires in the culture or society. Studies of cultural factors and context can often provide some information on why and how a practice exists, without ethically justifying the practice. In fact, cross-cultural moral criticism and normative judgments are often insightful in identifying the moral blind spots that every society or culture has. In ancient Greek and Rome, and in early periods of U.S. history, the morality of slavery was rarely questioned. In patriarchal societies, including China, belief in the social, moral, and intellectual inferiority of women is rarely contested. In ancient China, as in many other imperial systems, the political and moral authority of the emperor over his subjects was rarely challenged. The moral blind spots in each of these societies were rarely questioned, as reigning social practices and customs were taken for granted, even seen as the "natural" order. Such moral blind spots may be so well embedded in everyday social practice and long-rooted customs that it is difficult to identify them. Human beings depend upon customs and practices to simplify life by reducing the need for individual decision making about conduct in day-to-day living. Cross-cultural moral criticism and normative judgments can effectively reveal problems that hide, deeply rooted, in everyday practices.

HUMAN RIGHTS IN CHINESE CONTEXT

Since liberty, together with life and the pursuit of happiness, is defined as a "self-evident" endowment of all people in the Declaration of Independence, it is not surprising that the idea of individual rights or the natural rights of human beings plays such a dominant role in American political, moral, and sociocultural life, including the contemporary abortion debate. Although the labels "pro-life" ("fetuses' right to life") and "pro-choice" ("women's right to choose") have oversimplified and polarized the abortion debate in the United States, some common ground remains; that is, most people, whatever pole they occupy, are employing the same language—the language of human rights.

The discourse of human rights has never been so dominant in China as in the United States. In the perspective of the popular modern myth of a communitarian China, a striking feature of Chinese social and political life is the emphasis on the priority of common good and the state's authority. Ren-Zong Qiu (Qiu Renzong), a leading bioethicist and philosopher of science in China, summarizes this view:

A quasi-holistic social-political philosophy has been developed from Chinese cultural tradition. It is based on two thousand years of power-centralized, autocratic monarchy—one that has lacked any rights-oriented, individualistic, liberal democratic tradition. In recent decades, Marxism—rather, a mixture of Russian and Chinese versions of Marxism—has become the dominant ideology. The historicism and social holism of this system, interwoven with traditional ideas, puts the greatest emphasis on nation, society, and country rather than on individuals. (Qiu 1992: 170–71)

As a result of the combination of Chinese traditional "quasi-holistic sociopolitical philosophy" and Marxist holism in the recent decades, "Rights-oriented individualism is essentially alien to the Chinese" (Qiu 1990: 172). But, because the rights-oriented individualism is alien to contemporary Chinese official discourse does not necessarily mean that the concept of human rights does not apply to China. In fact, Qiu, as a major advocate of patient's rights in China, has significantly contributed to the ongoing Chinese human rights movement.

One of the popular arguments or theories to reject the relevance and applicability of the idea of human rights in the Chinese context builds upon cultural differences. In its typical form, the cultural-difference argument runs as follows:

First premise: The notion of human rights arose in and is a part of Western culture;

Second premise: The cultural tradition of China is fundamentally different from that of the West;

Conclusion: Therefore, the notion of human rights is neither relevant nor applicable to China.

Elsewhere, I have pointed out some intellectual flaws of rejecting the applicability of informed consent in China based on this cultural-difference argument (Nie 2002). As I see it, the cultural-difference argument relies on exaggerated assessments of the differences between Western and Chinese cultures; on wrong assumptions about the existence of a unified communitarian Chinese culture; and on essentialist presuppositions that claim Chinese culture and norms are unchangeable. The cultural difference argument assumes that all those who engage in a given moral practice (such as informed consent) must justify that practice with the same arguments or theories (such as liberal individualism). But this is not necessarily so.

The goal of this section is to further point out the problems that the popular myth of a homogeneous and collectivist China has introduced into cross-cultural discussions on human rights. To avoid misunderstanding, let me make two points at the outset. I do not think that abortion in China should be debated in the American way, that is, dominated by the language of human rights. Neither do I think that human rights can be applied and should be practiced everywhere in the same way regardless of cultural and sociopolitical differences in different countries or areas. Moreover, this section aims neither to prove positively the applicability of human rights in the Chinese context nor to explore the relationship between cultures and human rights in general. Rather, I will use traditional Chinese ethical thinking and the views of women and doctors who have expressed human rights violations associated with forced abortion to establish the need for attention to human rights in China. My argument is that to address human rights issues in China adequately it is necessary to take seriously the internal diversity of Chinese culture.

In my contribution to the recent anthology, *Linking Visions: Feminist Bioethics, Human Rights, and the Developing World,* edited by Rosemarie Tong, Anne Donchin, and Susan Dodds, I argue that Western feminism in general, and feminist bioethics and its language of human rights in particular, are relevant to Chinese women and China (Nie 2004a). First, Chinese women suffer even more than Western women the consequences of sexual inequality, injustice, and discrimination in every aspect of their economic, political, cultural, and domestic lives, including the health-care sphere. Western feminism offers Chinese women and men lenses through which they can see and understand their problems as well as powerful strategies and political means to change their unjust environment. Of course, as important as it is for China to learn about and use Western feminist theories and perspectives, it is even more important and urgent to focus on native problems as articulated through the voices and experiences of Chinese women, especially those who are underprivileged and deprived, and to develop a feminist language rooted in the indigenous Chinese moral and political traditions (Nie 2004a).

The previous chapters of this book have demonstrated that abortion is indeed *not* an issue of human rights in contemporary China—not in the official discourse, and not in the experiences of doctors and women. What does this mean? When people state that abortion in China is not an issue of human rights, they generally do not merely describe a matter of fact; they almost always express or support some normative view or moral judgment on the nature of abortion, human rights, and culture. Explicitly or implicitly, this statement, which appears purely descriptive, can mean very different things in different contexts and for different people. For some, stating that Chinese do not treat abortion as an issue of human rights may mean that abortion *should* be treated as an issue of human rights and that the Chinese are wrong, or even morally inferior, in failing to see it this way. For other people, it means that the Chinese way is morally acceptable or at least not morally wrong and that the American way of dealing with abortion—with heated and divisive debate—is problematic. For some people, the official Chinese discourse on abortion represents a human rights abuse because human rights are universal values and should be applied internationally, regardless of the cultural differences. For other people, the fact that abortion is not regarded as an issue of human rights in China simply provides evidence for their commitment that, due to obvious and profound cultural differences, the language of human rights is not universal and should not be universal. Very often, partly due to the influence of the popular myth of individualist West versus communitarian China, the fact that Chinese do not see abortion as an issue of human rights is associated with the following two propositions: (1) that Chinese people do not care about human rights and (2) that the language of human rights is alien to and even incompatible with Chinese culture.

However, the fact that abortion in China is not treated as a human rights issue does not mean that Chinese people do not care about human rights. They do care. When Li Xiaohua, who was pressured to have a mid-stage abortion, asked "Shouldn't this be regarded as murder?" (see introduction), she was crying for human rights protection, not only for herself but also for the fetus in her womb. As I reported in chapter 6, although most Chinese OB/GYN doctors realize that the size of China's population needs to be controlled if China is to prosper, a growing number of them have serious reservations about the *means* the government authorities have used and still use to achieve this goal. A salient example is Dr. Zhang, who admitted to me that she has had second thoughts about some of the "family planning" operations she performed in the past. She is especially uncomfortable with the role she has played and is asked to play in controlling other women's bodies. In retrospect, what bothered Dr. Zhang most about the operations she performed was that no attempt was made to secure the women's informed consent to sterilization or abortion. She was particularly troubled by her participation in a coercive late abortion in which the pregnant woman had no say. Therefore, she applauded enthusiastically a phenomenon called *zhiqing xuanze cun* (the village of informed choice), a social experiment carried out since the 1990s that gives rural women more freedom to choose their method of birth control, and she earnestly hoped that this kind of practice would expand (see chapter 5).

As Cecilia N. Milwertz (1997) discovered, most urban women in China complied with the birth control program despite their wish to have more than one child, not so much from fear or coercion as from "conscientious acceptance" (*zijue jieshou*). At the same time, Chinese women "experience a violation of their reproductive self-determination, but they do not have a concept with which to label the experience" (Milwertz 1997: 198). It seems to me that "Western" language of human rights can help Chinese women label their as-of-yet nameless problem, to express their sense of reproductive loss and possibility. Seen through the lens of human rights, it is difficult to think of forced abortions as a necessary evil, because the practice violates women's rights to personal privacy and bodily integrity. Here it is crucial to notice to whom the language of human rights appeals. As Marina Svensson sharply observes in her groundbreaking study of the Chinese debate on human rights since 1898, rights are usually called for by people whose rights are violated or who are deprived of them, and the individuals or institutions to whom these calls are directed seldom regard them as legitimate or valid (Svensson 2002).

Some evidence seems to support the claim that concern for human rights is historically absent in Chinese culture. For example, classical liberalism as a value system seems to be exceedingly eccentric to the native Chinese political-intellectual traditions. As early as the beginning of the twentieth century, Yan Fu (Yen Fu), the first Chinese intellectual to relate seriously to modern Western social and political thought, translated (or more exactly speaking, paraphrased in elegant classical Chinese) some key texts of classical liberalism, such as John Stuart Mill's *On Liberty*, C. L. Montesquieu's *The Spirit of the Laws*, Adam Smith's *The Wealth of Nations*, and Herbert Spencer's *A Study of Sociology*. Even for Yan, however, liberty was subordinated to the state; liberalism is a means to the end of the state power and wealth—the premier concern of twentieth-century Chinese intellectuals (Schwartz 1964).

It is incorrect, however, to claim that the notion of human rights is therefore alien to and incompatible with Chinese culture. First, as the pioneering work on human rights and Chinese thought by Stephen Angle (2002) has illustrated, there is a rich and distinctive rights discourse in China that can be traced back to seventeenth- and eighteenth-century Confucianism. Second, even closer approximations of rights talk are present in some modern Chinese works. In the late nineteenth century and the first half of the twentieth century, many Chinese publications advocated that women and men were equal and should enjoy equal civil and political rights, such as freedom of thought and speech. These rights were declared natural or heavenly (*tianfu zhi quanli*). The authoritarian and patriarchal elements in traditional Confucianism were seen as enemies of science, democracy, human rights, and the emancipation of all individuals, but particularly women, whose subjection was epitomized in the notorious practice of foot-binding (see Svensson 2002: 105–6). Were it not for developments in the second half of the twentieth century, such as the emergence of the Maoist cult, in which (understandably) human rights were totally rejected as part of "capitalist" and "antirevolutionary" theory, the Chinese may have learned to speak the language of rights as fluently as most Westerners do. Third, more and more evidence indicates that the notion of individual rights is at least compatible with many streams of Chinese thought, Confucianism in particular. One point of agreement among scholars is that Confucianism over the centuries has been involved with many of the same issues that have concerned Western human rights thinkers (de Bary and Tu 1998; for the East Asian challenges for human rights, see also wonderful essays collected in Bauer and Bell 1999; Jacobsen and Bruun 2000). There is a liberal tradition and individualism in classic Confucianism and especially neo-Confucianism (de Bary 1983, 1998). In other words, the fact that abortion in China is not treated as an issue of human rights does not mean that the notion of human rights is incompatible with Chinese culture.

Fundamentally different from economy-centered population control practice, Western feminism argues for a women-centered population policy and advocates to improve the general condition of women's rights. This feminist and human-rights-oriented approach appears to be directly against the current birth control program of China and incompatible or, in a fashionable term in various disciplines in humanities and social sciences, incommensurable with Chinese traditions, Confucianism included. However, some further study indicates that, despite apparent and significant differences between feminism and Confucianism, there is some striking key common ground, for instance, opposing instrumentalism in treating people, believing in the autonomy of the moral person, contesting force by promoting morality, and pursuing morally sound social policies. It is these common grounds that make what I call "a Confucian-Feminist approach to population control" possible and necessary (Nie 2004c).

In contemporary Western sociopolitical life in general and the American abortion debate in particular, privacy is a key notion. It has been widely held that Chinese society and culture do not have the concept of privacy at all. However, recent essays contributed by scholars from a variety of disciplines on Chinese concepts of privacy

> show that Chinese people at various times and places have demonstrated an acute awareness and appreciation of privacy; that there has been discourse on privacy at least since early Confucianism and possibly earlier; that there appears to be no major area of uniquely Chinese features of privacy, although experiences and awareness of privacy may differ from those familiar in Western countries; . . . and that there is no single Chinese concept of privacy (just as there is no single Western/British/English/Geordie concept of privacy). (McDougall and Hansson 2002: 24)

This conclusion is bound to be controversial. But recent scholarship has indicated beyond doubt that is superficial simply to claim that the concept of privacy is alien to and incompatible with Chinese culture.

Within China, one of the main objections to encouraging the use of the language of human rights is that China cannot afford to spend time and effort worrying about civil, political, and reproductive rights when its population lacks adequate food, clothing, shelter, employment, education, and basic health care. Indeed, not only Chinese state authorities but also the bulk of the Chinese people believe that economic interests or rights must take priority over civil and political rights, and that population control is more important than reproductive rights. In particular, it is a widespread view that to the Chinese people as a whole, especially those in rural areas where living standards are very low and illiteracy rates are very high, to talk about civil and political rights, particularly reproductive rights, is not only inappropriate but also destructive. Specifically, this view goes that letting illiterate rural people who believe that one can never have too many children make their own reproductive choices is to court disaster and to retard the development of China's economy, which cannot afford yet more mouths to feed. In all fairness, I am somewhat sympathetic toward this view, though I think that there are ways to nurture the growth of political, civil, and reproductive rights that do not jeopardize the country's economic development and social stability. Prominent economist Amartya Sen (1999) has argued not only that freedom should be the basic end of development, but also that freedom is the most effective means to overcome poverty and sustain economic growth. To claim that the Chinese people care only about the right to survival assumes that the Chinese people, especially rural folks, are not capable of active political participation and a decent civil life. Clearly, this view is factually wrong if my fellow Chinese peasants' participation in and enthusiasm for elections for local officials is any sign. According to the political and moral doctrines of Confucianism and even Marxism, people, Chinese included, are not simply animals for whom food is the be all and the end all; like all other human beings, Chinese are completely capable of decent political and civil life.

I have presented much evidence, both historical and contemporary, to dispute the claim that the concept of individual human rights is alien to and incompatible with Chinese culture. But there is a final stand to be taken—a philosophical stand. Even if the notion of human rights were both totally alien to and incompatible with Chinese culture, that does not mean that it *ought to be*. In fact, Chinese moral traditions, including Confucian, Daoist, and even Chinese-Marxist, emphasize the importance of critically engaging reality (what is) from various ethical perspectives (what ought to be). Classical Confucianism expressed by Confucius and Mencius, for example, calls people to reflect critically upon social reality, face squarely the immoral elements, and seek to reform society by cultivating moral characters and participating in everyday social and political activities. Therefore, Chinese thinkers, even if they mistakenly believe that rights-oriented individualism is alien to the Chinese political and cultural system, still may believe that China should develop the discourse of human rights because it is the right thing to do and desirable for Chinese people. I am aware that this philosophical stand opens the door to the controversial concept of the universality of human rights, a controversy I will not address here. My main objective in this section is illustrating the misleading nature of the myth of a homogeneous and communitarian China and the necessity of taking seriously the internal diversity of Chinese culture in cross-cultural discussions on human rights.

THE VALUE OF HUMAN AND FETAL LIFE

One of the commonly accepted views or stereotypes about China holds that individual human life is less respected in Chinese culture than in the West, the United States included. As mentioned in chapter 1, the wide sociopolitical acceptance of abortion in China on the one hand and the obvious lack of concern in the Chinese public discourse on the other hand have led Western observers and many overseas Chinese interviewed in my pilot study to this very conclusion. This view of the cheapness of human life in Chinese culture and the myth about China seem to reinforce each other. The question is: In what sense is human life in China not respected as highly as in the West? Is this a valid generalization on Chinese-Western cultural differences?

American legal and political philosopher Ronald Dworkin has imaginatively and forcefully argued in his work on abortion and euthanasia in the United States that the American abortion debate is based on a conviction shared by almost everyone: the *intrinsic* or *sacred* value of human life in any form. He claims that "The great majority of people who have strong views about abortion—liberal as well as conservative—believe, at least intuitively, that the life of a human organism has intrinsic value in any form it takes, even in the extremely undeveloped form of a very early, just-implanted embryo" (Dworkin 1993: 69). For Dworkin, the key question is not, as many hold, whether a fetus is a person with its rights and interests equal to other persons. Rather, the belief in the importance or sacredness of human life, including undeveloped fetal life, is the "undiscovered planet" or "gravitational force" that explains the otherwise inexplicable—why abortion is such a controversial issue for Americans.

If Dworkin's claim on the underlying conviction of the American abortion debate is valid, then there is a striking contrast between the American and Chinese views. In the contemporary dominant or official discourse, the idea of the intrinsic value of human life in any form, not only the embryo and fetus but also adults, does not exist. According to the official collectivist worldview, as chapter 2 illustrates, fetal life has little moral significance and every individual life is subject to the great cause of socialism and the interests of the state and the collective. A great number of Chinese seem to hold this perspective consciously or unconsciously. Evidence presented in the previous chapters has indicated that the ideas of eugenics are widely accepted and supported by contemporary Chinese. The survey results (see chapter 4) show that an overwhelmingly large majority of Chinese (over 90% of six hundred surveyed) believed that a pregnant woman should have an abortion for eugenic reasons under the following situations:

- if the fetus has a genetic disease (96%),
- if she will give birth to a malformed or defective baby (94%),

- if she suffers mental illness (93%),
- if she is mentally retarded (91).

A large majority of Chinese (over 70% but less than 80%) agreed that a pregnant woman should have an abortion for eugenic reasons under the following situations:

- if she is alcoholic (88%),
- if she smokes heavily (85%),
- if she may (but not certainly will) give birth to a defective baby (82%),
- if she has taken some medicine that may have an adverse influence on fetal development (73%).

In this age of information explosion, lay people often rely on professionals and specialists for the authoritative source of advice. So do Chinese. In the survey item that asked respondents whether the pregnant woman should terminate or continue pregnancy "if a fortune-teller concluded that the fetus is an abnormal or monster fetus, but the doctor finds that the fetus is perfectly normal," only 3% overall—none at all in five samples, including northern city, Buddhist, Catholic, and medical humanities scholar—preferred abortion. An international survey of nearly three thousand genetic professionals in thirty-six nations, including China and the United States, suggests that a type of libertarian or individual-choice-based eugenics, not imposed or coerced by the state, "survives in much modern genetic practice" (Wertz 1998). China stands out as the exceptional sample in which most geneticists did not reject government involvement in prenatal testing or sterilization. An overwhelmingly large majority of Chinese geneticists would give pessimistic information in their genetic counseling if any of six genetic disorders had been diagnosed: severe, open spina bifida (98%); trisomy 21 (Down's syndrome) (96%); cystic fibrosis (95%); sickle cell anemia (91%); achondra plasia (the most common form of dwarfism) (92%); and XXY (Klinefelter syndrome) (92%). A large or very large majority of Chinese geneticists would urge termination of pregnancy in the diagnosis of these six genetic disorders (respectively 89%, 90%, 82%, 67%, 77%, and 73%). This contrasts strikingly with the United States, where only a small minority of geneticists would give pessimistically slanted information after prenatal diagnosis of the six genetic diseases (respectively 28%, 13%, 9%, 6%, 6%, and 5%). In fact, China stands out as the country with the highest percentages of genetic professionals who support eugenics or at least falls in the class of countries including Cuba, India, and Greece with the highest percentages, while the United States falls in the class of countries, with Chile, Canada, the United Kingdom, and Germany, with the lowest support for eugenics (Wertz 1998; also Mao 1998; for a critical examination of the ideology of contemporary Chinese eugenic practice, see Nie 2003).

Unlike the issue of abortion, mercy killing or euthanasia (*anlesi*) has been one of the most prominent topics in Chinese medical ethics. Since the 1980s, this topic has attracted the attention of scholars and medical professionals as well as national and local media. While active euthanasia at the request of the patient or family members is illegal, withdrawing treatment is widely accepted and practiced. Many sociocultural and intellectual forces are leading toward the legalization of both passive and active euthanasia. The most widely accepted argument in favor of passive as well as active euthanasia for a number of patients, including seriously impaired newborns and people suffering from late-stage cancers and other terminal diseases, is that treating and caring for them poses an unbearable and unjustifiable burden on the health-care system and society. This argument for euthanasia reflects not only the official ideology of collectivism or socialism (in which individual human life should be subject to the interests of the state and society) and economic determinism, but also the recent revival of social Darwinism (see Nie forthcoming-a).

All these examples from the abortion and end-of-life debates seem to support the view that human life is cheap in China in comparison to the United States. However, the mainstream Chinese discourse in which fetal life in particular and human life in general are not as highly valued in China is only one of China's many voices. Chapter 2 shows that this official perspective does not necessarily accord with the historical understanding of China's many voices. The previous chapters illustrate that people in contemporary China have very different views of and feelings toward the fetus. Seventy percent of the subjects in the survey believed that human life begins some time before birth, and nearly half of the subjects surveyed thought that conception was the starting point of a human life, though it is not clear whether they considered this a reason to restrict abortion. The majority of Chinese surveyed believed in the existence of a soul in the human being but not in the fetus, while Catholics and Protestants strongly or very strongly believed in the existence of a soul in both. Most doctors who perform abortions and the majority of women who have had abortions rarely think of the aborted fetus. But a few doctors and some women have very strong feelings about the fetus and see the fetus as a growing human life or even as a child.

Although many Chinese consider conception the starting point of a human life and the fetus a human being, a dead fetus is rarely mourned with public rituals as is an adult, and people do not often say that a person or human being dies when an abortion, either spontaneous or induced, occurs. But it is also true that, according to deeply rooted practice, the age of a person is calculated on the understanding that he or she is already one year old at birth. Many people still calculate their ages in this way in many parts of China. According to my survey results, nearly half of six hundred Chinese believed that human life begins at conception; only less than one-third

(30%) believed that a human life begins at birth; the other one-fifth thought that a human life starts sometime between conception and birth.

People who accept and hold the Party line on fetal life may not necessarily agree with what the official views prescribe in dealing with the actual cases, or vice versa. Little systematic study has been done of the moral world of those Chinese cadres engaged in the national birth control program, how they function in what they have called the "number one difficult job in the whole world," and how they resolve various moral dilemmas they face. My survey results indicate that there are very few items on which Party members disagreed with non-Party members, and even then they disagreed only slightly. This means that many Party as well as non-Party members disagree with many official positions on the nature of abortion, fetal life, and related issues with which they are supposed to agree. In chapter 2, I report that, although fetal life is of no significant moral weight in the official discourse, local cadres may not necessarily think and act in the officially prescribed way. I will not be surprised if future systematic studies show that abortion, especially late abortion, is a terribly bitter experience, not only for the women and the doctors concerned but also for the family planning cadre.

As presented in chapter 3, it cannot be refuted that Chinese traditions exist in which human life is much more highly respected than it is in contemporary official discourse in which humans are mainly of instrumental value. In the West, human life is believed to be precious and sacred, mainly because, according to the Judeo-Christian tradition, the first man was created in the image and likeness of God. Many Chinese traditions agree in principle that human life must be respected and valued, but on different grounds. In chapter 3, I recount some Confucian reasons for the value of human life, for example, as a requirement of ancestor worship. In Chinese culture, the preciousness and even sacredness of human life is often believed to originate in nature, from which human beings come and on which human existence depends. In both Confucianism and Daoism, every individual's life, from the very beginning to the end, is seen to be closely and mysteriously related to nature, physically and spiritually understood.

As I left Texas for the airport to fly to China for fieldwork, I bumped into an American colleague and friend. Before she said "Good-bye" and "Have a great trip" in her regular tone of voice, she whispered into my ear: "Watch out for the spirits of fetuses in the streets!" Her extremely soft whisper had such a chilling and haunting effect that it still echoes in my ears. When hearing that, one of my initial tacit responses was that Chinese would not think in line with this intelligent American woman. Surely, in all of my field research, none of more than thirty doctors I interviewed seemed to share the view of my American friend about the existence of the spirit of the aborted fetus. At least, no doctor ever talked explicitly about the spirits of aborted fetuses. But, in interviewing women and doctors, I never asked any of them explicitly whether the aborted fetus has a spirit or not. Anyway, the historical evidence presented in chapter 3, such as the story against abortion in the ancient medical ethics text in which an abortionist was haunted at her deathbed by the spirits of the aborted "children," suggests that my American colleague's idea about the sprits of fetuses is not as alien to Chinese culture as it might appear. In fact, survey results presented in chapter 4 further show that at least a significant portion of Chinese believed that the fetus has a soul as any adult does.

In chapter 3, I cite the great historian of medicine and culture in China, Paul Unschuld (2001), who has boldly and insightfully argued that, "from studying the history of medicine and medical ethics in China it is obvious Chinese culture for at least two millennia has placed as much emphasis on the value of human individual life as has Western culture." He emphasizes that "the findings by Dorothy Wertz [on the acceptance of eugenics by contemporary Chinese genetic professionals; see Wertz 1998] and the medical media report on human rights violations in contemporary China" should not be interpreted as a logical consequence of Chinese culture, but originated in "a difficult contemporary situation." As a German scholar, he urges us: "Keeping in mind that in German history we have experienced only half a century ago a period where traditional cultural values were turned upside down." In other words, the contemporary practices in which human life is not respected as highly as it should be "are definitely not intrinsic elements of Chinese culture" (Unschuld 2001). Not only the forgotten controversies presented in chapter 3 but also the great diversity of voices reported in other chapters of this book support Unschuld's provoking general thesis.

It is impossible here to compare Chinese and American views on human life systematically. The aim of this section is not to pursue this task, however fascinating it may be, but to illustrate that stereotypes of Chinese, along with the popular myth of a collectivist China where individual human life is not highly respected, must be overcome in order to have a genuine cross-cultural dialogue with Chinese people.

BITTERNESS OF WOMEN'S EXPERIENCES

As already stated above, an interpretative approach to cultures, unlike modernist and postmodernist ones that focus on radical differences, pays close attention to both similarities and differences among different cultures, especially the differences in the similarities and the similarities in the differences. A rough comparison of American and Chinese women's experience helps to illustrate how similarly and how differently women experience abortion from one culture or society to another.

In the middle of the nineteenth century, Henry C. Wright wrote *The Un-welcome Child; or, the Crime of an Undesigned and Undesired Maternity*, in which he published letters from American women telling of their feelings about abortion and the circumstances under which they sought abortion. Most of the women who wrote these letters said that they "hated" having to do it (Mohr 1978: 110). Some condemned themselves for having no other choice than to "murder" their fetuses. One of the women wrote:

> I consulted a woman, a friend in whom I trusted. I found that she had perpe-trated that outrage on herself and on others. She told me it was not murder to kill a child any time before its birth. Of this she labored to convince me, and called in the aid of her "family physician," to give force to her arguments. He ar-gued that it was right and just for wives thus to protect themselves against the results of their husband's sensualism,—told me that God and human laws would approve of killing children before they were born, rather than curse them with an undesired existence. My only trouble was, with God's view of the case, I could not get rid of the feeling that it was an outrage on my body and soul, and on my unconscious babe. He argued that my child, at five months (which was the time), had no life, and where there was no life, no life could be taken. Though I determined to do the deed, or get the "family physician" to do it, my womanly instincts, my reason, my conscience, my self-respect, my entire nature, revolted against my decision. My Womanhood rose up in withering condemna-tion. (Mohr 1978: 111)

No matter how much she hated doing it, this American woman had not one but several abortions.

Many contemporary American women who have abortions are as conflicted about abortion as their nineteenth-century sisters. According to Carol Gilligan's famous study on women's moral universe (1993 [1982]), one woman going through an abortion was Sandra, a twenty-nine-year-old Catholic nurse. San-dra reports that she had always thought of abortion, as well as euthanasia, as a "fancy word for murder." The second time she became pregnant, she found that "keeping the child for lots and lots of reasons was just sort of impractical and out." She had only two options: terminating the pregnancy or offering the child for adoption. She had previously given up a child for adoption and found that "there was no way that I could hack another adoption." "There was just no way I was going through it again." Yet continuing pregnancy would hurt her parents and damage herself. Sandra explained why she decided to have an abortion: "I am doing it because I have to do it. I am not doing it the least bit because I want to." For her, "abortion is morally wrong, but the situation is right." Thus she had an abortion (Gilligan 1993 [1982]: 85–86).

Chinese and American women's moral experiences of abortion share some intriguing transcultural similarities and important cross-cultural differ-ences. Obviously, in both the United States and China, abortion is never merely a medical procedure or personal matter. For many American and Chinese women, abortion is a bitter experience, something they never wanted to do, though they have to under some conditions. These similarities are very striking, if we take into account the conspicuous differences in the role of the abortion issues in the social, legal, and moral life in the two countries. In other words, in spite of the obvious language difference, Chinese and American women who have had abortions are truly sisters in their suffering, no matter how different their sociocultural backgrounds are.

However, the moral reasons why American and Chinese women feel bitter about abortion may differ significantly. Many American women believe that aborting a fetus is murdering or taking a human life. To these women, abortion is against the law of God, their "womanly instincts," "reason," "conscience," "self-respect," "womanhood," and "entire nature," as the above quotation from the letter of the nineteenth-century American woman indicates. For most Chinese women who have had abortions, abortion is a bitter experience not so much because they feel they are committing murder but because it is physically painful and, more importantly, because they fear they might be jeopardizing their reproductive health, the ability to fulfill an essential womanly duty defined by the society (see chapter 5). Nevertheless, as we have seen, many Chinese women regret destroying a fetus, and abortion is against their personal conscience and "womanly instincts." These Chinese women view abortion as the taking of a growing human life, not one seen as the property of God, but one seen as a child that might have been, or a part of their own blood and flesh. Christian Chinese, on the other hand, would believe, as many Americans do, that the fetus is not merely a part of the mother's blood and flesh, but a gift from God.

One point I want to make here is that the differences between Chinese and American women's experiences of abortion are not necessarily as dramatic and fundamental as the differences within particular groups of Chinese women. As presented in chapter 5, the difference between the experiences of a well-educated and professional urban Chinese woman and a poor rural woman who nearly died in an attempt to have a son can be more striking than the difference between the experiences of a professional urban Chinese woman and a professional urban American woman.

Without detailed and systematic comparative studies, the above remarks on the similarities and differences of Chinese and American women's experiences are bound to be preliminary. Before ending this very tentative section, I would like to cite what a thirty-nine-year-old woman in Taibei, Taiwan, has said about her aborted fetus:

A few years ago I went to a hospital and killed the baby in my body. One day after several years I felt that something was wrong. I sensed that there was a boy who was always behind me. When I turned back to see, there was nothing. I didn't believe in ghosts until the spirits made me sick. My family took me to stay in a [Buddhist] temple instead of a hospital. After one month . . . I recovered. I didn't see the child in the temple because Buddha protected me when I was there. But when I went home I still felt there was someone behind me. I went to see a fortuneteller and the man gave me a talismanic paper. I stuck the paper on the door and burned incense to the ghost as the fortuneteller told me to do. The fortuneteller also told me to go to a temple and set up a memorial plaque for the dead child. He said it would be better for me if I went to the temple every year to see the dead child. I set a place for the child in a temple as the man said.

Now I am the mother of three children. I think that one of my three children might have the spirit of my dead child because I have never felt nor seen the child again. (Moskowitz 2001: 47)

Whatever the political status of Taiwan, more traditional Chinese norms and beliefs are alive there than in today's mainland China. This Taiwanese/Chinese woman's provocative experience of the haunting fetus, together with those presented in chapter 5 and above in this chapter, calls for further cross-cultural and cross-regional comparative studies on women's personal experiences of abortion in China, the United States, and other places. These personal experiences demonstrate that the popular dichotomous characterization of China and the United States as collectivism versus individualism will never be able to do justice to the richness and complexities of Chinese and American women's actual experiences of abortion.

CONCLUSION

This book has presented a wide range of Chinese perspectives on abortion and closely related issues such as fetal life and the national birth control program, highlighting areas of consensus as well as sharp disagreements. In this chapter, I have revisited some major conclusions and arguments of the study:

- The Chinese silence on abortion is eloquent, with multilayered meanings, indicating not only the acceptance of abortion and a number of complicated personal meanings, but also the widespread fear resulting from political repression.
- The official and public discourse emphasizes a collectivist and statistical ethics in which fetal life is not given significant attention and human life is not always accorded the highest respect. But the official standpoint on abortion, which has varied historically, is far from necessarily in accord with Chinese traditions such as Confucianism and the views of the contemporary majority.

- Chinese moral understandings of abortion, in both the past and the present, are not as "liberal" as usually assumed. Although abortion is acceptable legally and socioculturally in contemporary China, a significant proportion of the population, especially religious groups including Catholics, Buddhists, and Protestants, oppose it in principle.
- Chinese people differ greatly on the question of when a human life begins—whether at conception or at birth or sometime during pregnancy. Most consider the fetus a life. In other words, the great majority of Chinese believe that human life starts either at conception or sometime during pregnancy. Historically speaking, China owns its own sophistic knowledge on fetal development.
- Although most would prefer two children, Chinese people accept and support the national birth control program because the policy is viewed as being both necessary for the country and good for individuals. Due to the lack of full public discussions on all related issues, this acceptance and support is conscientious on the one hand and insufficiently informed on the other.
- The experiences of women who have had abortions are diverse and their narratives complex. For nearly all, the experience is both bitter and unforgettable. Some clearly see the aborted fetus as their lost "child."
- Most doctors who routinely perform abortion (almost all are female) exhibit no overt moral conflict in their professional work because they believe they are serving both women and the country. They usually neither have reservations about the national population policy nor express feelings about the aborted fetus. Nevertheless, at least one doctor felt that she was totally lost with her professional work because of her attitudes toward the fetal life, the methods employed in the birth control program, and the sufferings of her patients.
- Three sociological factors that have led to the practice of coerced abortion include the strong state control, the complexity and pressure in the local world, and people's support of the birth control program. Ethically speaking, it is highly objectionable, though not completely impossible to argue as a lesser evil, according to not only Western but also Chinese moral-political traditions.

The most important conclusion of this book, however, is on the great diversity of Chinese perspectives. In other words, as emphasized in this chapter,

- There does not exist, and there never has existed, a single and unified Chinese perspective on abortion. Despite the apparent silence, contemporary mainland Chinese speak with diverse and often radically different voices on abortion.

Furthermore, I have argued in this chapter:

- To develop an effective cross-cultural dialogue, the popular modern myth of a communitarian and homogeneous China, in striking contrast with an individualistic and plural United States (West), must be overcome. An interpretative approach, which maintains the crucial importance of taking seriously the various kinds of internal plurality within China, is needed.

Together with the two popular approaches to understanding cultures—modernist or ethnocentric and postmodernist or relativist—the modern myth of a communitarian and homogeneous China versus an individualistic and plural United States has seriously simplified and distorted the sociocultural reality of both cultures, but more especially, of China. It has created and reinforced many stereotypes of Chinese people and culture and produced a series of avoidable confusions in discussing such urgent political issues as the value of human life and human rights. By some preliminary comparisons of Chinese and American perspectives on abortion, I have shown that, to go beyond the popular myth and two conventional ways of thinking on cross-cultural differences, the first step is to take seriously the profound internal diversity in China. Materials presented in this book demonstrate beyond doubt that Chinese perspectives of abortion can never be justly understood if one does not pay close attention to those diverse, often conflicting and contradictory, views and experiences of different Chinese people.

Therefore, the crucial difference between the two nations with regard to sociocultural pluralism is *not* that China is homogeneous/communitarian and the United States heterogeneous/individualistic, but that the two nations view and deal with this diversity in quite different ways. Because diversity is acknowledged, accepted, and discussed constantly and widely in the public discourse and private lives of Americans, the United States has developed various means—ranging from legislation to cultural sensitivity training—to address differences in cultural background and other spheres of life. Of course, the progress has not been achieved without struggle, and fundamental problems remain to be solved. Still, by comparison with China in the twentieth century, the success of the United States in dealing with sociocultural diversity is rather remarkable.

For China, my motherland and the country my heart belongs to, it is far more urgent practically to take its internal plurality seriously. Viewing the history of China in the past two centuries, one is struck by the turmoil, disorders, violence, and destruction Chinese people have endured. There are many complicated sociopolitical and intellectual reasons for this distressing history; a major but often ignored source of these conflicts is the fact that China has not worked out a way of adequately addressing the ethnic, regional, sociocultural, economic, religious, and historical diversity of its people. On the one hand, there is the obvious, profound diversity among Chinese people in all spheres of life. On the other hand, the myth or dream or illusion of a united and homogeneous China persists. The inevitable result, as the history of modern China unfortunately proves, is either a forced unity by an authoritarian state or a country rent by disorder, chaos, and civil war. Without such diversity in all spheres of life among all her people, modern China would not have suffered so many irreconcilable civil conflicts and such internal turmoil. The tragic history of China in the second half of the twentieth century proved once again that the plurality within her society cannot be destroyed or even reduced, no matter how hard people like Mao and his cult may have tried. If, after two centuries of extraordinary hardship, China fails again to find an effective way of dealing with this plurality, Chinese people will be unable to avoid another massive social upheaval.

Appendix: The Pilot Study, the Survey, and the Interviews

THE PILOT STUDY

The pilot study was conducted in the summer of 1997. In total, twenty Chinese (eleven male and nine female) then studying, working, and living in the United States were interviewed by means of the semistructured interview. Most of the participants were scholars and students at the University of Texas Medical Branch at Galveston. All of them were born, grew up, and received all or most of their formal education in mainland China. Some had lived in the United States for several years while others had just arrived. All were very well educated even by American standards, with most having degrees beyond the bachelor's level. Several had received medical degrees in China and had practiced medicine there. Although personal information on abortion was not requested, several interviewees revealed their personal histories of abortion. Three informants said that they had performed abortions in China. One woman said she had had three abortions. Two men said their wives had had abortions. This willingness to reveal personal experiences indicates that abortion, especially if the woman is married, does not carry a stigma in contemporary Chinese society.

In the interviews, great efforts were made to keep the conversation open. The basic questions asked of the informants were: (1) "Under what situations would a Chinese woman have an abortion?" Or, "What are the reasons why a Chinese woman would have an abortion?" (2) "What would other people, including family members and friends, think and say about a woman who has had an abortion?" (3) "What are the reasons which account for the silence of Chinese people—no public discussion or debate—about the abortion issue?" (4) "When does a human life start? Is the fetus a 'ren' (human being or person)?" (5) "What do you think about the American controversy surrounding abortion? What is the controversy about; that is, what is the basis for opposition to abortion in the U.S.?"

THE SURVEY: QUESTIONNAIRE AND SAMPLES

The design of the questionnaire is based on my personal experience about abortion in China and, especially, the information obtained from the pilot study. The questionnaire has four parts. Part one solicits demographic information, including gender, age, ethnicity, education, religious background, marital status, number of children, political party membership, and occupation. In the second part, the informant is asked to give his or her own opinion concerning whether or not a woman should have an abortion in each of the thirty-six situations under which a woman might possibly terminate her pregnancy. The reasons offered as explanation for pregnancy termination in these thirty-six situations include social taboo, economic restriction, eugenic reasons, lifestyle of the pregnant woman, birth control, sex preference, personal convenience and preference, and possible influence on the woman's career. In the third part, the informants are asked to express their opinions by agreeing or disagreeing with thirty different ideas or statements on such topics as whether abortion is like killing, whether the fetus is a human life, whether the national population control policy is necessary, and whether the "one-child-per-couple" policy is beneficial to the family and individual. Part four consists of six multiple-choice questions on when human life begins, the ideal number of children the informant wants, whether and how many abortions a female informant has had in her life, and so forth. The order of all thirty-six items in the second part were randomized. So were the items in the third part, except the twenty-eighth and twenty-ninth statements, which were put together because both concern the "one-child" policy. For the exact Chinese version of the questionnaire I used in the survey, a complete English translation, as well as the primary data from the survey, including all demographical information, see the book's website at www.rowmanlittle field.com/ISBN/0742523705.

Because of the complex historical, political, and sociocultural factors, Chinese people are not accustomed to expressing their individual opinions. Many people are not familiar with or have not actually participated in surveys, especially those associated with social policy issues. In the instruction notes for part II and part III, special emphasis was given to the questionnaire's focus on the personal views of the informant. In the oral instruction before and during the informants' completion of the questionnaire, my assistants and I repeated the following message: "There is no standard correct answer to any item in the questionnaire. The survey is about *your own* opinions, not those of any other person, organization, or institution. What we want to know is *your own* points of view."

Since this subject matter is politically sensitive, the scholarly and academic nature of this study was emphasized in the questionnaire. For example, the general instruction included the statement, "The true information you provide is of great significance for this *scientific* research project." What I attempted to communicate here is not so much the scientific nature of this study as the scholarly nature. In spite of all these efforts, an informant still raised his concern to one of my assistants about the "political incorrectness" of this survey and considered it potentially dissident with the extant national policy of the PRC. Also, although the general instruction of the questionnaire stressed that each respondent would be anonymous, several informants wrote their names down on the front page of their completed questionnaires.

Although random sampling was not used (that is, all twelve samples in this survey were samples of convenience), effort was made to make the sample as diverse as possible. In contemporary China, about 70% of the total population lives in rural areas and works in farming and agriculture. In this survey, three rural samples came from villages in two different counties not very far away (several hours by driving) from a capital city of a Southern province in hinterland China. These villages were agricultural areas and had populations of about one or two thousand. My research assistants and I went to villagers' homes during the day to ask them to complete the questionnaire. Respectively, fifty-eight, fifty-four, and ninety completed questionnaires were gathered from Village A, Village B, and Village C.

Two urban samples came from the capitals of two provinces—one on the Northern coast and the other in the inland South. The questionnaires were gathered through the Institute for the Science and Technology of Family Planning located in the two cities—which also provided birth control service, including abortion. At each site, after being informed how the survey should be conducted, two physician–researchers from each of two institutes, who had had some empirical research experience, gave the questionnaire to people nearby—other doctors, patients, neighbors, and friends. A total of 106 completed questionnaires were collected in the Southern city and 46 in the Northern city.

Two Christian samples—Catholic and Protestant—came from the interior Southern city mentioned above. Most Chinese people view Catholicism and Protestantism as different religions. In the everyday Chinese language, the former is called *tianzhu jiao* (the religion of the Heavenly Master) and the latter *jidu jiao* (the religion of Christ). As a result, for many people, the *jidu jiaotu* (the believer of Christ, i.e., the Christian) does not include the *tianzhu jiaotu* (the believer of the Heavenly Master, i.e., the Catholic). Twenty-six subjects in the Catholic sample were clergy and nuns who were working at the Catholic Church or believers who attended the church worship activities. I gave the questionnaire to the participants and collected the completed ones by myself. The Protestant sample was obtained from two Protestant churches in the same city. Among forty-two completed questionnaires in this sample, twenty-four were obtained by myself from the attendees when a Friday evening Bible study meeting was over; ten were gathered by a young pastor at the other church from the clergy and church attendees; and eight were collected for me by two Protestants from their friends.

Three student samples were collected from two cities—one in the Northern coast and the other in the Southern coast. The medical student sample, twenty-eight respondents, came from an evening English class at a modern biomedical college in the capital city of the Northern coastal province mentioned above. In the class, three American visitors gave talks about the medical humanities. The traditional Chinese medical student sample came from a class at a university for Chinese medicine and pharmacology located in the capital city of the Southern coastal province. The sixty-one subjects were the second-year students who had just finished a lesson for the required course "The Fundamental Principles of Marxist Philosophy." The university student sample, forty-six completed questionnaires, came from the undergraduate and graduate students majoring in biology and anthropology at a well-known university in the same Southern coastal city from which the Chinese medical student sample came.

The medical humanities scholar sample, nineteen informants, came from the attendees of a national conference on the medical humanities and medical ethics held in another Northern coastal city. In the conference, several American scholars were invited to deliver lectures.

The last sample, twenty-four cases, came from miscellaneous sources. During the fieldwork, whenever it seemed appropriate, the questionnaires were given to the people I met. Several informants in this miscellaneous sample were people who attended activities at churches in the Southern inland city, but did not identify themselves as Protestants or Catholics in their completed questionnaires. Since this sample represents no particular population group, no particular discussion is made of them in this book.

There is no specifically selected Buddhist sample in this survey. In order to have a Buddhist sample, I went to a well-known temple in a Southern inland province. But my plan to have some Buddhists fill out the questionnaire and perhaps even to interview them was a total failure. In the temple, there were only three senior high school students who were asking blessing for passing the national admission exam to university and one middle-aged man who was requesting medicine for his mother's post-stroke problems from an old nun after a ritual. None of these four persons claimed to be Buddhists, while one high school student checked "Christianity (Protestantism)" as his religious belief on his completed questionnaire. Fortunately, there were twenty-seven informants among 601 subjects who claimed they believed in Buddhism. For the importance of Buddhism in Chinese society, as well as for convenience of discussion and comparison, these twenty-seven people were treated as an independent sample, although they were not sampled as a separate group in the actual survey.

Only a few samples and a few questions had greater than 5% missing responses. In this book, the percentages that are reported are calculated only upon those who responded, rather than upon the entire sample.

The following is the overall demographic description of all 601 subjects. Among 601 respondents, 39% were male and 61% were female. Most respondents were of childbearing age: 7% below twenty years old, 46% twenty to thirty years old, 25% thirty to forty years old, 16% forty to fifty years old, 7% over fifty years old. The majority of subjects were married. The marital status of the respondents was: 35% never married, 64% married, and 1% divorced and remarried. Over half the subjects (56%) had at least one child. Thirty-four percent had one child, 18% had two children, and 3% had more than two children. Forty-four percent had no child.

Ninety-seven percent of the respondents belonged to the Han nationality, the majority ethnic group, with only 3% belonging to minority ethnic groups. In China, there are fifty-six nationalities or ethnic groups. Ninety-two percent of the people belong to Han. Eight percent belong to the other fifty-five ethnic groups, among which are Mongel, Hui, Zhang (Tibetan), Uygur (Uighur), Miao, and Man (Manchu).

The overall educational level of respondents was much higher than the average educational level in China. The educational levels of the subjects were: 9% had no more than elementary school class work; 28% had graduated from junior middle school; 15% had graduated from senior middle school; 45% were university or college students or graduates; 2% had postgraduate education. Nationally, the educational levels of Chinese in 1990 were: 42.3% graduated from elementary school; 26.4% graduated from junior middle school; 9.0% graduated from senior middle school; only 1.6% graduated from college or university. The rate of illiteracy is 22.3% (Feng 1992).

The occupations of respondents included: 8% workers, 24% peasants, 10% national cadres (state-employed personnel), 14% medical students, 11% university and other students, 8% medical doctors, 8% nurses and other medicine-related professionals, 5% business persons, 3% teachers, 7% other occupations or no job.

In this survey, 80% of informants reported no explicit particular religious belief, 5% were Buddhists, 5% were Catholics, and 9% were Protestants. More than half of the informants were, at least at one time, officially associated with political organizations such as the Chinese Communist Party (CCP) and the Communist Youth League (CYL). The informant's party memberships were:

21% members of CCP, 44% members of the CYL, 1% members of democratic parties, and 34% without any party membership. Nationwide, the members of the CCP make up nearly 5% of the total population.

While every effort was made to secure the broadest possible sample from among those who had experienced and practiced abortion from the major regions of China and in city and countryside, this is neither a comprehensive nor a fully representative sample of the Chinese people or of Chinese views. It is, however, the first significant exploratory sample and one that casts much light on the diversity of Chinese abortion practices and opinions.

INTERVIEWS WITH WOMEN

The method of semistructured interview was used to talk with thirty women. They were living in five Chinese cities—three in the North and two in the South, including Qingdao, Dalian, Beijing, Changsha, and Guangzhou—and three villages in an interior southern province, Hunan. Most of the women were in their twenties or thirties. Several were in their forties or fifties. Their occupations included worker, farmer (villager), business person, teacher, medical professional, and other work roles. Among the thirty women interviewed were two doctors who also told me their own experiences of having abortions.

The basic interviewing strategy was to ask open-ended questions. The interview usually started with one of these questions: "Could you please tell me something about your own experience of abortion?" "I am very interested in your personal experience of abortion. Could you tell me about it?" The list of questions for interviewees included: "What reason(s) made you decide to have an abortion?" "How did you make the decision? Did you consult with someone—husband or boyfriend or mother or friend or someone else?" "How did you feel when experiencing the abortion? Was it painful?" "How did you feel after having the abortion?" "Did you see the aborted tissue?" "Do you sometimes think of the aborted fetus? How do you feel about the aborted fetus?" "How can doctors improve their medical services for women seeking abortion?" "Could you please tell me something more about your own experience of abortion?" "Could you tell some stories—yours or other people's—related to abortion?"

Putonghua (the standard Chinese) was the language for most interviews with women. But interviews with women, as with physicians, in the interior provincial capital and the three villages in the province, were conducted in the dialect spoken by the natives.

Before the field research, I had planned to train a female doctor or nurse or medical student as a research assistant to interview the women for me.

This plan was given up in field research for two reasons. First, after a few interviews I found that, partly because I am a medical doctor, the gender difference between interviewer and interviewees did not appear to be an obstacle in communication. In my oral introduction about myself and my project, I mentioned my previous medical background in China and current status of being a doctoral student from a medical school in Texas, U.S.A. This enabled the interviewees to talk to me as though talking to their physicians, even though I did not wear a white coat. Second, I wanted to know directly how Chinese women responded to my questions and how they spoke about their feelings and experiences. Although a female research assistant might gather some information usually shared only among women, I felt I would lose the direct touch with how the women narrated their personal world not only through words but also through body language and facial expression. In fact, most interviewees did not have obvious difficulties in conveying their opinions and experiences, partly because abortion is not at all a taboo topic among mainland Chinese people. Generally speaking, the women interviewed were very willing to talk. Their willingness to talk about rather private matters to a male stranger was, at times, amazing.

I had also planned to record all the interviews with women, just as I did while interviewing doctors. But this plan was changed, too. After two or three interviews, I realized that it was better not to record, but to take notes. Unlike with most doctors, recording the interviews usually made the women nervous and uneasy. Yet almost all the women who consented to be interviewed were very comfortable with my note taking. In fact, note taking had at least two advantages. First, it gave the interviewees time to recollect their experiences and to figure out ways to express their feelings and opinions. Second, watching me actually take notes helped to assure interviewees that I sincerely cared about what they were saying.

At the beginning of the field research, a couple of women were interviewed immediately after having completed the questionnaire, which included items on whether the fetus is a human being, whether abortion is equivalent to killing, whether the woman will mourn the aborted fetus, and so on. I soon realized that the questionnaire might suggest vocabulary and answers to my interview questions, and possibly distort their personal views and narratives. Thereafter, most interviewees did not complete the questionnaire at all, and no woman filled out the questionnaire before being interviewed.

Locations of interviewing varied: at the doctor's office of a clinic, at the woman's home, at the woman's workplace such as a lab or office. More than half the time, a female doctor or a female friend of the interviewee was present.

INTERVIEWS WITH DOCTORS

Thirty doctors were interviewed by the method of semistructured interviewing. Like women interviewed, they were living in five Chinese cities—three in
the North and two in the South, including Qingdao, Dalian, Beijing, Changsha, and Guangzhou—and three villages in an interior southern province,
Hunan. All the thirty OB/GYN physicians but one were female. The thirty
doctors ranged in age from their twenties to their early sixties, all performed
abortions as a routine part of their work, currently or not long before being
interviewed. About one-third (nine) were country doctors who worked at
township hospitals located in three different townships in an inland southern
province. Two-thirds (twenty one) were city doctors working at general hospitals, clinics of maternal and infant health, hospitals affiliated with colleges
or universities of modern biomedicine or traditional Chinese medicine, and
institutions called "Institute for the Sciences and Technology of Family Planning." A major routine task of these institutes is to provide medical service associated with birth control and to conduct some research. These hospitals, institutes, and clinics were located in two northern coastal (Dalian and Qindao),
one southern coastal (Guangzhou), and two inland cities with one in north
(Beijing) and the other in south (Changsha), and a county in Hunan.

Before going to China for field research, I was curious about the views and
experiences of male OB/GYN doctors, since I knew there were very few of
them in China. In the whole period of fieldwork, only one opportunity occurred for me to interview a male OB/GYN doctor. Unlike female physicians
interviewed, this one male doctor did not perform abortion routinely and
was not very willing to talk to me.

Once again, the basic interviewing strategy was to ask open-ended questions. The first formal question I posed was usually: "Could you please tell
something about your own experience related to your work, especially to
performing abortion?" Or I said, "I am very interested in your personal experiences of performing abortion. Could you tell me some?" If the person interviewed was not sure what I was asking and insisted that I asked more specific questions, which was quite often the case, I would ask the following
questions: "For what reasons might a woman demand an abortion?" "What is
your experience of performing the first abortion on a patient?" "How do you
feel about performing abortions? Do you feel any differences in performing
an early or late abortion?" "How do you feel about the aborted fetuses? Do
you sometimes think of them?" "As an OB/GYN doctor, what are the most rewarding aspects of your work?" "What aspects do you dislike most about
your work?" "Do you have any stories related to abortion—happy or sad or
interesting—that you want to share with others?"

As in interviews with women, *putonghua* (the standard Chinese) was the
language for most interviews with doctors. But interviews with physicians in

the interior provincial capital and the three villages in Hunan were conducted in the dialect spoken by the natives.

Compared with the female "patients" interviewed, doctors were much more comfortable with having interviews taped, less nervous in interviewing, and even more willing to talk. Their openness and frankness were often surprising. Nevertheless, compared with their city counterparts, country doctors in general seemed to be less active in talking about their views and experiences. As a result, almost all the interviews with city physicians were taped, but only two interviews with country doctors were taped.

The interviewing time varied from thirty minutes to two or three hours, depending on how much the doctor wanted to talk. Most interviewing occurred in the doctor's office, which was usually shared with other doctors. Sometimes interviews occurred as other doctors were coming or going. Three times, two doctors were interviewed together. A few interviews were carried out in doctors' homes.

References

Aird, John S. 1990. *Slaughter of the Innocents: Coercive Birth Control in China*. Washington: AEI.

———. 1994. "China's 'Family Planning' Terror." *Human Life Review* 20, no. 3: 83–104.

———. 1995. "Population Polices: Strategies of Fertility Control: D. Compulsion." In *Encyclopedia of Bioethics*, ed. Warren T. Reich, 2023–27. Revised ed. New York: Simon & Schuster, Macmillan.

Anagnost, Ann. 1989. "Family Violence and Magical Violence: The Woman as Victim in China's One-Child Family Policy." *Women and Language* 11, no. 2: 16–22.

Angle, Stephen. 2002. *Human Rights and Chinese Thought: A Cross-Cultural Inquiry*. Cambridge: Cambridge University Press.

Aristotle. 1995. Trans. Ernest Barker. Revised R. F. Stalley. *Politics*. Oxford: Oxford University Press.

Aron, Raymond. 1985. "Relativism in History." In *The Philosophy of History in Our Time*, ed. Hans Meyerhoff. New York: Garland.

Banister, Judith. 1987. *China's Changing Population*. Stanford, CA: Stanford University Press.

Bauer, Joanne R., and Daniel A. Bell, eds. 1999. *The East Asian Challenge for Human Rights*. Cambridge: Cambridge University Press.

Baum, Richard, and Alexei Shevchenko. 1999. "The 'State of the State.'" In *The Paradox of China's Post-Mao Reforms*, ed. Merle Goldman and Roderich MacFarquhar, 333–60. Cambridge, MA: Harvard University Press.

Beauchamp, Tom L., and James F. Childress. 2001. *Principles of Biomedical Ethics*. 5th ed. Oxford: Oxford University Press.

Becker, James. 1996. *Hungry Ghosts: Mao's Secret Famine*. New York: Free Press.

Bei, Dao. 2001. *The August Sleepwalker*. Trans. Bonnie S. McDougall. New York: New Directions.

Bellah, Robert N., Richard Madsen, William M. Sullivan, Ann Swidler, and Steven M. Tipton. 1985. *Habits of the Heart: Individualism and Commitment in American Life*. New York: Harper & Row.

Bernstein, Richard. 1992. *The New Constellation: The Ethical–Political Horizons of Modernity/Postmodernity*. Cambridge: MIT Press.

Bond, Michael H. 1996. "Chinese Values." In *The Handbook of Chinese Psychology*, ed. Michael H. Bond. Hong Kong: Oxford University Press.

Bray, Francesca. 1997. *Technology and Gender: Fabrics of Power in Late Imperial China*. Berkeley: University of California Press.

Brokaw, Cynthia J. 1991. *The Ledgers of Merits and Demerit: Social Change and Moral Order in Late Imperial China*. Princeton, NJ: Princeton University Press.

Bu, Ping, ed. 2003. *Yixue Lunlixue* (Medical Ethics). Beijing: Higher Education Press.

Calabresi, Guido, and Philip Bobbitt. 1978. *Tragic Choices*. New York: Norton.

Callahan, Daniel. 1970. *Abortion: Law, Choice and Morality*. New York: Macmillan.

Cao, Kaibin, Shichang Qiu, and Minsheng Fan, eds. 1998. *Yixue Lunlixue Jiaocheng* (Textbook of Medical Ethics). Shanghai: Shanghai Medical University Press.

Carson, Ronald A. 1990. "Interpretive Bioethics: The Way of Discernment." *Theoretical Medicine* 11: 51–59.

———. 1999. "Interpreting Strange Practices: A Commentary to Nie on 'Human Drugs' in Chinese Medicine." In *Confucian Bioethics*, ed. Ruiping Fan. Dordrecht, Netherlands: Kluwer.

———. Forthcoming. *Medical Ethics as Moral Works*. Book manuscript.

Chai, Ch'u, and Winberg Chai, eds. and trans. 1965. *The Humanist Way in Ancient China: Essential Works of Confucianism*. New York: Bantam.

Chan, Wing-tsit. 1963. *A Source Book in Chinese Philosophy*. Princeton, NJ: Princeton University Press.

Chen, Banxian, eds. 1982. *Ershiliushi Yixue Shiliao Huibian* (Materials on Medicine from the Official Histories of Twenty-Six Dynasties). Beijing: Chinese Academy of Traditional Chinese Medicine.

Chen, Menglei. 1962 [1723]. *Gujin Tushu Jicheng Yibu Quanlu* (Collection of Ancient and Contemporary Books, The Part of Medicine), Book 12: General Discussions (Vols. 501–520 in original). Beijing: People's Health Press.

Cong, Ya-li. 2003. "Bioethics in China." In *The Annals of Bioethics: Regional Perspective in Bioethics*, ed. John Peppin and Mark Cherry, 229–60. Lisse, Netherlands: Swets & Zeitlinger.

Croll, Elisabeth, Dalia Davin, and Penny Kane, eds. 1985. *China's One-Child Family Policy*. New York: St. Martin's.

Dai, Xinyi. 1992. "Inverse Elimination Is a False Alarm." In *Zhongguo Renkou Shenghuo Zhiliang Yanjiu* (Research on the Quality of Life of China's Population), ed. Feng Litian, 310–15. Beijing: Beijing College of Economics Press.

Davis, Deborah, and Stevan Harrell, eds. 1993. *Chinese Families in the Post-Mao Era*. Berkeley: University of California Press.

de Bary, Wm. Theodore. 1983. *The Liberal Tradition in China*. Hong Kong: Chinese University Press; New York: Columbia University Press.

———. 1998. *Asian Values and Human Rights: A Confucian Communitarian Perspective*. Cambridge: Harvard University Press.

de Bary, Wm. Theodore, and Richard Lufrano. 2003. *Sources of Chinese Civilization.* Vol. 2. Columbia University Press.

de Bary, William Theodore, and Tu Weiming, eds. 1998. *Confucianism and Human Rights.* New York: Columbia University Press.

Dikötter, Frank. 1998. *Imperfect Conceptions: Medical Knowledge, Birth Defects and Eugenics in China.* New York: Columbia University Press.

Döring, Ole, ed. 2002a. *Ethics in Medical Education in China: Distinguishing Education of Ethics from Moral Preaching.* Hamburg: Mitteilungen des Instituts für Asienkunde.

———. 2002b. "The Meaning of 'Cultural Values' in Approaching Issues of Medical Ethics in Contemporary China." *Estudos Sobre a China 6.*

———. 2003. "China's Struggle for Practical Regulations in Medical Ethics." *Nature Review* (Genetics) 4 (March): 233–39.

Döring, Ole, and Renbiao Chen, eds. 2002. *Advances in Chinese Medical Ethics: Chinese and International Perspectives.* Hamburg: Mitteilungen des Instituts für Asienkunde.

Dorland's Illustrated Medical Dictionary. 2000. Philadelphia: Saunders.

Drake, Kate. 2001. "Abortions: No Question Asked." *Time,* August 6, 27.

Du, Chungwen. 1997. "The Lonely Grave Mound." *Dangdai* (The Present Time), no. 1: 174.

Dworkin, Ronald. 1993. *Life's Dominion: An Argument about Abortion, Euthanasia, and Individual Freedom.* New York: Knopf.

Editorial Committee. 1996. *Zhongguo Jihuashengyu Shouce* (Handbook of Family Planning Work). Beijing: Population Press.

Edwards, Red B., and Edmund L. Erde. 1995. "Freedom and Coercion." In *Encyclopedia of Bioethics,* ed. Warren T. Reich. Revised ed. New York: Simon & Schuster Macmillan.

Fairbank, John K. 1987. "The Reunification of China." In *The Cambridge History of China.* Vol. 14: *The People's Republic of China;* Part I: *The Emergence of Revolution,* ed. John K. Fairbank and Denis Twitchett. Cambridge: Cambridge University Press.

Fan, Ruiping. 1997. "Self-determination vs. Family-Determination: Two Incommensurable Principles of Autonomy." *Bioethics* 11 (3–4): 309–22.

Fan, Ruiping, and Julia Tao, eds. 2004. *Informed Consent and the Family: A Cross-Cultural Study.* Issue of *Journal of Medicine and Philosophy* 29, no. 2.

Feng, Litian, ed. 1992. *Zhongguo Renkou Shenghuo Zhijiang Yanjiu* (Research on the Quality of Life of China's Population). Beijing: Beijing College of Economics Press.

Feng, Zhong-Hui, and Charles H. C. Chen. 1983. "Induced Abortion in Xian City, China." *International Family Planning Perspectives* 9: 81–85.

Fingarette, Herbert. 1972. *Confucius—The Secular as Sacred.* New York: Harper and Row.

Fox, Renee C., and Judith P. Swazey. 1984. "Medical Morality Is Not Bioethics: Medical Ethics in China and the United States." *Perspectives in Biology and Medicine* 27: 336–60.

Fung, Fu-lan. 1952. Trans. Derk Bodde. *A History of Chinese Philosophy.* Vol. I. Princeton, NJ: Princeton University Press.

Furth, Charlotte. 1987. "Concepts of Pregnancy, Childbirth, and Infancy in Ch'ing Dynasty China." *Journal of Asian Studies* 46, no. 1: 7–35.

———. 1995. "From Birth to Birth: The Growing Body in Chinese Medicine." In *Chinese Views of Childhood*, ed. Anne Behnke Kinney, 157–91. Honolulu: University of Hawai'i Press.

———. 1999. *A Flourishing Yin: Gender in China's Medical History, 960–1665.* Berkeley: University of California Press.

Gates, Hill. 1993. "Cultural Support for Birth Limitation among Urban Capital-Owning Women." In *Chinese Families in the Post-Mao Era*, ed. Deborah Davis and Stevan Harrell. Berkeley: University of California Press.

Geertz, Clifford. 1973. *The Interpretation of Culture*. New York: Basic.

———. 1983. *Local Knowledge*. New York: Basic.

Gernet, Jacques. 1996. Trans. J. R. Forster and Charles Hartman. *A History of Chinese Civilization*. 2d ed. Cambridge: Cambridge University Press.

Gilligan, Carol. 1993 [1982]. *In Different Voice: Psychological Theory and Women's Development*. Cambridge, MA: Harvard University Press.

Gilmartin, Christina K., Gail Hershatter, Lisa Rofel, and Tyrene White, eds. 1994. *Engendering China: Women, Culture, and the State*. Cambridge, MA: Harvard University Press.

Ginsburg, Faye D. 1989. *Contested Lives: The Abortion Debate in an American Community*. Berkeley: University of California Press.

Goldman, Merle, and Roderich MacFarquhar, eds. 1999. *The Paradox of China's Post-Mao Reforms*. Cambridge, MA: Harvard University Press.

Gordon, Linda. 1977. *Woman's Body, Woman's Right: A Social History of Birth Control in America*. Harmondsworth: Penguin.

Greel, G. Herrlee. 1953. *Chinese Thought: From Confucius to Mao Tse-Tung*. Chicago: University of Chicago Press.

Greenhalgh, Susan. 1993. "The Peasantization of the One-Child Policy in Xhaanxi." In *Chinese Families in the Post-Mao Era*, ed. Deborah Davis and Stevan Harrell. Berkeley: University of California Press.

———. 1994. "Controlling Birth and Bodies in Village China." *American Ethnologist* 21, no. 1: 3–30.

Hai, Zi. 1997. Ed. Xi Chuan. *Hai Zi Shi Quanbian* (The Complete Poems of Hai Zi). Shanghai: Sanlian Bookstore.

Harvey, Peter. 2000. *An Introduction to Buddhist Ethics*. Cambridge: Cambridge University Press.

He, Huaihong. 1998. *Liangxin Lun* (On Conscience: The Social Transformation of the Traditional Concept of Liangzi). Shanghai: Sanlian Bookstore.

He, Lun, and Shi Wenxin, eds. 1989. *Xiandai Yixue Lunlixue* (Modern Biomedical Ethics). Hangzhou: Zhejiang Education Press.

Henshaw, Stanley K., and Evelyn Morrow. 1990. *Induced Abortion: A World Review (1990 Supplement)*. Washington, DC: Alan Guttmacher Institute.

Himes, Norman E. 1970 [1936]. *Medical History of Contraception*. New York: Schocken.

Honig, Emily, and Gail Hershatter. 1988. *Personal Voices: Chinese Women in the 1980's*. Stanford, CA: Stanford University Press.

Hsiao, Kung-chuan. 1979. Trans. F. W. Mote. *A History of Chinese Political Thought*. Vol. 1: *From the Beginnings to the Six Century A.D.* Princeton, NJ: Princeton University Press.

Hsu, Francis L. K. 1970 [1953]. *Americans and Chinese: Reflections on Two Cultures and Their People*. New York: American Museum Science Books.

Huang, Shu-min. 1989. *The Spiral Road: Change in a Chinese Village Through the Eyes of a Communist Party Leader*. Boulder: Westview.

Hui, Edwin. 2000. "Jen and Perichoresis: The Confucian and Christian Bases of the Relational Person." In *The Moral Status of Persons: Perspectives on Bioethics*, ed. Gerhold K. Becker, 95–118. Amsterdam: Rodopi.

Jacobsen, Michael, and Ole Bruun, eds. 2000. *Human Rights and Asian Values: Contesting National Identities and Cultural Representation in Asia*. Surrey, England: Curzon.

Jennings, William H. 1999. "Commentary on Jing-Bao Nie's Article 'The Problem of Coerced Abortion in China and Related Ethical Issues.'" *Cambridge Quarterly of Healthcare Ethics* 8, no. 4.

Ji, Jun. 1998 [1800]. *Yuewei Caotang Biji* (The Notes from the Reading-Subtlety Hut). Shanghai: Shanghai Press for Ancient Books.

Johnson, Elizabeth. 1975. "Women and Childbearing in Kwan Mun Hau Village: A Study of Social Change." In *Women in Chinese Society*, ed Margery Wolf and Roxane Witke. Stanford, CA: Stanford University Press.

Kafka, Franz. 1970 [1936]. Trans. Willa Muir and Edwin Muir. *The Great Wall of China: Stories and Reflections*. New York: Schocken.

Kane, Penny. 1987. *The Second Billion: Population and Family Planning in China*. Ringwood, Australia: Penguin.

Keown, Damien. 1995. *Buddhism and Bioethics*. Hampshire: St. Martin's.

Kleinman, Arthur. 1986. *Social Origins of Distress and Disease*. New Haven, CT: Yale University Press.

———. 1988. *The Illness Narratives*. New York: Basic.

———. 1995. *Writing at the Margin*. Berkeley: University of California Press.

———. 1999. "Moral Experience and Ethical Reflection: Can Ethnography Reconcile Them? A Quandary for 'The New Bioethics.'" *Daedalus* 128 (no. 4): 69–97.

Kong, Yun Cheung, Jing-xi Xie, and Pual Pui-Hay But. 1986. "Fertility Regulating Agents from Traditional Chinese Medicines." *Journal of Ethnopharmacology* 15, no. 1: 1–44.

LaFleur, William R. 1992. *Liquid Life: Abortion and Buddhism in Japan*. Princeton, NJ: Princeton University Press.

Lee, Tao. 1943. "Medical Ethics in Ancient China." *Bulletin in the History of Medicine* 13: 268–73.

Li, Benfu, and Qiang Leng. 1993. "The Influence of Religions over the Abortion Debate." *Zhongguo Yixue Lunlixue* (Chinese Medical Ethics), no. 1 (February): 41–42.

Li, Shizhen. 1988 [1592]. *Bencao Gangmu* (The Great Pharmacopeias). Beijing: Chinese Bookstore.

Li, Virginia C., Glenn C. Wong, Shu-hua Qiu et al. 1990. "Characteristics of Women Having Abortion in China." *Social Science and Medicine* 31, no. 4: 445–53.

Li, Yinhe. 1998. *Zhongguo Nüxing de Qinggan yu Xing* (Love and Sexuality of Chinese Women). Beijing: Today's China.

Lin, Yü-sheng. 1979. *The Crisis of Chinese Consciousness: Radical Antitraditionalism in the May Fourth Era*. Madison: University of Wisconsin Press.

Liu, Zheng. 1984. "Population." In *China's Socialist Modernization*, ed. Yu Guangyuan. Beijing: Foreign Language Press.

Lu, Qihua, ed. 1999. *Yixue Lunli Xue* (Medical Ethics). Wuhan: Huazhoang University of Science and Technology Press.

Luk, Bernard Hung-kay. 1977. "Abortion in Chinese Law." *American Journal of Comparative Law* 25: 372–90.

Luker, Kristin. 1984. *Abortion and the Politics of Motherhood*. Berkeley: University of California Press.

Luo, Guojie, ed. 2002 [1989]. *Lunlixue* (Ethics). Beijing: People's Press.

Luo, Guojie, Ma Boxuan, and Yu Jing. 2004 [1986]. *Lunlixue Jiaocheng* (Textbook of Ethics). Beijing: People's University Press.

Luo, Lin, Wu Shi-zhong, Chen Xiao-qing, and Li Ming-xiang. 1999. "Induced Abortion among Unmarried Women in Sichuan Province, China: A Survey." In *Abortion in the Developing World*, ed. Axel I. Mundigo and Cynthia Indriso, 337–45. London: Zed for World Health Organization.

Ma, Bo-Ying. 1994. *Zhongguo Yixue Wenhuashi* (The History of Medicine in Chinese Culture). Shanghai People's Press.

Madsen, Richard. 1955. *China and the American Dream: A Moral Inquiry*. Berkeley: University of California Press.

———. 1984. *Morality and Power in a Chinese Village*. Berkeley: University of California Press.

Mann, Thomas. 1969. Trans. H. T. Lowe-Porter. *The Magic Mountain*. New York: Vintage.

Mao, Xin. 1998. "Chinese Geneticists' Views of Ethical Issues in Genetic Testing and Screening: Evidence for Eugenics in China." *American Journal of Human Genetics* 63: 688–95.

McDougall, Bonnie S., and Anders Hansson. 2002. *Chinese Concepts of Privacy*. Leiden, Netherlands: Brill.

McNicoll, Geoffrey. 1995. "Strong Persuasion." In *Encyclopedia of Bioethics*, ed. Warren T. Reich. Revised ed. New York: Simon & Schuster Macmillan.

Mencius. 1970. Trans. D. C. Lau. *Mencius*. London: Penguin.

Milwertz, Cecilia N. 1997. *Accepting Population Control: Urban Chinese Women and the One-Child Family Policy*. Surrey: Curzon.

Mohr, James C. 1978. *Abortion in America: The Origins and Evolution of National Policy, 1800–1900*. Oxford University Press.

Mosher, Steven W. 1983. *Broken Earth: The Rural Chinese*. New York: Free Press.

———. 1993. *A Mother's Ordeal: One Woman's Fight against China's One-Child Policy*. New York: Harcourt Brace Jovanovich.

Moskowitz, Marc L. 2001. *The Haunting Fetus: Abortion, Sexuality, and the Spirit World in Taiwan*. Honolulu: University of Hawai'i Press.

Mueggler, Erik. 2001. *The Age of Wild Ghosts: Memory, Violence, and Place in Southwest China*. Berkeley: University of California Press.

Nanjing College of Chinese Medicine. 1981. *Huangdi Neijing Suwen Yishi* (The Yellow Emperor's Medical Classic with Annotations and Modern Chinese Translation). 2nd ed. Shanghai: Shanghai Science and Technology Press.

Nie, Jing-Bao. 1999a. "'Human Drugs' in Chinese Medicine and the Confucian View: An Interpretative Study." In *Confucian Bioethics*, ed. Ruiping Fan, 167–206. Kluwer Academic.

———. 1999b. "The Myth of *the* Chinese Culture, the Myth of *the* Chinese Medical Ethics." *Bioethics Examiner* 3, no. 2 (Summer): 1, 2, 5.

———. 1999c. "The Problem of Coerced Abortion in China and Related Ethical Issues." *Cambridge Quarterly of Healthcare Ethics* 8, no. 4 (Fall): 463–75. Reprinted in Belinda Bennett, ed. 2004. *Abortion*. International Library of Medicine, Ethics and Law series. Hampshire, England: Ashgate, pp. 427–39. Also reprinted in Larry May, Shari Collins-Chobanian, and Kai Wong, eds. *Applied Ethics: Multicultural Approach*. 4th ed. Englewood Cliffs, NJ: Prentice Hall, 2005.

———. 2000. "The Plurality of Chinese and American Medical Moralities: Toward an Interpretative Cross-cultural Bioethics." *Kennedy Institute of Ethics Journal* 10, no. 3 (September): 239–60. The Chinese and modified version, translated by Wang Jin and Chen Rongxia, was published in *Chinese and International Philosophy of Medicine* 3, no 4 (December 2001): 135–58.

———. 2001. "Is Informed Consent Not Applicable to China?: Intellectual Flaws of the Cultural Difference Argument." *Formosa Journal of Medical Humanities* 2, no.1–2: 67–74. (The Chinese and modified version, translated by Mingjie Zhao, was published in *Yixue Yu Zhexue* [Medicine and Philosophy] 23, no. 6 [December 2002]: 18–22.)

———. 2002. "Bringing Ethics to Life: A Personal Statement on Teaching Medical Ethics." In *Ethics in Medical Education in China: Distinguishing Education of Ethics from Moral Preaching*, ed. Ole Döring, 63–74. Hamburg: Mitteilungen des Instituts für Asienkunde.

———. 2003. "The Ideology of China's Eugenics Program." Paper presented at the 3rd International Convention of Asian Scholars (ICAS III), Singapore, August 19–22. Also presented at the National Conference for Civic Education on "Good Gene, Bad Gene?" Bremen, Germany, September 15–17.

———. 2004a. "Feminist Bioethics and Its Language of Human Rights in the Chinese Context." In *Linking Visions: Feminist Bioethics, Human Rights, and the Developing World*, ed. Rosemarie Tong, Anne Donchin, and Susan Dodds, 73–88. Lanham, MD: Rowman & Littlefield.

———. 2004b. "What China Can Learn from the Eugenic Program in Nazi Germany." Paper presented at the International Symposium on Science, History and Culture in Germany, Chinese Academy of Science, Beijing, May 17–19.

———. 2004c. "China's Birth Control Program and Western Feminism: Toward a Confucian–Feminist Population Policy." A paper presented at the Congress of International Network of Feminist Approach to Bioethics, Sydney, November 13–14.

———. 2005. "Why Reproductive Rights Matter in the Chinese Context." A key-note address delivered at the Second Nordic–China Women and Gender Studies Conference on Gender and Human Rights, Sweden, August 7–10.

———. Forthcoming-a. *Medical Ethics in China: Major Traditions, Contemporary Issues, and Dialogue with the West*. Washington, DC: Georgetown University Press.

———. Forthcoming-b. "The Moral Discourses of Practitioners in China." In *A History of Medical Ethics*, ed. Robert Baker and Larry McCullough. New York: Cambridge University Press.

Nisbett, Richard E. 2003. *The Geography of Thought: How Asians and Westerners Think Differently . . . and Why*. New York: Free Press.

Noonan, John T., Jr. 1970. "An Almost Absolute Value in History." In John T. Noonan Jr., ed. *The Morality of Abortion: Legal and Historical Perspectives.* Cambridge, MA: Harvard University Press.

Nussbaum, Martha C. 1997. *Cultivating Humanities.* Cambridge, MA: Harvard University Press.

Overmyer, Daniel L., ed. 2003. *Religion in China Today.* Cambridge: Cambridge University Press.

Pan, Guiyu, ed. 2001. *Zhonghua Shengyu Wenhua Daolun* (Introduction to Chinese Reproductive Culture). 2 vols. Beijing: China Population Press.

Pan, Zhongdan, Steven H. Chaffee, Godwin C. Chu, and Yanan Ju. 1994. *To See Ourselves: Comparing Traditional Chinese and American Cultural Values.* Boulder: Westview.

Peng, Peiyun, ed. 1997. *Zhongguo Jifa Shengyu Quanshu* (The Complete Book of Family Planning in China). Beijing: China Population Press.

Perry, Elizabeth J., and Mark Selden, eds. 2000. *Chinese Society: Change, Conflict and Resistance.* London: Routledge.

Pillsbury, Barbara. 1978. "'Doing the Month': Confinement and Convalescence of Chinese Women after Childbirth." *Social Science and Medicine* 12: 11–22.

Poston, Dudley L., and David Yaukey, eds. 1992. *The Population of Modern China.* New York: Plenum.

Potter, Sulamith H., and Jack M. Potter. 1990. *China's Peasants: The Anthropology of a Revolution.* Cambridge: Cambridge University Press.

Pye, Lucian W. 1985. *Asian Power and Politics: The Cultural Dimensions of Authority.* Cambridge, MA: Belknap.

———. 1992 [1968]. *The Spirit of Chinese Politics.* New ed. Cambridge, MA: Harvard University Press.

Qiu, Ren-Zong. 1987. *Shengmin Lunlixue* (Bioethics). Shanghai: Shanghai People's Press.

———. 1992. "Medical Ethics and Chinese Culture." In *Transcultural Dimensions in Medical Ethics,* ed. Edmond D. Pellegrino et al., 155–74. Frederick, MD: University Publishing Group.

———, ed. 2004. *Bioethics: Asian Perspectives: A Quest for Moral Diversity.* Dordrecht, Netherlands: Kluwer Academic.

Qiu, Ren-Zong, Chun-Zhi Wang, and Yuan Gu. 1989. "Can Late Abortion Be Ethically Justified?" *Journal of Medicine and Philosophy* 14, no. 3: 343–50.

Qiu, Ren-Zong, and Albert Jonsen. 2003. "Medical Ethics, History of: Contemporary China." In *Encyclopedia of Bioethics,* ed. Stephen G. Post. 5 vols. 3d ed. New York: Macmillan.

Qiu, Xiangxing, et al. 2003. "Ethical Issues of Human Stem Cell Research: A Survey and Discussion." *Yixue yu Zhexue* (Medicine and Philosophy) 25, no. 1: 9–11.

Reiser, Stanley J., and De-bing Wang, ed. 2004. "A Global Profession: Medical Values in China and the United States." Special Supplement of *The Hastings Center Report* 28, no. 4: S1-S48.

Rigdon, Susan M. 1996. "Abortion Law and Practice in China: An Overview with Comparison to the United States." *Social Sciences and Medicine* 42: 543–60.

Rodman, Hyman, Betty Sarvis, and Joy Walker Bonar, eds. 1987. *The Abortion Question.* New York: Columbia University Press.

Savage, Mark. 1988. "The Law of Abortion in the Union of Soviet Socialist Republics and the People's Republic of China: Women's Rights in Two Socialist Countries." *Stanford Law Review* 40: 1027–117.

Scharping, Thomas. 2003. *Birth Control in China 1949–2000: Population Policy and Demographic Development*. London: RoutledgeCurzon.

Schwartz, Benjamin. 1964. *In Search of Wealth and Power: Yen Fu and the West*. Cambridge, MA: Belknap.

Schwarz, M. Roy, and David T. Stern, ed. 2004. *The Use of Human Subjects in Research Conference: Comparing Core Values in the People's Republic of China and the United States*. Special Issue of *Journal of Clinical Ethics* 15, no. 1.

Sen, Amartya. 1999. *Development as Freedom*. New York: Anchor.

Shapiro, Ian, ed. 1995. *Abortion: The Supreme Court Decisions*. Indianapolis: Hackett.

Shi, Wenxin, He Lun, and Huang Gang. 1998. *Shengwu Yixue Lunlixue* (Biomedical Ethics). Hangzhou: Zhejiang Education Press.

Shue, Vivienne. 1988. *The Reach of the State: Sketches of the Chinese Body Politics*. Stanford, CA: Stanford University Press.

Song, Shugong, ed. 1991. *Zhongguo Gudai Huangshi Yangsheng Jiyao* (Main Collections of Ancient Literature on the Bedroom Hygiene). Beijing: Chinese Medical Science and Technology Press.

Stacey, Judith. 1983. *Patriarchy and Socialist Revolution in China*. Berkeley: University of California Press.

Stephen, James F. 1967. *Liberty, Equality, Fraternity*. Cambridge: Cambridge University Press.

Svensson, Marina. 2002. *Debating Human Rights in China: A Conceptual and Political History*. Lanham, MD: Rowman & Littlefield.

Tang, Kailin. 2002. "Ethical Dimensions of Yousheng (Healthy Birth or Eugenics): The Perspective of a Chinese Ethicist." *New Zealand Bioethics Journal* 3, no. 3: 9–14.

Tang, Kailin, and Xiao Long. 1992. *Chaoyue Weiji de Xuanzhe: Renkou Daode* (The Choice beyond the Crisis: Ethics of Population). Changsha: Hunan Normal University Press.

Tien, H. Yuan. 1991. *China's Strategic Demographic Initiative*. New York: Praeger.

T'ien, Ju-K'ang. 1988. *Male Anxiety and Female Chastity: A Comparative Study of Chinese Ethical Values in Ming-Ch'ing Times*. Leiden: Brill.

Tietze, Christopher, and Stanley K. Henshaw. 1986. *Induced Abortion: A World Review*. 6th ed. Washington, DC: Alan Guttmacher Institute.

Tribe, Laurence H. 1992. *Abortion: The Clash of Absolutes*. New York: Norton.

Tu, Wei-ming. 1992. "A Confucian Perspective on Embodiment." In *The Body in Medical Thought and Practice*, ed. Drew Leder. Dordrecht, Netherlands: Kluwer Academic.

Tucker, Robert, ed. 1978. *The Marx–Engels Reader*. 2d ed. New York: Norton.

———. 1993. "Confucianism." In *Our Religions*, ed. Arvind Sharma, 139–228. San Francisco: HarperSanFrancisco.

United Nations, Department of Economic and Social Development. 1992. *Abortion Policies: A Global Review*. Vol. 1: Afghanistan to France. New York: United Nations Publications.

Unschuld, Paul. 1979. *Medical Ethics in Imperial China*. Berkeley: University of California Press.

————. 1985. *Medicine in China: A History of Ideas*. Berkeley: University of California Press.

————. 1995. "Confucianism." In *Encyclopedia of Bioethics*, ed. Warren T. Reich. Revised ed. New York: Simon & Schuster Macmillan.

————. 2001. "Chinese Medical Ethics and the Role of Medical History." *Acta Medica Nagasakiensia*, Suppl. 46 (October): 14–18 (English), 46–50 (Japanese).

U.S. Congress. House of Representatives. Committee on International Relations. Subcommittee on International Operation and Human Rights. 1998. *Forced Abortion and Sterilization in China: The View from the Inside* (Hearing before the Subcommittee on International Operation and Human Rights of the Committee on International Relations, House of Representatives, 105th Congress, Second Session). Washington, DC: U.S. Government Printing Office.

Wang, Feng. Forthcoming. "The Rise of Abortion in Modern China." In *Abortion and Infanticide in East Asia*, ed. James Lee and Osamu Saito. Oxford: Oxford University Press.

Wang, Maohe. 1995. *Taoyu Xuanji* (The Secrets of Fetal Life and Children's Growth) (Collected Traditional Works). Zhengzhou: Zhongzhou Ancient Books Press.

Weller, Susan, and A. Kimball Romney. 1988. *Systematic Data Collection*. Newbury Park, CA: Sage.

Wertheimer, Alan. 1990. *Coercion*. Princeton, NJ: Princeton University Press.

Wertz, Dorothy C. 1998. "Eugenics Is Alive and Well: A Survey of Genetic Professionals around the World." *Science in Context* 11, nos. 3–4: 493–510.

White, Tyrene. 1992. "Family Planning in China" (English translation of original Chinese materials). *Chinese Sociology and Anthropology* 24, no. 3.

————. 1994. "The Origin of China's Birth Planning Policy." In *Engendering China: Women, Culture, and the State*, ed. Christina Gilmartin et al., 250–78. Cambridge, MA: Harvard University Press.

————. 2000. "Domination, Resistance and Accommodation in China's One-Child Campaign." In *Chinese Society: Change, Conflict and Resistance*, ed. Elizabeth J. Perry and Mark Selden, 102–19. London: Routledge Press.

Wittfogel, Karl A. 1957. *Oriental Despotism: A Comparative Study of Total Power*. New Haven, CT: Yale University Press.

Wolf, Margery. 1985. *Revolution Postponed: Women in Contemporary China*. Stanford, CA: Stanford University Press.

Wolf, Margery, and Roxane Witke. 1975. *Women in Chinese Society*. Stanford, CA: Stanford University Press.

Xu, Ling, Xinyan Liu, and Liandi Lou. 1996. "Condition and Psychology of Youth Abortions: A Survey." In *Shengyu Jiankan yu Lulixue* (Reproductive Health and Ethics), ed. Ren-Zong Qiu, 108–12. Beijing: Beijing Medical University and China Union Medical University Joint Press.

Yan, Yunxing. 2003. *Private Life under Socialism: Love, Intimacy, and Family Change in a Chinese Village, 1949–1999*. Stanford, CA: Stanford University Press.

Yang, C. K. 1961. *Religion in Chinese Society*. Berkeley, CA: University of California Press.

Yü, Ying-Shih. 1964. "Life and Immortality in the Mind of Han China." *Harvard Journal of Asiatic Studies* 25: 80–122.

Zhang, Hongzhu, and Zhang Jingzhong, eds. 1995. *Yixue Lulixie Guangyao* (An Outline of Medical Ethics). Tianjing: Tianjing Academy of Social Sciences Press.

Zhou, Guoping, 1997. *Zhou Guoping Wenji* (Collected Works of Zhou Guoping). Vol. 2. Xi'an: Shanxi People's Press.

Zhou, Wei-jin, Gao Er-sheng, Yang Yao-ying, Qin Fei, and Tang Wei. 1999. "Induced Abortion and the Outcome of Subsequent Pregnancy in China: Client and Provider Perspectives." In *Abortion in the Developing World*, ed. Axel I. Mundigo and Cynthia Indriso, 228–44. London: Zed for World Health Organization.

Zhuang Zi (Chuang Tzu). 1968. Trans. Burton Watson. *The Complete Works of Chuang Tzu*. New York: Columbia University Press.

Index

abandonment, 50, 189, 197
abortifacients, 69, 70, 75, 76, 78
abortion (*duotai* or *rengong liuchan*,
   abbreviated as *renliu*): 1950s
   permission for, 42; agents involved
   in, 198, 199–200; ancient,
   controversies, 91; anecdote in
   Zhang's ethical text, 73; through
   assault in ancient China, 71;
   biomedical student's perspective
   regarding, 59–60; Chinese opposition
   to, based on fetal development,
   79–84; complex meanings of Chinese
   silence on, 11, 17, 30, 31–36, 195;
   cost of, 13, 37n1; delivering babies
   vs., 1–2, 166; descriptive phrases
   regarding, 135, 137; diverse attitudes
   toward, 93–94, 146; diversity
   contained in Chinese experience of,
   10–11; doctor's manner during, 142,
   143, 146, 161; forced, 15, 16, 56, 58,
   163, 166, 193, 207, 215, 219, 238;
   guilt about, 5–6; historical
   complexity of, controversies, 92;
   historical review of, policies and
   laws, 40; induced, 6, 28, 44, 61, 87,
   88, 119, 140, 145, 150, 169; late, 2,
   28, 34, 38n4, 58–61, 88, 119, 156,

166, 174–75, 178–82, 186–88n1, 189,
   198, 204–5, 210, 239; moral problem
   deserving of academic attention, 8;
   official sanctioned understandings
   of, 63; performed by female doctors,
   163; performed on *getihu*, 102;
   perspectives on, 14, 69, 70–72,
   88–89, 224, 251–52; reasons for, 6,
   27–29, 99–106, 117, 126, 136, 147–50,
   168–69, 244; as risk factor for
   reproductive capabilities, 140, 144;
   selective, 49, 59; Shi, He, and Huang,
   on, 28, 30–31; sociocultural issues
   surrounding, 131, 141, 190–92, 198,
   200; support of loved ones during,
   139, 142, 143–44; therapeutic, 71;
   traumatic experience of, 112–13,
   140–47. *See also* cases, desperate;
   coerced abortion; human life;
   pregnancy; termination
Abortion: The Clash of Absolutes
   (Tribe), 13
acupuncture, 69, 70, 81
Aird, John S., 16, 193, 194, 205, 206,
   224, 225
America: China's culture vs., 226–32;
   Chinese and, women's experiences
   of abortion, 247–49

276

Acknowledgments

It has taken nearly ten years to make this book. First of all, I owe a special debt to all the Chinese people—nearly seven hundred in total—who directly participated in this research project by agreeing to be interviewed and to complete my questionnaire. This work is not so much mine as theirs. I can never thank them enough for the trust they put in me and for what they taught me.

Quite a few Chinese friends and colleagues helped tremendously with my fieldwork. Although I want to list their names here, I do not do so, not right now at least, because I am not sure that they will not face any political difficulties as a result of the political sensitivity and the critical stance of this book.

One of the greatest good fortunes of my academic life was being mentored and supported by my U.S. professors, Harold Vanderpool, Arthur Kleinman, Susan Weller, Ronald Carson, and Michelle Carter. Series editor Mark Selden played a crucial role in revising my manuscript for publication with his general guidance, intellectual insights, and detailed comments. Mark, along with Susan McEachern of Rowman & Littlefield, have been extraordinarily patient.

I am grateful for the financial and academic support of the Institute for the Medical Humanities and the Graduate School of Biomedical Sciences at the University of Texas Medical Branch, the Center for Bioethics of the University of Minnesota, the Institute for the Studies of World Politics in Washington, DC, and the Chun Ku & Soo Yong Huang Foundation in Hawaii. The Dunedin School of Medicine and the Asian Studies Research Centre of the University of Otago provided financial assistance for the professional editing of the manuscript.

Faith Lagay in the United States and Paul Sorrell in New Zealand provided invaluable editorial advice. If this book is not very unreadable, or there are not too many unbearable language errors in it, it is mainly due to their capable assistance.

I am also very grateful to my colleagues and supervisors at the University of Otago for their support, including Donald Evans, Neil Pickering, Grant Gillett, Gareth Jones, Robert Walker, William Gillespie, John Adam, Rick Garside, Lynley Anderson, Barbara Lee, and Vicki Lang. Brian Moloughney helped in many ways, from finding a publisher to cotranslating the Chinese poetry that opens chapters 1, 4, and 7.

Many other individuals and friends have given not only moral support but also generous, concrete aid, including U.S. friends Kirk Smith, Lexi Bambas, Kayhan Parsi, Faith McLellan, and Trammi Nguyen. Carl Elliott in the United States and Ole Döring in Germany read my initial study and provided thoughtful suggestions for revision. To all my friends in the different parts of the world, I would like to cite a well-known Chinese poem: "If in this world an understanding friend survives, / Then the ends of the earth seem like next door."

Of course, I myself take full responsibility for any errors that remain in this book.

I would also like to take this opportunity to extend my heartfelt thanks and deep respect to all my teachers and mentors since the beginning of my school career at the age of five. Besides those mentioned above, they include my father, Zhou Yimou, and Yuan Lidao at the Human College of Traditional Chinese Medicine in Changsha; Ma Kanwen, then at the Chinese Academy of Traditional Chinese Medicine in Beijing; Jim Maxwell, Roberta Hamilton, Bin-ky Tan, Annette Burfoot, David Lyon, and Robert Arnold at Queen's University in Canada; Chester Burns, Ann H. Jones, William Winslade, Thomas Cole, John Duard, Mary Winkler, and Allen More at the University of Texas Medical Branch in Galveston. In imperial China, in the celebration activities such as the Spring Festival (Chinese New Year), the teacher stood side by side with Heaven, the earth, the emperor, and parents (and ancestors) for receiving thanks and respect. A wonderful Chinese proverb says: "A teacher for one day is like a parent for a lifetime."

I cannot imagine how unbearable my life would be without the emotional and other support from my wife, daughter, son, parents, parents-in-law, and younger brother and sister. I express my deep gratitude here partly because in China it is not a custom to express thanks directly to family members.

Some material in this book, in earlier versions, has been published in journals or anthologies or presented at professional conferences. Parts of chapters 3 and 5 appeared respectively in *New Zealand Bioethics Journal* 3, no. 3 (2002): 15–31, and in Rosemary Tong, ed, *Globalizing Feminist Bioethics: Women's Health Concerns Worldwide* (Boulder, CO: Westview,

2000), pp. 151–64. Portions of chapter 8 were published in *Cambridge Quarterly of Healthcare Ethics* 8, no. 4 (1999): 463–79; this article "The Problem of Coerced Abortion in China and Related Ethical Issues," was later reprinted in Belinda Benett, ed. *Abortion*, a volume in the International Library of Medicine, Ethics and Law (Hampshire, England: Ashgate, 2004), pp. 427–39, and in Larry May, Shari Collins-Chobanian, and Kai Wong, eds., *Applied Ethics: Multicultural Approach*, 4th edition (Englewood Cliffs, NJ: Prentice Hall, 2005). Several paragraphs in chapter 9 appeared in *Bioethics Examiner* 3, no. 2 (1999): 1–2, 5, and *Kennedy Institute of Ethics Journal* 10, no. 3 (2000): 239–60. A summary of the study appeared in Ole Döring and Chen Renbiao, eds., *Advances in Chinese Medical Ethics: Chinese and International Perspectives* (Hamburg, Germany: Mitteilungen des Instituts fur Asienkunde, 2003), pp. 279–89. An overview will appear as a part of chapter 5 in "Medical Ethics through the Life Cycle in China," in Robert Baker and Larry McCullough, eds., *A History of Medical Ethics* (New York: Cambridge University Press).

About the Author

Nie Jing-Bao is senior lecturer in the Bioethics Centre, Dunedin School of Medicine, University of Otago, New Zealand. He is also adjunct/visiting professor or faculty associate at several Chinese institutions, including Wuhan and Beijing universities. He obtained a bachelor of medicine degree in traditional Chinese medicine (equivalent to an MD) and a master of medicine degree in Chinese medical history from Hunan College of Chinese Medicine in China (1983, 1986); an MA in sociology from Queen's University in Canada (1993); and a PhD in the medical humanities from the University of Texas Medical Branch in the United States (1999). He was the postdoctoral fellow in bioethics at the University of Minnesota in 1998–1999 and a lecturer at Hunan College of Chinese Medicine in 1988–1991. He was born and grew up in a remote village in south-central China; he worked as a "peasant" at the bottom of Chinese society.

Dr. Nie has coauthored a book on comparative Chinese-Western medicine (Shenyang, 1990) and published nearly sixty journal articles and book chapters on bioethics, Asian/Chinese studies, and the history of medicine. He is finishing *Medical Ethics in China: Major Traditions, Contemporary Issues and Dialogue with the West* (2006). His current major research is on the ethical, sociocultural, and historical dimensions of Japanese wartime medical atrocities, on which he has a monograph and an coedited volume in progress.

Dr. Nie coedited the "Liuyedao" (Lancet) translation series (Qingdao, 1999–2000) and is editing the "Yinairenshu" (Medicine as the Art of Humanity) book series (Hunan Science & Technology, 2005–). He also coedits the *International Journal of Chinese and Comparative Philosophy of Medicine* and serves on the editorial or advisory boards of seven major English and Chinese periodicals in bioethics and related fields. He is a member of the Board of Directors of the International Association of Bioethics and a coordinator of the Sixth World Congress of Feminist Approaches to Bioethics (Beijing, 2006).